CELEBRATIONS

CELEBRATIONS

A unique treasury of holiday ideas featuring appetizing recipes, family games, gala decorations and easy craft activities for over 25 special occasions

BECKY STEVENS CORDELLO

Butterick Publishing

To Anthony and Jennifer

ACKNOWLEDGEMENTS

The efforts and interest of many people have made "Celebrations" possible. Among the most important are those who cannot be thanked: the nameless magazine editors of long ago who preserved or developed many of the ideas collected in this book. My debt to them is great indeed.

There are, however, other individuals and institutions whose assistance can be specifically acknowledged:

For research assistance: Vera Stewart of the Butterick Archives; Janet Blatter of YIVO, Institute for Jewish Research; Rabbi Allan Schranz and the Sisterhood of Temple Israel and the Jewish Community Center, Ridgewood, New Jersey; Jeff and Willa Speiser; Rebekah Levine.

For cooperation with outdoor photographs: Dr. Charles Abate, Laura Nagle, and students Julie Brewer, Elaine and Vivian Bell, Jennifer Cordello, Andre Lewis, Jonah and Lewis Meyersn and Victoria Wilkinson of the Orchard School, Ridgewood, New Jersey.

For fabrics and frames: Continental Felt Company, New York, New York; Arthur Zeiler Woolens, New York, New York; Prints n' Things, New Jersey.

For crafting items for photography: Paula Bell, Evelyn Brannon, Linda Crane, Mary Hoff, Andy, Beth, and Jane Ross, Jessica Stevens, Mildred Vinson, Barbara Weiland, and Sunny Lee who adaptd the "Keepsake" designs and worked many of them.

Very special thanks must go to my neighbors who became involved with this project at the very beginning and subsequently tasted, tested, glued, stitched, and proofread their way across these pages and thus have made the fact of this book a kind of celebration of friendship. In particular to Paula Bell, Jane Ross, and Arlene Meyers go my sincere gratitude.

My greatest debt, finally, is to my husband Anthony whose ability to see the forest in spite of the trees and considerable writing and editorial skills helped shape this book.

B.S.C.

Histories
TONY CORDELLO
Illustrations
JANET LOMBARDO

Patterns and Graphs
PHOEBE GAUGHAN
Photography
BOB CONNOLLY
ROBIN FORBES

Editor
EVELYN L. BRANNON
Cover design
WINIFRED YOUNG

Book design **SALLIE BALDWIN**

Library of Congress Catalog Card Number 77-89714
International Standard Book Number: 0-88421-034-0
Copyright © 1977 by Butterick Publishing
161 Sixth Avenue, New York, New York 10013
A Division of American Can Company

Contents

Acknowledgements   III

Introduction   VII

1 The New Year   2
   Keepsake   6

2 Groundhog's Day   13

3 Saint Valentine's Day   14
   Keepsake   16

4 President's Birthdays   35

5 Purim   38

6 Saint Patrick's Day   42

7 April Fool's Day   46

8 Easter   48
   Keepsake   53

9 Pesah (Passover)   71

10 Arbor Day   75

11 May Day   76

12 Mother's Day   81

13 Memorial Day   83

14 Flag Day   85

15 Father's Day   87

16 Independence Day   90
    Keepsake   92

17 Labor Day   104

18 Rosh ha-Shanah
    and Yom Kipper   106

19 Columbus Day   111

20 Halloween   112
    Keepsake   116

21 Thanksgiving Day   132
    Keepsake   134

22 Hanukkah   152

23 Christmas   160
    Keepsake   164

24 Personal Celebrations:
    Birthdays & Wedding
    Anniversaries   206
    Keepsake   208

25 Gifts   223

26 Craft Basics   282

    Material Source List   308

    Index   309

Color Plate List

Following page : 55

COLOR PLATE 1   The New Year
COLOR PLATE 2   The New Year
COLOR PLATE 3   Saint Valentine's Day
COLOR PLATE 4   Saint Valentine's Day

COLOR PLATE 5   Easter
COLOR PLATE 6   Easter
COLOR PLATE 7   April Showers
COLOR PLATE 8   May Day

Following page : 151
COLOR PLATE 9   Independence Day
COLOR PLATE 10   Independence Day
COLOR PLATE 11   Halloween
COLOR PLATE 12   Halloween
COLOR PLATE 13   Thanksgiving
COLOR PLATE 14   Thanksgiving
COLOR PLATE 15   Christmas
COLOR PLATE 16   Christmas

Following page : 183
COLOR PLATE 17   Christmas
COLOR PLATE 18   Christmas
COLOR PLATE 19   Birthday
COLOR PLATE 20   Wedding and Anniversaries

COLOR PLATE 21   Gifts
COLOR PLATE 22   Gifts
COLOR PLATE 23   Gifts
COLOR PLATE 24   Gifts

Following page : 247
COLOR PLATE 25   Cards
COLOR PLATE 26   Cards
COLOR PLATE 27   Cards
COLOR PLATE 28   Cards
COLOR PLATE 29   Keepsakes
COLOR PLATE 30   Keepsakes
COLOR PLATE 31   Keepsakes
COLOR PLATE 32   Keepsakes

Recipe List

Apple and Celery Stuffing, 189

Baked Apple Variations, 118
Bread Stuffing, 141

Candied Orange Peel, 191
Candied Pumpkin Chips, 144
Cape Cod Cocktail, 143
Challah, 108
Chestnut Stuffing, 141
Cider Flip, 118
Cranberry Frappe, 143
Cranberry Jelly I, 142
Cranberry Jelly II, 142
Cranberry Sauce I, 142
Cranberry Sauce, II, 142
Cranberry Tarts, 143

Dark fruit Cake, 192
Date and Cranberry Marmalade, 143
Decorations for Cakes and Cookies, 192–193

Egg Nests on Toast, 56
Eggs Susette, 56

Famous Christmas Punch, 10
Fricaseed Pecans, 190
Fruit Caramels, 190
Fruited Christmas Crescent, 188

Gelatin Eggs, 57
Giblet Gravy, 142
Glacé Nuts and Fruits, 191

"Half-Dozen" Punch, 10
Hamantashen, 41
Hot Cross Buns, 54

Indian Pudding, 143–144

Lemonade, 95
Light Fruit Cake, 192
Lollipops, 191

Mincemeat (with meat), 144–145
Mincemeat (without meat), 145
Mincemeat Pielets, 145

Mince Pie, 145

Nut Turkey Roast, 146

Oyster Stuffing, 141

Parisian Figs, 191
Plum Pudding, 189
Popcorn Balls, 119
Potato Latkes, 157
Prince of Wales Punch, 11
Pumpkin Pie, 144
Pumpkin Pie with Extra Cream, 144
Pumpkin Pie with Nuts, 144

Roast Turkey, 141

Salted Peanuts, 191
Spiced Cranberries, 142
Stirred Egg Omelet, 56

Taffy Apples, 118–119

Virginia Chicken Pie, 143

Introduction

With only a few exceptions, the days that we celebrate as holidays have their origins in seasonal changes. This results from the fact that agriculture was the mainspring of society supplying its sustenance and its main employment, and the seasons are a crucial factor in agricultural success. Not understanding the physical world around him, the ancients did not know why the seasons changed nor that they would continue in cycle. Therefore, when summer arrived and the wheat began to turn golden yellow, man celebrated to thank his God and hoped, as well, that if his celebration were sincere, autumn would follow.

As time progressed the customs surrounding holiday celebrations changed to reflect different social and religious traditions. One finds, for example, many pagan customs in religious holiday observances because Christianity found it impossible to exorcise these secular ceremonies and so gave them religious meanings. Also, when Pope Gregory III changed the Julian calendar year a number of holidays were repositioned in the calendar year and customs associated with different holidays became intermingled.

Patriotic and personal events are also sources of major celebrations. And they often assume seasonal characteristics in their observances.

Celebrations concentrates its attention on holiday celebration ideas which were presented in the "ladies" magazines of the period 1835-1935, primarily "The Delineator," a Butterick publication, and "Godey's Lady's Book", the first woman's magazine in the United States, both of which are preserved in the Butterick Archives.

In addition to information regarding the latest clothing and home decorating fashions, gift ideas, crafts, and recipes, which both magazines contained in abundance, "Godey's Lady's Book" was characterized by sentimental poetry, romantic adventure stories and an occasional cause, such as the famous crusade of its editor Sarah Josepha Hale to have Thanksgiving become a national holiday. "The Delineator" began in 1875 as a fashion publication containing a catalog of the latest Butterick patterns and evolved into a magazine concerned with such relevant problems as child care and woman's suffrage. The Delineator Institute, which was operated by the publishers of "The Delineator", developed recipes and cooking techniques, produced numerous party and craft booklets and published a cookbook. Magazines such as "The Delineator", "Godey's Lady's Book" and others played a vital role in passing on traditions and establishing new ones in a rapidly changing world.

The time span covered by this book was an era of great change in America. Massive immigration occurred during this period, breathing life into the spiritless celebrations resulting from the austerity of our Puritan heritage. There were wars which diverted national interest and raw materials, resulting in recipes such as cranberry sauce sweetened with corn syrup and the exhortation to "use the wool yarn for the boys in the trenches and reknit old garments for the folks at home." Tremendous improvements in household methods, hygiene, and appliances—from wood stove, to coal, to oil, to gas and electric in 75 short years—enabled recipes to contain standard language of weights, measurements and temperatures and success no longer depended on the cook who could "tell when it looks right". Craft materials changed as did tastes . . . glue replaced sewing in some projects, glitter replaced tin shavings, beads and tassels fell from favor for home decor. Women got the vote and many went to work, leaving little time to carry on family holiday traditions. The magazines we surveyed tried to chronicle the old traditions, retaining the best for the future and at the same time presenting new ideas for new life styles.

Throughout the time period covered by this book, a high premium was placed on any work—needlework, gift making, card making, cooking—done by the individual. Readers were repeatedly urged to make a special personal effort in order to receive full measure in return. Today, many people have rediscovered the deep satisfaction of "making" as opposed to "buying" and more than ever, hand work is especially prized. Our early forebearers, lacing television, radio, movies and easy mobility, turned to home celebrations for entertainment. Elaborate parties were held on the slightest pretext, and people became personally involved in the most minute preparations for these get-togethers.

Celebrations considers both major and minor holidays. The greatest emphasis, as would be expected, is on the more widely celebrated holidays of the year such as Thanksgiving, Christmas, and Easter. Aside from holidays which we celebrate together as a nation or as religious groups, the book also explores the personal holidays of birthdays and wedding anniversaries. Other interesting holidays have been discussed because of their historical significance or the importance which they once enjoyed. Some holidays have been included which are of special interest to segments of our population; among these are St. Patrick's Day, Columbus Day, and several Jewish holidays but the book does not attempt to explore the contributions of individual ethnic groups to our national celebrations, beyond specific illustrations in the historical development of each holiday.

The book includes all facets of a holiday celebration. Each chapter begins with a brief history tracing the evolution of the holiday and its observance in America. There are party plans complete with decorations, games, and menus; suggestions for family meals and activities; gift projects; traditional holiday menus and foods with recipes; greeting card designs; gift wrapping ideas. Customs which have come to use from all over the world through our emigrating ancestors are explored.

Of special interest are the "Keepsakes". This series of eight designs, one for each of the major celebrations in this book, can be interpreted in a choice of several needlework forms according to the preference and skill of the worker. The designs are presented as framed pictures to be hung in the home during the appropriate season. Since the designs are all the same size, a single frame can be used for all. They will become a treasured part of a family's holiday tradition.

Since gift giving is such an important part of the celebration of many holidays, this book contains over fifty gift projects which can be crafted at home. These projects are complete with illustrated instructions. The gift ideas have been adapted from gift projects contained in the pages of the ladies' magazines during 100 years of our history.

Techniques for crafting the gift and holiday projects in this book are carefully explained and illustrated in the "Craft Basics" chapter of this book. In most instances special skills are not required to interpret the ideas contained in <u>Celebrations</u>.

The projects in this book have been adapted only as much as necessary to make them relevant—many times an interesting idea required updating in intent, materials, or technique. Wherever possible, however, the original has been left intact. The recipes have been tested and adjusted to modern ingredients and cooking methods.

Throughout the book drawings, engravings, page embellishments, color illustrations, poetry, and quotations are reproduced from the pages of the original magazines to convey the spirit of these historical treasures, the high level of design, and evolving art styles. Many of the page decorations can be adapted to craft projects, gifts, and card designs.

Some full color cover or page illustrations have also been reproduced from these periodicals and are intended to convey the feeling of how certain holidays were regarded at various times. These have been supplemented by color photographs of many of this book's projects which show suggested ways of interpreting many of the ideas presented in the text.

A writer in "Godey's Lady's Book" in 1896 wrote of holidays "We have had too much evolution. The trouble with us is that we know too much." Unfortunately, this may be true where holiday observances are concerned for it is hard to take seriously such traditions as Halloween's expansive predictions of one's fate or St. Valentine's Day's coy sentimentality. There are, however, many good reasons for celebrating these religious, patriotic, or personal days. As "Godey's Lady's Book" quoted in 1852

Festivals, when duly observed, attach men to the civil and religious institutions of their country; it is an evil, therefore, when they fall into disuse. Who is there who does not recollect their effect upon himself in early life?

Tradition is the stuff of celebrations. Don't, however, be so bound by it that you are unable to discard those habits of which you have truly grown tired or never enjoyed anyway. We have searched through many nostalgic resources to find ideas that are fun, interesting, and, often surprisingly relevant to a modern society. Some will be new to you, some familiar. Choose what interests you from the documented customs and make it part of your own celebration.

BECKY STEVENS CORDELLO

"RESOLUSHUNS"

By Margaret G. Hayes

Illustrated by Grace G. Drayton

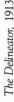

He'd quit a-teasin' 'ittle girls
Wif catty-pillers in their curls.
When Sister's best beau comes to call
He'd never hide—an' tell—*a-tall*;
He'd never climb on kitchen roofs
To hide his Granny-ma's false toofs;
He'd never take Aunt Belle's gold puffs,
An' stuff 'em in her new beau's cuffs.
Green apples? No, he'd never steal,
Nor monkey wif Big Bruvver's wheel:
He'd clean his teef, an' scrub his neck,
An' never sulk the leastes' speck,
When comp'ny comes an' he's helped last.
Folks 'll forget his naughty past.
These resolushuns, when he maked 'em,
He meaned to keep—but oh, he breaked 'em!
So now he says: "Folks, do not fear!
I'll make a bran' new set—Nex' Year."

ONCE'T ther' was a 'ittle boy—
    What maked some resolushuns,
On New Year's Day—'at he would stop
    A-bein' sech a "Noo-sanse."
He sed, he'd start in takin' bafs
    Without no drivin' to it;
He sed, he'd go to bed at night
    Soon as he's telled to do it.
An' after this he'd stick to trufe,
    'An never tell a fib;
He never more'd put a frog
    In baby sister's crib;
He'd never take the cookie box
    When Cook had jus' fresh filled it;
He'd alway say: 'at it was *him*
    Took Muvver's c'lone, an' spilled it.
He'd let the poor cat live in peace,
No more fill Gran'dad's pipe wif grease:

1

The New Year

Celebrated January 1
New Year's Eve celebrated December 31

The actual date on which the new year begins has varied considerably through history, although the day has been universally celebrated as a jubilant time when one turns one's back to the past and looks optimistically to the future. The different societies that celebrated New Year's Day generally believed the day to have particular significance in their lives.

The Romans, for example, began the new year on the anniversary of the day when they originally laid the foundation of their great city. The Jews regard the day of the creation of Adam, according to the book of Genesis, as the commencement of a new year. (The Jewish New Year, Rosh ha-Shanah, occurs on the first day of the lunar month Tishri, falling in mid-September). In 1793, the French decreed that the new year begins on the anniversary of the date on which they inaugurated their new system of government, the twenty-second of September, the autumnal equinox. The French, after the Revolution, restructured the entire year, dividing it into twelve months of thirty days each, with the five or six days left over celebrated as holidays dedicated to the ideals of the Revolution: virtue, labor, genius, and opinion.

The Chinese New Year is based on a different calendar and occurs sometime between January 21 and February 19. Among the more important aspects of the celebration is the idea of wiping the slate clean, which is accomplished by settling debts and acquiring new clothing. On the last day of the year the family gathers to celebrate and exchange gifts. There are also fireworks in the evening to chase away the evil spirits that have accumulated through the year.

Early Christians, using a calendar devised by Julius Caesar, had varying preferences, considering either the birthday of Christ or Easter (Resurrection Day) as New Year's Day. In 1582, Pope Gregory XIII settled the matter by designating January 1 as New Year's Day. This date gradually became accepted in continental Europe. It was only in the year 1752, however, that England and the American colonies proclaimed this date to be New Year's Day.

Because the coming of the new year has been almost universally celebrated from earliest times, characteristics of the various celebrations have found their way into many other traditional celebrations. The Druids, a pre-Roman Celtic religious sect, observed New Year's Day by giving gifts of mistletoe to friends. The Druids believed that mistletoe held great religious significance.

The Romans dedicated the day to Janus, their deity with two faces looking in opposite directions. The temple to Janus was closed during times of peace and opened in times of war. Because of the importance of Janus to the well-being of their society, the Romans dedicated feasts and made sacrifices to Janus before every undertaking and on New Year's Day. Similar celebrations occurred when newly appointed or elected officials were installed. At the same time, and for reasons which are lost to history, the custom developed of giving gifts such as dates, figs, prunes, and little cakes to one another.

In the earlier days of the Roman Empire, there arose the custom of the Emperor receiving gifts from his subjects, in return for which he would grant pardons. From simple gilded fruits, small coins to be kept for good luck, and oranges stuck with cloves (pomanders), this practice developed eventually to the point where the Emperor was demanding heavy tribute which became burdensome to his subjects. The result was that, ultimately, New Year's Day ceased being a day of happiness and rejoicing in Rome.

The English sovereigns also developed the practice of receiving tribute on New Year's Day from their vassals who, in turn, were given tribute by the tenant farmers who worked their land. These tributes served an important economic and political purpose in the early days of the English monarchy. By the time of Queen Elizabeth I, these gifts had become more frivolous and extravagant, involving vast quantities of jewelry, delicacies, and other luxuries. The practice of giving extravagant gifts became more widespread and it was common for ladies of position to receive, on New Year's Day, a pair of gloves or a dozen dressing pins, which were useful and highly prized at that time and considered to be very generous gifts. Bonbons or cakes in fancy boxes were also suitable gifts.

As the importance of Christmas as a religious holiday grew, the practice of gift giving among Christians shifted to Christmas. Closely related to the custom of gift giving has been the practice of exchanging messages of goodwill and congratulations. This custom has continued to modern times, to the extent that such greetings are often incorporated into messages sent at Christmas time.

Another New Year's custom which has developed in nearly all countries over the years and is especially important to the Jewish and Chinese celebrations is the wearing of new garments on the first day of the year. This practice symbolizes the beginning of a new phase and the forgetting of past ills.

Among some regional groups, it is traditional to eat certain foods on New Year's Day. Southerners feast on black-eyed peas (symbolizing pennies) and greens (symbolizing dollars) in the hope of influencing their fortune in the coming year. The Pennsylvania Dutch eat sauerkraut to assure having money all year.

Customs for the celebration of New Year's Eve also developed. Many religious groups held Watch Night services in which the congregation met and prayed together until five minutes before midnight. During these moments before the clock tolled the new year, there would be silence and private prayer. On the last stroke of the gong, the congregation broke into a joyous hymn. This service is still held in some churches today. The sounding of bells at midnight represented to the early Christians the battle between good and evil and the ultimate victory of good. The idea of using the annual midnight which comes between the old and new year as a time to banish evil spirits can also be seen in the Norse custom of using horns, shouts, drums, and cymbals to celebrate the coming year.

The modern custom of people meeting at each other's homes on the last evening of the year to await the new year and exchange affectionate greetings can be traced to Norway and Sweden. These gatherings were intended to reaffirm mutual friendship for the next twelve months. The American practice of having gay and boisterous parties on New Year's Eve came from the Dutch and their love of beer, wine, and joviality. This extended to the custom of having open houses on New Year's Day, when friends could freely visit each other without previous invitation. In New York City in the 1870's, this day was also called "Gentleman's Day," since it was the custom for men to take the liberty of making brief and friendly visits to their female acquaintances.

It was considered essential to have an open house on New Year's Day in order to maintain one's social status in the community. Initially formal attire and lavish buffets were the order of the day for these events, although simple menus were also socially acceptable. Because of the tendency of many young gentlemen guests to take advantage of the generous offerings of food and drink, open houses became open "by invitation only," and the charming custom gradually died out almost completely. New Year's Day, however, remains in one sense "Gentleman's Day," with its prolific offerings of televised football which so many men—and women—find compelling. Perhaps the old custom could be reversed: the men could stay home with the TV set while women go a-calling!

Until 1934, it was the practice for the President to hold an open house in the White House. This custom probably began with the presidency of Andrew Jackson.

A relatively new custom is the making of New Year's resolutions. Considering the historical spirit of New Year's Day, this practice is clearly based on the wish to make the new year better and to turn a new leaf in one's life.

Each grid square is equal to one square inch.

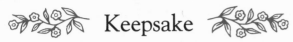

Keepsake

HAPPY NEW YEAR COLOR PLATES 31 and 32

Based on page decorations appearing in *Needle-Art*, 1924, and *The Delineator*, 1926, this design is worked in three simple embroidery stitches. See Embroidery, page 289.

MATERIALS:
 1 piece fine white linen, 15″ × 18″
 Persian yarn: bright golden yellow, light brown, dark brown, black, and red
 crewel needle
 marking equipment
 2 11″ and 2 14″ canvas stretchers
 staple gun or thumb tacks

STEP-BY-STEP:
 Note: Use 1-ply yarn for this project.
1. Enlarge design to 11″ × 14″. .
2. Transfer design to center of white linen.
3. Embroider design as follows:
 banner and words red yarn, backstitch
 cupid (body) black yarn, backstitch
 (hair) light brown yarn, backstitch
 hourglass (all outlines) black yarn, backstitch
 (top and bottom) light brown yarn and dark brown yarn, satin stitch
 (side bars) black yarn, satin stitch
 sand bright golden yellow yarn, French knots
4. Clean and block if necessary.
5. Stretch and frame.

New Year's Wishing Tree

Because New Year's follows as closely as it does on the heels of Christmas, holiday wreaths and greens will still be plentiful in the house and will provide suitable New Year's decorations. After Christmas, the Christmas tree is often ignored, no longer an object of great fascination now that the mysterious bundles it so carefully guarded have been opened. But the job of the tree doesn't have to be over. By transforming the Christmas tree into a New Year's Wishing Tree, the importance of the tree as a center of activity continues and the joy and pleasure the tree provides is lengthened while the task of packing away the decorations and disposing of the tree is postponed.

A primary activity at New Year's is making resolutions for changes in the coming year and extending the wish that the new year will be happy, healthy, and prosperous. The Wishing Tree, from a 1923 *Delineator*, provides each guest a random prediction for the future, a fulfillment (in spirit) of some fond wish, and a charm for good luck in the coming twelve months. The Wishing Tree is a suitable center of activity either for New Year's Eve and New Year's Day festivities or for visitors.

Decorating the Wishing Tree

Remove a few Christmas decorations from the tree to provide space for the wishing ornaments to be added. Leave garlands, tinsel, lights, and balls in place. Many of the ornaments which follow may be seen in Color Plate 2.

Walnut Fortunes, *The Delineator*, 1901
Carefully pry walnuts open so there will be two perfect half shells each. Remove nut meat. Inside shell, place a fortune written on a piece of paper or some symbol indicative of a prediction for the year (Illustration 1-1):

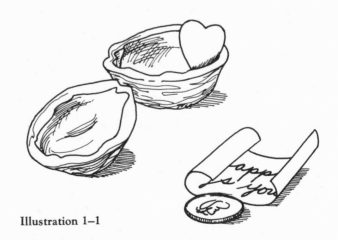

Illustration 1–1

- coin for wealth
- tiny doll for a baby
- valentine for marriage
- candy for a sweet year
- bit of map for a long trip

For children, let the symbols indicate future interest or activities:

- paint brush for art
- tiny ball for sports

Paint walnut shell halves. Glue halves together, enclosing at the stem end of the walnut the ends of a 10″ string or ribbon to use as a hanger (Illustration 1-2). Guests choose fortunes from tree at random. **Note:** Differentiate between adults' and children's fortunes in some way. Hanger colors may differ, or use gold paint for adults and silver paint for children.

Illustration 1—2

Wishing Cards, *The Delineator,* 1923

On tiny cards write for each expected guest a prophesy of the fulfillment of some dearest wish. The prophesies can be outlandish and should be tailored for each recipient:

- "You will win at Wimbledon" for the tennis player
- twenty cashmere sweaters for some lucky lady
- a sports car for the owner of the most dilapidated vehicle in the group

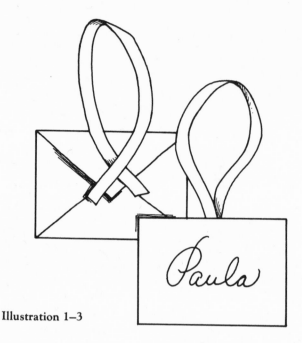

Illustration 1—3

Slip the card into an envelope, address it, and hang it from the tree with a ribbon. (Illustration 1-3)

Lucky Charms, *The Delineator,* 1923

- **Cutout Ornaments** Cut four-leaf clovers and horseshoes (Design Sheet, page 12) out of shirt cardboard and cover. Use textured or non-textured ornament method and gild (see page 172). Hang with gold cord, or red ribbon.
- **Rabbit's Foot** Hang white or brightly colored rabbit's feet by hangers made of red ribbon.
- **Good Luck Coins** Attach red ribbon hangers with white glue and hang.
- **Wishbones** Boil and scrub clean turkey and chicken wishbones to remove grease and cartilage. When dry, gild with spray paint. Tie a red velvet bow on each and hang. Since it will take some time to collect a number of wishbones, start early in the year and enlist the help of your neighbors.

Other items have special significance at the New Year as tree decorations, favors, or even gifts, should you wish to revive the ancient custom of exchanging New Year's gifts. Some suitable gifts may be seen in Color Plate 2.

Pomanders

MATERIALS:

oranges, lemons, or kumquats
whole cloves
cinnamon, orris root (optional)
red ribbon about ¼" wide, to fit around fruit
   twice plus 12"
ice pick

Pierce skin of fruit with ice pick and insert whole clove into each hole. Fruit should be densely studded (Illustration 1-4). Tie ribbon around fruit in opposite directions with a loop hanger at the top. Hang from tree. At one time, a pomander presented by a guest to a New Year's hostess was floated in the holiday punch bowl! Today, the pomander is often used to freshen a linen closet or drawer. Pomanders for this purpose may be dusted with a mixture of equal parts of cinnamon and orris root after cloves are inserted.

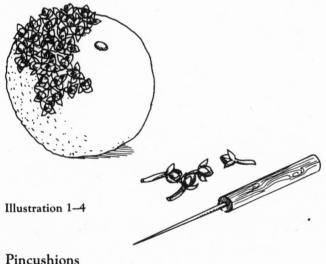

Illustration 1—4

Pincushions

MATERIALS:

pins
pincushions as desired
ribbon hangers, about 12" long

When pins were a luxury, as few as a dozen were considered to be a prized gift. Small pincushions make charming tree decorations or favors, particularly when made up in seasonal colors. Filled with pins, they handsomely revive the ancient custom of giving pins at the New Year. Use pincushions from the gift section (pages 228–231.)

Bonbons

MATERIALS:

homemade candies
bonbon bags or boxes

The early extravagant custom of gilding figs, dates, and other dried fruits gave way to the less wasteful custom of presenting sweetmeats in elaborate or gilded bags or boxes. For candy recipes, see page 190; bonbon bags, page 176; bonbon boxes, page 197.

Cake

MATERIALS:

chunks of rich cake
small white cake boxes
gold or red ribbon to tie

Cut pieces of fruitcake (see page 192) or other rich cake and package in small white boxes for guests to take home. Cake makes an appropriate hostess gift.

New Year's Eve Celebration

New Year's Eve historically has had a celebration of its own, ranging from the religious, such as Watch Night church services, to the merry, with noise to expel evil spirits at the beginning of the new year. There were many practices which were believed to assure good fortune in the coming year. Some of these were:

- Flinging open the front door to shout "Welcome, Welcome" to the new year.
- Arranging for a "first footer." It was considered unlucky for anyone to leave the house until someone from outside had entered—and that person had best be a dark-haired male, for maximum good luck. As a *Godey's Lady's Book* article in 1896 put it, "darkhaired folk could earn money and intoxication by well-timed calls."
- Having the first footer carry with him bread, to guarantee food for the year; money or salt, to guarantee wealth; and coal, to guarantee warmth.

• Having the head of the household throw a cake against the door to guarantee against hunger.

Dinner Party

A *Delineator* party plan from 1928 flatly states, "this night was made for gaiety; this night you may be naughty, even slightly devilish, a little mad. . . . Begin with a dinner and have a dance. One always dresses for New Year's Eve, and you may invite your guests either in masquerade costumes or in evening clothes. Why not suggest that all of them come as their own most powerful inhibition . . . and see how many Greta Garbos there are!"

In most of today's homes it is impossible to hold a dance, much less to have room left over to set up a formal dinner. Modern New Year's Eve celebrations have become more informal, but just once it might be fun to relive some of the formal elegance of days gone by. Don't have the dance, don't require the costumes, but do stick with the formal dress and plan an elegant dinner.

Decorations

Plan a sophisticated black and white color scheme with just a touch of red here and there. On a snowy white tablecloth arrange white carnations in a white or silver vase. Run black ribbon streamers from the base of the vase to each place, where they are tied to vivid red crepe-paper baskets filled with red and white mints. Your very best silver, china, and glassware should complete the setting.

Food

The same *Delineator Institute* booklet of 1928 which proposed the idea of a formal New Year's Eve provided this menu to put their philosophy into practice.

FORMAL DINNER

Oyster Consommé

Olives   Curled Celery   Radishes

Roast Duck

Orange Fritters   Candied Sweet Potatoes

Eggplant-and-Pimiento Timbales

Blackberry Jelly   Bread Sticks

Cranberry-and-Fruit Salad   Cheese Wafers

Mincemeat Tarts à la Mode

Salted Nuts   Sugared Dates

Coffee

Activities

The Wishing Tree

See the section on the Wishing Tree earlier in this chapter. In keeping with the black/white/red color scheme, the wishing ornaments may be colored silver, red, or white instead of gold.

New Year's Day Celebration

The custom of open and generous hospitality offered in one's home on New Year's Day has survived in much the same form through many generations. What more auspicious beginning could there be for the New Year than the happy wishes and Godspeed of friends and family? The French called it *jour de l'an* ("day of the year") to mark it as an occasion of particular happiness dedicated to friendship and the renewal of social relations. And on this day, visiting was considered the principal duty among all classes.

Tasty refreshments for the visitors were to be "conveniently arranged for gloved fingers" and placed on a table as far as possible from the front entrance to "the drawing room" yet within sight. In a 1877 *Delineator* article suggests choosing a lavish buffet menu from among these foods:

• salads and sweetbreads in fancy paper cups
• first and second joints of birds, cooked and cold, folded about the bone with fringed tissue paper
• boned turkey, spiced salmon, pickled oysters, chicken croquettes, ham, tongue

• Charlotte Russe, jellies, and other sweets
• sandwiches of grated ham or tongue with mayonnaise on thin bread, fancily trimmed or cut
• grapes, bananas, and other fruits

The offering of alcoholic beverages was discontinued when it became the fashion for young men to race from house to house, leave a calling card, quaff a drink, and dash off again as if on a marathon. After twenty such calls, their deportment left much to be desired. Hot coffee, hot chocolate, iced Apollinaris water, and hot lemonade came to be considered proper and fashionable drinks.

Open House

Decorations

Festoon the tablecloth with green vines caught at the corners with holly and mistletoe and at the edges with sprays of holly. Use red candles and set a vase of red and white flowers in a wreath of holly. (Illustration 1-5)

Illustration 1–5

Food

The same 1877 *Delineator* article that offered the preceding lavish menu also admitted that in some households "they consider the day too pleasant to waste upon wearing formalities" and served coffee, chocolate, and sandwiches. Try this tea menu from 1928:

TEA TABLE

Chicken-and-Almond Sandwiches
Orange Marmalade Sandwiches
Decorated Cakes   Flourless Oatmeal Wafers
Salted Pecans
Russian Tea   Hot Chocolate

Since this menu was offered in the middle of Prohibition, the hostess could not legally offer an alcoholic libation, and the magazines certainly could not give recipes for spiked punches.

Back in the Gay Nineties, however, things were different and one of the punch potions from that era might be just the thing to spark up a simple New Year's Day buffet of holiday dessert goodies:

DESSERT BUFFET

Candied Orange Peel[1]

Glacé Nuts and Fruits[2]   Parisian Figs[3]
Fricasseed Pecans[4]   Roasted Peanuts[5]
Fruit Cake[6]   Mincemeat Pielets[7]   Plum Pudding[8]
Hot Cider Flip[9]   Punch*

*See below.
[1]See recipe, page 191   [4]See recipe, page 190   [7]See recipe, page 145
[2]See recipe, page 191   [5]See recipe, page 191   [8]See recipe, page 189
[3]See recipe, page 191   [6]See recipe, page 192   [9]See recipe, page 118

A FAMOUS CHRISTMAS PUNCH
The Delineator Holiday Souvenir, 1899-1900

3 qt. claret
⁴/₅ qt. rum
1 qt. club soda
4 oranges (1 chopped, 3 squeezed)

4 lemons (1 chopped, 3 squeezed)
1 pt. fresh or frozen whole strawberries

Mix ingredients together. Makes a very nice dry punch. To sweeten, add ½ cup sugar to chopped fruit and juices and let stand a few hours. Another option is to add 1 cup of brandied fruit and syrup. Makes 40 4-oz. servings.

A "HALF-DOZEN" PUNCH
The Delineator Holiday Souvenir, 1899-1900

1 pt. claret
2 oz. rum
1½ oz. whiskey
1 oz. Benedictine
3 lemons

1 pt. to 1 qt. club soda
½ cup sugar
A few brandied cherries or one brandied peach, coarsely chopped

Mix ingredients and serve ice cold. Serves the number mentioned in the name. With the rum and whiskey omitted, this makes a nice light punch.

PRINCE OF WALES PUNCH
The Delineator Holiday Souvenir, 1899-1900

1 bottle champagne ⎫
1 bottle burgundy ⎬ approximately equal size bottles
1 bottle rum ⎭
10 lemons
2 oranges
3½ cups sugar

Squeeze oranges and lemons into punch bowl, add sugar, and let mixture stand for 36 hours, stirring often. Pour in the liquor and let the mixture stand for another 24 hours. Ice and serve.

Punch Bowl Decorations

- Prepare frozen rings of appropriate fruit juices or wines to cool punch without diluting.
- Place alcohol-saturated cotton bits in walnut halves; float in punch and ignite.

Activities
The Wishing Tree
Let each guest choose fate, fortune, and favors from your Wishing Tree. (See page 6.)

Children's Corner

Sunshine Diary, *The Delineator,* 1901
MATERIALS:
92 sheets unlined notebook paper, 3-hole punch, about 8″ × 10″
yellow cardboard folder, about 8″ × 10″, to hold paper
red and black fine felt-tip markers

STEP-BY-STEP:
1. Decorate cover with the words *Sunshine Diary* and sun and rays in black. (Illustration 1-6)

Illustration 1–6

2. Write your name, age, day, month, and year on first page of diary.
3. Turn page and rule a red line across the middle of the first right-hand page. At top of page write in red day of week, date, and year. Under red line do the same for the next day. (Illustration 1-7)

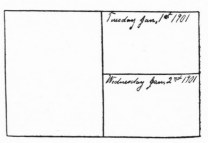

Illustration 1–7

4. In diary, write only the kindest and most pleasant things said and done during that day. Each day must reflect only beautiful thoughts. Nothing else is allowed in the Sunshine Diary.

Calendar, *The Delineator,* 1901
MATERIALS:
13 pieces fairly stiff colored paper, about 4″ × 6″
2 pieces of ribbon, 12″ long × ¼″ wide
magazines or greeting cards or other sources of brightly colored pictures
scissors, hole punch, glue
small printed calendar, about 2″ × 3″ (available in stationery stores or as promotional gifts from dry cleaners, etcetera)
Note: Printed calendars come in many sizes, so adjust paper size of this project to suit the printed calendar you will be using.

STEP-BY-STEP:
1. Cut out a picture you consider appropriate for each month.
2. Glue picture to top half of paper and glue proper calendar month on bottom half. (Illustration 1-8)
3. Glue another picture to remaining sheet for cover and write year on cover sheet.
4. Punch two holes on top of each sheet, stack in correct order, and tie in two loops, as shown.

Hold the two loops together at the top and hang calendar.

5. Mark family birthdays and anniversaries, school holidays, national holidays, and other dates you consider especially important.

A New Year's Wish

What better wish can be given you than that in the coming year you may never lose an old friend, but gain many new; that you may never do an unkindness, for which you would be sorry; that while God's sunshine is upon you, then will not be forgotten the blessing of it; that when clouds arrive, you will think with joy of the possibility of sunshine; and that on the gay opening day of the year, you will remember

'If all the year were playing holidays,
To sport would be as tedious as to work.'

The Delineator, 1882

Illustration 1–8

DESIGN SHEET

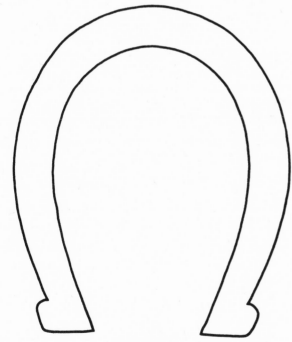

Horseshoe,
page 7

Half Scale

Four-Leaf Clover,
page 7

Half Scale

2
Groundhog Day

Celebrated February 2

Groundhog Day is connected with a traditional weather superstition brought to the United States by English and German settlers, who called the day Candlemas. It is thought that various hibernating animals come to the surface of the ground on this day to observe the condition of the weather. If the groundhog, hedgehog, or badger sees the sun, he becomes frightened by his shadow and crawls back into his hole to sleep for six more weeks. In this event, the farmer expects cold weather for the next six weeks and a poor crop for the year. If the skies are cloudy, however, the groundhog stays above ground and this is a harbinger of an early spring. This is a rare instance in which sunshine is a bad omen.

Pennsylvania has become the home of groundhog fables and many groundhog clubs have been organized to observe the movements of the groundhog and predict the weather. After stalking the groundhog at sunrise, these clubs fill the day with merriment and celebration, all with a slight touch of self-mockery.

Candlemas Day originally had considerable religious significance. It is also known as the Feast of the Purification of the Virgin. The name *Candlemas* comes from the fact that one of the rituals observed on that day was the blessing of candles. Among the British, Candlemas was considered the end of the holiday season. They believed it was unlucky for Christmas decorations to remain up after this day. The religious significance of the day was considerably diminished after the Reformation.

3 Saint Valentine's Day

The origin of this holiday is lost in history and many different theories have been suggested. Probably the most commonly accepted theory is that it originated with the ancient Roman holiday Lupercalia.

Lupercalia was a holiday dedicated to young lovers and it was the custom for young men to place the names of young women in a box and then draw a name at random. The couples who were matched in this way were considered betrothed and were expected to remain together at least until the following Lupercalia. The Lupercalia was celebrated on February 15.

During the third century A.D., a Christian priest named Valentine was martyred by being stoned to death. February 14 was probably set aside in dedication to his memory. Another possibility is that a Christian bishop named Valentine was so beloved by the people that they began to celebrate his birthday. Pope Galasius in 496 changed the Lupercalia on February 15 to Saint Valentine's Day on February 14, although the celebration retained the character of the pagan holiday.

Whatever the origin, it is clear that the holiday was firmly established in England and Scotland by the Middle Ages. As it evolved, an important element of the celebration continued to be the ceremony of young men drawing the names of young women from a box. As a result, the *love billet*, a slip of paper bearing the girl's name, took on considerable significance as a declaration of affection and esteem.

From the notion of not leaving to chance the selection of one's beloved, the tradition arose that a man would write his name on a piece of paper and present it to his chosen girl as early as possible on Saint Valentine's Day. In time these love billets were embellished with fragments of poetry.

Another quite different tradition was prevalent in Elizabethan times in connection with Saint Valentine's Day. It was thought that when an unmarried person went outside his home on the morning of Saint Valentine's Day, he would find his true love in the first person of the opposite sex encountered to whom he said the words, "Good morning, 'tis Saint Valentine's Day."

There is no common agreement on the derivation of the present custom of sending Valentine's Day greetings. What is clear, however, is that the purpose of the greeting was to profess one's affection. As customs developed, these greetings began to be accompanied by flowers, candy, or simple gifts, all with the purpose of reinforcing the message.

Godey's Lady's Book, 1848

Keepsake

TO MY VALENTINE COLOR PLATE 30

A mixed-media design based on a 1920 *Delineator* page decoration, this piece combines crochet, embroidery (page 289), and stuffed appliqué (page 284) to create an old-fashioned valentine. The design can also be executed in needlepoint, embroidery, or a combination of the two. Purchased elements, such as lace, can be incorporated into the design.

MATERIALS:
    2 balls white pearl cotton
    1 crochet hook, size C or other as needed for
        gauge
    1 piece fine red linen, 15″ × 18″
    1 large scrap white satin
    cotton embroidery floss: red, golden yellow,
        dark brown, white
    small amount of polyester fiberfill
    marking equipment
    white sewing thread, needle, embroidery
        needle
    2 11″ and 2 14″ canvas stretchers
    staple gun or thumb tacks

STEP-BY-STEP:
    Crochet Lace, Hearts, and Flowers. Gauge: 7 sc = 1″, 9 rows = 1″

Lace Mesh Ring (Make 1)
Round 1 Ch 160 (about 22″ long).
Round 2 Join to form a ring. Ch 6, skip 2 ch, dc in next ch, *ch 3, skip 2 ch, dc in next ch, repeat from * around. Ch 3, sl st to join to the 3rd ch from ch 6.
Rounds 3, 4 Ch 7, dc in next dc, *ch 4, dc in next dc, repeat from * around. Ch 4, sl st to join to the 3rd ch from ch 7.
Rounds 5, 6 Ch 8, dc in next dc, *ch 5, dc in next dc, repeat from * around. Ch 5, join to the 3rd ch from ch 8.

Round 7 *3 sc, ch 3, sl st to the first ch to form a picot, 3 sc in ch 5 mesh, repeat from * around. Sl st to join to the 1st sc. Fasten off.

Heart (Make 4)
Row 1 Ch 4, sc in 2nd ch from hook and next 2 ch, ch 1, turn. (3 sc)
Row 2 2 sc in 1st ch, and 1 sc in every st, 3 sc in last st, ch 1, turn. (6 sc)
Row 3 Sc in 1st and every st, 2 sc in last st, ch 1, turn. (7 sc)
Row 4 2 sc in 1st st, sc in every st, 2 sc in last st, ch 1, turn. (9 sc)
Row 5 Sc in 1st and every st, 2 sc in last st, ch 1, turn. (10 sc)
Row 6 2 sc in 1st st and sc in every st, 1 sc tog in last 2 st, ch 1, turn. (10 sc)
Row 7 1 sc tog in 1st 2 st, and sc in every st, 2 sc in last st, ch 1, turn. (10 sc)
Row 8 1 sc tog in 1st 2 st, and sc in every st, 2 sc in last st, ch 1, turn. (10 sc)
Row 9 2 sc in 1st st, and sc in every st, 1 sc tog in last 2 st, ch 1, turn. (10 sc)
Row 10 1 sc tog in 1st 2 st, and sc in every st to end, ch 1, turn. (9 sc)
Row 11 1 sc tog in 1st 2 st, sc in every st, 1 sc tog in last 2 st, ch 1, turn. (7 sc)
Row 12 1 sc tog in 1st 2 st, sc in every st to end, ch 1, turn. (6 sc)
Row 13 1 sc tog in 1st 3 st, 1 sc in next st, 1 sc tog in last 2 st. Fasten off.

Small Flower (Make 6)
Round 1 Ch 11, sl st to join to the 1st ch to form a ring.
Round 2 18 sc into center of ring.
Round 3 *(sc, dc) in first st, 3 trc in next st, (dc, sc) in 3rd st, repeat from * until 6 petals are formed.

Large Corner Flower (Make 4)
Round 1 Ch 11, sl st to join to the 1st ch to form a ring, ch 3.
Round 2 23 dc into center of ring. (24 dc)
Round 3 *(sc, dc) in 1st st, (dc, 2 trc) in 2nd st, (2 trc, dc) in 3rd st, (dc, sc) in 4th st, repeat from * until 6 petals are formed.

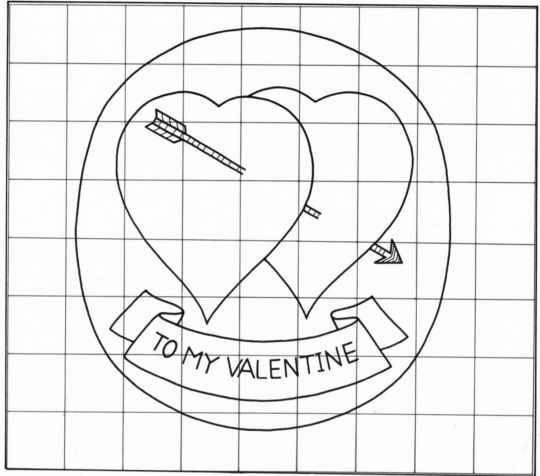

Each grid square is equal to one square inch.

Central Design

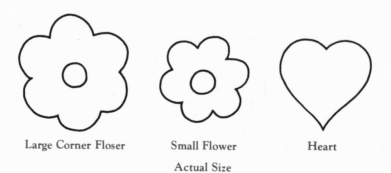

Large Corner Floser   Small Flower   Heart

Actual Size

Central Design

1. Enlarge design if desired. Central motif is given in correct size for 11″ × 14″ picture. Transfer placement of heart, arrow point, banner, and inner edge of ruffle to center of red linen. Corner motifs can be positioned by eye.

2. Cut two single hearts out of white satin, adding ¼″ all around. Cut one banner shape, adding ¼″ all around, also out of white satin. Transfer arrow shape to hearts and words to banner.

3. Placing stitches in directions shown, embroider as follows:
   arrow shaft 2 strands, golden yellow, satin stitch
   feathers 2 strands, dark brown, satin stitch.

4. Appliqué hearts, using turned-edge method (see page 282). Lap hearts and slipstitch in place, padding with a small amount of fiberfill. Do not pad too high. Take one tiny stitch at base of arrow embroidery on each heart to depress heart a bit.

5. Embroider arrow point on linen as follows, in stitch directions shown:
   shaft 2 strands, golden yellow, satin stitch
   point 2 strands, dark brown, satin stitch

6. Embroider letters on banner in 2 strands, red, backstitch. Appliqué banner using turned-edge method (see page 282). Slipstitch banner in place on red linen.

7. Using running stitch, sew inner edge of ruffle to red linen on placement line. Arrange small flowers and hearts on ruffle according to design and stitch in place. Stitch four large hearts in corners.

8. Stretch and frame.
   Note: If purchased lace is used (or perhaps a bit of heirloom lace you have stashed away), you will need about 22″ of lace about 2½″ wide; 4 embroidered motifs about 2″ in diameter; and 10 embroidered motifs about 1½″ in diameter, 4 of one design and 6 of another.

Valentine Cards

Originally these unabashedly sentimental professions of affection were sent only by men. The cards were handmade (presumably by the sender), secured with sealing wax, and hand delivered. The poetry in the cards was usually sentimental and florid, often copied from booklets of verse which were commonly available (*Godey's Lady's Book* dismissed these verses as "printed doggerel"). But sometimes the poetry was composed by the swain, if he were particularly clever. The verses were usually rendered in most careful penmanship. Early designs were simple and a variety of card-making techniques was utilized, including watercolor, pen and ink, pinprick, and cutouts, which sometimes featured silhouettes. Folded rebuses with numbered verses created a valentine puzzle for the receiver to solve. Early cards were often ornamented with tintypes or mirrors, or with painted silk or satin centers.

Handmade valentines had largely disappeared by the 1850's as imported lithographed cards became widely but expensively available. In the 1850's, an enterprising young American woman began to market valentines which she assembled of cutout lithographed flowers, bouquets, birds, swags, and similar design elements which she imported. These she pasted to paper lace, which was similar to modern doilies. Often, the cards were highlighted with color underlying the lace or with ribbons or tassels, and the sender could sometimes select a preferred verse from a catalogue and paste it into the card, thus personalizing the card as much as a hand-assembled card could be. In the 1860's, valentines began to be lithographed in the United States and became less expensive to purchase than the earlier imported lithographed cards, so that interest in hand crafting valentines declined.

Comic valentines have long been on the card scene, although they were neither as ornate nor as popular as the sentimental ones. Usually containing sharp caricatures or barbed humor, they were generally sent unsigned.

In the late Victorian era, handmade valentines were rapidly replaced by the machine-made variety. Although valentines reflected the general decline of taste of this period, there remained the essential charm and character of the earlier handmade and hand-assembled versions. Shadow boxes containing portraits and having ornately ornamented covers were popular and, for the first time, valentines began to feature children.

The turn of the century did finally bring a marked change in valentine style: lithography was the technique; more and more often children were featured; and such novel features as pull-outs and moving parts came into vogue. World Wars I and II, like the Civil War, inspired special groups of cards reflecting the concerns of the day.

Your Own Hand Assembled Valentine Cards

To make a really *old* old-fashioned valentine requires artistic skill and, at the very least, excellent penmanship. For those who are simply ingenious, without being artistically skilled, the hand-assembled varieties from the mid-nineteenth century can be easily and charmingly duplicated, using paper doilies, real lace, ribbons, gummed stickers, or designs cut out of used greeting cards or wrapping paper.

The multi-media Keepsake for Valentine's Day, for which the pattern is given in this section, can be reduced in size and composed entirely of purchased or cut and pasted elements producing a lovely sentimental card. The basic shape, which was inspired by a *Delineator* page decoration, is a very typical one and will serve well as a basis for countless variations. The first four designs which follow use this basic shape. Before beginning to craft valentine cards, please read Card Making, pages 284–288, for important information on paper selection, pointers on planning card and envelope size, and printing methods.

Golden Lace
COLOR PLATE 26
MATERIALS:
    1 sheet stiff white paper, 12″ × 6″
    2 French lace paper doilies, gold, 6″ diameter
    1 purchased embroidered heart, about 1½″ at
        widest point

    4 purchased embroidered roses, about ¾″ long
    4″ white satin ribbon, ¼″ wide
    bits of red tissue paper or ribbon
    rubber cement, sharp scissors
    red acrylic paint, fine paintbrush
STEP-BY-STEP:
1. Fold white paper in half to form 6″ square.
2. Cut center out of one doily. Separate doily ring that remains into four sections and arrange on paper. Glue in place, applying glue to inner edge of doily only. (Illustration 3-1)

Illustration 3–1

3. Cut 4 motifs from the other doily and glue to card to fill in corners in previously glued design. (Illustration 3-2)

Illustration 3–2

4. Glue bits of tissue paper under doily in selected spots.
5. Glue heart and roses in center of doily.
6. Paint "Be Mine" in center of ribbon with acrylic paint and notch ends (Illustration 3-3). Fold ribbon under so ends extend beyond folds and glue ribbon to heart. (Illustration 3-4)

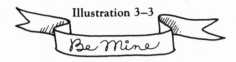

Illustration 3–3

Illustration 3–4

7. Write message inside card.

Ruffles and Violets

COLOR PLATE 26

MATERIALS:

    1 correspondence card, about 3¾" × 5¾"

    12" purple ribbon, about ¼" wide

    4 purchased embroidered violets, about 1" long

    5 purchased embroidered nosegays, about ½" diameter

    15" gathered lace, about ½" wide

    scraps of lace to cover one paper heart

    1 small sheet purple construction paper

    rubber cement, compass, needle and thread

    white acrylic paint, fine paintbrush

STEP-BY-STEP:

1. With compass, draw a 3½" diameter circle on purple construction paper. Draw another circle inside first circle, ½" smaller. Cut out circles, leaving a ½" ring intact (Illustration 3-5). Cut out 2 purple paper hearts, about

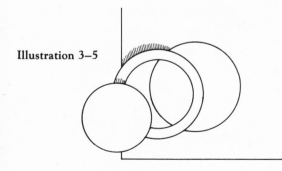

Illustration 3–5

1¼" at widest point. Cover one heart with lace scrap.

2. Glue paper ring to card slightly lower than center of card. Lap lace-covered heart over plain one and glue both to card inside ring. (Illustration 3-6)

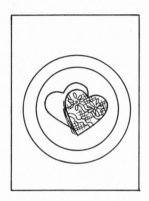

Illustration 3–6

3. With needle and thread, gather edge of lace to fit inside circle and glue in place.

4. Cut 4¼" length of ribbon. Paint "Be My Valentine" on ribbon with acrylic paint. Notch ends and glue ribbon across circle. (Illustration 3-7)

5. Make tiny bow with remaining ribbon. Notch ends and glue in place at top center of card.

6. Glue 4 violets in corners of card.

7. Space and glue 5 small nosegays evenly on lace ruffle, having 2 slightly overlapping ribbon banner. (Illustration 3-8)

Illustration 3–8

Illustration 3–7

White Lace

COLOR PLATE 26

MATERIALS:

> 1 folded plain note paper, about 2¾″ × 4¼″
>
> 1 paper doily, 8″ diameter
>
> 1 gummed sticker, violets or other symbol of the day
>
> rubber cement, sharp scissors

STEP-BY-STEP:

1. Cut rectangle out of doily slightly smaller than card.
2. Lightly brush rubber cement on back of doily and glue to card. (Illustration 3-9)
3. Cut motifs from remaining doily pieces and glue over doily edges on card. Glue sticker to center of card. (Illustration 3-10)
4. Write message inside card.

Illustration 3—9   Illustration 3—10

Forget-Me-Not

MATERIALS:

> 1 sheet extra heavyweight drawing paper, 9″ × 12″
>
> 4 forget-me-not flower stickers
>
> scraps of light blue paper or fabric to match stickers
>
> 1 paper doily, 8″ diameter
>
> 7″ white satin ribbon, about ¼″ wide
>
> rubber cement, sharp scissors

STEP-BY-STEP:

1. Fold paper in half to form 9″ × 6″ rectangle (a). Fold again to measure 4½″ × 6″ (b). Place card with first fold at top and second fold at left and work on front of card to make valentine. (Illustration 3-11)

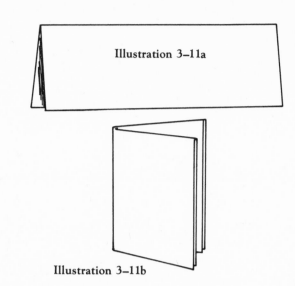

Illustration 3–11a

Illustration 3–11b

2. Draw a heart about 2¼″ at widest point on front of card and cut from top layer of paper only. (Illustration 3-12)

Illustration 3–12

3. Cover front of card with doily, positioning doily so that selected sections may be highlighted with paper underlays. When a satisfactory position is determined, cut doily to fit card front. Tack doily in place lightly with dots of rubber cement.
4. Cut colored paper to fit under desired doily sections and glue in place under doily.
5. Lightly brush back of doily with rubber cement and press in place. Cut doily away from heart cutout. (Illustration 3-13)
6. From doily scraps, cut out small segments of the motif and glue around heart cutout as an edging.

Illustration 3—13

7. Glue flower stickers on doily as desired.
8. Tie a tiny bow and glue to card at lower point of heart.
9. Tape colored paper or a photograph behind heart cutout, centered in the heart. (Illustration 3-14)
10. Write message inside card.

Illustration 3—14

Woven Paper Valentine, *Godey's Lady's Book,* 1871
MATERIALS:
   2 strips lightweight construction paper,
      3″ × 7″, one red, one white

STEP-BY-STEP:
1. Fold each strip in half to form 3″ × 3½″ rectangle. From folded end, make 2 straight cuts, each 2¼″ deep, ¾″ apart (1⅛″ from either edge). (Illustration 3-15)

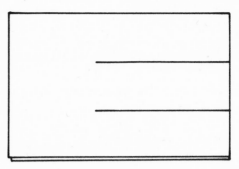

Illustration 3—15

2. Weave the strips into each other so that the folded end of one strip encloses the open side of the other. (Illustration 3-16)

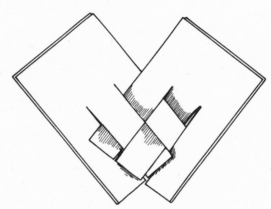

Illustration 3—16

3. Trim open ends into valentine curves. (Illustration 3-17)

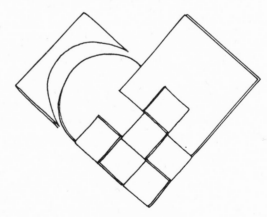

Illustration 3—17

4. Write message on small slip of paper and tuck inside woven heart.
Note: Experiment by cutting more strips into

the folded paper for a more complex design. Also try using felt or leather strips. This design was originally presented as a pen wiper.

Heart Frame, *The Delineator,* 1891
MATERIALS:
  1 piece mat or illustration board
  1 piece heavy paper
  1 small portrait photo or dime store mirror
  utility knife, glue, assorted trimmings to ornament card, fine felt-tip markers or pen and ink, rubber cement

STEP-BY-STEP:
1. Cut one heart out of mat board larger than photo or mirror being used. Cut another, very slightly larger, out of heavy paper.
2. On back of paper heart, lightly trace around photo or mirror (Illustration 3-18). Draw a heart smaller than the tracing over the outlines of the tracing and cut out heart. (Illustration 3-19)

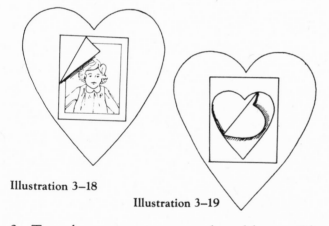

Illustration 3–18

Illustration 3–19

3. Trace heart cutout on mat board heart. Glue mirror or photo on to mat board heart, centering face (if a photo) over tracing of heart cutout. (Illustration 3-20)
4. Glue paper heart to mat board with cutout framing mirror or photo.
5. Decorate with ribbons, cutout pictures, drawings (Illustration 3-21). If a mirror has been used, the following verse may be lettered on the frame:

> *Look into this mirror clear*
> *And my true love will appear.*

Illustration 3–20   **Illustration 3–21**

6. Apply an easel back (see page 233).
   Note: A mirror valentine should be hand delivered to prevent breaking in the mail.

Children's Corner

Simple Valentines

Double Heart, *The Delineator,* 1894
MATERIALS:
  2 pieces red construction paper, 3″ × 4″
  1 piece yellow construction paper, 6″ × 1¼″
  1 8″ × 10″ sheet stiff white paper
  white glue, scissors, ruler
  heart gummed stickers

STEP-BY-STEP:
1. Cut two hearts (Design Sheet, page 34), 3″ wide at the widest part, from red paper. Cut a ¼″ diamond-shaped hole in the center of each heart. (Illustration 3-22)

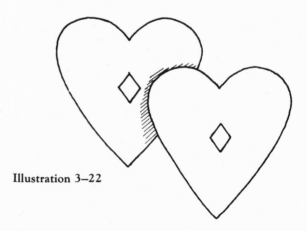

Illustration 3–22

2. Cut an arrow (Design Sheet, page 34) out of yellow paper. Fold arrow in half lengthwise and cut feather shape and arrow point.

3. Insert arrow through holes in hearts. Flatten crease in arrow and fringe end to "feather."

4. Arrange hearts and arrow and glue in place in the center of white sheet of paper. (Illustration 3-23)

Illustration 3—23

5. Write valentine message on paper, fold and seal with a heart sticker. (Illustration 3-24)

Illustration 3—24

Valentine Puzzle, *The Delineator,* 1916
MATERIALS:
    Several sheets white paper
    1 sheet red gummed paper
    fine felt-tip markers or pen and ink

STEP-BY-STEP:
1. From white paper, cut squares progressively

smaller by ½″, the largest being 8½″, the smallest 1″. Cut a quantity of hearts from gummed paper sized similarly.

2. Find the center of each square and fold in corners until they touch, forming an envelope shape. (Illustration 3-25)

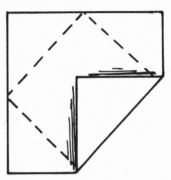

Illustration 3—25

3. Into the smallest square, insert a tiny heart lettered "I love you". (Illustration 3-26)

4. Fasten the envelope with a small gummed heart and insert it into the next larger envelope. (Illustration 3-27)

Illustration 3—26

Illustration 3—27

5. Fasten it and continue the process of nesting envelopes until all envelopes are placed one inside the other. (Illustration 3-28)

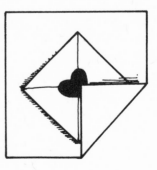

Illustration 3—28

6. Seal the large outer envelope and send it along.

Valentine Card Sachet, *The Delineator,* 1908

MATERIALS:

    1 white envelope, about 3″ × 5″
    small quantity polyester fiberfill
    sachet powder or perfumed dusting powder
    fine felt-tip markers, or laces, stickers, ribbons
       and white glue to ornament as desired
    straight pin

STEP-BY-STEP:

1. Draw or assemble valentine on front of envelope.
2. Fill with scented fiberfill, taking care not to fill too full.
3. Seal envelope.
4. With pin, prick holes in the padded envelope, following the lines of your designs or creating a design with the pricks. Pinholes should occur about every ½″ to allow fragrance to escape from envelope.

Valentine Sentiments

To a friend:
We scrap and fight
But just the same,
I love you best—
Now guess my name!

The Delineator, 1927

The rose is red,
And the violet blue;
Sugar is sweet
And so are you.

Metropolitan, 1873

If you love me as I love you,
No knife can cut our love in two.

Metropolitan, 1873

Ef you don't sheer mi luv,
ile soon be found,
Eggzactly 6 feet under the erth.

Metropolitan, 1873

For Father:
What can you give to a man like a king,
With dimes in his pockets and everything?
Well, even a king wouldn't turn up his nose
If loving Me sends a Valentine Rose.

The Delineator, 1927

If you love us as we love you,
Though far away, we're always true.

The Delineator, 1927

I wish I were the valentine
I'm sending you today,
I'd nestle close against your heart
And love you dear alway.

The Delineator, 1918

A hundred hearts would be too few
To carry all my love for you
The one I send is true as gold
And gives itself a hundred fold.

The Delineator, 1918

Flowers I'm sending you today,
Because my lips won't tell
What these blossoms boldly say,
I love you all too well.

The Delineator, 1918

My heart is broke, and you have done it,
By them little eyes you carry under your bonnet;
And, if you don't mend it by loving me straight,
I shall die of the trouble, and you'll be too late!
So take me then quickly, and you'll be in time
To have a good-looking feller for your Valentine.

Godey's Lady's Book, 1852

For teacher:
My teacher's gay and wise and good—
I don't obey her as I should,
But cross my heart, I never knew
A lady half so sweet as you.

The Delineator, 1927

For Mother:
My heart for you, oh Mother mine,
Forever sings
Sweet loving things,
Till every day is Valentine.

The Delineator, 1927

The world is large
   come, let us go
To Loveland
   across ice and snow

The Designer, 1909

Give me your heart and by its aid
I'll quickly find where mine has strayed.

The Designer, 1909

Valentine Gifts

Gift giving on Valentine's Day became popular in the 1880's. As an 1886 *Delineator* put it:

St. Valentine's day is becoming more and more a gift-giving day, and instead of the valentine of ye olden time, which, although costly, was of little use, dainty, useful articles are now sent; and oftentimes these souvenirs of affection are made by the donors, thus rendering them more valuable in the eyes of the recipients.

Many of the small personal items in the Gifts section, pages 223–280, are appropriate for Valentine's Day, especially the photograph frames and sachets. Candy is another popular valentine gift, and recipes for homemade candies are given on pages 190–191. To present the candy, use paper doilies generously in a box, both between candy layers and over the top. Decorate the box lid with one of the fancy valentine card designs in this chapter and you will have a delightful and sweet valentine! (Illustration 3-29)

Illustration 3—29

Valentine Celebrations

Valentine's Day is a good excuse for a party in February, which is a cold bleak month in many parts of the country. Little girls will be more likely to appreciate the dainty decorations in the party plan for children which follows. And, although they may giggle at the sentimental theme of many Valentine's games and activities, both boys and girls will participate with gusto, so plan hearty—but yummy—food. If you think the boys on your list will resist sentimentality, tone down the frills and change the details of some of the games, and they'll be sure to enjoy the party, too.

For adults, Valentine's Day has long been thought of as an obvious occasion for a card party. Since the principal symbol of the day is hearts—which is both a card suit and a card game—there are many opportunities for creative exploitation of this motif. And for those years when February's usual dreariness is prolonged for an extra day, there is a Leap Year Frolic from 1920 for teens and adults.

For any Valentine's fete, or simply to bring some of the merry spirit of the occasion into your home for a few days, decorate with hearts, the colors red and white, doves, flowers, cupids, and anything frilly and dainty. Heart-shaped cookies, cakes, rolls, sandwiches, even meatloaf, will carry out the theme.

Valentine Party for Children

Invitations

On smooth but slightly stiff white paper, trace a heart shape about 5″ at the widest point. Write the following verse from *Day Entertainment for Children*, 1898, in the center of the heart:

> On Valentine's Day,
> Your books put away,
>   And let your hearts gladden with joy.
> The school-room forsake,
> Your Valentine take.
>   We'll welcome each girl and each boy.

In the lower corners of the sheet, put date, time, address, host(ess). Decorate the corners of the heart with smaller hearts cut out of gummed paper, then spread a line of white glue on the outline of the heart and sprinkle with gold glitter (Illustration 3-30). When dry, shake off excess. In the manner of old-fashioned valentines, fold and seal each invitation with sealing wax (or hearts cut out of gummed paper) (Illustration 3-31) and hand deliver them. Or, for a simpler invitation, cut a single heart out of white paper and punch two holes in the top. Tie a red ribbon

Illustration 3—31

through the holes and write the message in red (Illustration 3-32). Slip into envelopes, seal, and deliver.

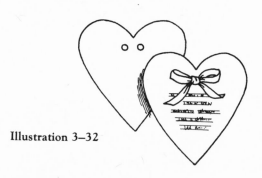

Illustration 3—32

Decorations

String the whole house with red hearts as the primary form of decoration. Glue hearts to narrow red ribbon or string and festoon from picture to picture (Illustration 3-33). Hang bunches of hearts from the overhead lights (Illustration 3-34) and in doorways (Illustration 3-35), garlands of hearts around lamp shades.

Illustration 3—30

Illustration 3—33

Illustration 3—36

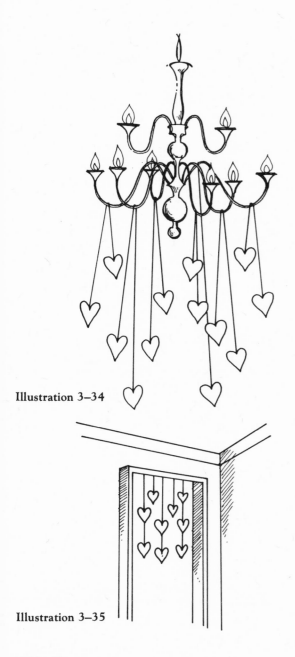

Illustration 3—34

Illustration 3—35

Table Decorations
COLOR PLATE 4

Cover table with a red cloth. Use white napkins with valentine stickers. Run strings of hearts of various sizes from above the table to a point between each place setting. The centerpiece is a Jack Horner pie in a heart shape. To make it, cover a heart-shaped container (cake pan, old candy box, etcetera) with white tissue or crepe paper and trim with red (Illustration 3-36). For each guest, wrap assorted candies (hearts with mottoes, candy kisses) or other appropriate valen-

tine favors in red tissue and staple a red ribbon to each. Run the remaining end of each ribbon through the tissue paper which covers the top of the pie and thence to each respective place setting (Illustration 3-37). On a signal, guests will

Illustration 3—37

pull the ribbons and receive their party favors. **Note:** The Jack Horner pie, named after the nursery rhyme in which a young boy stuck his thumb into a pie and speared a plum, occurred time after time in the magazines in various guises. It was a very popular children's decoration/activity and may be customized to any holiday by changing the shape or colors.

Lollipop Doll Place Card, The Delineator, *1918*

Lollipop dolls are appropriate on this day for which candy has become a symbol of affection. Directions which follow are for one lollipop doll with 2″ diameter head and 3″ stick.

MATERIALS:
    1 round flat lollipop, 2″ diameter, red
    1 white pipe cleaner
    5″ square white construction paper
    large scraps crepe and tissue paper, metallic paper, yarn, cotton, fabrics, red gummed paper, metallic trims
    white glue, acrylic paints, transparent tape, toothpicks, stapler

STEP-BY-STEP:

Note: Dimensions given below will vary if lollipop size differs from above.

1. Wind pipe cleaner around stick at base of candy to form arms. (Illustration 3-38)

Illustration 3–38

2. To enable doll to stand, round off one corner of construction paper square and trim opposite corner slightly (Illustration 3-39). Roll to form a cone, overlap edges, and tape or staple together. Insert lollipop stick into cone and figure will stand. Tape stick to inside of cone in balanced position. (Illustration 3-40)

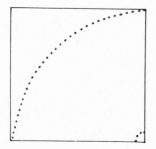 

Illustration 3–39   Illustration 3–40

3. Dress dolls according to illustrations:

King Machine gather long edge of 4″ × 10″ piece white crepe paper and glue to cone around neck. Cover arms with tube of 2″ × 2″ white crepe paper glued at shoulder. Make a hinged heart-shaped collar, 2″ wide, and slip over king's head to rest on shoulders. Glue a small heart to toothpick to make scepter and glue in king's hand. Glue on yarn hair and beard and paint on face. Cut metallic paper crown and glue in place.

Queen Glue tiny red hearts around long edge of 4″ × 10″ piece white crepe paper. Machine gather opposite edge of paper and glue to cone at neck. Make royal cape by gluing metallic trim to one long and both short edges of a 4″ × 10″ piece of red crepe paper. Gather ½″ from undecorated edge. Arrange cape around queen, open in front, making holes for arms, and tie with gathering threads at neck. Glue tiny bow of metallic trim at neck. Flute neck edge of cape. Glue on yellow crepe paper curls for hair. Paint on face. Cut metallic paper crown and glue in place.

To make place cards, write boy's name across king's heart-shaped collar. For girls, let the queen hold a narrow card bearing the guest's name in her hands (Illustration 3-41). In one hand, the lollipop doll may carry the guest's ribbon from the Jack Horner centerpiece.

Illustration 3–41

Games

My Heart is Gone, The Delineator, *1912*

All players except one leave the room. The one who remains hides a tiny stuffed heart, no longer than a thimble, *in plain view*. When the heart is hidden, the player calls:

> *My heart is gone*
> *And I'm forlorn*
> *Who'll be the first to find it?*

The others then come in to hunt and each, upon seeing the heart will say, without pointing to it and even looking the other way to deceive the rest:

> *Your heart I spy,*
> *With my blue (brown) eye,*
> *I hope you do not mind it.*

When all have found the heart, the one who saw it first has a chance to hide it next.

Pin the Valentine, The Delineator, *1912*

As a variation on the classic theme, have each player, in turn blindfolded and turned about three times, attempt to pin a valentine closest to the slot on a mailbox painted on corrugated cardboard. (Illustration 3-42)

Illustration 3—42

Stolen Hearts, Day Entertainments for Children, *1898*

Blindfold one player and hand him a heart-shaped bean bag. Other players circle around him, chanting:

> *Alack-a-day! Alack-a-day!*
> *Some one has stolen your heart away;*
> *But dry your eyes and calm your grief,*
> *And see if you can catch the thief.*

At this point, one player snatches the bean bag and hides it behind his back. The other players hold their hands behind their backs, also. The player in the center is unblindfolded and must guess who has stolen the heart. If he guesses right, the guilty one is blindfolded in turn.

Heart Hunt, The Designer, *1906*

Wrap mottoed candy hearts in tissue paper and hide them all over the party area. Award a prize to the one who finds the most hearts in a predetermined length of time.

Valentine Writing Contest

Older children may enjoy composing valentine verses to be read aloud and judged for prizes.

Heart Darts, The Designer, *1908*
COLOR PLATE 4

A harmless dart game with a fabric board to receive round darts with Velcro® covering will be enjoyed long after Valentine's Day has passed.

DART BOARD

MATERIALS:
¾ yd. red velour fabric
½ yd. white velour fabric
white thread
large sheet paper to cut pattern
4 canvas stretchers, each 22″ long
staple gun or masking tape

STEP-BY-STEP:

1. Trace dart board heart from Design Sheet, page 34, to make pattern for central heart (1), add ½″ all around heart tracing, except along foldline. To make pattern for outer heart ring, add ½″ seam allowance to inner and outer outlines of larger heart (2)

2. Fold white velour on lengthwise grain. Place heart pattern on fabric with center line of heart on fold, smoothness of nap running from bottom of heart to top. To cut out heart and heart ring, cut on all 3 lines according to diagram. (Illustration 3-43)

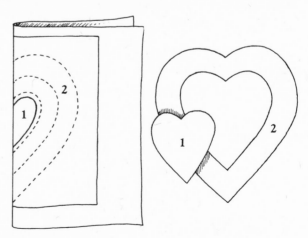

Illustration 3—43

3. Machine stitch ½" from edge of heart and inner and outer edges of heart ring. Press edges to wrong side of fabric on stitching line, trimming points, clipping and notching curves as necessary. Trim edges to ¼". (Illustration 3-44)

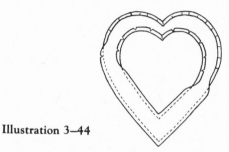

Illustration 3—44

4. Cut red velour into a piece 26" × 26". Locate exact center of red velour and exact center of small white heart, and pin white heart on red velour with red nap running from bottom of heart to top. Machine edgestitch (about ⅛"from folded edge) in place. Pull thread ends to wrong side and tie.

5. Place heart ring on red velour with small heart centered inside. Pin and edgestitch. (Illustration 3-45)

Illustration 3—45

6. Fit stretchers together to form frame and staple corners together. Center heart design, stretch, and staple or tape to back of frame.

DARTS

MATERIALS:
    1 Ping-Pong ball
    8" Velcro® self-gripping fastener
    household cement

Note: materials list is for one dart. As many as three are a good idea for full enjoyment of the game.

STEP-BY-STEP:
1. Separate Velcro® fastener and cut hook part of fastener in half, lengthwise, to form 2 8" strips.
2. Cut 1 strip to fit around circumference of Ping-Pong ball and cement in place.
3. Cut two strips and glue in place perpendicular to first. (Illustration 3-46)

Illustration 3—46

4. Cut 4 more short strips to fit in remaining sections. Let cement dry thoroughly. (Illustration 3-47)

Illustration 3—47

THE GAME

Hang the dart board at a comfortable height flat against wall. Stand about four feet from the board. Gently but firmly toss each dart underhand at the board. Give point values to the heart sections:

    outer ring: 1 point
    middle ring: 2 points
    bull's-eye: 3 points

The 1908 *Designer* dart board from which this one was adapted designated the outer ring "friendship", the middle ring "admiration," and the bull's-eye (naturally) "love."

Food

PARTY MENU

Heart-shaped Red Jelly Sandwiches Tied with Narrow
Red Ribbon
Cherry Gelatine in Heart-Shaped Molds with
Whipped Cream
Heart-Shaped Cake with White Frosting and Red
Sugar
Lemonade with a Red Cherry

Adult Card Party

Invitations

Cut hearts out of poster board, then cut each apart with jagged lines as though it had been broken. Be certain that no two hearts are cut apart in exactly the same pattern (Illustration 3-48). Write the complete invitation message on the back of each part and send only one half to each guest. When the guests arrive, the search will be on to match halves to form a complete heart. Invitations, card partners, and ice breaker all in one!

Illustration 3–48

Decorations

Decorate the serving table by using a white lace tablecloth with a red underlay. For a centerpiece, use a large bouquet of scarlet carnations with baby's breath and fern, with streamers of red baby ribbon, a tiny heart at the end of each, extending out to all parts of the table in a casual flowing manner (Illustration 3-49). Serving bowls may be decorated by cutting red hearts out of stiff paper and tying as many as necessary together at the top to fit around the bowl (Illustration 3-50). For decorating individual card tables, cover each with a lace paper tablecloth and paste a very large red heart to the center, thus creating large "valentines."

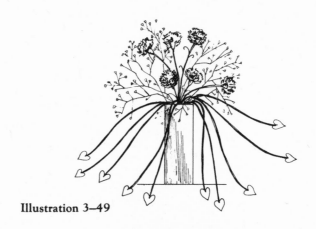

Illustration 3–49

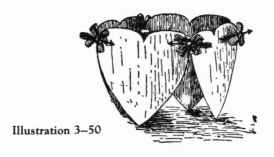

Illustration 3–50

An elegant card-party plan in 1894 used quite a different color scheme, concentrating on mauve and lavender colors and using violets (which mean "love" in the language of flowers), gilded cupids with quivers and arrows, and similax as accent greens. Scorecards were cut from pale-violet card stock and ornamented with artificial violets and cupid's arrows. To each a dainty pencil was tied with baby ribbon. Score pads were pasted on the reverse of each card. (Illustration 3-51)

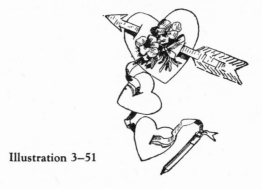

Illustration 3–51

Games

Hearts is the obvious choice of card games, followed (on a somewhat different level) by Old Maid, but any preferred card game is suitable.

Prizes which reflect the special theme of the day are books of love poems, boxes of candy, heart-shaped sachets, jewelry, and pincushions.

Food

PARTY MENU

Fruit Cocktail
Cream Cheese with Olive Sandwiches
Chicken Salad Sandwiches
Red Jelly
Hot or Cold Potato Salad
Strawberry or Cherry Mousse
or
Raspberry Ice with Angel Food Cake

Leap Year Frolic

Invitations

Decorate the edges of correspondence cards with a border of tiny red hearts (Illustration 3-52) stamped with art gum or cork stamp, (see page 286). In red ink, write to the men this doggerel:

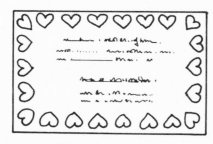

Illustration 3—52

On Valentine night, at candlelight,
  Your presence, lad, I crave;
And lest you fear the darkness, dear,
  I send a maiden brave!

To the members of the "brave sex" send this verse:

On Valentine night, at candlelight,
  Your presence, lass, I crave;
The lad below fears darkness, so
  Protect him, maiden brave!

And, of course, the name of the boy whom each girl is to bring is written on her card.

Decorations

Red paper lanterns, bobbing strings of cardboard hearts, red lamp shade covers.

Games

Sea of Matrimony, The Delineator, 1920

Each male guest is given a large cardboard heart and a pencil and each girl is given a necklace of ribbon strung with a number of small hearts (Illustration 3-53). On their hearts, the

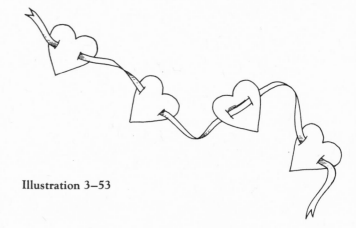

Illustration 3—53

men must describe themselves: hair and eye color, height, disposition, habits, past record in love affairs, future hopes. After a certain time, the hostess collects the hearts and places them in a large container which is labeled:

The water's fine,
Cast in your line,
And bring to land a valentine!

Each girl fishes and lands a heart—and must then find the man who seems to answer the description on the heart. When the hostess rings a bell, it is the signal for a proposal. If the girl proposes to the wrong man, she gives up a heart from her necklace. And the game continues until the bell rings again. The girl with the most hearts on her necklace at the end of the game is the winner.

Additional games may be adapted from the children's party, if desired.

Food

Foods suggested for the adult card party are suitable.

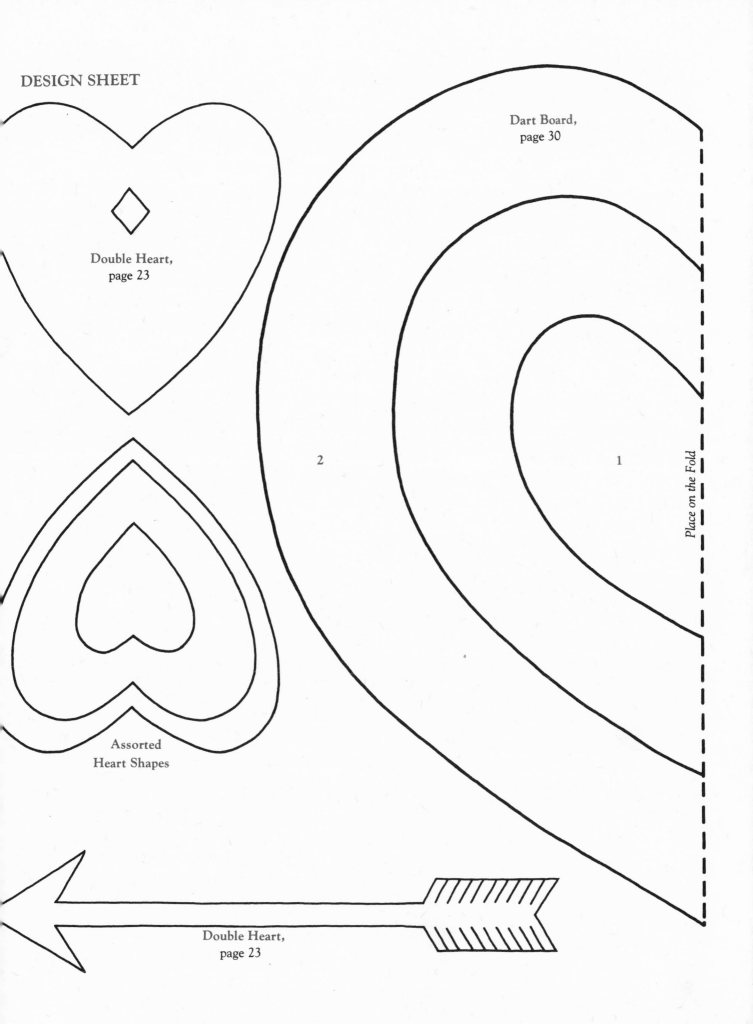

DESIGN SHEET

Double Heart,
page 23

Assorted
Heart Shapes

Double Heart,
page 23

Dart Board,
page 30

2

1

Place on the Fold

President's Birthdays

4

Abraham Lincoln's Birthday celebrated February 12
George Washington's Birthday celebrated February 22 with
Federal Observance 3rd Monday in February

Only two of our presidents are honored by having their birthdays celebrated as national holidays; they are Abraham Lincoln and George Washington. Both days occur in February.

Abraham Lincoln's birthday was first commemorated on February 12, 1866, and had more of the character of a memorial service. By the one hundredth anniversary of his birthday, in 1909, the memory of Lincoln had become an important part of the nation's heritage and private and unofficial celebrations of the day had taken place before then. In 1892 the state of Illinois, where Lincoln spent his youth, and where his grave is located, declared the anniversary a legal holiday. The 1909 centenary was celebrated in Springfield, Illinois; in Washington, D.C., where President Theodore Roosevelt presided; and in New York City, where one million people attended ceremonies at Cooper Union, where Lincoln had made a memorable speech during the years before his presidency. Major celebrations also occurred in Boston, Gettysburg, and Pennsylvania, and in certain cities in the South: Birmingham, Little Rock, and New Orleans. Today, thirty-three states of the union have declared Lincoln's birthday a legal holiday.

It is difficult to pinpoint the date when the first celebration of Washington's birthday occurred, because there were many unofficial, semi-public events commemorating his birthday. One of the earliest was a dinner given for French and American officers by the commander of the French forces aiding the colonies in the American Revolution. What is generally considered to be the first official celebration of Washington's birthday took place in New York City on February 22, 1783, when a group of people met at a hotel for a banquet and made speeches in praise of Washington. By 1791, there were celebrations in various cities of the country, as well as a parade in Philadelphia, then the nation's capital.

The centennial and bicentennial anniversaries of his birthday in 1832 and 1932 played important parts in the recognition of Washington's birthday as a national holiday. By 1961, Washington's Birthday was observed all over the country in schools, banks, libraries, and government offices.

Lincoln's Birthday Celebration

Lincoln's Birthday calls to mind the cabin in which he was born. Family meals on this day should be hearty and wholesome. The log cabin theme can be used throughout the celebration for a centerpiece or for food presentation.

Decorations

Place Cards, The Delineator, *1918*

To folded cards, affix gummed stickers of Lincoln's likeness. Or glue a shiny Lincoln penny on each card. Choose brief and pithy quotations from Lincoln and write one on each card along with the person's name.

Log Cabin Centerpiece, The Delineator, *1913*

MATERIALS:

> brown construction paper strips, 2½″ × 8″ and 2½″ × 6″
> construction paper as desired for roof, doors, windows
> white glue
> shirt cardboard at least 9″ × 7″, for cabin foundation
> large pencil

STEP-BY-STEP:

1. Roll the construction paper strips into cylinders, using the pencil as a foundation for rolling.
2. Glue 2 cylinders to the cardboard, crossed at the corners in log cabin fashion, to make the foundation of the house.
3. Continue in this manner until house is desired height.
4. Fashion roof and other details as desired. (Illustration 4-1)

Illustration 4–1

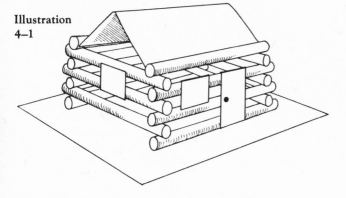

Food

LINCOLN'S BIRTHDAY FAMILY DINNER

Tomato Soup
Bread Sticks
Pork Chop and Potato Casserole
Little Corn Pones   Green Salad
Mincemeat Pielets**
Coffee

**See recipe, page 145.

Washington's Birthday Celebration

There are two popular themes for celebrating this day. One uses the elements of the famous legend in which young George Washington admits to having chopped down a cherry tree with the words "I cannot tell a lie." Games involving truth are played; hatchets and cherries become decorative symbols; and cherries figure prominently in foods both as an ingredient and as ornamentation. The other popular theme is Colonial times, with costumes, sophisticated foods, and games whose names commemorate some of Washington's exploits. Elements of the two themes may be combined as well.

Decorations

Gumdrop Tree Centerpiece, The Delineator, *1923*

MATERIALS:

> several short branches, spray painted brown or green
> floral wire
> green tissue paper or artificial leaves
> flowerpot of dirt
> circle of cardboard, painted green, to cover top of flowerpot
> red gumdrops, small
> needle and thread

STEP-BY-STEP:

1. Wire several branches together to look like a tree and set securely in pot of dirt through a hole cut in the cardboard covering.

2. To make "cherries," thread pairs of gumdrops with flat ends facing about 5″ apart. Knot and cut the thread at the small end of each gumdrop, leaving them attached in pairs.

3. Twist two pairs and a spray of leaves together and hang over a branch. (Illustration 4-2) Place a tiny hatchet at the base of the tree if desired.

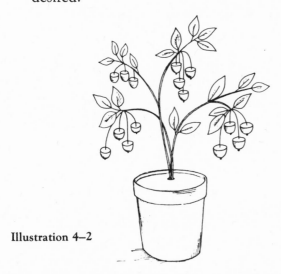

Illustration 4–2

Cocked Hat Napkin Fold

Follow the instructions for Cocked Hat (page 100), using napkins. Ignore the references to stapling and pompoms.

Games

Crossing the Delaware, The Delineator, *1921*

Divide the group into two teams, each with a captain. Stretch two strings the length of the room as far apart as possible, leaving spaces on the sides for the players to stand on the "banks." One captain starts the game by saying "A is coming to help Washington cross the Delaware." The first player starts across, acting out some adverb beginning with *a,* the action having been previously decided upon by the captain and the team. The object is to cross the "Delaware" and return before the other team can guess the word being acted. If they guess, the player must join their side. The side having the most players when the entire alphabet has been gone through is the winner.

Food

Plan a menu of sweets from the following foods:

- Lady Baltimore cake, angel food cake
- Bavarian creams
- Cherry tarts
- Red jelly sandwiches, pimiento cheese sandwiches
- Lemonade with cherry garnish

5
Purim

Celebrated the 14th day of the lunar month Adar
(February-March)

Purim, the Feast of Lots, is a joyous festival on the Jewish holiday calendar and commemorates the story of Esther in the Old Testament. The Book of Esther is the story of a beautiful Jewish girl who was taken as queen by the Persian King Ahasuerus without his knowing of her Jewish background. Esther's cousin, Mordecai, a learned and devout Jewish leader, refused to pay homage to the King's minister Haman and as a result earned Haman's ire. Haman persuaded the King to annihilate the Jews. A lot (*Pur* in Persian) was cast and the thirteenth day of the month of Adar was chosen as the day of the annihilation.

Hearing of this, Mordecai begged Esther to go to the King and persuade him to save her people. With much fear, Esther finally informed the King of her Jewish heritage and begged him to spare the Jews. Since he had come to love her very much, the King acceded to her wish and ordered Haman hanged.

According to the Persian law, a decree once issued could not be changed, so the attack had to proceed. The King, however, gave arms to the Jews and they were able to defend themselves and defeat their attackers. Mordecai then became minister to the King in place of Haman, and later he and Esther wrote the story in a megillah ("scroll") so it might be read on the fourteenth day of Adar, a day of triumphal celebration, from then on.

The Megillah of Esther is one of the symbols commonly associated with Purim. The megillat have always been beautifully illustrated manuscripts and the cases which contained them were often objects of the finest artistry and craftsmanship.

Purim is a carnival festival, not unlike the Christian Mardi Gras celebrated at about the same time, and may in some way relate to ancient pagan spring rites or to the ancient Persian new year festival. It is a festive holiday, greatly enjoyed by children. During the readings of the megillah, the congregation attempts to obliterate the name of Haman by making loud noises at the mention of it. Traditional wooden noisemakers called *gragers* are used as well as shouts and stamping of the feet.

Children particularly enjoy the tradition of masquerading, which grew out of the dramatization of Purim's exciting tale by roving troupes of actors. Although the children may costume as anything they like, the most popular

38

characters are the ones from the legend—Esther, Ahasuerus, Mordecai—and the selection of a Queen Esther as a form of beauty contest is often a part of the children's activities. School carnivals are popular events.

The giving of gifts to the poor and to friends is another tradition. One custom is to give to at least two poor people; another is to give two food items to at least one friend. Where these customs are widely observed, costumed children dash about delivering the white-covered bundles (called *shalachsmanos*) of cakes and other sweets. Hamantashen, a poppy-seed filled cookie shaped like Haman's hat, and kreplach, of the same shape, are traditional foods. Often family and friends gather for a feast on the afternoon of Purim. Sweets and hamantashen (see recipe below) are suitable for the shalachsmanos offerings.

Purim represents the resilience of the Jewish culture in the face of prejudice and discrimination and relates another reassuring instance of the triumph of good over evil.

Purim Costumes

Several of the Halloween costumes (see page 121) can be adapted for Purim masqueraders.

Queen Esther

The Fairy Queen makes a perfect Queen Esther. Different placement of the trim (Illustration 5-1) will give a more authentic Persian look to the gown, although authenticity is certainly not essential. Use the same crown and royal cape designs as for the Fairy Queen costume.

King Ahasuerus

Cut the costume according to the measurements for the Skeleton but construct it as a skirt, not pants, to fall knee length, giving a toga-like effect. Do not put elastic casing at sleeve edges. Apply trim as shown here, to imply a toga swept up and caught at the waist. Use a rope belt. Gold trim on white fabric is a good color combination. Use the crown instructions from the Fairy Queen costume, but adapt the shape as shown here. Make a royal cape if desired. (Illustration 5-2)

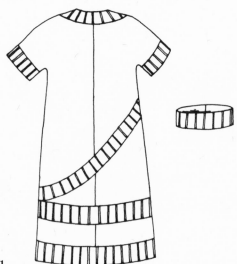

Illustration 5—1

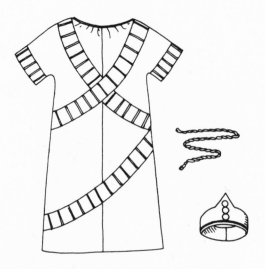

Illustration 5—2

Mordecai

Dress this devout old man solemnly in black. Using the Skeleton base, make a skirted costume as for King Ahasuerus, floor length. The cape should be black and worn closed, like a cape rather than a royal cloak. Using instructions for the witch's hat as a guide, make a hat by putting a 3"-high crown on to a 3"-wide brim, all black. (Illustration 5-3)

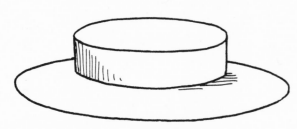

Illustration 5–3

Purim Grager

This traditional wooden noisemaker is adapted from a design which appeared in *The Young Judaean*, a magazine for children and young people. Other suitable noisemakers are metal-topped cans (spice cans, some tea and coffee containers, tobacco tins) containing coins, screws, or beans; aluminum pie pans banged together; or dried and decorated gourds. All may be painted with desired symbolic decorations. Purchased noisemakers from New Year's Eve and Halloween may be similarly decorated to customize them for Purim.

Grager, *The Young Judaean*, 1925
MATERIALS:
1 small wooden spool (Wooden spools are available in craft shops.)
2 wooden tongue depressors, about ¾" wide and 6" long
1 strip wood ¾" × ½" × 13" long
6 1" lightweight finishing nails
1 dowel, about 9" long, to fit snugly in spool
drill, drill bit slightly larger than dowel, file, white glue, chisel, hammer, fine sandpaper, saw

STEP-BY-STEP:

1. Cut 13" strip into one 7" piece and two 3" pieces. With chisel, chunk out a space in the middle of each 3" piece of wood ¼" deep and ¾" wide (Illustration 5-4). Sand as necessary.

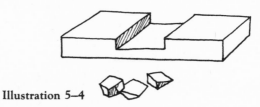

Illustration 5–4

2. Glue tongue depressors to one 3" piece on either side of carved-out space. Glue one end of 7" strip into depression. Glue remaining 3" strip over first glued strip. (Illustration 5-5)

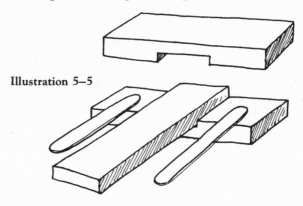

Illustration 5–5

3. When glue is dry, strengthen by nailing 2 nails through each tongue depressor and through center strip. (Illustration 5-6)

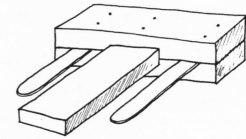

Illustration 5–6

4. Saw spool in half across the middle. With file, notch lip ends of spool. (Illustration 5-7)

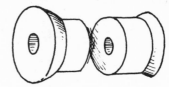

Illustration 5–7

Illustration 5—7

5. Using one spool as a guide, fit tongue depressor into one groove and note position of spool hole on wooden 7″ strip (Illustration 5-8). Drill a dowel hole in this spot through strip (Illustration 5-9). Sand dowel or hole as necessary so that dowel moves freely in hole.

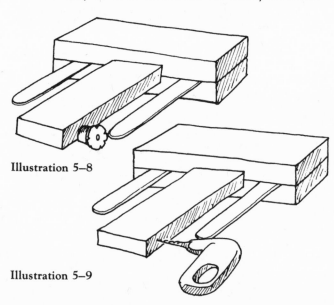

Illustration 5—8

Illustration 5—9

6. Fit dowel through spool hole, and other spool as shown. Glue one spool half onto dowel with teeth side up. Glue remaining spool half with teeth side down. Do not let glue ooze under strip as free dowel movement is essential. (Illustration 5-10)

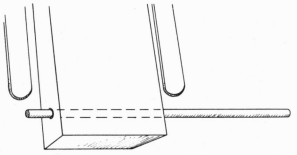

Illustration 5—10

7. When glue is thoroughly dry, grasp dowel firmly and swirl around to make noise. Stain or paint as desired and decorate as desired with appropriate symbols. (Illustration 5-11)

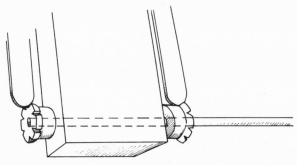

Illustration 5—11

Hamantashen

Although shaped like Haman's hat, these cookies are named after Haman's pockets.

TRADITIONAL HAMANTASHEN

3 cups sifted flour (approximate)	1 cup oil or shortening
3 eggs	3 tsp. baking powder
¼ cup warm water	pinch salt
1 cup sugar	prune or poppy seed filling
1 tsp. vanilla	(canned or prepared as below)

Put flour in large bowl and scoop out center; put remaining ingredients (except fillings) into center of the flour. Mix to the right consistency for kneading. If more flour is required, add a little at a time. Knead thoroughly and roll out on floured board to ¼″ thickness. Cut out 3″ to 4″ rounds with a glass. Place 1 tsp. filling on center of each round. Fold in thirds toward the center and pinch sides up tightly. Bake at 350° on greased cookie sheet until light brown (about 10 minutes).

Prune Filling   Mix cooked dried prunes with ground nuts and orange rind or use prune jam.

Poppy Seed Filling   Boil 1 cup milk with 4 tbs. sugar, 1½ cup poppy seeds, and 1 tbs. butter. Reduce heat and cook gently until milk is absorbed. Add 3 tbs. raisins, 4 tbs. honey, 2 tsp. lemon juice, 1 tsp. grated lemon rind, and mix well. Cool before using.

6

Saint Patrick's Day

Celebrated March 17

Although the celebration of Saint Patrick's Day in the United States is a happy and frivolous occasion, in Ireland the day has considerably more religious significance because Saint Patrick is credited with bringing Christianity to Ireland.

During the early history of Ireland, the religion of the land was that of the Druids, a highly ritualistic sect based on sun worship and belief in the immortality of the soul. The Druids were also very politically powerful and formed a confederation which fostered revolt against ancient Rome.

The exact date of Saint Patrick's birth, somewhere in Scotland, is unverified. His name at birth, however, was Maewyn and the time was between 373 and 395. Whatever facts are known regarding his life are obtained from his *Confession,* an explanation of his actions to his religious superiors. At the age of sixteen, he was captured by Irish marauders and sent to Ireland, where he spent six years in captivity tending sheep. It was during this period that he had the first of frequent visions which were to guide his life and which, at this time, assisted his escape.

For the next eighteen years, he remained on the Continent, studying at the monastery of Saint Martin of Tours in France. Later he entered the priesthood and ultimately became a bishop. Subsequently, Pope Celestine I named him Patrick and sent him to Ireland as a missionary.

It was during his campaign to convert the inhabitants from Druidism to Christianity that the legends regarding Saint Patrick arose. The shamrock was used by Saint Patrick to explain the concept of the Trinity, that one unity can have three equal components. The three leaves joined at the stem symbolized this idea. It is interesting to note, however, that the shamrock was also used in ancient Celtic fertility rites.

On his missionary travels, Saint Patrick was preceded by a drummer to announce his arrival. And, according to legend, it was with drumming that he banished all the snakes from Ireland. He had to dupe the last snake by luring him into a box, which he then hurled into the sea.

The first United States observance of Saint Patrick's death in 493 A.D. occurred in Boston in 1737 and was sponsored by the Charitable Irish Society of Boston. In Philadelphia in 1780, the Friendly Sons of St. Patrick began celebrating the day in that city, and its branch in New York began celebrating in 1784. These societies were fostered to a great extent by the Irish veterans of the American Revolution.

An important part of the American celebration of Saint Patrick's Day is a parade. Parades are seen today in Philadelphia, Boston, Savannah, Atlanta, Los Angeles, Cleveland, and New York City. The largest and most elaborate of these is the one staged in New York, where many thousands of people participate and upwards of one million people view the parade.

The festivities of Saint Patrick's Day are shared by everyone who feels the Gaelic spirit. It is common, for instance, for people to wear a green item of clothing and a green carnation. Drinking is a popular part of the gaiety of the day, and many bars serve beer that has been tinted green with food coloring.

Saint Patrick's Day Celebration

Saint Patrick's Day is a time of great merriment which may be observed by a special family meal or may serve as a reason for a party. For a family tired of the traditional corned-beef-and-cabbage year after year, try this menu from 1927:

FAMILY MEAL

Clam and Mushroom Soup
Baked Spinach Soufflé   Lamb Steaks
Cloverleaf Rolls
Celery   Olives   Radishes
Green Bonbons and Mints
Salted Pistachio Nuts
Chocolate Ice Cream   Mint Marshmallow Sauce

Saint Patrick's Day Party

Young people, especially, will enjoy the activities at this party. The menu is suitable for adults as well as children.

Invitations, *The Delineator,* 1919

Come a-wearing of the green
Every lad and gay colleen,
With song and game we'll celebrate
The birthday of fair Erin's saint.

Write the invitations in green on white paper. Ornament the paper with shamrocks (see Card Making, page 284). Fold and seal with green sealing wax.

Decorations

Use tiny pots of live shamrocks (or maidenhair fern, which gives a similar effect). Contrast with bunches of daffodils. If possible, provide a pot of shamrocks for each guest as a favor. Other symbols of the day are the harp, a man's pipe, snakes, potatoes, the flag of Ireland, and the shillelagh (walking stick).

Food

SAINT PAT'S PARTY MENU

A Platter of Thinly Sliced Boiled Ham
Potato Salad   Hot Oatmeal Muffins
Whole Wheat Pancakes with Maple Syrup
or
Raisin Pudding with Hard Sauce

Games
Wearing of the Green, The Delineator, *1898*

As each guest is greeted, he or she must show some touch of green in the clothing. If none is found, the guest must wear a huge shamrock cut from green paper for the remainder of the evening.

Orange and Potato Race, The Delineator, *1920*

In this relay, the object is to roll either an orange or a potato down a line marked on the floor (use masking tape) using a shillelagh, which may be any fairly thick, knotted stick.

Shamrock Walk, The Delineator, *1920*

Also a relay, each team is given two large green shamrocks cut from poster board, green felt, or vinyl fabric. The players move toward the finish line by taking each step on one of the shamrocks and moving the other forward for the next step. The contestant is never permitted to step off a shamrock.

Limerick, The Delineator, *1898*

This popular verse form bears the name of a county in Ireland, thus its relevance for the day.

Distribute to each player a paper on which the following terminal words of a limerick are written:

_____ *cow,*
_____ *row,*
_____ *light,*
_____ *flight,*
_____ *how?*

Each player writes in a first line, then turns the paper down so that what has been written will not show and passes the paper to the next player, who writes in the second line and so on until all limericks are completed. There will be one limerick for each participant. When read aloud, the poem which seems to make the most sense is the winner and the five people responsible for it are awarded prizes.

DESIGN SHEET

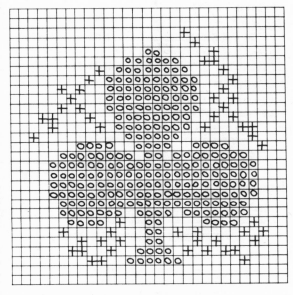

Counted Thread Shamrock Design
(Use for linens, cards, or clothing.)

⊡ = kelly green ⊞ = light green

Shamrocks

APRIL DAY SPORTS.

7

April Fools' Day

Celebrated April 1

There are many explanations of the origin of April Fools' Day, none of which has been satisfactorily authenticated. The day most probably relates to an ancient New Year's festival held on the vernal equinox, March 21, the beginning of the new year according to the pre-Gregorian calendar. In France, the custom of April fooling developed after the implementation of the Gregorian calendar by Charles IX in 1564 moved the beginning of the new year to January 1. Prior to the change, it had been customary to exchange New Year's gifts on April 1. When the date was changed, people began to send mock gifts on April 1. It was only sometime later that the custom made its way to England and Scotland. In Scotland, one of the favorite pranks is to send someone off to hunt a *gowk* ("cuckoo"). The word *gowk* is derived from *geck*, which means "someone who is easily imposed upon." The prank was so common that in Scotland the day is known as April's Gowk Day.

In the United States, the day is observed primarily by the young and the inveterate practical jokers. It is considered humorous to put a "kick me" sign on someone's back or to place a brick in a hat on the ground and to have a person stub his toe as he indulges in the common temptation to kick the hat. Another favorite prank is to tie a string to a wallet placed alluringly on the ground and to jerk it away abruptly as someone bends over to pick it up.

Another possible origin of April Fools' Day is that it is a remnant of the Cerelia, the ancient Roman feast which celebrated the story of Proserpina. According to the legend, Proserpina was abducted by Pluto while she was gathering lilies and violets in the valley of Enna. Distraught to hear the news of her daughter's disappearance, Ceres began a futile search for Prosperpina's voice. Because of the hopelessness of her mission, Ceres' quest has gone down through history as a "fool's errand."

It has also been suggested that April Fools' Day is a carry-over of Hilaria, the ancient Roman festival in honor of the nature goddess.

GATHERING EASTER EGGS.

Godey's Lady's Book, 1872

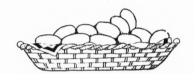

8
Easter

Celebrated on the Sunday following the first full moon
after the vernal equinox, between March 22 and April 25

The Easter season is the spring festival of Christendom, commemorating the Resurrection of Jesus Christ. In pre-Christian times, the season was celebrated as a time of renewal of nature's beauty and vitality after the deathlike sleep of winter. In fact, the English word *Easter* comes from the Saxon goddess of spring, Eostre, who, according to the Venerable Bede, opened the gates of Valhalla for Baldur, the Sun God who brought light to mankind. The festival to Eostre was celebrated at the vernal equinox, March 21. It is this date as well that fixes the Sunday upon which Easter is celebrated.

The exact time when Easter should be celebrated was for a long time the subject of considerable conflict. It was only during the reign of Constantine in A.D. 325 at a Council held in Nice that the date was finally fixed as the first Sunday after the full moon occurring at the time of the vernal equinox, which is also referred to as the fourteenth day of the Paschal moon. Therefore, Easter may occur as early as March 22 or may not be celebrated until April 25.

The Eastertide begins on Ash Wednesday, which is the beginning of Lent. The word *Lent* derives from the Anglo-Saxon *lencten*, meaning "spring." Lent is observed as a period of forty days, excluding Sundays, of fasting and penitence in preparation for the Easter. The period of forty days is believed to commemorate Jesus' forty-day fast in the desert after his baptism.

In the early Christian church, the Latin word for Lent, *Quadrigesima*, referred to the forty hours of fasting that traditionally preceded the baptism of converts on Easter Eve. In fact Paschas, the period from Good Friday to Easter Day, was expanded to six days to symbolize the six weeks of training required to instruct converts about to be baptized.

Later, as Christianity became more widespread and important, the fasting and penitence of Lent was applied to all Christians, rather than to the converts only. Gradually the importance of convert baptism as a part of the Lenten period diminished, to the point where today only vestiges of the practice remain in most Christian churches. It was sometime before the year 330 that Lent was fixed at forty days, excluding Sundays. Sundays were excluded because they are never fast days.

Penitence took on greater importance as an element of this period as time progressed. It was seen as a time when all Christians shared the sorrows

and sufferings of Christ. People who had sinned were reconciled with the Church by the end of the Lenten period, specifically on Maundy Thursday.

Later in England, in the fourteenth century, Lenten fasting was decreed by law and gluttony was punishable by fine and imprisonment. Even as late as 1688, King James II proclaimed publicly that Englishmen should abstain from eating meat. Lenten fasts continue to this day as a part of the celebration of Lent. Today, however, fasting is done primarily on a voluntary basis.

The association of ashes with the beginning of Lent, as is seen on Ash Wednesday, symbolizes the concept that man is born of dust and shall return to dust. The custom of anointing the forehead with the ashes of the palm leaves from the previous Palm Sunday was initiated by Pope Gregory (590–604).

The somberness and travail associated with the Lenten season has traditionally been anticipated by a feast representing the last moment of gaiety before the long hour of repentance. Shrove Tuesday is the best-known name given this day in the Anglo-Saxon countries. Its name comes from the fact that the old English practice was to confess one's sins in preparation for Lent. The verb *to shrive* (past tense, *shrove*) means both "to confess" and "to pardon" and evolves from the word *scribe*, that is to "prescribe penance." Shrove Tuesday also became known as Pancake Day because pancakes and other rich foods were prepared on this day in an effort to use up forbidden Lenten foods such as fats, eggs, and butter. To this day many Episcopal churches have pancake suppers on this day.

Mardi Gras, or Carnival, has a longer tradition. The words Mardi Gras refer to the attempt to use up forbidden Lenten food and are French for "fat Tuesday." Carnival, from the Latin *carnevale*, means "farewell to meat." Before the Gregorian calendar was adopted, the new year began at the vernal equinox. It was required that a number of days be inserted at this time to make the lunar year coincide with the solar year. Since this period was not reflected in the calendar, it was believed that the normal structure of society did not prevail on these days. The feasts, as in the old Roman Saturnalia, involved the reversal of social roles and standards and it was customary for the masters to serve the slaves. Many of the elements of this Roman feast are apparent today in Mardi Gras and Carnival, the main feature of which is the crowning of the Lord of Misrule, the Abbot of Unreason, the Bishop of Fools. Coming at the time of the vernal equinox, it was also a celebration of the coming of spring and traditionally included the killing or banishing of winter in a sham burial or by burning an effigy.

All these feasts and fasts, however, are in preparation for Holy Week, the most important time in the Christian calendar, starting on Palm Sunday and culminating with the greatest feast day of all, Easter Sunday.

Palm Sunday is the Sunday before Easter and derives from the New Testament description of Jesus' return to Jerusalem on the Sunday before his crucifixion. According to Matthew 21:8, when Jesus entered the city on the back of a mule, the people spread their garments and cut branches from the trees and placed them before Him as He passed. It is not certain when Palm Sunday first began to be celebrated. The Palm Sunday ceremony, however, has been recorded as early as the fourth century. Because palm leaves were not accessible in all the countries of early Christendom, this feast goes by different names. For instance, it is called the Sunday of the Willow Boughs or Olive Sunday in England and Blossom Sunday in Germany. In some areas of Europe, a Passion Play is performed with amateur actors recreating the trial, suffering, and death of Jesus.

Monday, Tuesday, and Wednesday of Holy Week are not celebrated as important feasts. Maundy Thursday, or Holy Thursday, is a celebration of the Last Supper when Christ offered the first Eucharist. The word *maundy* is thought to derive from the Latin word *mandatum*, meaning "commandment," and refers to John's account of the Last Supper at which Jesus gave a new commandment, "that ye love one another; as I have loved you" (John 13:34).

Two ceremonies have arisen over the years in celebration of Maundy Thursday. The first relates to the fact that Jesus washed the feet of His apostles. As a commemoration of this act, early English and French sovereigns would wash the feet of some of their poor subjects and in some churches today the practice may still be carried on. Later this developed into gift giving by the monarch, which is done to this day in a symbolic way. Another ceremony is the extinguishing of candles to symbolize the victory of evil and darkness represented in the betrayal of Jesus.

In early Christendom, Paschas was considered the feast to commemorate both the crucifixion of Christ and the Resurrection. Today, however, Good Friday commemorates the crucifixion and Easter celebrates the Resurrection. No authority is certain from where the name Good Friday derives and it is referred to by different names in different countries.

The most important feature of the observance of this day in many Roman Catholic churches is a three-hour service starting at noon and lasting until three o'clock during which passages from the New Testament which retell the story of the crucifixion are read. Attendance at this service is not compulsory today, although many Catholics try to pay a visit to a church during this service.

A custom which has become closely associated with Good Friday is the eating of hot cross buns. It is uncertain how this tradition arose, although it undoubtedly derives from pre-Christian times. The ancient Greeks used cross-marked cakes in celebration of Diana, the goddess of the hunt. The Egyptians used a similar cake in the worship of Isis, the mother goddess. To early Christians, these cakes symbolized the unleavened bread that Jesus ate during the Last Supper. Unleavened bread came to represent the Eucharist.

Aside from being the traditional breakfast food on Good Friday, a hot cross bun was hung in the home throughout the year to bring good luck to the household. This was a custom followed by seamen as well. The buns supposedly did not become moldy.

Holy Saturday, the day before Easter Sunday, became a separate feast day about the same time Good Friday was defined as a distinct feast. On the day before the Resurrection, according to Matthew 27:66, guards were placed at the tomb where Jesus' body had been interred, and the stone blocking the opening was sealed. No special service is performed on this day and this feast

is primarily a Roman Catholic observance. Following earlier traditions, the Episcopal churches perform convert baptisms on this day.

The culmination of pre-Lenten, Lenten, and Holy Week festivities is, of course, Easter Sunday. The traditional celebration of Easter is the dawn service which probably derives from the telling of the story of Easter in Luke 24:1–2, when he says, "very early in the morning, they came to the sepulchre . . . and they found the stone rolled away." These sunrise services may also relate to the Druid springtime fires. These rites, performed when the vernal equinox was considered the beginning of the new year, welcomed the sun, which was thought to dance just at the moment of sunrise. These services were held on a hill top and translated themselves into outdoor sunrise services which are still held in certain parts of the United States.

There are many symbols and traditions associated with Easter which, like the Easter lily, have no special significance. The Easter rabbit, on the other hand, is a symbol that pre-dates the Christians. The date on which Easter is celebrated depends upon the position of the moon, and the hare is the classic symbol for the moon, since it is born with its eyes open—suggestive of the full moon. The rabbit has no such significance, being born blind, and probably replaced the hare through a linguistic accident. Being highly prolific, the hare, along with the egg, was a symbol of the Anglo-Saxon fertility goddess, Eostre.

Throughout pre-Christian societies, the egg had profound significance. Many cultures held the belief that the universe derived from the egg. It was generally considered a symbol of rebirth and regeneration and it is fitting that it should play an important role in the celebration of the springtime feast of Resurrection. Another reason for the importance of the egg at Easter is the fact that, at the end of the Lenten fast period, it was once again permitted to indulge in this opulent food.

Dyeing eggs was not known in Europe prior to the Middle Ages and it is thought that the custom may have been brought back to Europe by the Crusaders, as it was common practice among the Egyptians, Persians, Phoenicians, Greeks, and Romans to dye eggs for their spring festivals.

There were several traditional reasons for coloring eggs: to suggest joy, to anticipate the bright colors of coming spring, or to symbolize the blood of Christ. It was also common to give these brightly and later artistically colored eggs as gifts. This practice was followed in all of Christian Europe and the ancient world. The custom of egg rolling was brought to the United States from England, and the first White House Egg Roll was held during the presidency of James Madison (1809–1817). It has continued since, except during times of war. The egg hunt, as well, was imported from Europe and is enjoyed today in many private homes.

The custom of sending greetings and gifts at Eastertime probably originated when the vernal equinox was the new year celebration. This custom is not strictly adhered to and it is not considered a social breach to ignore it. The wearing of new clothes at Easter also derived most likely from the ancient New Year rite.

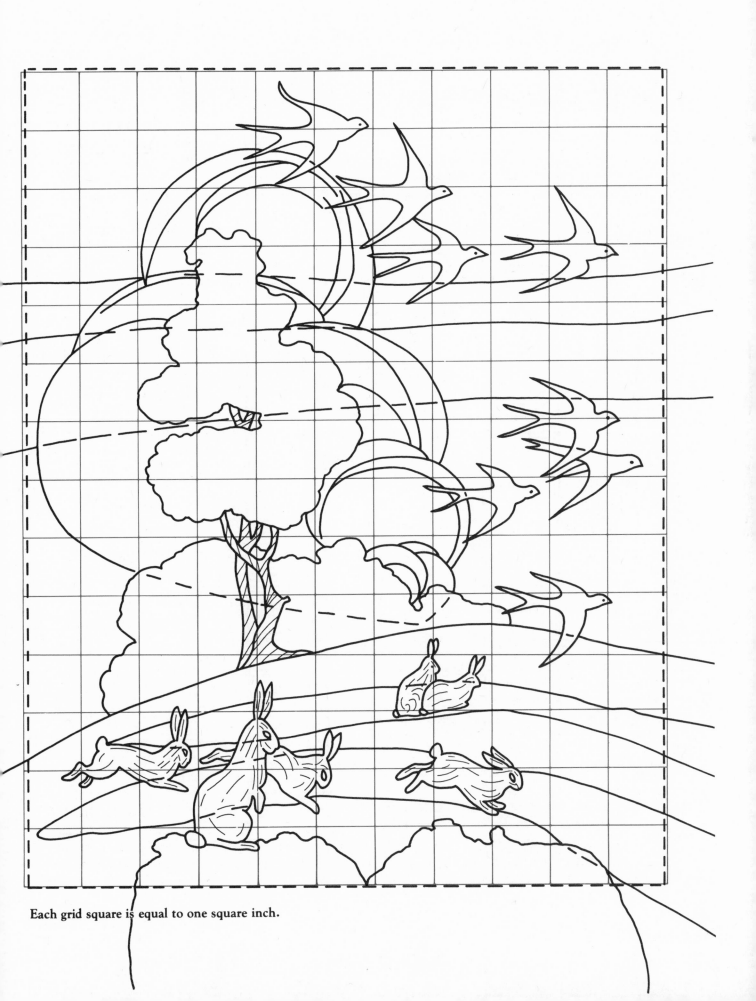

Each grid square is equal to one square inch.

 Keepsake

SPRING FROLIC COLOR PLATE 30

An appliqué interpretation of a 1910 illustration in *The Delineator*, this design may also be worked in needlepoint. See Appliqué (page 282) and Embroidery (page 289).

MATERIALS:

large cotton fabric scraps as follows:

sky medium blue (color 1), light blue (color 2), pale blue (color 3)

grass medium green (color 4), light green (color 5)

bushes and tree dark print (color 6), medium print (color 7), light print (color 8)

cloud white chintz (color 9)

bird light gray felt (color 10)

Persian yarn: white, pink, medium brown

cotton sewing thread: light blue, medium green

marking equipment

needle, thread, embroidery needle, sewing machine, white glue

2 11" and 2 14" canvas stretchers

staple gun or thumb tacks

STEP-BY-STEP:

Note: Use Appliqué with Turned Edge technique (page 282) for bushes, tree, grass, and cloud.

1. Enlarge design to measure 11" × 14".
2. Cut appliqué shapes out of appropriate fabrics, adding ¼" seam allowance all around on tree, bushes, and cloud, and on long edges of sky and grass. Light green should be cut in one large piece, as medium green will be appliquéd on top. Transfer cloud details and medium green grass placement to appropriate pieces.
3. Machine stitch seams of blue pieces, right sides together, to make sky. Transfer cloud and bird placement to sky pieces.
4. Using light blue thread, machine appliqué cloud in position and machine stitch cloud

details. Transfer tree and background bush placement to sky pieces.

5. Machine appliqué medium green grass pieces to light green piece. Transfer rabbit shapes and foreground bush placement to grass pieces. Machine stitch grass and sky sections together.
6. Slipstitch tree and bushes in place. It is not necessary to turn under lower edge of foreground bushes (light print fabric). Transfer tree trunk shape to cloud and background bushes.
7. Embroider as follows, making stitch strokes as indicated in illustration:

   tree trunk 1 strand, medium brown, backstitch outline, satin stitch filling

   rabbits (body) 1 strand, white, backstitch outline, split stitch filling

   (eyes) 1 strand, pink, French knot
8. Glue birds in position.
9. Clean if necessary and press lightly from wrong side.
10. Stretch and frame.

Easter Celebration

The many interesting food customs associated with Easter and Lent relate directly to the fact that Lent was, at one time, a period of strict fasting. The feasting and revelry of Mardi Gras were part of a frenzied last fling before the deprivations of Lent. The Lenten fast began on Ash Wednesday. In old English times, the week was ushered in by Collop Monday (collops are small slices of bacon) and was the day on which people ate meat for the last time before the fast. The following day, Shrove Tuesday, was observed by pancake suppers, the purpose of which was to dispose of fats, eggs, and butter before the fast.

Although Lent is no longer widely observed by fasting, the Shrove Tuesday pancake custom is one which can be revived as a family tradition or for an evening's entertainment. For a formal evening, simply translate *pancakes* into *crepes*.

Shrove Tuesday Pancake Party

In the invitations, ask each guest to bring a cook's apron and cap. Provide a pancake turner for each couple and batches of batter. The 1909 *Delineator* instructed the hostess to "have a good fire in the range." That advice isn't necessary for today's hostess but you will need several griddles, "as the shrine appropriate to the pancake rite." Each couple takes turns baking a griddleful of cakes. Prizes may be awarded for the most symmetrical, most tender, brownest, or most quickly baked. Suitable prizes would be a cookbook or a small frying pan. Eat in the kitchen so the pancakes can be served piping hot, fresh from the griddle. Quartered lemon is a traditional condiment, although sugar or maple syrup may be preferred.

If your kitchen won't hold a lively flapjack-flipping group, make a stack of crepes, keep warm, and serve buffet style with assorted fillings. For dessert, spread a crepe with softened, tart fruit jelly and roll while hot. Place side by side on a platter, lapped side down to prevent spreading. Dredge with granulated sugar and, with a red-hot wire rack, burn lines on the sugared crepes so the lines show distinctly. This gives a slight taste of caramelized sugar.

Good Friday Hot Cross Buns

The Good Friday custom of eating hot cross buns has continued to the present. In ancient times, the sign of the cross on the bun made it a Christian cake. Often the housewife used to make the cross on a loaf of bread to prevent the devil from interfering with her baking—and since Good Friday was supposed to be the most unlucky day of the year, she naturally took every precaution to guard against evil influences and make her baking a success.

HOT CROSS BUNS
The Delineator, 1895

3 cups scalded milk
2 pkg. dry yeast
1 cup flour (approximate)

Scald milk. When lukewarm, add yeast and enough flour to make a thick batter. Beat well; cover and place in a warm place overnight to form a sponge. Next morning add:

1 cup sugar
½ cup melted lukewarm
  butter
½ tsp. nutmeg

1½ tsp. salt
4–5 cups flour to form a
  soft dough

Knead well and let rise for 5 hours. Punch down and roll out ½" thick. Cut into 2" rounds. Place on buttered cookie sheets and let rise in a warm place ½ hour. Lightly make cross on each bun with sharp knife or razor blade. Bake at 350° for 20 minutes or until lightly brown. When done, brush with egg white mixed with a little sugar or glaze with a little molasses and milk. If desired, form white sugar crosses by drizzling the following glaze over warm bun: 1 cup confectioners' sugar, sifted, mixed with 1½ tbs. milk and ¼ tsp. vanilla. Makes 2½ dozen buns.

Family Easter

Although Easter has great religious significance, it also falls during that time of the year when Mother Earth and Father Sun are busy changing the drab attire of their children to lighter and gayer garb. Thus, "spring time" tends to be the favorite theme for Easter decorations in the home. This in spite of the fact that Easter may fall as early as late March when quite unspringlike weather is possible. Traditional symbols, of course, are the Easter lily and other flowers, young animals, rabbits, and colored and decorated eggs, most of which exemplify in some way the resurgence of life, which occurs in springtime as well as in the Resurrection of Christ which the Easter holiday observes.

Decorations
Pussy Willow, The Delineator, *1911*

A charming centerpiece can be made by wiring pussy willow twigs together to form a nest. Inside the nest, stand a few twigs, bending a few to appear to form a basket handle for the nest. Fill the nest with small blooming boughs or violets and place tiny Easter chickens among the flowers and on the twigs (Illustration 8-1). A place card

Illustration 8–1

for the Easter dinner might be a small pussy willow twig with a chick balancing on it, and tied around his neck a card with the guest's name. (Illustration 8-2)

Illustration 8–2

Fortune Eggs, The Delineator, 1894

Children never seem to tire of a centerpiece which incorporates brightly colored eggs. To vary this favorite theme, try an idea from 1894 and prepare "Fortune Eggs." Dye blown eggs (see directions in this chapter) and into the hole of each, insert a tiny roll of paper bearing a written fortune. Coordinate the fortunes to the egg color. Some fortunes used in 1894 were:

The one who gets a golden egg
Will plenty have and never beg.

The one who gets an egg of blue
Will find a sweetheart fond and true.

The one who gets an egg of green
Will jealous be and not serene.

The one who gets an egg of white
In life shall find supreme delight.

The one who gets an egg of red
Will many tears of sorrow shed.

Who gets an egg of purple shade
Will die a bachelor or old maid.

A silver egg will bring much joy!
And happiness without alloy.

A lucky one—the egg of pink
The owner ne'er sees danger's brink.

The one who gets an egg of brown
Will have establishment in town.

The one who speckled egg obtains
Will go through life by country lanes.

A stripèd egg bodes care and strife,
A sullen man or scolding wife.

The one who gets an egg of black
Bad luck and troubles ne'er will lack.

Display the eggs on a bed of artificial grass or in a small decorative basket. Or suspend each from flowering branches arranged in a vase (Illustration 8-3). To suspend, tie thread to half a toothpick and push toothpick entirely into hole in egg so that thread remains hanging out, to be tied to the branch (Illustration 8-4). The section on Eggs and Egg Containers (page 66) has other ideas to adapt for table decorations.

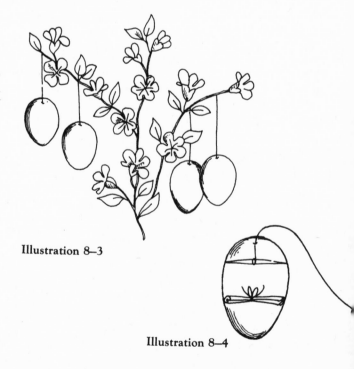

Illustration 8–3

Illustration 8–4

COLOR PLATE 1/The New Year
The Designer, January, 1923

COLOR PLATE 2/The New Year
On the table: Star Pincushions, page 231; Pansy Pincushions, page 230; Bonbon Bags, page 176; Round Pincushions, page 228; Pomanders, page 8.

On the tree: Walnut Fortunes, page 6; Wishing Cards, Cutout Ornaments, Rabbit's Foot, Good Luck Coins, Wishbones, page 7; Cut Paper Chain, page 169; Snowballs and Medallions, page 173; Peanuts, page 177.

COLOR PLATE 3/Saint Valentine's Day
The Delineator, February, 1918

COLOR PLATE 4/Saint Valentine's Day
Valentine Party for Children, pages 27-32.

COLOR PLATE 5/Easter
The Delineator, April, 1904

COLOR PLATE 6/Easter
Top: Hanging Eggshell Basket and Hanging Egg, page 62; Dangling Eggs, page 65.
Middle: Bunny Box, page 67; Rose, page 64; Lily Basket, page 66.
Front: Lace and Rickrack Eggs, page 61; Berry Basket, page 68; Egg Satchel, page 67; Egg Vase, page 65.

COLOR PLATE 7/April Showers
The Designer, April, 1920

Color Plate 8/May Day
Needle-Art, March, 1922

Food

EASTER FAMILY BREAKFAST

Grapefruit

Oatmeal	Cream	Brown Sugar
Eggs	Ham or Bacon	Hot Biscuits
Coffee	Milk	

At one time, eggs were a forbidden food during Lent, so they were served in fancy abundance on Easter Sunday. *The Delineator* gave some interesting recipes for preparation of eggs which might be incorporated into a breakfast menu.

EGG NESTS ON TOAST

The Delineator, 1912

1 egg, separated
1 thick slice bread
salt and pepper to taste

Toast bread, trim crusts, and butter lightly. Press center of toast in lightly without poking a hole in the slice. Season egg white lightly with salt and beat until stiff. Place white in a ring on slice of toast and into the center depression drop egg yolk. Sprinkle with salt and pepper and bake in 375° oven about 5 minutes until egg is set. A tasty and very pretty way to serve an egg. Makes one serving.

EGGS SUSETTE

The Delineator, 1912

1 large potato
1 small egg
1 tsp. minced ham, cooked chicken, or sautéed mushrooms

butter, cream, salt and pepper

Bake the potatoes 40 min. to 1 hour at 425°. (May be done ahead.) Slice thin section from the side of each potato and scoop out the center, taking care not to break the skin. Mash potato, season with butter and cream, and add ham, chicken, or mushrooms. Fill skins with this mixture, making indentation in top, and drop in raw egg. Bake at 375° for about 5 minutes or until egg is cooked as delicately as though lightly poached. Makes one serving.

STIRRED EGG OMELET

The Delineator, 1914

2 eggs   **1½ tbs. butter**
3 tbs. grated Swiss cheese

Put butter and cheese into pan over medium heat. As they begin to melt, break in eggs and stir briskly until well mixed and eggs are set. Season with salt and pepper and serve. Makes one serving.

For a large family gathering, these hearty menus from 1912 will be appreciated on a day which begins early in households with children.

FORMAL EASTER BUFFET BRUNCH

Grapefruit or Orange with Fruit Salad

| Consommé | Printanière[1] |
| Yellow Radishes | Olives |

Lobster Patties à la Newburgh[2]
Chicken Croquettes Jardinère[3]
Pineapple Sherbert
Loin of Spring Lamb
Asparagus Tips Salad

| Strawberry Baskets | Assorted Cakes |

Yellow Candied Violets
Candied Kumquats
Coffee

[1]Assorted early mixed vegetables cut in similar size small shapes (cubes, balls, disks) cooked separately in water and topped with butter
[2]Sherry flavored cream sauce
[3]Fresh vegetables cut into small regular shapes, cooked separately, and arranged as a garnish in separate groups around the main dish

EASTER DINNER

Clam Cocktails
Salted Almonds and Olives
Cream of Celery Soup

| Planked Shad[1] | Cucumbers |

Roast Saddle of Spring Lamb, Mint Sauce

| Parslied Potatoes | Peas |
| Apricot Punch | Asparagus Salad |

Toasted Wafers and Cheese

| Ice-Cream | Strawberries |
| Fancy Cakes | Gelatine Eggs* |

Coffee

[1]Marinated, medium-sized fillets baked or grilled on a buttered wooden plank and garnished with lemon and parsley
*See below.

Gelatine Eggs, The Delineator, *1900*

Although they are not really appropriate on such an elegant menu, the children will get a kick out of these. With a safety pin, poke a hole in the *side* of a raw egg and carefully pick away bits of shell to enlarge the hole to about dime size (Illustration 8-5). Remove the egg through the hole

Illustration 8—5

and clean the shell. The shells must be wet on the inside when the prepared gelatine is poured in. Prepare gelatine according to package directions. Select flavors with springtime colors: lemon, lime, cherry, peach. Set shells on their sides in an egg carton, fill them carefully, and place them in the refrigerator to set. For serving, dip each eggshell into warm water briefly to make removal of the shell easier. Decorate with whipped cream if desired. Present the shimmering pile in an orange gelatine ring, garnished with parsley "grass." (Illustration 8-6)

Illustration 8—6

Games

Egg Hunt

The first activity of the day, except perhaps in those homes where Easter sunrise services are attended, is the traditional and obligatory hunt for the colored eggs hidden about the house by the Easter Bunny. And this hunt at dawn will be the first of many held throughout the day, as friends and relatives visit and children come together to compare and share their Easter surprises and hide the eggs from each other. The egg hunt ritual can be varied for groups by designating certain col-

ored or marked eggs for special consideration: prizes, points, etcetera. Or set a time limit for the hunt.

Egg Roll, The Delineator, *1908*

Another very old traditional activity for this day is the egg roll. One version has each player rolling a hard-boiled egg downhill without breaking it. At the least crack, the player must leave the game. In another version, partners, each with an egg, sit on the floor facing each other. Then the partners roll the eggs to each other very fast, trying not to break them and catching them every time. When an egg is broken, it is retired and when both are broken, the team retires.

Egg Toss, The Delineator, *1901*

Tossing an egg into the air to another player or to oneself is a popular Easter pastime, the object being to avoid cracking the egg. Among experienced players, the preference is to use an uncooked egg.

Rabbit Hunt, The Delineator, *1913*

Little white paper rabbits (see Design Sheet, page 69), each numbered one, five, or ten (Illustration 8-7), are hidden all about the house, with just the tips of their ears sticking out. The hunt lasts ten minutes and the player with the highest total of points is the winner.

Illustration 8—7

Children's Corner

Fluttering Butterflies, *The Delineator, 1901*

The butterfly is another emblem particularly appropriate to Easter, as it changes from an insignificant worm in a deathlike sleep into a radiant winged creature.

MATERIALS:

    yellow, orange, light blue, white tissue paper scraps

    fine black thread and needle

    stick about 16″ long

STEP-BY-STEP:

1. Cut one butterfly (see Design Sheet, page 69) out of each color tissue paper.
2. Thread needle and put a large knot in one end. Sew through center of one butterfly body. Repeat for each. Thread lengths should vary from 6″–13″. (Illustration 8-8)

Illustration 8–8

3. Tie threads to stick, about 4″ apart.
4. If the heat is still on, hold the stick near a register or radiator and move it about until it is positioned in a gentle heat, which will cause the butterflies to flutter up and down. If the weather is warm, take the toy out-of-doors where a gentle breeze will cause the desired movement.

Easter Top, *The Delineator,* 1901

MATERIALS:

    1 colored hard-boiled egg

    4½″ square shirt cardboard or poster board

    white glue

    felt-tip markers (optional)

STEP-BY-STEP:

1. Cut a disk 4½″ in diameter out of cardboard. In the center, cut a hole 1¼″ in diameter. Slash edges of inner circle about ¼″ deep all around and bend tabs up. (Illustration 8-9)
2. Decorate disk with felt markers if desired.
3. Fit disk onto egg with narrow end of egg

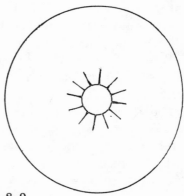

Illustration 8–9

down. Disk should fit snugly near middle of egg. Cut slashes deeper if necessary. Glue cardboard tabs in place on egg. (Illustration 8-10)

Illustration 8–10

4. To use top, twirl around with the fingers. Take care not to drop top onto floor when beginning spin.

Easter Gifts

At one time it was considered quite appropriate to send Easter gifts, which were generally adapted to the special nature of the holiday. By far, the most popular gifts were egg-shaped items such as photo frames, pincushions, or ornamented eggs made of actual blown eggs or on papier-mâché shapes. These eggs were especially valued when they were decorated by hand. In keeping with the feeling of hope and gaiety which spring promotes, frivolous trinkets were popular as well. Leading the gift list in an 1886 *Delineator* article were jewel boxes, scent bottles, decorated gauze fans, and sachet bags.

    Because of the deep religious significance of the day, many preferred to give such articles as prayer-book markers, prayer books, Easter calendars, Bibles, or other religious articles.

The Easter lily, in spite of its lack of documented importance as a real Easter symbol, was and is perhaps the most popular flower gift. One legend does say that it never bloomed until the death of Jesus Christ and since then it has been used in token of the Resurrection. Other spring flowers, particularly violets (the color signifying "sacrifice") were also popular. Cut flowers, which die after breathing out their sweetness for this special day, appear to make a fitting and happy sacrifice at Easter.

By 1905, however, although the custom of gift giving remained in practice, it was not considered bad form to ignore the practice or to confine it to immediate family and intimate friends. The sending of Easter cards seemed to be a good way to continue the exchange of Easter hospitality and good cheer in lieu of gift giving, and cards increased in popularity as gift giving declined.

Easter Cards

Early Easter cards were richly ornamented with silk and satin fringes and, in the best Victorian tradition, the decorations quickly became overwhelming. Most cards featured the usual symbols, hand painted on fabric or heavy paper and used in combination with fabric, ribbon, fringes, etcetera. Popular themes were eggs, egg rolling, the Easter Rabbit, lilies, the coming of spring, and birds, especially the robin and the dove (symbol of gentleness). Less well known symbols were the lion (a medieval symbol of the Resurrection), the peacock (symbol of immortality), and the serpent (symbol of regeneration).

Several *Delineator* designs for Easter cards are described below. Some of these are pictured in Color Plate 26. Please read Card Making, page 284, before making any of these cards for important information on paper and envelope selection and printing techniques.

Easter Chicks, *The Delineator,* 1891
COLOR PLATE 26
MATERIALS:
    1 sheet stiff paper, 5½″ × 7″
    2 chenille chicks, about 1½″ beak to tail

a few sprays dried grasses and straw flowers
white glue

STEP-BY-STEP:
1. Fold paper in half to measure 5½″ × 3½″.
2. Arrange and glue grasses and flowers on front of card.
3. Glue chicks on card. (Illustration 8-11)

Illustration 8–11

4. Print the following verse inside the card:

> *Each fluffy little chicken*
>   *Is peeping, "We are here;*
>   *The Eastertide has come at last,*
>   *The sweetest time of year."*

Bunny and Chick, *The Delineator,* 1925
MATERIALS:
    1 correspondence card about 3¾″ × 5¾″
    1 art gum eraser 1″ × 2″
    1 cork about ¼″ diameter
    artist's knife
    fine felt-tip markers
    violet foam stamp pad, black foam stamp pad

STEP-BY-STEP:
1. Carve bunny and chicken on opposite sides of art gum. Carve one flower petal on cork end (see Design Sheet, page 70).
2. Print bunny and chicken on card according to design.
3. Print 3 flowers, 4 petals each, in center of card.
4. With markers, color in flower centers, stems, chicken beak, ribbon, and message. (Illustration 8-12)

Illustration 8–12

Easter Greeting, *The Delineator,* 1888
MATERIALS:
  1 sheet watercolor paper
  metal ruler
  3″ square silk fabric
  1 purchased embroidered appliqué, about 1½″
    diameter
  fine felt-tip markers or pen and ink
  rubber cement

STEP-BY-STEP:
1. Tear watercolor paper into a 5″ square, using
   metal ruler as an edge to tear against.
2. Fold corners of paper toward center 1¾″, then
   fold points back ¾″. Crease well.
3. Fringe fabric ¼″ on each side. Lightly glue
   points of fabric to card, leaving fabric slightly
   puffy.
4. Glue paper folds to fabric.
5. Glue appliqué to fabric.
6. Letter message on points of paper as desired.
   (Illustration 8-13) **Note:** The original design
   featured pansies on a lavender background.

Illustration 8–13

Forget-me-nots and lilies-of-the-valley would
also be lovely, on pale blue or pink fabric
backgrounds.

Decorated Eggs

Eggs may be hard-boiled, dyed a pretty color, and
left at that—and children will be delighted. But
with a little extra effort, Easter eggs can be turned
into objects of fragile beauty. There are two ways
to prepare eggs for ornamentation:

Preparing Eggs for Ornamentation

Hard-Boiled
  Place eggs in a saucepan and cover with cold
water. Bring to a boil. Reduce heat and simmer
about 15 minutes. Plunge into cold water to prevent yolk from discoloring.

Blown
1. Use a large sharp safety pin to make holes in
   egg. Gently push the pin into one end of the
   egg. Repeat on the other end of the egg and
   enlarge this hole a bit by breaking off tiny
   pieces of shell with pin point. Step-by-step
   directions will specify whether the larger hole
   should be in the narrow or wider end of the
   egg. Poke the pin into the hole to break the
   membrane surrounding the egg yolk.
2. Shake the egg, then place the smaller hole
   against your mouth and blow the contents
   into a bowl. (Illustration 8-14)

Illustration 8–14

3. To clean the inside of the shell, suck soapy water in through the larger hole, shake, blow out the water, then repeat with clean water.

4. Rinse the outside of the shell, dry, and place upright (large hole down) in an egg carton. **Note:** Start blowing eggs well before Easter to accumulate as many as you'll need while using the contents at a comfortable pace. No mass inundation of omelets and soufflés!

The advantages of using blown eggs instead of hard-boiled eggs is that they may be stored and used year after year as part of your family Easter tradition. The eggs may even be used as Christmas tree ornaments. On the other hand, hard-boiled eggs are somewhat less fragile and young children will be able to hold, play with, and enjoy them more than blown ones.

Coloring Eggs

Techniques for coloring eggs have varied over time. Before the development of special dyes for Easter eggs, the ingenious homemaker had a few clever methods of her own. One way to dye eggs was to sew a calico print around the eggs, then to boil them half an hour or so. In the days before colorfast fabric dyes, the color, even the design itself, would transfer to the egg. Another method was to boil various vegetable matter with the eggs: onion skin for yellow orange, saffron for yellow, spinach and parsley for delicate green, beets for red colors. Inscribing names or designs on an egg with liquid fat before dyeing caused the inscription to remain white, as the dye would not penetrate the fat. Wax crayons are used today with the same results. To color eggs, use special egg dye or food coloring.

Easter Egg Dye
Follow package instructions.

Food Coloring
To ½ cup boiling water, add 1 tsp. white vinegar and about 20 drops of desired color. Dip eggs until desired shade is obtained. Dry thoroughly before handling. Check food coloring package for variations from this formula.

Ornamenting Eggs

Lace and Rickrack, *The Delineator,* 1881
COLOR PLATE 6
MATERIALS:
   1 hard-boiled egg, colored
   artist's knife
   or
   7″ of flexible lace ¾″ wide
   15″ baby rickrack
   or
   Paraffin or wax crayon

In the original version, the design for this egg was scratched on the shell of a dyed hard-boiled egg with a sharp instrument. To do this, lightly draw design (see Design Sheet, page 70) on shell with pencil. Use an artist's knife to scrape away dye. (Illustration 8-15)

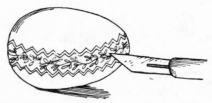

Illustration 8–15

Another version of the same design uses ¾″ wide flexible lace with contrasting flower design glued diagonally around a blown egg, covering blow holes. Rickrack is glued along each edge of the lace. You will need about 7″ of lace and 15″ of baby rickrack, depending on size of egg. (Illustration 8-16)

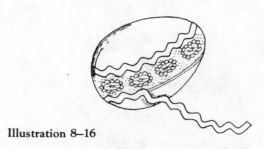

Illustration 8–16

Yet another way to use this design on an egg is to paint the design on the shell with melted wax or wax crayon. When the egg is dyed, color will not stick to the waxed areas.

The latter two methods may be worked on blown eggs or cooked eggs; the former on hard-boiled eggs only.

Hanging Egg, *The Delineator,* 1881
COLOR PLATE 6
MATERIALS:
  1 large blown egg with enlarged hole at narrow end
  ½″ trim about 7″ long or to fit around egg
  4 tassels, about 1″ long
  single fold bias binding, about 7″ long or to fit egg
  18″ soutache to match trim
  white glue
  permanent felt-tip markers, fine point

STEP-BY-STEP:
1. Glue bias binding around egg, slightly above center line.
2. Glue trim around egg, overlapping bias binding so about half of binding width is exposed. (Illustration 8-17)
3. Color designs (see Design Sheet, page 70) on top and bottom of egg.
4. Cut soutache in half and string two tassels on each piece. Spacing the four ends equally around the egg, glue ends of soutache to bias binding, tucking ends under trim. (Illustration 8-18)

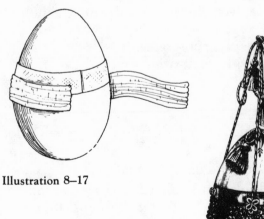

Illustration 8–17

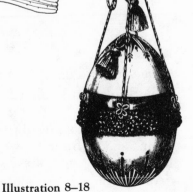

Illustration 8–18

5. Tie soutache loops together at top. Position tassels as desired and hold in place with a dab of glue.

Hanging Eggshell Basket, *The Delineator,* 1881
COLOR PLATE 6
MATERIALS:
  1 large blown egg with enlarged hole at wider end (or plastic egg-shaped stocking container)
  single fold bias binding, about 7″ or to fit around egg
  ½″ wide lace, about 7″ or to fit around egg
  4 ft. ¼″ ribbon in white
  1 ft. ¼″ ribbon in pink
  2 small pompoms (balls cut from ball fringe are fine)
  20″ soutache
  permanent felt-tip markers, fine point
  white glue, fine sharp scissors

STEP-BY-STEP:
  Note: Omit steps 1 and 2 with plastic egg.
1. Soak eggshell in hot water to make it easier to cut. Lightly pencil mark circumference of egg at widest point.
2. Cut so that the narrow end will form the basket. A bit at a time, cut away pieces of eggshell until you have cut fairly close to the marking. (Illustration 8-19)
3. Glue bias binding around opening with one narrow fold extending over jagged edge to outside of shell. (Illustration 8-20)
4. Color design on bottom of egg (see Design Sheet, page 70).

Illustration 8–19

Illustration 8–20

5. Divide opening into quarters and lightly mark on edge. Glue pieces of ribbon around egg in zigzag pattern from quarter to quarter. (Illustration 8-21)

6. Cut soutache in half and tie one pompom near the center of each piece. Mark opposite sides of the rim. Glue ends of soutache on either side of these marks.

7. Glue lace around rim.

8. Tie four bows from remaining ribbon and glue bows at points of zigzag.

9. Position pompoms on soutache as desired and hold in place with a dab of glue. Tie soutache together at top. (Illustration 8-22)

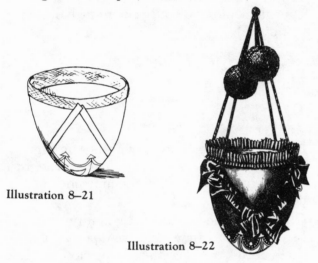

Illustration 8–21

Illustration 8–22

Radish, *The Delineator,* 1902
MATERIALS:
   1 red-dyed blown egg with enlarged hole on wider end
   green crepe paper scraps
   bit of cotton
   white glue

STEP-BY-STEP:
1. Enlarge leaf pattern (see Design Sheet, page 69) proportionate to eggshell being used. Cut 5 or 6 leaves out of green crepe paper.

2. To give leaves a realistic crinkle, fold each lengthwise over a straight edge (a). Hold one end in place and gradually push the other end up on the edge with the other hand (b) Straighten out leaf slightly. (Illustration 8-23)

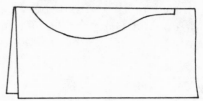

Illustration 8–23a

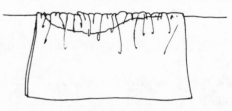

Illustration 8–23b

3. Glue leaves to wide end of eggshell.

4. Glue a bit of cotton to narrow end of "radish." Pull gently and twist cotton end to look like radish root. Dip root into egg dye. (Illustration 8-24)

Illustration 8–24

Plum, *The Delineator,* 1902
MATERIALS:
   1 purple-dyed blown egg with enlarged hole at wide end
   green crepe paper scraps
   branch with small twigs attached
   white glue

STEP-BY-STEP:
1. Prepare several leaves following direction for Radish.

2. Glue wide end of egg to small twig.

3. Glue leaves on branch for foliage as desired. (Illustration 8-25) **Note:** An unusual centerpiece would be a pile of radishes or a branch of plums made from blown eggs. Made from hard-boiled eggs, these might serve as an "April Fool" food presentation!

Illustration 8–25

Rose, *The Delineator,* 1888
COLOR PLATE 6
MATERIALS:

> 1 blown egg with enlarged hole at narrow end
> green floral tape (or 1″ wide bias strips of green
>   crepe paper)
> pink crepe paper
> green crepe paper
> thin branch
> rubber cement
> materials to paint face on egg as desired
>   (acrylics, watercolors, felt-tip markers)

STEP-BY-STEP:

1. Enlarge petal and leaf patterns (see Design Sheet, page 70) to fit egg chosen. Cut 11 petals out of pink crepe paper. Cut 6 green leaves.

2. Paint face on wide end of egg.

3. Glue petals in place, placing glue at middle and at narrow end of egg. Overlap and pleat petals as necessary. (Illustration 8-26)

Illustration 8–26

4. Cut two strips of green crepe paper 4″ long and 1″ wide. Cut points at ends. Glue strips crossed over narrow end of egg, leaving points free. (Illustration 8-27)

Illustration 8–27

5. Wind floral tape around narrow end of egg. Wind floral tape around branch, attaching leaves in clusters of 3 as desired. (Illustration 8-28)

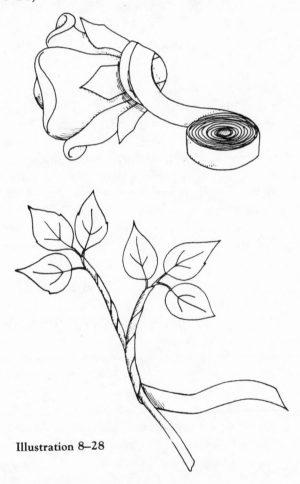

Illustration 8–28

6. Attach flower to branch with floral tape.

7. Stretch edges of petals and open out to form attractive shape. Stretch green points on back of flower. (Illustration 8-29) **Note:** Caricature was, for a long time, an extremely popular manner in which to decorate eggs in those

Illustration 8–29

gentle days when many ladies cultivated artistic skill with the paintbrush. The caricatures were usually broad parodies of familiar types such as military men, babies, ethnic groups, clowns, etcetera, set on paper stands or, like this one, in a paper flower. By changing the petal shape, different types of flowers could be designed: roses, daisies, chrysanthemums.

Dangling Eggs, *The Delineator,* 1893
COLOR PLATE 6
MATERIALS:

   7 blown eggs, small, with enlarged holes at narrow end, dyed three different shades
   2–3 ft. baby ribbon for each egg to match egg colors
   7 pompoms or tassels to match ribbons
   white glue

STEP-BY-STEP:
1. To tie one egg: Place a dab of glue at top and bottom of egg and glue a piece of ribbon around egg. (Illustration 8-30)

Illustration 8–30

2. Attach pompom about 4″ from end of remaining piece of ribbon and tie ribbon around egg so that pompom will be at bottom (wide end) of egg. (Illustration 8-31)

Illustration 8–31

3. Tie ribbon at top of egg, leaving a long end.
4. To make bunch: Catch long ribbon ends together at top and tie into a pretty loop. Adjust lengths of individual eggs as desired before tying together. (Illustration 8-32)

Illustration 8–32

Egg Vase, *The Delineator,* 1902
COLOR PLATE 6
MATERIALS:

   3 blown eggs, same size with enlarged hole at narrow end
   dye (optional)
   white glue, small sharp scissors, safety pin

STEP-BY-STEP:

1. With a safety pin, bit by bit pick away the shell from small end of egg until scissors can be used to cut the opening as evenly as possible. Diameter of holes should be about 1″. (Illustration 8-33)

Illustration 8—33

2. Dye eggs if desired.
3. Place the shells close together as shown and where the sides touch, glue together. (Illustration 8-34)

Illustration 8—34

4. Fill with paper or fabric flowers.

Egg Containers

Lily Basket, *The Delineator*, 1910
COLOR PLATE 6
MATERIALS:

    3 sheets heavyweight paper, 9″ × 12″ (watercolor paper is fine)
    6 feet thin flexible wire
    white plastic tape, about ¾″ wide
    1 round cereal box, 4″ diameter
    1 sheet green construction paper, 9″ × 12″
    white glue

STEP-BY-STEP:

1. Enlarge lily petal pattern (see Design Sheet, page 70) to 11″ long and cut 6 out of white paper.
2. Tape wire down center of underside of each petal. (Illustration 8-35)

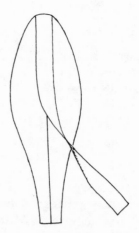

Illustration 8—35

3. Cut round box to measure 4″ high and cover outside with green paper, tucking paper over top edge of box. (Illustration 8-36)
4. Glue bottom of wrong side of petals to inside of box around the bottom. (Illustration 8-37). Shape petals as desired by bending the wires. (Illustration 8-38) **Note:** Basket will hold a dozen eggs and makes a pretty centerpiece.

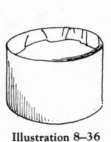

Illustration 8—36

Illustration 8—37

Illustration 8—38

Bunny Box, *The Delineator,* 1910
COLOR PLATE 6
MATERIALS:

    1 sheet poster board, 22″ × 28″, pastel color
    2½ ft. ribbon, about ¾″ wide
    2 puffs cotton (optional)
    rubber cement
    felt-tip markers (optional)
    artificial grass

STEP-BY-STEP:

1. Enlarge bunny pattern (see Design Sheet, page 70) to measure 17″ from back feet to front feet (Illustration 8-39). Cut 2 bunnies out of poster board.

2. Cut a strip of poster board 18″ long × 3″ wide. Clip and fold strip according to diagram. (Illustration 8-40)

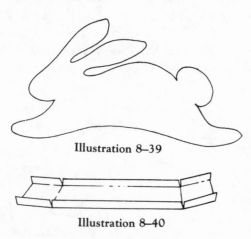

Illustration 8–39

Illustration 8–40

3. Glue one bunny to each side of strip. (Illustration 8-41)

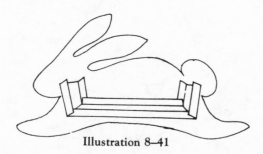

Illustration 8–41

4. Draw eyes and nose on bunny if desired. Glue optional cotton to tail on each side. Tie ribbon in pretty bow around neck.

5. Partially fill box with artificial grass so that eggs will be visible when bunny is filled. (Illustration 8-42)

Illustration 8–42

Egg Satchel, *Peterson's Magazine,* 1882
COLOR PLATE 6

This charming and unusual egg bag would make a novel centerpiece or place to tuck the hot cross buns.

MATERIALS:

    2 pieces cotton flannel, white, 12″ square
    1 piece polyester fleece, slightly smaller than 12″ square
    green embroidery cotton
    2 purchased embroidered appliqués, Easter theme, about 2½″ in diameter
    1 white shank bottom, about ½″ in diameter

STEP-BY-STEP:

1. Slipstitch purchased appliqués in place on opposite corners or satin stitch embroider bunny and eggs. On remaining corners, embroider design using feather stitch.

2. Sandwich fleece between two layers of flannel, embroidered side up.

3. Blanket stitch layers together all around. (Illustration 8-43)

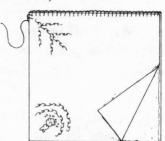

Illustration 8–43

4. Sew button on at one corner. Make ½″ loops at other 3 corners. (Illustration 8-44)

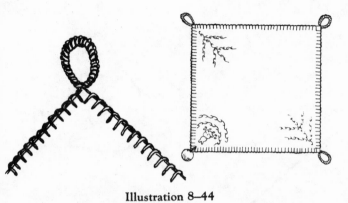

Illustration 8–44

5. Fold and button three corners. Fill with eggs (satchel will hold about 12) and button remaining corner.

Berry Basket, *The Delineator,* 1887
COLOR PLATE 6

This simple project originally involved weaving ribbons through the mesh of a wire broiler basket. Adapted to a plastic berry basket, it creates a lovely egg container. There are many other uses for this basket, for example, as a centerpiece filled with fresh or dried flowers.

MATERIALS:
 1 small berry basket
 spray paint (optional)
 1 yd. each of 3 colors satin ribbon, about ⅝″ wide or to fit between basket spokes (yardages will vary with basket sizes)

STEP-BY-STEP:
1. Spray-paint basket if desired.
2. When thoroughly dry, weave ribbons in and out and tie a bow at the end of each row. Experiment at the corners to get desired effect. Take care to keep ribbon untwisted as you weave. (Illustration 8-45) **Note:** A small basket will hold about 8 eggs.

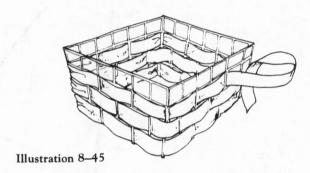

Illustration 8–45

Oh, what am I, whom children hide,
Round, hard and smooth, yet soft inside?
Who's born all white, yet, strange to say,
Turns red and blue on Easter day?
Who has a yolk, but not a shirt,
Whose head when cracked does not feel hurt?
Who's boiled alive, unless too bad,
Whose dyeing makes the children glad?
Now, what am I? Pray guess, I beg.
Of course I am an ——— ———!

The Delineator, 1923

DESIGN SHEET

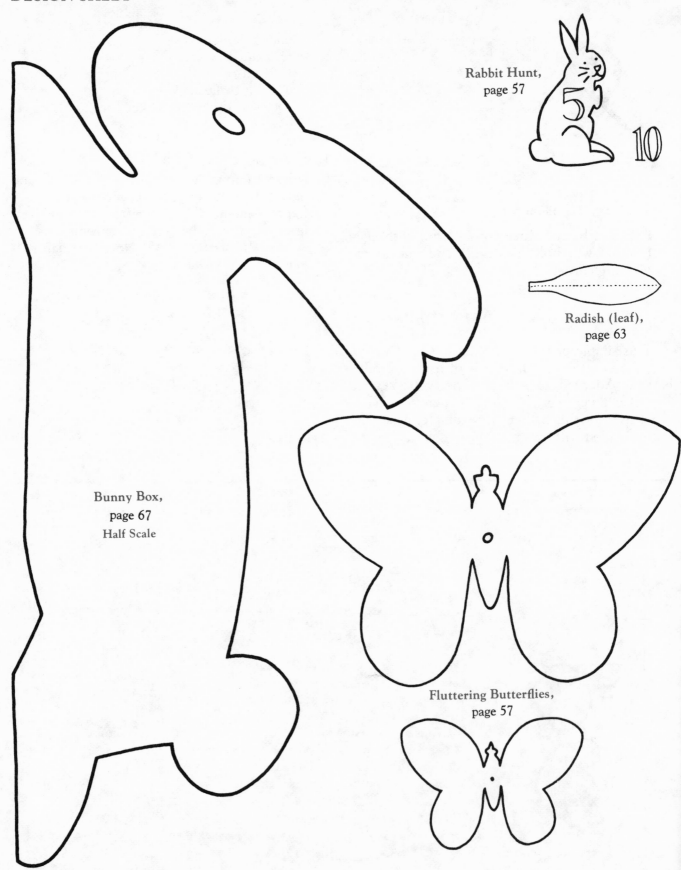

Rabbit Hunt,
page 57

Radish (leaf),
page 63

Bunny Box,
page 67
Half Scale

Fluttering Butterflies,
page 57

DESIGN SHEET

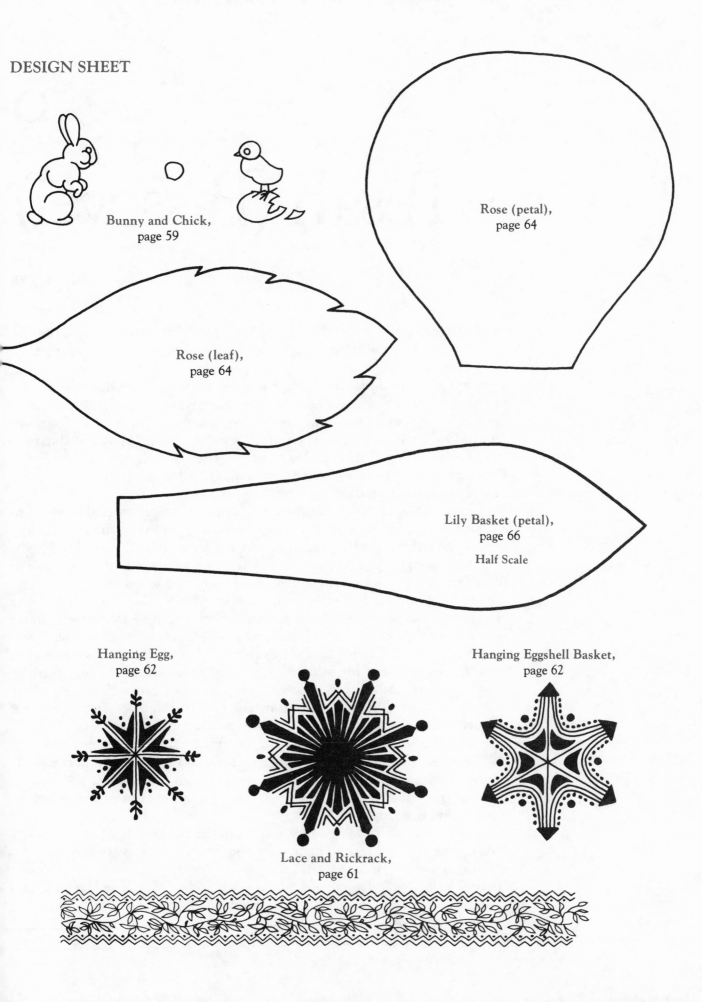

Bunny and Chick,
page 59

Rose (petal),
page 64

Rose (leaf),
page 64

Lily Basket (petal),
page 66

Half Scale

Hanging Egg,
page 62

Hanging Eggshell Basket,
page 62

Lace and Rickrack,
page 61

9
Pesah (Passover)

Celebrated beginning with the eve of the 15th day of the lunar month of Nisan (March-April)

Pesah (Passover), a major Jewish festival, commemorates the story of the flight of the Hebrews from Egypt and celebrates the joy of freedom from slavery. After living many years in Egypt under the Pharaohs in peace and with religious freedom, the Hebrews were decreed to be slaves and were forced to labor to build temples and cities. Successive Pharaohs became more cruel and life became harsher. The Old Testament describes how Moses was sent by God to the people and performed miracles that proved to the Pharaoh that it was God's will that the Jews be free. The Pharaoh was unmoved until God sent the last of many plagues, one which killed the eldest son in every household, including the Pharaoh's.

To spare the Hebrew families from this curse, Moses ordered the Jews to sacrifice an unblemished lamb and rub its blood on the door mantel as a sign to God and the Angel of Death would pass over that household. This is where the word *Passover* comes from. After the final plague, and the death of the Pharaoh's own son, the Hebrews were permitted to leave.

Fearing the further effects of this last plague, the Pharaoh bid the Hebrews to escape in haste. Consequently they had time to mix only water and wheat, without yeast, for bread and bake it under the rays of the desert sun. Before the Jews were able to cross the Red Sea, the Pharaoh's awe turned to wrath and he sent his soldiers in pursuit. Facing the Red Sea with the Pharaoh's troops behind him, Moses, as an agent of God, performed another miracle and parted the sea, permitting the Hebrews to cross. As the soldiers pursued them, the sea closed, destroying the Pharaoh's army.

Well before the historical significance of the Exodus was connected with the Passover feast, however, the ancient Jews had celebrated other festivals during the same season. Two festivals merged with the Exodus, which took place at the same time of year, to create a joyous festival of regeneration, rebirth, and freedom.

The Seder is a ritualized feast central to the celebration of Passover. It is held on the first and second nights of Passover (Reform Jews hold a Seder on the first night only). The word *Seder* means "order" and there is, indeed, a strict order of the Seder fixed by religious law and custom. The Haggadah is a special book which contains the Seder service.

71

The Seder

The Seder table is set with the household's finest linens and may be decorated with spring flowers. Candles are an adornment decreed by religious law. All tableware is specially cleaned for the occasion or perhaps a special set, used only for Passover meals, is placed on the table. As the service begins, the table is set with a Haggadah for each person, matzot (often in a special three-layer cover), wine for all (including a cup filled for Elijah, who according to tradition may arrive at any moment during the feast), and the Seder plate. The Seder leader, usually the head of the household, sits ensconced with pillows, the comfort of which is a reminder of the freedom gained against slavery.

On the Seder plate, which is often handsomely designed, are the roasted lamb shankbone, a reminder of the sacrificial lamb; a hard-boiled egg, symbol of life; greens such as parsley, representing the new hope brought by spring; bitter herbs such as horseradish, a reminder of the bitterness of slavery; haroset (a nut-apple-wine mixture) representing the mortar used to build the Pharaoh's cities; and salt water, symbolizing the tears the Jews shed while in slavery. At appropriate points in the evening, amid blessings and the traditional questions and answers between father and child as contained in the Haggadah, each participant tastes the greens (first dipped into salt water), bitter herbs, and haroset, and drinks four cups of wine, symbol of joyfulness. The often elaborate Seder feast, which may consist of favorite family foods, is eaten slowly, in the manner of a free man.

Every effort is made to hold the attention of the children during the Seder service, one function of which is, after all, to pass from generation to generation the story of the Exodus. The afikoman-hiding custom is one means, the alert waiting for signs that the invisible Elijah has arrived is another.

Matzah

The unleavened bread matzah plays several roles in the Passover celebration. It is reminiscent both of the ancient agricultural feast and of the bread eaten on the Exodus. Jewish law forbids the possession of even a crumb of leavened food during Passover, and in a special ceremony the night before Passover, the house is searched. Symbolic crumbs are found, collected, and burned the next day. The ban against leavened foods creates many challenges for the Jewish cook during Passover, and the effort to purge one's house of leavening can result in a thorough spring cleaning.

At the Seder table, the matzot are often placed in a special three-compartmented container which may be richly embroidered. The middle matzah is broken in two at the beginning of the service and the larger piece (the *afikoman*) is tucked away to be eaten at the end of the meal. During the course of the evening, however, it is customary for the younger children to steal the afikoman and hide it, returning it only upon reaching an agreement with the Seder leader for a suitable reward. When it has been returned, the afikoman is shared by all the Seder participants and eaten. The remaining matzot are blessed and eaten during the Seder service.

Compartmented Matzah Cover, *Adapted from the Yivo Collection*

The original cover was worked on golden yellow cotton sateen with a gold-colored fringe border and brightly colored embroidery. Embroider yours in classic blue on white or to coordinate with Passover china. The words, translated loosely, mean "Tonight we eat matzot" and the foods on the Seder plate are listed.

MATERIALS:
1 yd. fine white linen or other fabric as desired
cotton 6-strand embroidery floss: copen blue
1¼ yd. fringe, ½"–¾" wide
white thread, sewing machine, embroidery needle

STEP-BY-STEP:
1. Cut fabric into 4 pieces, each 10" × 10".
2. Press one edge of each piece under ½". Press raw edge under again ¼" and edgestitch in place to hem. (Illustration 9-1)

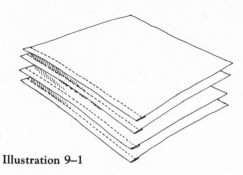

Illustration 9–1

3. Embroider design (see Design Sheet, page 74) on right side of one hemmed cloth. Keeping in mind the need for a ½" seam allowance on all raw edges, position design as though the hemmed edge were the line upon which the message is written.

4. Work cross-stitch design in method preferred.

5. To construct cover, stack 4 pieces together right sides up, with the embroidered piece second from bottom. Stitch together around 3 unhemmed edges, using a ½" seam allowance. Clip corners and trim seam to a scant ¼" (Illustration 9-2). Turn so that embroidered piece is on top and press. (Illustration 9-3)

6. Slipstitch fringe to top around edges, mitering corners, taking care not to sew the opening of the cover closed.

7. To use, insert one matzah into each pocket and place on table with embroidered side up.

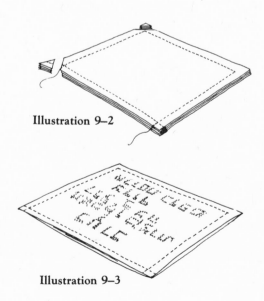

Illustration 9–2

Illustration 9–3

Activities

The game below was suggested by *The Young Judaean* as a game to be played during the Passover holiday. The game could also be constructed and played by adapting the Heart Darts technique, page 30.

Nut Game, *The Young Judaean,* 1925
MATERIALS:

  1 piece corrugated cardboard, about 3 ft. square
  artist's knife
  7 ½ gal. plastic food storage containers (ice cream, etcetera) *exactly alike* in size and shape
  acrylic paint for numbers (paint for board, optional)
  nuts for each player

STEP-BY-STEP:

1. Draw a 6-pointed star on cardboard and cut out with knife. Star should be as large as cardboard will permit. (Illustration 9-4)

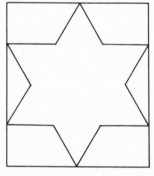

Illustration 9–4

2. Arrange the seven containers top down on star in design shown and trace around each one. Cut out each circle slightly inside tracing, as each container must fit snugly into its hole when board is assembled.

3. Paint board if desired and assign a number value to each hole (Illustration 9-5). Fit a plastic container into each hole. Game will be supported by the containers serving as legs. (Illustration 9-6)

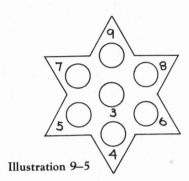

Illustration 9–5

4. To play game: One player acts as banker. Other players in turn toss a nut at the board from a distance of about 10 feet. If the nut goes into the pocket, the banker pays the player the number of nuts indicated on the board for that hole. If the nut misses, the banker keeps it. Countless variations in play are possible: most points, first to reach a certain score, etc. Younger children may enjoy the game, too, by standing closer to the board.

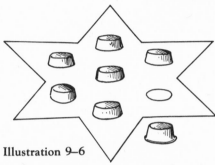

Illustration 9–6

DESIGN SHEET

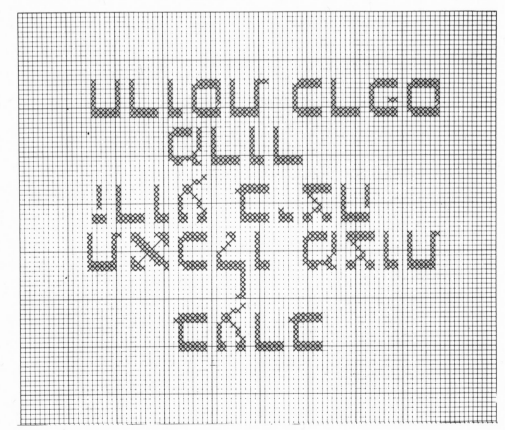

Matzah Cover,
page 73

10
Arbor Day

Celebrated variously according to state although April 22 is often chosen

The planting of a tree to commemorate an event is a tradition that goes back to early civilizations and reflects man's recognition that he must regenerate nature.

In the United States people celebrate Arbor Day for the sole purpose of designating a special day for the planting of trees. The greatest impetus to celebrate a particular day for this purpose came from the efforts of J. Sterling Morton. A year after graduating from Union College in Michigan in 1854, Mr. Morton settled in the Nebraska Territory. There he noted the absence of trees and realized the need for trees as protection against land erosion from blizzards and wind storms and the need for lumber for homes, barns, and fence posts. As editor of the *Nebraska City News*, he promoted this cause. First as a member of the Territorial Legislature and, after Nebraska entered the Union, as a part of the Cabinet of President Cleveland, he pursued the idea of setting a day aside exclusively for the purpose of planting trees.

In 1872, a resolution was passed by the Nebraska State Board of Agriculture and the first Arbor Day was celebrated on April 10 of that year, when over a million trees were planted. Finally the Nebraska State Legislature in 1885 declared the day a legal holiday and in recognition of Mr. Morton's work, set the date as April 22, his birthday. So many trees were being planted in Nebraska at this time that it earned the name Tree Planter's State. Ultimately, other states followed suit.

Another important part of the Arbor Day tradition is the legend of Johnny Appleseed. The early colonists frequently planted orchards to offset the relative lack of fruit trees they found on this continent. A New Englander named John Chapman set about roaming through the colonial settlements of Pennsylvania and Ohio around 1797, planting apple trees. While living on the fringes of these settlements, Chapman would clear some ground in the forest, surround it with a brush fence, and plant seeds. He would repeat his procedure twenty miles or so down the road. As a result, he provided the settlers with seedlings and vivid tales of his exploits.

11
May Day

Celebrated May 1

The ancient Romans observed the coming of spring in their festival honoring Flora, the goddess of flowers. The central feature of this celebration was the abundant use of blossoms in parades and dances. The festivities spanned the period from April 28 to May 3, the high point of which was May Day, the first of May, when the slaves were set free for the day after promising to return to their masters' houses that evening.

The greatest influence on our present-day celebration of May Day is the Druid spring festival called *Beltane,* "Bel's fire," after the custom of lighting fires on hill tops to honor the sun.

When the Romans occupied the British Isles, elements of the Roman and Druid feasts merged and the bringing in of the Maypole from the woods was added as an important element of the festivities. During the medieval and Tudor periods, May Day was one of the most important holidays.

The Maypole was set up by each village in the town square, and in medieval England, the towns competed to see which could produce the tallest one. In London, the Maypole was secured into the ground, and in 1661, London boasted one of the tallest, measuring 134 feet. Traditionally, the tree was adorned with three gilt crowns, streamers, flags, garlands of flowers, and other adornments. During the course of the celebration, which lasted almost the entire month of May, the Maypole became the center of activity. Games were played and jousts were undertaken and a special Robin Hood play was performed. The Robin Hood legend is very much a part of the May Day festivities. He is considered the Lord of May in all the games and the Queen of May is his faithful Maid Marian. Their attendants, dressed in green, are other Robin Hood characters such as Little John, Friar Tuck, and Will Stukeley.

Although May Day was an important holiday in England, it never became significant in the United States, especially as a home celebration, because the Puritan settlers frowned upon the Maypole and on dancing as frivolous. In time, however, the charming custom of May baskets, which are made and filled with flowers by children who then distribute them in the neighborhood in the early morning, has been adopted in many parts of the country. Schools throughout the country normally celebrate the day with field days and similar sporting events. Often, at these events, a May Queen is named and there is a traditional Maypole dance.

The Queen of May

Godey's Lady's Book, 1851

May Baskets

The May baskets which follow are quick to make. The size of each may be adjusted to suit available flowers. The cornucopia may be adapted to serve as a May basket (see page 174). Baskets should be filled with fresh flowers immediately before delivery. The flower ends may be enclosed in plastic wrap to help prevent wilting and to protect the basket against dampness. In the absence of fresh flowers, artificial flowers may be easily fashioned out of crepe paper, floral wire, and tape. The flowers need not be botanically correct, merely pretty and colorful. Since delivery should be made in secret, hang the basket on a door knob, ring the door bell, and run!

May Basket I, *The Delineator*, 1901
MATERIALS:
 1 piece lightweight construction paper, 6″ × 3″, pastel color
 2 pieces ribbon, 12″ long, about ¼″ wide, color to match paper
 stapler or glue

STEP-BY-STEP:
1. Bring ends of one long side of the paper together and overlap slightly. Staple or glue in place.

2. Staple or tie ribbons in place at each point of basket opening (see May Basket II). (Illustration 11-1)

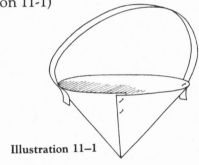

Illustration 11–1

3. Fill with flowers.

May Basket II, *The Delineator*, 1905
MATERIALS:
 circle of lightweight cardboard (shirt cardboard), 1¾″ in diameter
 4″ square construction paper, pastel color
 14″ ribbon about ¼″ wide or pretty color string or yarn
 hole punch, glue, scissors

STEP-BY-STEP:
1. Fold the paper in half each way to make four small squares.

2. Open out and glue the cardboard circle exactly in the center. (Illustration 11-2)

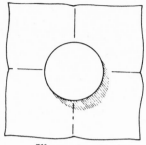

Illustration 11–2

3. Cut down each fold line to the circle, bend up the four flaps just made, lap the edges a little, and glue in place.

4. Punch a hole in two opposite corners and tie one end of ribbon loosely in place through each hole. (Illustration 11-3)

5. Fill with flowers.

Illustration 11–3

May Basket III, *The Delineator,* 1923
MATERIALS:
    8″ square lightweight construction paper, pastel color
    sharp scissors

STEP-BY-STEP:
1. Fold paper in half diagonally (Illustration 11-4) then in half three more times. Cut off extra bit of paper at end of fold.

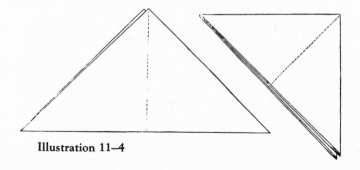

Illustration 11–4

2. Carefully cut through folded paper just up to but not through folds, cutting alternately from each side. Cuts should be about ⅜″ apart. (Illustration 11-5)

3. Carefully unfold paper and stretch basket open. Put something slightly heavy, like a small stone, in the bottom to weight it down before filling with flowers. (Illustration 11-6)

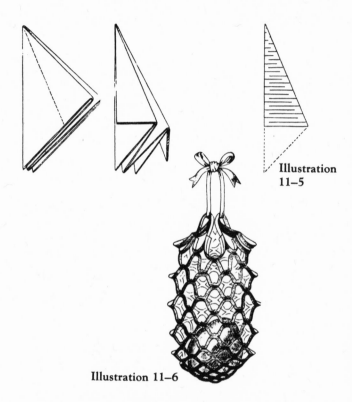

**Illustration
11–5**

Illustration 11–6

May Day Celebration

When May Day falls on a weekend, revive the May basket custom and distribute breakfast invitations as you make the early morning deliveries. Invitations can be written on a roll of paper tucked among the flowers or verbal. Since the guests are apt to straggle in, keep the occasion informal but do set a pretty table with flowers and a Maypole centerpiece.

Decorations
Maypole Centerpiece, The Delineator, *1907*
MATERIALS:
    box about 1″ high, about 6″ square
    ½″ diameter dowel, about 12″ long

6 different colors pastel ribbon about ¼″ wide, 2 feet long each

6 small bunches artificial flowers to coordinate with ribbons

1 garland of small flowers to twine around dowel

white and green acrylic paint, glue, scissors

STEP-BY-STEP:

1. Paint dowel white and box lid green to simulate grass. Cut a hole in the box lid just large enough to fit dowel into snugly.

2. With lid on box, force dowel in hole and glue to bottom of box. Wind garland around dowel and glue in place top and bottom.

3. Bunch ribbons together and tie about 3″ from one end. Drape knot over top of dowel and glue in place.

4. Glue one single flower of matching color to each short ribbon end. Arrange long ribbon ends evenly around pole on "grass" and glue in position along with bunch of matching flowers (Illustration 11-7). **Note:** In the original 1907 version of this centerpiece, small dolls

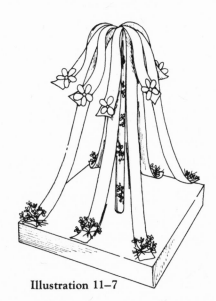

Illustration 11-7

were dressed in pastels to match the ribbons and flowers and were arranged around base of Maypole as if they were performing the Maypole dance. Lollipop Dolls (see page 28) or Cornhusk Dolls (see page 137) might be adapted for this use.

Food

Cook, as the guests arrive, this springtime menu from 1931.

INFORMAL BREAKFAST

Strawberries with Cream

Waffles   Honey or Syrup

Bacon

Coffee

Activities

Maypole Dance

The pole, which need not be over seven feet high, must have an even number of gaily-colored ribbons tacked around and near the top. Ornament the top of the pole with colored streamers and suspend a wreath of flowers by means of two ribbons crossed and nailed on the top of the pole. Fasten the four ribbon ends to the flower wreath. The dancers stand facing alternately right and left, each holding a ribbon in the hand nearest the pole. Each dancer facing right passes under the ribbon held by the dancer opposite, then allows the next dancer to pass under his ribbon. In and out, over and under, the ribbons weave.

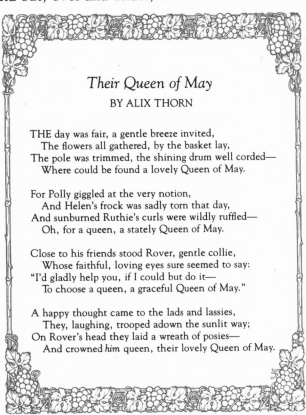

Their Queen of May

BY ALIX THORN

THE day was fair, a gentle breeze invited,
   The flowers all gathered, by the basket lay,
The pole was trimmed, the shining drum well corded—
   Where could be found a lovely Queen of May.

For Polly giggled at the very notion,
   And Helen's frock was sadly torn that day,
And sunburned Ruthie's curls were wildly ruffled—
   Oh, for a queen, a stately Queen of May.

Close to his friends stood Rover, gentle collie,
   Whose faithful, loving eyes sure seemed to say:
"I'd gladly help you, if I could but do it—
   To choose a queen, a graceful Queen of May."

A happy thought came to the lads and lassies,
   They, laughing, trooped adown the sunlit way;
On Rover's head they laid a wreath of posies—
   And crowned *him* queen, their lovely Queen of May.

12
Mother's Day

Celebrated second Sunday in May

Three years after the death of her mother in May, 1905, Miss Anna M. Jarvis arranged to have her church in Grafton, West Virginia, dedicate a Mother's Day service to her mother's memory. Because her mother loved and cultivated carnations, everyone in attendance that Sunday was given one of these beautiful flowers.

From that day on, Miss Jarvis, who never married, waged a relentless campaign to have a day set aside to honor mothers. She wrote letters and enlisted the support of influential people. Gradually, more and more states proclaimed a Mother's Day, usually a Sunday in May. At the same time, the carnation became inextricably associated with the day, red blooms worn to honor mothers who are living and white those who have died.

On May 9, 1914, President Woodrow Wilson issued the first Mother's Day Proclamation, designating the second Sunday in May as a day set aside to express "our love and reverence for the mothers of our country." Every year a similar proclamation is issued by the President. Despite the success of her efforts, Miss Jarvis ultimately became disillusioned with the commercialism that began to surround the day and died bitter and disappointed.

The idea of honoring mothers did not originate with Anna Jarvis. The Romans celebrated a spring festival dedicated to the mother goddess, Cybele. This three-day festival, called the Hilaria, started on the ides of March.

Early Christendom celebrated Mothering Sunday on the fourth Sunday in Lent to worship Mary, the Mother of Christ. This holiday became important later to children in domestic service, living in the master's household, as an opportunity to return to their families to see their mothers. It was customary for these children to bring gifts. The simnel cake, a small hard cookie made of simila, a high-grade wheat flour, was especially popular as a gift to mother. The English poet Robert Herrick refers to this cake in his poem, "To Dianeme."

A Mother's Day celebration today honors mother by giving her special attention. She will receive cards and gifts and most certainly a corsage of carnations. If her children do not live at home, they will call or pay a visit. The family will make a special effort to relieve her of her household duties and breakfast will be served to her. In the evening, she will be treated to dinner at her favorite restaurant. And, of course, many churches hold services honoring motherhood, preserving the spirit of the day as envisioned by Anna Jarvis.

81

Mothers
by Mary Carolyn Davies

Mothers!

The gray-haired mother, whose successful sons and happy daughters bring flowers and love—

The young girl-wife, with her first baby in her arms—

The mother of seven, struggling against poverty. and fear and want, but keeping the six patched and mended and in school, and the baby clean—

The mother in the shack on the prairie, in the homestead on the range, in the mountains far from church or neighbors, who becomes church and neighbors and civilization to her children—

The average mother of the average family, with the average amount of bills and worries over Johnny's measles and Mary's beaus—

Mothers!

May Providence strengthen them to go on with high hearts for another year—when we will again bear loving gifts of white carnations or, if far from them, send our grateful telegram.

Mothers! God bless them.

The Delineator, 1925

13
Memorial Day

Celebrated May 30, federal observance last Monday in May

The custom of honoring the dead has been a part of every civilization. The ancient Greeks and Romans honored the dead by decorating their graves. Memorial services were held in the monasteries during the Middle Ages at Whitsuntide.

Exactly where or how the custom of nationally honoring the dead began in the United States is uncertain. It is known, however, that the origin of Memorial Day was a commemoration of those who died during the Civil War. It is commonly accepted that the first memorial service of this kind occurred in April, 1866. The ladies of Columbus, Mississippi went to the Friendship Cemetery, containing 1,500 Confederate and 100 Union graves of those who had fallen during the Battle of Shiloh, and walked indiscriminately among the graves strewing flowers. Since this ceremony occurred during the Reconstruction, there was great uncertainty as to how the gesture would be viewed. The *New York Herald Tribune* recorded the event and interpreted it as an act of reconciliation.

Later, on May 5, 1868, General John A. Logan, Commander-in-Chief of the Grand Army of the Republic, an organization of Union veterans, sent an order to all the local posts of the Grand Army ordering them to decorate the graves of comrades on May 30, 1868. New York, in 1873, was the first state to legalize Memorial Day, and most of the other states followed suit. It is not, however, a national legal holiday.

Other tributes to war dead have been made in the course of our history to commemorate the dead of subsequent wars. On Memorial Day 1958, the coffins of two unidentified soldiers, one from World War II and one from the Korean War, were transported from their battle-site graves to Arlington National Cemetery and reinterred in the Tomb of the Unknown Soldier.

A traditional part of today's celebration of Memorial Day is the 500-mile race at the Indianapolis Motor Speedway, culminating a month of festivities. Marking the beginning of the summer season in the United States, this day is usually the occasion of the year's first picnic. There are also parades and special ceremonies commemorating the war dead. In the past, children would be sent to gather armfuls of flowers for the graves. The flag is flown at half-staff until twelve noon.

In some areas, the day is referred to as Decoration Day, which was its original designation.

Then Strew Bright Flowers on Every Grave
by Miss P. A. Culver

From hill, and dale, and glen, bring flowers
  To strew each soldier's bier,
In ev'ry springtime's golden hours,
  In ev'ry coming year.
Bring laurel, emblem of their fame,
  And myrtle, of our love,
Let violets remembrance name,
  And amaranth, life above.

Chorus

Then strew bright flow'rs on ev'ry grave
  Wherein a hero lies,
And let the dear old banner wave
  'Neath freedom's sunlit skies.

The first clear notes the bugle blew,
  Were special calls to them,

And with their country's weal in view,
  They went forth strong, armed men.
Left fathers, mothers, sisters, wives,
  And children young and pure,
And held as naught their precious lives,
  That homes might still endure.

Chorus

To them be honor, earnest, true,
  And may we ne'er forget:
They died for me, they died for you,
  Where hostile armies met.
Come, lay upon each grassy bed
  A garland rich and rare,
Wherever sleep our soldier dead,
  Let them this tribute share.

Chorus

Godey's Lady's Book, 1876

The Delineator, 1916

14

Flag Day

Celebrated June 14

Despite the fact that the United States is one of the newest countries in the industrialized world, its flag is one of the oldest, being older than the present Union Jack and the French and Italian flags. June 14 is celebrated every year as the birthday of Old Glory.

The nickname *Old Glory* was given to the flag by a sea captain who received a large flag from a group of ladies upon his departure for a round-the-globe journey. When the flag was hoisted on the mast, the captain exclaimed "Old Glory, Old Glory." The appellation has remained ever since.

In 1775, the Continental Congress named a committee including Benjamin Franklin to propose a design for a national ensign. Some two years later, on June 14, 1777, in Philadelphia, the present flag was adopted. George Washington later said the stars were taken from heaven, the red from our mother country, separated by white stripes to signify that we have separated from her. The five-pointed star instead of the six-pointed star of Britain may have been chosen for its similarity to that used by France, then our only ally.

The first design had thirteen stars, arranged in a circle. When Vermont and Kentucky later joined the Union, two stars and two stripes were added. It was this fifteen-star and fifteen-stripe flag which was flying over Fort McHenry during the War of 1812 when Francis Scott Key wrote "The Star-Spangled Banner." As more states became part of the Union, it was decided to maintain thirteen stripes for the original thirteen colonies and to add a star for each new state. Any such change would take effect on the Fourth of July of the succeeding year. In 1818, during the administration of President Monroe, Congress enacted a law to this effect. The flag underwent many changes until Arizona entered the Union in 1912. From 1912 to 1959, the flag remained unchanged until Hawaii and Alaska became states.

In 1877, one hundred years after the adoption of the flag, Congress declared that it should be flown over public buildings on June 14 of that year. Various school districts around the country began to have special ceremonies on June 14. In 1916, President Wilson proclaimed that Flag Day should be celebrated every year on June 14. Subsequently, in 1926, the first Flag Week was declared (May 23–30) to promote greater love and respect for the Stars and Stripes.

The story of Betsy Ross and the first American flag is a very popular legend, according to which Betsy Ross, a well-known seamstress in Philadelphia, was commissioned by the Continental Congress to sew the first flag. Also, it is believed that she demonstrated to a special committee how easy it was to fashion a five-pointed star. Unfortunately none of this charming legend can be supported by historical fact. Indeed, there is no record that the Continental Congress gave such a commission.

Flag Display

The United States flag may be displayed on all days except when the weather is inclement. Customarily, it is flown only from sunrise to sunset unless illumination is provided after dark. When the flag is flown at half-staff, it is first raised to full staff then lowered to half-staff (half the distance between the top and bottom of the staff). The flag is again raised to the peak before it is lowered for the day. The flag is flown at half-staff until noon on Memorial Day and on other days by order of the President. Holidays and certain other days are special favorites for flying the flag. Some of these are:

New Year's Day, January 1
Inauguration Day, January 20
Lincoln's Birthday, February 12
Washington's Birthday, third Monday in February
Easter Sunday, variable
Mother's Day, second Sunday in May
Armed Forces Day, third Saturday in May
Memorial Day, last Monday in May (half-staff until noon)
Flag Day, June 14
Independence Day, July 4
Labor Day, first Monday in September
Constitution Day, September 17
Columbus Day, second Monday in October
Navy Day, October 27
Veterans' Day, November 11

Thanksgiving Day, fourth Thursday in November
Christmas Day, December 25
Dates of admission to Union of states
State holidays

Over the street, the flag is suspended vertically, with the union (the blue field) to the north in an east and west street, to the east in a north and south street.

When displayed with another flag against a wall from crossed staffs, the United States flag should be on its own right, with its staff in front of the other flag's staff.

When flown on the same halyard with a state or city flag or pennant, the United States flag should always be at the peak.

When suspended over a sidewalk from a rope extending from a house to a pole at the sidewalk, the flag should be hoisted out, union first, from the building.

When displayed from a staff projecting horizontally or at an angle from a building, the union should be at the peak of the staff unless the flag is at half-staff.

When displayed other than from a staff, indoors or out, the flag should be flat. Horizontally or vertically against a wall, the union should be uppermost to the observer's left. In a window, it should be displayed in the same manner with the union to the left of the observer in the street. Bunting may be used for festoons, rosettes, or drapings but never the flag.

15
Father's Day

Celebrated third Sunday in June

A day for honoring fatherhood is of more recent derivation than Mother's Day and has no comparable feast among the ancients. Credit for promoting this cause is generally given to Mrs. John Bruce Dodd of Spokane, Washington. The idea occurred to her in 1909 as a suitable way to honor her father, who had reared his six motherless children on a Washington farm after his wife died at an early age. Mrs. Dodd brought her idea to Rev. Conrad Bluhm, president of the Spokane Ministerial Association, and to the Spokane YMCA, both of whom began to publicize it. The day chosen was June 5, Mrs. Dodd's own father's birthday. The first Father's Day commemoration occurred in 1910.

In 1916, President Wilson participated in the Father's Day celebration in Spokane by pushing a button in Washington, D.C., which unfurled a flag in Spokane.

It was only in 1972 that a Congressional resolution permanently established the date as the third Sunday in June. Senator Margaret Chase Smith made a major contribution to having the day officially recognized.

The National Father's Day Committee, formed in New York City in 1936, has promoted the idea of Father's Day by selecting a "Father of the Year." Presidents Truman and Eisenhower, Dr. Ralph Bunche, and General Douglas MacArthur are among those Americans given this prestigious designation. The day is generally celebrated by sending gifts or cards to one's father or making a fitting tribute to a father who has died. Many families gather on this day to honor the fathers among them.

The charming piece which follows was an editorial in *The Delineator* in June, 1915. Note the reference to women's struggle for the right to vote.

Fathers' Day

June is the month not only of roses and weddings, but it is the month that celebrates a far less frequently sung fete. Fathers' Day comes this month on June 22nd. The rose, any kind or color, is the emblem of Fathers' Day, and all who wear one on June 22nd will be known to be paying tribute to Father, living or dead. Father himself was not the inventor of this celebration. It was a woman who devotedly admired her father and her husband who made the suggestion. Happy and admiring daughters and wives all over the country have taken it up. There is a slow but sure gathering feeling among women that in spite of the heavy artillery used against men in the fight for suffrage, after all, Father is a pretty fine old Father, and that we will tell him so once a year, no matter how we ignore and maltreat him the remaining three hundred and sixty-four days.

The Delineator, 1915

16
Independence Day

Celebrated July 4th

It was on July 4, 1776, that John Hancock signed the Declaration of Independence in Philadelphia after a long and heated debate among the representatives of the thirteen colonies that were then under the oppressive political and economic sway of England. The Continental Congress was not unanimous and only nine colonies voted in favor of the Declaration. Ultimately, it was carried, and signed by John Hancock, president of the Congress, to make the act official. That night the document was printed in handbills and posted and distributed the next day.

The full text appeared in the *Pennsylvania Evening Post* on July 6, 1776, and on July 8 the Declaration was read publicly for the first time in Independence Square. There were bonfires and the ringing of church bells to celebrate the occasion. General George Washington had the document read "in a clear voice" to his troops in City Hall Park in New York on July 9, and Boston celebrated its adoption on July 18 with the firing of cannons and the pealing of church bells. On the nineteenth of July the Declaration was put on parchment and signed by all members of the Continental Congress.

The feeling of irrevocable commitment that prevailed in the gathering can be sensed in John Hancock's remark, that "we must all hang together," to which Benjamin Franklin replied, "If we don't, we shall all hang separately." The Fourth of July has been celebrated ever since as the anniversary of our independence.

Following the spontaneous celebrations that occurred on the original Fourth of July, early Independence Day festivities included cannon fire, bonfires, fireworks, and public readings of the Declaration of Independence. Since the Revolutionary Army was not disbanded until November 5, 1793, the early celebrations had a distinct military character, of which the traditional Fourth of July parade is a carry-over. Also, when the Army was disbanded, the soldiers carried these traditional forms of celebration with them throughout the colonies and beyond, to the frontiers of Ohio and Kentucky and to the Mississippi River.

Oratory, a form of entertainment in the days before radio and television, was an important part of the early Independence Day celebrations. It was a great honor to be asked to deliver a Fourth of July speech, and a two-hour speech was the minimum requirement.

As the frontier moved farther west, the celebration of Independence

Day followed, and the military tradition was carried with it as festivities were enjoyed in the frontier outposts. The first celebration of the Fourth of July on the West Coast occurred in 1847 at Fort Moore, Los Angeles.

Another important influence on the way we celebrate the holiday is the fact that children are generally not in school in July, with the result that this is very much a family celebration with picnics and community gatherings.

In recent years, the fireworks and other military features of the celebration have diminished in importance and have given way to forms of celebration devoted to children and family activities. In many states, the possession of fireworks by individuals has been banned as being too dangerous. Many communities, however, have continued the tradition by sponsoring fireworks displays under the supervision of the local fire department. In 1919, gaily-colored floats were added as a feature of the traditional Fourth of July parade in Washington, D.C., as an expression of appreciation by the foreign governments the United States aided in World War I.

This celebration has often been used to promote a cause, such as women's suffrage, or to collect alms for orphanages and other worthy causes.

The Centennial celebration in 1876 featured the first American International Exposition. Such an exposition was then a showcase for the progress made by the nation sponsoring it. There had previously been expositions in London, Paris, and Vienna. The American Exposition was held in Philadelphia on a 236-acre site in Fairmount Park. Twenty-four states and nine foreign countries erected buildings and thirty-five foreign nations were represented in total. The Exposition was opened on May 10, 1876, by President Grant and closed on November 10, 1876, during which time almost a million people attended.

On Independence Day, 1966, President Lyndon Johnson established the American Revolution Bicentennial Commission for the purpose of planning and developing observances and activities commemorating the two hundredth anniversary of American independence with a view to reaffirming the ideals which underlie the nation's heritage. Subsequently, bicentennial commissions were set up by each state to plan activities reflecting its unique character.

The events that took place on July 4, 1976, were extensively covered by the national media, and special television programs broadcast the key attractions of the festivities in each of the major American cities. One of the more spectacular of these was the procession of 129 sailing ships from almost thirty nations. The tall ships and smaller vessels sailed past the Statue of Liberty and up the Hudson River to the northern end of New York's Manhattan Island. President Gerald Ford was among the many public officials who viewed the spectacle from the deck of a U.S. Navy aircraft carrier. Many local communities observed the day with parades, picnics, concerts, and fireworks displays.

Throughout the entire year there were special television programs and promotional announcements concerning American history. It was generally agreed that the Bicentennial year was a great success, and Americans gained a greater appreciation of the nation's heritage from it.

Keepsake

Freedom's message rings out in this 1857 alphabet from *Godey's Lady's Book.* The border is taken from a page decoration in a 1904 *Delineator.* The motto is worked on perforated paper (see Embroidery, page 290). This needlework form was a popular one with Victorian ladies for mottoes. The design may be worked in needlepoint or cross-stitch embroidery. Use the fancy alphabet in composing alternate messages.

MATERIALS:

  1 sheet perforated paper, size 15″ × 18″
  cotton 6-strand embroidery floss: red, white, blue
  metallic embroidery yarn
  masking tape
  permanent felt-tip markers, fine point
  fine embroidery needle

STEP-BY-STEP:

1. Transfer design to perforated paper using permanent markers. Tape all edges to prevent tearing.

2. Embroider letters first, then border. Be very gentle. Work as follows:
   letters (upper half) 6 strands, blue, half cross-stitch
   (lower half) 6 strands, red, half cross-stitch
   6 strands, white, half cross-stitch
   3 strands, red, backstitch
   (points) 1 strand, metallic yarn, half cross-stitch
   stars 3 strands, white, cross-stitch
   fire crackers (body) 6 strands, red, half cross-stitch
   (outline) 3 strands, blue, backstitch
   flag poles 1 strand, metallic yarn, straight stitch

3. Frame. Use cream colored mat behind embroidered piece.

Independence Day Celebration

Celebration of this holiday was urged by *The Delineator* in 1894.

The patriotic American mother is anxious to celebrate Independence Day in such a manner as will impress her children with a sense of the freedom and independence which are their birthright. It devolves upon her to stimulate and encourage the patriotism of the younger members of the family by bringing to their minds as impressively yet as gayly as possible the significance of the anniversary, and this she can do by an artistic decoration of the home with the national colors, and by a menu and table ornamentation that will be viewed with delight and remembered ever after with joy.

In 1914, *The Delineator* noted that "picnics, excursions, lawn-parties, and village gatherings, with open-air programs and plays, are now increasingly popular on the Fourth of July, and to be commended."

A Neighborhood Party

Combining the best features of past observances can arouse the commendable feelings of love of home and country and be a lot of fun as well.

Invitations, *The Delineator*, 1914

Make giant firecrackers by covering empty 1½" paper tubes with red paper, tucking in the ends. Glue a string "fuse" in one end. Write invitations in blue ink on white paper, roll, and tuck into the tube (Illustration 16-1). Ask children to toss a firecracker at each home. They will think it fun and, of course, these firecrackers are safe. Ask everyone to wear only red, white, or blue clothing.

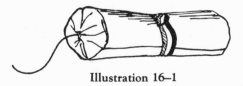

Illustration 16–1

Decorations

Red, white, and blue, of course, are the colors which give any gathering patriotic overtones for Americans. Use flags, shields, stars, liberty bells, and paper fireworks and firecrackers. Put streamers and flags on fence posts, pillars, and in other suitable spots.

Table Decorations

Set the buffet table with seasonal flowers in the national colors: geraniums, roses, poppies, daisies, alyssum, larkspurs, cornflowers. Use whatever is blooming in abundance, or use crepe and tissue paper or purchased printed paper decorations, striped ribbons and streamers, stickers, or flags.

A pretty table in a 1907 *Delineator* combined flowers and paper decorations. To duplicate it, cover the table with a white cloth. Stretch tricolored streamers down the middle of the table. Place a vase of red and white flowers arranged with American flags as a centerpiece. Use a blue container or cover the container with a blue crepe-paper ruffle. Around the overhang of the tablecloth, arrange a zigzag of streamer by folding and pinning the points to the tablecloth. Finish off the upper points with rosettes made by gathering the long edge of a 17" × 2" red crepe-paper strip, pulling up tight, and stitching the ends together. Cut out a white star, 3" across (see page 101) and glue it in the center of each rosette. Instead of flowers, a large bunch of paper skyrockets (see page 99) makes a dramatic centerpiece.

Wrap silverware in napkins and insert into paper-covered tube "firecrackers" made in the same way as the invitations. Pile firecrackers at one end of the table.

Food

Buffet service will be most satisfactory for a large gathering. Give some thought to the food presentation. Use red, white, and blue dishes, cut sandwiches in shield shapes, tie sandwiches or cookies with tri-colored ribbon, wrap candies in tissue paper and stick flags in radishes.

The July 1912 *Delineator* termed the following menu "a good Fourth of July picnic."

FOURTH OF JULY PICNIC

Deviled Eggs

Radishes   Homemade Pickles
Cold Fried Chicken   Sandwiches
Baking Powder Biscuits
Gingerbread   Sugar Cookies
Lemonade*

*See below.

LEMONADE
The Delineator, 1912

3 lemons, rinsed and   desired
   scrubbed   1 qt. boiling water
Granulated sugar as

Chip off thin outer skin of 2 of the lemons and steep 10 minutes in a little water. Cut 2 thin slices from the center of each lemon and set aside. Juice the remaining lemon pieces. Add sugar to the juice as desired, then add the boiling water and the strained water from steeped peel. Let stand until cool, then refrigerate until needed. Serve with slices of lemon and chipped ice. A little currant, strawberry, or raspberry juice may be added. Slices of banana, strawberries cut in quarters, or raspberries or pitted cherries on cocktail skewers make attractive garnishes. *The Delineator* flatly stated in the article accompanying this recipe that "the best lemonade is that made with boiling water instead of cold." Makes 1 qt.

Another approach to the menu is to let the food reflect the red, white, and blue spirit of the day, within the bounds of taste appeal. As blue is not a color found frequently in food, it should be used sparingly. An early food editor suggested blueberry juice as a suitable blue food coloring. The July 1912 *Delineator* offered a list of foods from which the hostess could plan her "American Flag Dinner." Among the choices for this red, white, and blue feast were:

- appetizers: red radishes, cocktail onions, salted popcorn
- soups: tomato soup, lobster bisque, cream of clam
- fish: bluefish
- salads: fruit salad of red raspberries, currants, and cherries; tomato and cream cheese
- entrees: very rare roast beef, chicken fricasee, cold Virginia ham
- vegetables: mashed potatoes, buttered beets, cauliflower
- desserts: steamed blueberry pudding, strawberry and lemon ices, white frosted cake with violet and cherry decorations
- beverages: grape-juice punch with cherry and grape garnish

Games

Hold the party outside in the beautiful July weather that is found throughout the country and plan games and activities for a wide range of interests and ages. In the past, familiar games were frequently adapted to the occasion by giving them new names or using props appropriate to the theme of the party. End the festivities with patriotic songs.

Flag Tag, The Delineator, *1914*

Played like tag. The tagger has a flag to use in tagging the players. This game is best for older children who can handle the flag safely.

Flag Hunt, The Delineator, *1914*

Hide various-sized flags throughout the yard. Have prizes for greatest number found, least number found, largest, smallest.

Pin the Star on the Flag, The Delineator, *1905*

Paint an American flag on corrugated cardboard. Adjust the dimensions a bit to provide a larger blue field. Omit one star from the field (Illustration 16-2). Write each player's name on

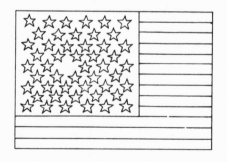

Illustration 16—2

separate stars and, blindfolded, have each player attempt to pin his star in the empty spot on the flag. The winner is the player who comes closest to the empty space.

States, The Delineator, 1904

Have each guest name the fifty states on paper; set a time limit. Increase the difficulty of the game by requiring state capitals, as well.

Revolution Relays

Adapt standard relay races by using red, white, and blue bean bags to conduct the contests. Several relay favorites are:

- passing the bags along the lines
- walking with bags balanced on the head
- tossing at holes in a heavy cardboard shield (Illustration 16-3)

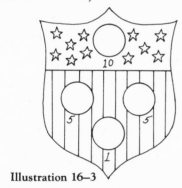

Illustration 16–3

Red, White, and Blue Darts, The Delineator, 1906

Use Skyrockets (see page 99) which have perhaps been slightly damaged in firing or make darts from red, white, and blue tissue paper (Illustration 16-4). Each player should have one dart of each color. The object of the game is to toss the darts to stand upright in bushes or grass. A dart is considered upright when a flat hand can be placed under the wings without moving the dart.

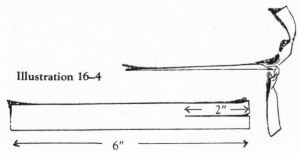

Illustration 16–4

Scoring Red: 10 in grass, 5 in bush
White: 7 in grass, 3 in bush
Blue: 5 in grass, 1 in bush

Flag-Guessing Contest, The Delineator, 1917

Display flags of other nations to be identified in writing.

Charades

One team acts out an historical event to be guessed by the other team.

Paper Fireworks

These will amuse children and adults alike. Older children may enjoy constructing the fireworks; invite them to do so a few days before the party. Make many skyrockets, cut lots of confetti. Many of the paper fireworks can be seen in Color Plate 10.

Roman Candles, The Delineator, 1902

MATERIALS:
1 sheet red, white, or blue construction paper, 6″ × 9″
confetti or small bits of brightly colored paper
transparent tape

STEP-BY-STEP:
1. Roll construction paper into a tube approximately 1″ diameter × 9″ long. Tape edge of paper to roll. Fold in tube at one end (Illustration 16-5).

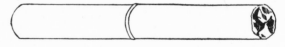

Illustration 16–5

2. Load the candle loosely with confetti.
3. To send off candle, hold it in one hand and swing it around. The paper "sparks" will fly out and scatter festively.

Note: This is messy but fun, especially for the little ones.

Sparkling Calumet, The Delineator, *1902*

MATERIALS:

    1 tube from paper towels, etcetera, approximately 11″ × 1½″ diameter

    2 sheets red, white, or blue construction paper, 9″ × 12″

confetti or small bits of brightly colored paper
white glue, stapler

STEP-BY-STEP:

1. Cover tube with one sheet of paper, cutting away excess. Cut a hole the diameter of a dime on the side of the tube opposite paper seam, about 2″ from the end. Squeeze end of stem near bowl together and staple. (Illustration 16-6)

2. To make pipe bowl, cut a quarter circle from the corner of the remaining paper with the radius 5″ long, as shown. Curve out the point. (Illustration 16-7)

3. Form funnel shape by bringing the two sides together with a 1″ overlap. Glue edge together. Slash lower edges of funnel, bend up slashes and glue to inside of pipe stem through hole. (Illustration 16-8)

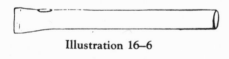

Illustration 16–6

Illustration 16—7

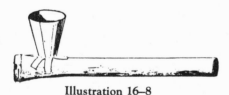

Illustration 16—8

4. Half-fill pipe bowl with bits of paper. Blow through open end of tube to scatter confetti. This, too, is messy but fun! (Illustration 16-9)

Illustration 16–9

Note: A *calumet* is a tobacco pipe smoked by the Indians on ceremonial occasions, especially in token of peace.

Disk Pinwheel, The Delineator, *1900*

MATERIALS:

    yellow, red, green, and blue construction paper, 9″ × 12″

soft string, approximately 34″
1 large, flat button with big holes
tapestry needle with eye large enough for string
rubber cement

STEP-BY-STEP:

1. Cut 2 circles (3½″ diameter and 2″ diameter) from yellow paper. Cut 2 circles (3″ diameter and 1″ diameter) from red paper. Cut 2 circles (2½″ diameter) from green paper. Cut 2 circles (1½″ diameter) from blue paper.
   Cut 2 circles (1½″ diameter) from blue paper.

2. Glue these two sets of disks together by placing one over another, forming two varicolored disks exactly alike.

3. Stack disks wrong sides together and push needle through on either side of center point. Sew string through one disk, through one hole

of button, and through other disk. Bring needle back through second disk, button, and first disk and tie string ends together. (Illustration 16-10)

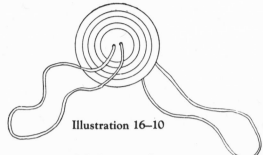

Illustration 16–10

4. Glue edges of disks together.
5. To use pinwheel, place the first two fingers of the right hand in one loop and the same fingers of the left hand in the other, give the string a twirl and pull the hands apart quickly. The motion causes the string to twist, allowing the hands to come nearer together; another outward motion of the hands and the pinwheel will revolve rapidly in other direction. **Note:** Pinwheel may be decorated with stars, spirals, or other motifs instead of disks.

Three-Star Pinwheel, The Delineator, *1901*
MATERIALS:
    3″ square red construction paper
    4″ square white construction paper
    5″ square blue construction paper
    hat or corsage pin with 2¾″ shaft
    2 corks, ½″ long, about ¼″ in diameter
    ¼″ balsa stick, about 12″ long
    scissors

STEP-BY-STEP:
1. Mark exact center of each square.
2. Cut from each corner of each square to within ¼″ of center. (Illustration 16-11)

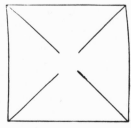

Illustration 16–11

3. From behind, pierce consecutive points of the smallest square (red) on to the hat pin, then push pin through center of square and slide star up to head of pin. (Illustration 16-12)

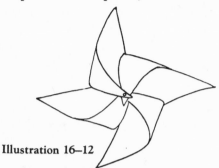

Illustration 16–12

4. Thread on 1 cork, allowing a little tolerance above the cork.
5. Repeat steps 3 and 4 with white square.
6. Repeat step 3 with blue square.
7. Insert pin into end of stick, leaving a little tolerance between star and stick. (Illustration 16-13)

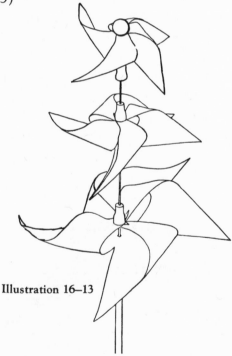

Illustration 16–13

Comet, The Delineator, *1902*
MATERIALS:
    rubber ball, about 3″ in diameter
    1 sheet each blue, orange, and red tissue
        paper, 30″ long
    white glue

STEP-BY-STEP:

1. Cut two strips 4″ wide the entire length of the sheet from each color tissue paper. Leave paper folded for cutting.
2. Glue same color strips together at one end forming three 60″-long strips. Fold each strip, leaving about 3 inches free at one end (Illustration 16-14) and cut fringe through folded edge, having strands about ½″ wide. (Illustration 16-15)

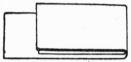 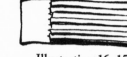

Illustration 16–14   **Illustration 16–15**

3. Glue red tail to ball (Illustration 16-16). Then glue on blue tail, partly beyond and partly overlapping the red paper. Apply orange tail in the same manner.

Illustration 16–16

4. Let comet dry completely. Handle tail carefully to prevent tangles.
5. To use outside, throw ball up as far as possible. It will sail down with a brilliant streak of color streaming behind it (Illustration 16-17). Avoid trees, bushes, and wires. **Note:** The tail may be made longer by using three instead of two lengths of tissue paper.

Illustration 16–17

Skyrocket, The Delineator, *1900*
MATERIALS:

    foil-coated gift wrap paper (red, white, blue silver, or assorted colors), each piece 3″ × 20″
    1 large wooden spool
    5″ length of elastic or rubber band, ¾″ wide
    1 regular rubber band

STEP-BY-STEP:

1. To make skyrocket, fringe strip of foil paper 7″ along one long side, cutting fringe ¼″ wide about 2″ deep. (Illustration 16-18)
2. Starting at corner diagonally opposite fringed corner, tightly roll strip up. Fold over top end to keep it in place (Illustration 16-19). Make a large number of skyrockets.

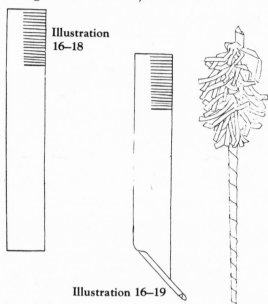

Illustration 16–18

Illustration 16–19

3. To make firing device, wrap elastic or large rubber band loosely over one end of spool. Fasten securely by wrapping regular rubber band tightly around spool. (Illustration 16-20)

Illustration 16–20

4. To fire, place one skyrocket through hole in spool, fringed end out. Grasp tip end in the elastic, pull the skyrocket back toward you and let it fly like an arrow from a bow (Illustration 16-21). If end bends on landing, simply tear it off to use skyrocket again. Caution

Illustration 16–22

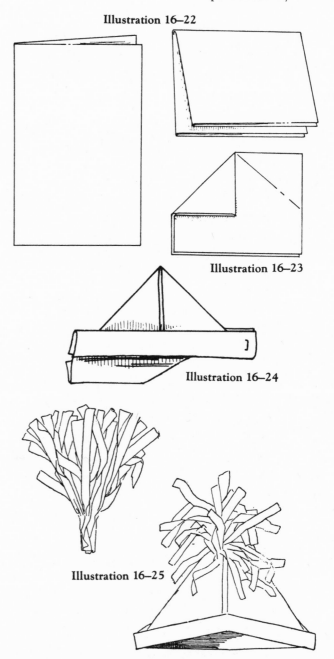

Illustration 16–23

Illustration 16–24

Illustration 16–25

Illustration 16–21

children to carefully aim skyrockets away from people when firing. **Note:** The skyrockets are attractive enough to be used in bunches as table decorations.

Children's Corner

Cocked Hat, The Delineator, *1900*

MATERIALS:

    1 sheet newspaper, approximately 23″ × 29½″

    1 red, 1 white, and 1 blue tissue paper strip, each 12″ × 5″

    stapler

STEP-BY-STEP:

1. Fold newspaper in half and in half again. (Illustration 16-22)
2. Fold folded corners toward center (Illustration 16-23). Adjust hat size by folding corners closer together or further apart as needed. Fold up bottom twice on each side. Staple ends near opening. (Illustration 16-24)
3. To make pompom, stack tissue paper strips and cut fringe on one long edge, 3½″ deep. Roll uncut edges tightly together and staple pompom to top of hat. (Illustration 16-25)

Head Wreath, The Delineator, *1900*

MATERIALS:

    1 red, 1 white, and 1 blue tissue paper strip each, 30″ × 3″

    1 white and 1 blue tissue paper strip, each 10″ × 3″

    1 red tissue paper strip, 20″ × 3″

    stapler

STEP-BY-STEP:

1. Fold one end of each 30″ strip roughly into thirds. Stack and staple folded ends together. (Illustration 16-26)
2. Braid, crushing paper gently into puffy strips. (Illustration 16-27)
3. Staple ends of braided strip into wreath. Stretch or compress wreath to adjust fit.
4. To make bow, notch one end of white and blue 10″ strips. Fold unnotched ends of these strips together and staple to wreath at overlap.
5. Fold ends of 20″ red strip toward center, overlapping about 3 inches. Do not crease folds. Crush strip together in center and staple to wreath over blue and white streamers. (Illustration 16-28)

Illustration 16—26

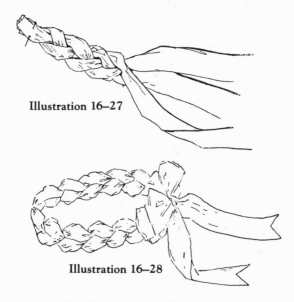

Illustration 16—27

Illustration 16—28

Star Badge, The Delineator, *1901*

MATERIALS:
    4″ square gold paper
    4″ square shirt cardboard

1 safety pin, about 1½″ long
masking tape, white glue, scissors
1 red, 1 white, and 1 blue ribbon or tissue paper strip, 7″ long × ½″ wide

STEP-BY-STEP:

1. Cut star out of gold paper (see instructions below).
2. Glue gold star to cardboard and cut out.
3. Notch one end of each ribbon or strip. Glue unnotched ends to star back. (Illustration 16-29)

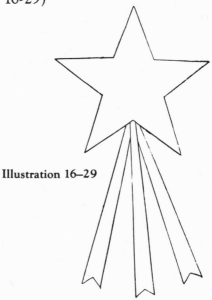

Illustration 16—29

4. Tape safety pin to back of star.

Stars

Stars are a prominent symbol for Independence Day and other holidays as well. A quick method for cutting a symmetrical star may prove most helpful.

MATERIALS:
    square paper
    scissors

STEP-BY-STEP:

1. Fold a square piece of paper exactly in half.
2. Fold again according to the dotted line in Illustration 16-30, which will result in Illustration 16-31.

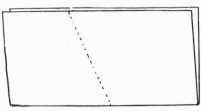

Illustration 16–30

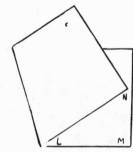

Illustration 16–31

3. Turn back the lower triangle LMN, and Illustration 16-32 will result.

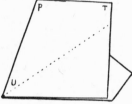

Illustration 16–32

4. Bend over forward the portion PTU on dotted line and it will result in Illustration 16-33.

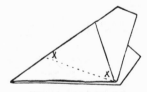

Illustration 16–33

5. Cut along the dotted line XX. The size of the star will be twice the length from X along the bottom fold to the point.
6. Unfold.

Clothespin Soldiers, The Delineator, *1914*
MATERIALS:
    wooden clothespins (no springs)
    white glue
    2″ × 3″ corrugated cardboard pieces
    felt-tip markers, fine and wide points

    bits of metallic soutache and other narrow trims
    scraps of large ball fringe for hats

STEP-BY-STEP:
1. Draw simple face on head of clothespin, arranged so that legs are properly positioned.
2. Color soldier costume with markers. Glue trims in place for pants stripes, chest stripes, and epaulets. (Illustration 16-34)

3. Glue 1 ball from fringe on top of head for hat.
4. Glue soldier to cardboard piece to stand. **Note:** These soldiers create a most unlikely regiment and provide fun for young patriots if Independence Day dawns rainy.

Living Flag

In Monterey, Cal., in 1896, a beautiful living flag was formed by two hundred little girls. Those dressed in red were arranged in rows for the red stripes, those in white fell in line for the white stripes, while others dressed in blue and wearing large flat hats, on the top of which were fastened the stars, were grouped for the blue field dotted with white stars. One of the Southern cities gathered a thousand children for her living flag. Each of the forty-five representing the stars bore the ensign of one of the States, the Governor of each State being asked to present a State emblem for the purpose; doubtless, you know that each star stands for a State and whenever a territory is admitted into the Union as a State a new star is added to the galaxy on the banner.

The Delineator, 1901

The Delineator, 1900

17
Labor Day

Celebrated first Monday in September

By the middle of the nineteenth century, industrialization had progressed to the point where a working class had defined itself. The cult of honest, manly labor had gained considerable prominence, especially in the United States. The labor movement had, as well, a messianic fervor and conceived of itself as the vanguard of all social progress. Consistent with the optimism of the time, it was believed that society could be made nearly perfect if the idealism of the labor movement could hold sway over society.

In this environment, it was natural for the labor movement to want to set a day aside to commemorate the working man. In fact, the idea was first proposed by Peter J. McGuire, a leader of the Knights of Labor and the founder of the United Brotherhood of Carpenters and Joiners of America. It was in 1882 that Mr. McGuire made his proposal to the Central Labor Union in New York City and on September 5 of that year, ten thousand workers marched around Union Square in New York City and staged the first Labor Day Parade. Oregon was the first state to recognize Labor Day on February 21, 1887, and it was made a national holiday by Act of Congress in 1894.

With time, the association between Labor Day and the labor unions has diminished to the point where, today, it is a general family holiday. It is considered the last holiday of summer, when traditionally there is a picnic or outing to have one last celebration before fall.

Picnics

A picnic is a marvelous way to celebrate summer and summer holidays. On Labor Day, an outdoor meal, even if it is just in one's own back yard, is always fun. In 1898, not long after Labor Day became a national holiday, a *Delineator* article included the following thoughts on "Picnic-Giving." Many of the ideas are relevant for modern picnics; others are interesting as a measure of how times have changed.

The Picnic Spot

Not the least important item to be considered in planning one of these *al fresco* merrymakings is the place in which to give it. This should not be too difficult of access, for it must be remembered that the guests, and particularly the juvenile ones, are likely to be wearied by their day's outing and will not care to make a tiresome journey at nightfall. There must be plenty of shade, and the chosen spot should be on the bank of a river or lake, near the ocean, in a glen or on a mountain, whichever is most convenient.

Clothing

The sensible woman who attends a picnic is sure to wear comfortable raiment that cannot be easily injured. The best gown for the purpose is the popular outing suit, which consists of a skirt and jacket of some serviceable woolen, like storm serge, and a silk or linen shirt-waist. The light-hued cottons are liable to be defaced by grass and other stains, and besides they would not be warm enough in case of a sudden fall in the temperature. A large hat should never be worn at a picnic. A close turban or sailor hat, with a parasol for shade, means a comfort and a serenity of mind that the most picturesque large hat could never yield. A gauze veil is an excellent protection against sunburn and is not as warm as the more closely woven varieties.

Food

The pièce de résistance of the picnic lunch is obviously the sandwich. There was a time when the only known form of sandwich was made by simply placing a slice of meat between two slices of bread, which was fresh or stale according to circumstances; but nowadays the advanced housekeeper scorns such a crude production and prepares instead sandwiches that are marvels of daintiness and goodness. Fresh biscuit, or bread that is just old enough to slice neatly, should be used for sandwiches. Cut the bread in the thinnest possible slices, butter lightly, and cut the slices square, removing all the crust; then cut them diagonally through the center, thus producing the fashionable three-corner shape.

Whatever filling is used, it should be chopped very fine, mixed with a mayonnaise dressing (which may be homemade), and spread lightly upon the bread. Chicken, ham, and tongue sandwiches are the kinds generally offered, and it is possible to purchase deviled ham and tongue in cans, all ready to spread upon the bread. Sardines that have been boned and cut into small bits make an excellent filling, and *pâté de foie gras* is liked by many, but is, of course, expensive. Watercress . . . chicken filling . . . Gruyère cheese . . . are delightful different kinds of sandwiches.

Nothing is more enjoyable at a picnic than nicely fried or broiled chicken, which should not be at all greasy when it is eaten cold. Deviled eggs . . . plain hard-boiled eggs shelled and wrapped in waxed paper with twisted and fringed ends . . . cold fried oysters . . . should have a place in every luncheon basket. Cold sweetened tea is refreshing. . . . lemonade is popular. A block of ice can be taken a considerable distance in the hottest weather, if wrapped in an ice blanket.

Although all picnickers should expect to endure many little inconveniences without complaint and should be willing sometimes to use their fingers in place of knives and forks, they should not be compelled to eat a luncheon composed of foods that have had their original flavors impaired or wholly changed by too close contact with one another. See to it that the viands are properly packed, and then the success of your picnic will be assured.

18
Rosh ha-Shanah

Celebrated tenth day of the lunar month of Tishri
(September-October)

and Yom Kippur

Celebrated beginning on the first day of the lunar month of Tishri
(September-October)

The ancient Jewish calendar contained four new-year days, each of which related to a particular phase of the agricultural cycle. As time passed and probably because it fell at the beginning of a month that contained Yom Kippur and Sukkot, Rosh ha-Shanah became the generally accepted beginning of the new year. It also ushers in the ten Days of Penitence, a time when God looks into the hearts of men to judge not only their acts, but their intentions and motives as well. The High Holy Days climax on the tenth day with Yom Kippur, the holiest day of the Jewish year.

The purpose of the High Holy Days is to examine the relationship of man to God and to other men. Not only must a person be sorry for the wrong he has done, he must ask God's forgiveness and he must also be ready and willing to do better. On Rosh ha-Shanah, God judges the individual, considering his acts of the past year. During the Days of Penitence the worshipper, through prayer, confession, and fasting, attempts to prove his sincere repentance, hoping to favorably affect God's final judgment for the coming year which is made on Yom Kippur.

An important symbol of the holiday season is the *shofar* ("ram's horn"). In the hills of ancient Judea, the shofar was a method of communicating from one hill top to another. It is used today to call the worshippers together and as a reminder of several great events in Jewish history. The shofar is sounded in the synagogue on each day for the month preceding Rosh ha-Shanah as a harbinger of the coming of the High Holy Days, so that the worshippers can prepare themselves emotionally and psychologically. The shofar is sounded at the beginning of the High Holy Days as part of the Rosh ha-Shanah services; a shofar blast on Yom Kippur marks the final sealing of the heavenly gates for the coming year and thus ends the High Holy Days.

The sending of greeting cards at Rosh ha-Shanah is a popular way of entering into the celebration of the period. Even though it is a solemn and introspective time, it is celebrated in joyful anticipation of forgiveness and renewal, since it is the beginning of a new year. Each greeting card bears the message *Leshanah tovah tikatevu*, which means "May you be inscribed (in the Book of Life) for a good year." The greeting after Rosh ha-Shanah is *Gemare hatimah tovah*, meaning "May the good judgment be confirmed."

Rosh ha-Shanah, although essentially a synagogue celebration, is also observed in the home with special foods. On Rosh ha-Shanah Eve, family and friends gather after services for a special meal. The finest table appointments are used. Honey cake and apple slices dipped in honey as they are eaten are important foods at this meal, symbolizing the hope for sweetness in the year to come. Traditional foods of the fall harvest such as carrots and sweet potatoes are served in abundance, symbolizing the hope for a bountiful harvest. The challah (bread) is baked in a round loaf to symbolize the wholeness of the coming year or in a braided ladder or is decorated symbolically with birds and ladders to help prayers to rise to God and His blessings to descend. Orthodox and Conservative Jews celebrate the second day of Rosh ha-Shanah as an equally holy day and at the evening meal, one fruit or vegetable which has not yet been served that season is eaten.

Yom Kippur is a day of total fast for all except persons under the age of thirteen and the sick and the weak. The final family meal preceding the Yom Kippur observance is served prior to sundown on the ninth day, and is considered to be especially important, as it must sustain the worshippers during the fast. After the close of Yom Kippur (sunset on the tenth day) a light meal is served to break the fast.

Yom Kippur is the most solemn day of the Jewish calendar. In addition to the fast, no work is done or business transacted by the Jewish community on this day. This last of the ten Days of Penitence is spent in synagogue services, beginning with the Kol Nidre service at sunset on Yom Kippur eve and continuing throughout the next day until sunset. White is worn by many people as a symbol of purity and innocence and is used in the synagogue adornments. Memorial prayers for the dead are included during the day and the book of Jonah is read. The sounding of the shofar ends the service at sunset.

The greater part of the High Holy Days celebrations occurs in the synagogue. The services for this period are among the most intricate of the entire Jewish liturgy. Through the act of communal atonement, the community reaffirms its ties to God and rededicates itself to His service. And individuals, with the past year's sins reconciled, may start the new year, determined and eager to make it a better one than the last.

Challah

With its special shapes, challah assumes a symbolic role at Rosh ha-Shanah. Some cooks like to add raisins to this basic recipe.

TRADITIONAL CHALLAH

1 oz. fresh yeast or 1 pkg. dried yeast	1½ tsp. salt
1 cup warm water	½ cup salad oil
4 cups flour (unsifted)	3 eggs (set aside 2 tbs. for glaze)
⅓ cup sugar	

Blend yeast in water until dissolved. Combine flour, sugar, and salt. Make a hole in the center of flour mixture and put in yeast, eggs, and oil. Blend all together and knead until dough is smooth and elastic. Add a little more flour if dough is sticky as you knead. Let rise in warm place until doubled in bulk. Punch down and knead slightly. Divide dough into 3 smaller pieces and roll each piece into a long rope of even thickness. Pinch the ends together and braid, or overlap ropes in center and braid toward the ends, pinching to hold together. For round shape for Rosh ha-Shanah, shape the braid into a ring and pinch the ends together, or working with 2 ropes, circle each about itself to form dome-shapes. Let rise for about 1 hour on greased cookie sheet. Add some water to the 2 tbs. egg and brush gently on dough. Bake at 350° until top is brown, about 40 minutes.

Challah Covers

Challah covers make excellent gifts at this period and do much to enhance the Rosh ha-Shanah table. Since challah loaves vary in size and shape, plan the dimensions of the challah cover you make for the size loaf you most often bake. For a long loaf, use the entire cross-stitch design and make a rectangular cover; for a round loaf, use the central menorah motif and make a square cover. For the Rosh ha-Shanah cover, white floss (silk perhaps) embroidered on white fabric would be especially appropriate. The border design may also be used at the ends of a long, self-fringed cloth.

Challah Cover, *The Young Judaean,* 1924

MATERIALS:
    1 yard fine fabric (linen or even-weave cross-stitch fabric)
    embroidery floss: color to match decor
    lace trim to fit around edges of cover, unruffled (optional)

STEP-BY-STEP:
1. Cut fabric in size necessary to fit over loaf, allowing 1½″ all around for hem.
2. Press edges under 1½″ and press raw edge under again ¼″. Miter corners and hem.
3. Work embroidery design in preferred cross-stitch method (see Design Sheet, page 109). Borders may be easily expanded to fit your cloth; menorah candlesticks may be lengthened to better fill a square space, if necessary.
4. Stitch lace around edges of cover mitering corners (optional).
5. To use, place challah on table and cover with cloth.

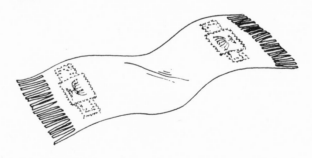

Rosh ha-Shanah Cards

There are many symbols which can be utilized in Rosh ha-Shanah cards. Each card must contain the greeting in Hebrew לשנה טובה תכתבו , which means "May you be inscribed for a good year." Suitable symbols are the shofar, kiddush (wine cup), Magen David, challah, circles, menorah, dove, tall white candles, seasonal vegetables, scales of justice. Before beginning card making, please read pages 284-288 for information on paper and envelope selection and printing techniques.

Magen Davids, *The Young Judaean,* 1920–1925
COLOR PLATE 26

These designs from the Twenties could be executed in silk screen, block printing, or cut paper or embroidered on perforated paper (see Design Sheet, page 110).

Menorah, *The Young Judaean,* 1924

This design is suitable for stamping with art gum eraser if the fine details are omitted. Or enlarge the design to fit a single one on a card and block print it (see Design Sheet, page 110).

Menorah

The graph design for the challah cover, below, would be suitable for interpretation in embroidery on perforated paper.

Fruits of the Season, *The Young Judaean,* 1926

Use this design in pen and ink drawing or linoleum block printing (see Design Sheet, page 110).

DESIGN SHEET

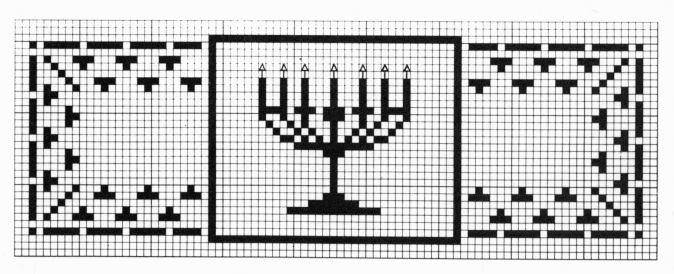

Challah Cover,
page 108

DESIGN SHEET

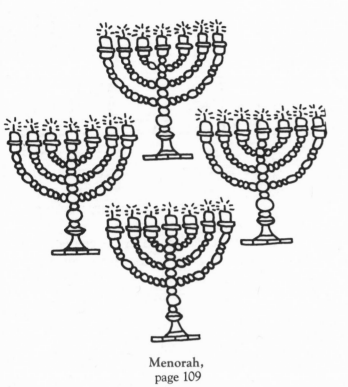

Menorah,
page 109

Fruits of the Season,
page 109

Magen David,
page 109

Magen David,
page 109

19
Columbus Day

Celebrated October 12, Federal observance second Monday in October

It is generally believed that the first celebration of the discovery of America by Christopher Columbus occurred three centuries after the event on October 12, 1792. The Order of Columbia, otherwise called the Society of Saint Tammany, held a dinner in New York City to commemorate the event that evening. New York City was at that time the only place to have a statue of the great discoverer. The Society of Saint Tammany was founded by William Mooney and named after an Indian sage to ridicule the societies named for Saint George, Saint Andrew, and Saint David.

Little is known of any celebrations honoring Columbus during the next hundred years. There was, nonetheless, a growing popularity of the name Columbia. King's College in New York City became Columbia College and the nation's capital was named the District of Columbia. In 1876, during the great Centennial Exhibition, a statue of Columbus was erected by the Italian citizens in Philadelphia at the site of the exhibition in Fairmount Park.

It was the four-hundredth anniversary of Columbus' landing that provided the greatest impetus to the holiday. In 1890, the House of Representatives designated Chicago as the site of the World's Columbian Exposition of 1892 and appropriated $10 million for the purpose. After a somewhat late inauguration, the fair opened in May, 1893, and was a tremendous success, with twelve million people attending. New York City honored Columbus by erecting a statue of Columbus and building Columbus Circle in honor of the four hundredth anniversary of the landing.

In 1905, Colorado was the first state to celebrate the anniversary. Subsequently, other states followed until 1934, when President Franklin D. Roosevelt issued a proclamation asking all the forty-eight states to observe October 12 as a national holiday.

Today most of the states of the Union have designated October 12 as Columbus Day and observance is usually highlighted by a parade and commemorative ceremonies. Probably the most well known Columbus Day Parade is the one which marches up Fifth Avenue each year in New York City. The parade is followed by a gala banquet for the purpose of raising money for scholarships.

111

20

Halloween

Celebrated October 31

The Druids have influenced many modern celebrations. In no holiday, however, is their impact more greatly felt that on Halloween. Druidism was the religion of the Celtic people who lived in Northern France and the British Isles. With the advance of the Roman Empire and the subsequent spread of Christianity, the Celts and Druidism receded into history. They left behind, nonetheless, distinctive traces of their presence. Druidism celebrated two important feasts, Beltane on May 1 and the autumn festival, Samhain, on the last day of October. Occurring after the gathering of the harvest, the Samhain feast marked the end of the growing and harvest seasons and the beginning of winter and the new year.

The highly mystical Druids worshipped nature and imbued it with supernatural qualities. They attributed great spiritual significance to certain plants (mistletoe is a prime example) and worshipped the Sun God and the Lord of Death. During the Samhain festival, the Druids appeased the Lord of Death, since it was believed that he allowed the spirits of those who had died that year to return to earth for a few hours to warm themselves by the fireplace and to mingle with their families once again.

Another important rite practiced during this holiday was the lighting of great bonfires on hill tops to honor the Sun God and to frighten away evil spirits, as it was thought that ghosts and witches fear fires. For days before, children would go around begging for material for the fire. The concept of witches developed among the Druids from their belief that there were women who had sold themselves to the Devil. This idea was also common among the early Egyptians and Romans. And ghosts were considered to be the souls of the dead. Samhain was a night on which bats, black cats, elves, and fairies stalked about. With visions of ghosts, witches, and other spirits filling their minds, people would dance and sing around the bonfire. Some people would dash through and over the flames.

When the Romans occupied Britain, it was inevitable that elements of the Roman harvest feast of Pomona, the fruit goddess, would intermingle with those of the Druid festival. For this reason fruit centerpieces, apples, and nuts feature prominently in our present-day festivities. The popular game of bobbing for apples was played by the ancient Romans and cider was drunk. Nuts are symbolic of food stored for the winter.

Since Samhain marked the beginning of the new year, there was interest in making predictions for the coming year, and fortune-telling became an

The Delineator, 1919

important part of this holiday. Among the Druids, it was the custom to tell the future from the peculiar shapes of various fruit and vegetables. Young women would try to discover who their husbands would be, and young men would peel apples in the hope that the shape of the peels would reveal the initials of future sweethearts.

Pope Gregory III in the eighth century designated November 1 as All Saints' or All Hallows' Day. By the Middle Ages, October 31 was known as All Hallows' E'en (*e'en* representing the shortening of *evening*). Today this is further contracted to Halloween.

Not being a particularly Protestant or Anglo Saxon feast, Halloween was not celebrated to any great extent during the early years of America's history. With the influx of Irish Catholics around 1848, however, Halloween became more widely celebrated.

Halloween costumes, which are an important part of our present day celebration, are connected with the belief that the souls of the dead return as ghosts and visit their families on this day. The custom may also derive from the practice among early Christians of displaying relics of saints on All Saints' Day. Among the poorer churches, which did not have relics to display, processions were held in which parishioners would dress like saints, angels, or the devil.

Today, the custom of wearing costumes is not closely associated with religious ceremonies and has taken on different characteristics. The children who parade in the streets on Halloween today are more likely to be dressed as Superman or Captain Kidd; at least for one evening, the child can live in the world of his imagination. Some children costume themselves as "what they want to be when they grow up," unconsciously acting out a foretelling of the future, in the best traditional Halloween spirit.

Going from door to door seeking alms goes back to the Druids' practice of begging for material for the bonfire. The *trick* feature of trick or treating results from the belief that the ghosts and witches created mischief on this night, so that any practical joke could be blamed on these supernatural forces.

The influence of the Irish immigrants on the celebration of Halloween can be seen in the jack-o'-lantern. The jack-o'-lantern comes from the legend of an Irishman named Jack who lured the Devil up a tree to fetch an apple and then cut the sign of the cross on the bark to prevent him from coming down. Jack forced the Devil to promise never to seek his soul. When Jack died, he was turned away from Heaven because of his drunken and nasty ways. Seeking a place to go, Jack went to hell but the Devil would have no part of him and, as Jack was walking away, the Devil threw a hot coal from the fires of hell at him. Jack was eating a turnip at that moment and caught the hot coal with it. Jack has wandered the earth with his jack-o'-lantern ever since, seeking a place to rest.

Each grid square is equal to one square inch.

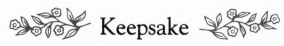

Keepsake

THE NICE OLD WITCH COLOR PLATE 31

This design appeared on the cover of the October, 1926, *Little Delineator,* a magazine for children contained within the pages of *The Delineator.* It has been worked in needlepoint, in the original colors. The design can also be worked in felt appliqué.

MATERIALS:

10 mesh needlepoint canvas, size 15" × 18"
Persian yarn: black (color 1)
           bright red orange (color 2)
           spruce green (color 3)
           royal blue (color 4)
           white (color 5)
           light tan (color 6)
           medium tan (color 7)
           medium brown (color 8)
           gray (color 9)
           yellow (color 10)
           red (color 11)
11" × 14" very heavy cardboard, strong thread, and needle

STEP-BY-STEP:

Note: Design in photo is worked in half cross-stitch. Yardages for yarn will vary according to size and stitch(es) selected. Design is worked in 3-ply yarn.

1. Enlarge design to 11" × 14".
2. Transfer design to canvas.
3. Work design in half cross-stitch or basket weave stitch. Work small areas, then details, then background areas.
4. Clean if necessary and block.
5. Stretch and frame.

Halloween Celebration

Halloween is a great time for a party. It is a season surrounded by quaint traditions which will appeal to every age group. And, in the absence of gift giving, more time is available to spend on party preparations. Children will enjoy the fun of a spooky cobweb party. Teens and adults will be amused and entertained by the fortune-telling traditionally favored on this day. These activities, combined with barn dancing (associated with Halloween harvest traditions), make an excellent, roof-raising neighborhood or club celebration.

Children's Cobweb Party

Invitations

Cut a black bat out of construction paper (see Design Sheet, page 130). Write message on white paper attached to the reverse side of the bat. Ask each guest to come dressed like a ghost.

Decorations

Use the inevitable motifs long associated with Halloween to set a spooky tone for the party: jack-o'-lanterns, witches, black cats, and bats (see Design Sheet, page 130). The major decoration will be the string cobweb, which will also be the center of the Ghost Walk, the evening's primary activity.

Table Decorations

Set the food table with a white cloth with a 7"–8" overhang all around. Enlarge the patterns (see Design Sheet, page 130) to fit the tablecloth overhang; then cut cats, bats, and witches from black construction paper and pumpkins from orange paper, adding details with a black felt-tip marker. Fasten cats, bats, witches, and pumpkins to the tablecloth and arrange black streamers between them. Plan to have two or three large motifs on each side, depending on the size of the table. Make a witch centerpiece by dressing a doll in black and orange crepe paper. Cover the doll's face with a plastic bag, then model a witch's face on the doll using cornstarch clay (see page 288). Use bits of apple skin for the eyes and mouth, accentuate the nose and chin. Tie broomstraws or twigs to a stick to make a witch's broom. Stand the witch in a glass, weighted if necessary, and place her in the center of the table. Cut two black construction-paper cats 3" or 4" long for each guest and glue on each side of a paper cup filled with Halloween candies and run a black ribbon leash from the witch to each cat. Make a cauldron for each guest by blackening three wooden skewers for each and tying them together to form a tripod. Hang a black cup from each and fill with salted nuts. Put one cauldron at each place. Cut a number of black construction-paper bats in various sizes and hang by threads from the ceiling to fly around the witch's head. Make place cards of 3" or 4" bats and hang from each guest's glass by means of a tab on the back (Illustration 20-1).

Illustration 20–1

Games
Ghost Walk, The Delineator, 1913

Since this is to be the high point of the evening, take pains to set it up carefully. For each guest, string throughout the house a cobweb. The string for each should be different in some way (color or texture) for easy identification and should be fairly sturdy. String each cobweb on a different route, overlapping and duplicating trails at times but making them different enough to have the "ghosts" following different routes on their walk. Go upstairs, around furniture, into closets, etcetera. Label the start of each string with a guest's name with a Halloween appellation: Jennifer Jack-o'-lantern, Spooky Julie, Witch Mary, Beth the Bat, etcetera. At the end of each string, in some hidden recess of the house, will be an appropriate favor for each ghost and perhaps a Halloween prophecy for the future. Use very low lights, or preferably none at all (and provide a flashlight for each guest) to add to the ghostly atmosphere for the parade. Consider stationing a few surprise "spirits" in the closets along the trail for a little good-natured spooking.

Bobbing for Apples

Hands tied behind their backs, guests try to bite apples floating in a tub of water. Make this a fortune-telling game by inserting a fortune written on a piece of paper into each apple or by marking some apples with "yes" and some "no" cut into the peel. The apple successfully bitten or removed from the water then indicates the answer to a previously asked yes-or-no question. Another fortune-telling method requires a set of apples with girls' names and another with boys' names. The girls bob for the apples with boys' names, the one they remove holding the name of their true love. Boys then bob for girls' names.

Snatching at Fate, The Delineator, 1913

Stretch a string tightly across a doorway and from it, on strings, hang a doughnut, a cotton ball, an apple, and an orange. With eyes closed, players try to catch one of the swinging items in their mouth. If the orange is caught, the player will enjoy wealth; the doughnut, an easy, sweet life; the apple, happiness; cotton, an unwed life.

Food

The menu for a Halloween celebration should be a homey one, utilizing for the first time the foods stored for the winter. Nuts and apples, because of their use in fortune-telling, are important foods. This menu combines the traditional Halloween foods.

HALLOWEEN FEAST

Apple and Nut Salad
Sandwiches
Baked Apples*   Taffy Apples*
Fortune Cake*   Gingerbread   Doughnuts
Popcorn Balls*   Nuts
Hot Chocolate   Cider Flip*

*See below.

Walnuts with fortunes hidden inside may be scattered among the edible nuts (see page 6). Tie sandwiches with orange and black ribbons, serve salad in hollowed-out oranges from which sections of the outer peel have been removed to form grinning jack-o'-lanterns. (Illustration 20-2)

Illustration 20–2

CIDER FLIP

The Delineator, 1901

2 qts. sweet cider
Several lemon slices
Juice 3 lemons

Place cider in tall pitcher. Add lemon slices. Just before serving, add lemon juice. Serve with straws in glasses. Can be served hot. Cider must be fresh and very sweet.

FORTUNE CAKE

The Delineator, 1923

Wrap a sterilized metal button, metal thimble, coin and ring in aluminum foil and drop into any cake batter (devil's food cake is especially appropriate for Halloween). Warn guests to be on the lookout for these items as they eat the cake. The button predicts hard work for fortune or fame, the thimble predicts a spinster or one who will work hard for a living, the coin is for wealth, the ring predicts an early marriage. Other charms with appropriate symbolic meanings may be used as well. For cupcakes, insert a fortune into each cake. Bake and frost the cake with white frosting, retaining a bit of the frosting. Thin the extra frosting and flavor it with chocolate. Drizzle threads of the frosting irregularly on top of the cake to suggest cob webs. (Illustration 20-3)

Illustration 20–3

BAKED APPLE VARIATIONS

The Delineator, 1920

• Fill center with small red cinnamon candy instead of sugar.
• Fill center with chopped nuts, raisins, and brown sugar.
• Fill center with sections of banana and top with nuts or raisins.
• Make a syrup of 1 cup water, 1/3 cup sugar, and juice and rind of 1/2 lemon. Add 2 tbs. each chopped raisins, candied orange peel, pineapple, and nuts. Cook slowly until thickened. Fill baked apples with chopped fruit and pour syrup over them. Serve cold with whipped cream or marshmallow whip.

TAFFY APPLES

The Delineator, 1920

1 cup granulated sugar	**1/2 cup water**
1 cup brown sugar	**Apples, firm and red**
1/2 cup vinegar	**Skewers**

Mix ingredients and cook until candy thermometer registers 300°. Insert skewer into end of each apple. Dip entire apple in syrup until well coated. Place on waxed paper to harden. Skewer is left in to hold apple when eating. Apples are merely coated, not cooked.

POPCORN BALLS
The Delineator, 1926

½ cup molasses	1½ tbs. butter
½ cup dark corn syrup	6 cups popped popcorn
½ tbs. vinegar	

Mix molasses, corn syrup, and vinegar. Cook, stirring occasionally, until candy thermometer registers 270°. Constant stirring is needed after 240°. At 270°, add butter, stirring just to mix, then pour syrup slowly over popcorn. Press into balls and place on waxed paper to cool. A simple prize may be placed inside each. Makes 10 balls, 2½" diameter.

Occult Party

Referring to the Halloween tradition of gazing into the future, an 1891 *Delineator* article said:

Since the spread of intelligence has robbed the old observances of their serious import, the night has been held in great regard as a time for universal jollity and for working charms, spells, and divinations.

Even though most people do not truly believe in the occult and in fortune-telling devices, it is fun, and sure to provide an evening's amusement.

Invitations
Write in white ink on black paper with frayed or burned edges, or write with lemon juice on white paper and indicate that the paper is to be ironed to reveal the message.

The hand of fate beckons!
At the hour of _____
On the eve of the last day of October,
At the _____ house from the corner
On the _____ hand side of the street called _____.

Appear in costume weird and ghostlike.
Ignore the summons at your peril!

Decorations
Concentrate on black in the decorations. Use bats, witches, jack-o'-lanterns, and black cats (which herald the coming of evil). Add a witch's cauldron, staffed by a real "witch" stirring a gooey mess and muttering dark and disastrous fortunes in a deadly voice. The table decorations from the preceding Cobweb Party would be suitable.

Games
Fortune-telling may be presented as games or individual activities. Include fortunes to predict the future, reveal hidden aspirations, or answer questions about one's true love. Many methods of fortune-telling are simple enough for children to enjoy.

Lighted Candle, The Delineator, *1891*
In turn, each player is blindfolded, turned around three times, and set free to find the lighted candle and blow it out, without using his hands. Those who succeed will be free for the ensuing year from witches and evil spirits, which are driven out with the candle's light.

Shoe Toss, The Delineator, *1905*
Each player tosses a pair of slippers lightly into the air. The manner in which the slippers land on the floor tells the fortune. The code is:

- both upside down and not touching: player will travel far and have no settled home.
- both right side up and not touching: player will go on the stage
- left slipper upside down: future mate will be unselfish and kind
- right slipper upside down: future mate will be cross and selfish
- both slippers crossed: early marriage
- toes point in opposite direction—marital differences of opinion
- toes point in same direction: congenial spouse
- soles cross one on another: player will own a gold mine

Three Cups, The Delineator, *1906*
Under each of three inverted cups, place a marble: one crystal, one brown, one black. The blindfolded player chooses a cup, and with it his fortune. The code is:

- crystal: young spouse, happy life
- black: middle-aged spouse, hard life with fame at the end
- brown: aged spouse, adventurous life

Saucer Luck, The Delineator, *1900*
Place sand in one saucer, flour in another, and leave a third empty. In turn, each blindfolded player chooses a saucer and thereby a fortune. The code is:

- flour: player will be the only love of his future lover
- sand: player will marry a widow(er)
- empty: player will enjoy single blessedness

A variation is to use salt, cornmeal, and one empty saucer, the code being:

- salt (representing silver) for a comfortable but not luxurious life
- cornmeal (representing gold) for wealth
- the empty saucer meaning the player will work hard for a living

Three Glasses, The Delineator, *1911*
Prepare one glass of clear liquid, one cloudy liquid, and one empty glass. In turn, each blindfolded player takes three steps forward and three steps backward and reaches out to touch a glass with the left hand. The code is:

- clear: a life free from sorrow and worry
- cloudy: many anxieties
- empty: player will make few friends

Nut Roasting, The Delineator, *1891*
Each player names two nuts, one for himself and the other for a friend. The nuts are placed on a shovel over a fire and as they heat the prophecy begins:

- if the nuts burn gently, the friendship will be long and tranquil
- if the nuts burst, the friendship will come to grief

Another tradition connected with nut roasting is that maidens who sleep with the ashes of roasted nuts under their pillows on Halloween night will dream of their future love.

Apple Peeling, The Delineator, *1891*
Each guest peels an apple, being careful to keep the paring in an unbroken strip. Each player then tosses the peel over the right shoulder and another designated player determines which letter of the alphabet it resembles, the letter being the initial of the tosser's future love.

Apple Seeds, The Delineator, *1900*
Place one apple seed on each eyelid. Name one "home" and the other "travel." The seed which adheres longer makes the prophecy. Another apple seed fortune requires that the apple be eaten and the seeds counted. The number of seeds gives important information on the fortune seeker's loved one, according to an old verse:

> One I love,
> Two I love,
>   Three I love, I say;
> Four I love with all my heart and
>   Five I cast away.
> Six he loves,
> Seven she loves,
> Eight they both love;
>   Nine he comes,
> Ten he tarries,
>   Eleven he courts and
> Twelve he marries.

Apple at Midnight, The Delineator, *1898*
Eat an apple at midnight, then walk backward down the stairs carrying a lighted candle and a hand mirror. The face of one's true love will reflect in the mirror.

Halloween Harvest Frolic
A different type of Halloween celebration deals with that aspect of the holiday which re-

joices over the safe return of the flocks and herdsmen from their summer quarters to the safety of their winter homes.

Invitations

Write on paper decorated with calico (Illustration 20-4) to suggest that the guests dress in

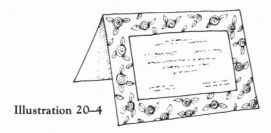

Illustration 20-4

calico and denim for the evening's entertainment of square dances, Virginia reels, and other folk dances, as well as selected traditional Halloween games and fortune prediction activities.

Decorations

Use piles of pumpkins, melons, squashes. Sheaves of wheat or dried grass and stalks of dried corn are also decorative and suggestive of plenty for man and beast during the coming winter.

Table Decorations

A suitable centerpiece for the food table on such an occasion would be a pumpkin carved into a basket, polished with a soft cloth until shiny, and filled with similarily polished autumnal fruit. Set the pumpkin basket on the table and surround it with a wreath of autumn foliage. (Illustration 20-5)

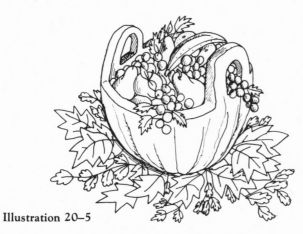

Illustration 20–5

Food

The food suggestions for the Cobweb Party would be suitable for this one, too.

Halloween Costumes

The custom of costumes, masks, and disguises, like trick or treating, has its essential roots in the ancient New Year's celebrations, when Druids costumed themselves to represent the souls of the dead who had visited the New Year's feast of their families. Costumes and disguises can be devised simply and quickly from materials and clothing on hand, or they can be elaborately and sturdily constructed. The costumes which follow fall somewhere in between. During the 1920's, there was great interest in costume parties and masquerades and the *Delineator Institute* published several small catalogues devoted entirely to costume patterns for Halloween, Carnival, and parties. The selection was extensive and the designs often quite artistic.

Materials

For many costumes, crepe paper can be used and it was, in fact, a popular costume material in the early 1900's, especially for impromptu creations by children. The main drawback to crepe paper is that it is fairly fragile and the colors run when wet. The best approach, especially for costumes worn to parties, which are more likely to receive hard wear than those worn just for the trick or treat parade, is to use the cheapest fabric available. Old sheets can be dyed to desired colors. Some fabric shops run special sales at Halloween featuring garish colors of sleazy fabric at cheap prices. Since the costumes aren't being made to last forever, these fabrics are often entirely suitable. The next best solution may prove to be cheap lining fabric, which comes in a wide range of colors and is lightweight, shiny, and easy to work with. Hemmed edges are necessary if the fabric ravels badly. Hats can be fashioned from poster board or construction paper.

In the interest of safety for nighttime masqueraders, masks should fit closely, with ample eye and nose room for unobstructed vision—or makeup can be used in lieu of masks. Costume colors should be bright or highlighted both front and back with reflective tape or paint. Lengths should be determined by the agility of the wearer. It is a good idea to provide a small flashlight for each trick or treater and under no circumstances should lighted candles be allowed. (They were once suggested for "torchlight processions.") Trick or treat tote bags in light colors or decorated in light or reflective colors are another safety aid.

Design

The Halloween costume designs selected for this book are based on Butterick costume patterns from the 1920's. Since, today, it is children who are the most likely to be interested in masquerading, these costumes are directed toward them. A printed commercial pattern may be used, with the unique aspects of these designs added, or a pattern may be easily cut from newspaper. These costumes have been simplified so that all have the same shape and basic pattern piece and the same neck construction. Variations occur in fullness and in sleeve, skirt, or pants finishes. The costumes are generously cut to ensure comfort, to facilitate pattern drafting, and to permit the wearing of sweaters or other warm clothing underneath the costume, should Halloween weather be cool.

Basic Pattern

1. Have child lie on his back on a large piece of paper (taped newspaper works well) with arms spread, one leg straight and the other slightly ajar. (Illustration 20-6)
2. With felt-tip marker, trace around straight-leg half of the body from neck to crotch, excluding hands and feet. Indicate on tracing neck, elbow, wrist, crotch, knee, ankle.
3. Straighten line from hip to ankle and continue line up through shoulder.

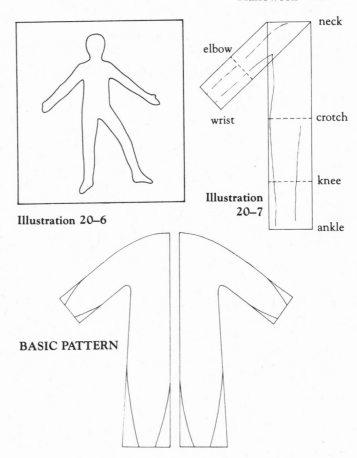

Illustration 20–6

Illustration 20–7

BASIC PATTERN

4. Straighten out underarm line similarly. (Illustration 20-7)
5. Shoulder line will vary with individual costume design selected and will be drawn in later.

Create Desired Costume

• Draw on the newspaper over body tracing according to the variations on the chart below, measuring from straight line.
• The variations are based on actual body measurements of the child.
• In most cases, body circumference becomes the flat pattern measurement.
• Use a tape measure to measure around head, thigh, upper arm, neck, ankle, wrist.
• As costume pattern is drafted over tracing, fullness is added to outside line of arm and inside line of leg thus maintaining underarm curve and adding necessary ease to pattern length and for seam allowances.

• The drafted shoulder line should continue across the body the added width from traced body line.

• Costume should be tried on during construction to shorten sleeves and pants legs if necessary.

• Yardage requirements can be determined by measuring the drafted pattern, keeping in mind the fact that each drafted piece must be cut out 4 times, or twice on doubled fabric, to provide for right front, left front, right back and left back pieces.

Chart of Costume Measurements

	LEGS		SLEEVES		OTHER
	Width	*Length*	*Width*	*Length*	
Clown	thigh meas.	add 4″ to bottom	upper arm meas.	add 5″ to bottom	Ruff: 9″ wide × 3 times neck meas. (cut 2)
Skeleton	thigh meas. minus 4″	ankle	upper arm meas. minus 2″	add 2″	upper arm meas. minus 2″
	Skirt		*Sleeves*		
Witch	thigh meas.	just below knee	upper arm meas.	between elbow and wrist	Cape: 2 full widths fabric × ankle-to-shoulder meas. plus equal amount fabric for lining
Fairy Queen	thigh meas.	between ankle and knee	upper arm meas.	between elbow and wrist	Belt: Waist measurement plus 8″ Cape: Same as witch
Ghost	thigh meas.	between ankle and knee	upper arm meas.	taper from elbow to wrist	Hood: head meas. plus 4″ at top and 16″ at bottom

Clowns: Diamond and Harlequin

COLOR PLATE 11

MATERIALS:

2 pieces black ribbon, 1½ yd. each, ¼″ wide
black and orange bias seam binding
¼″ elastic
stapler
masking tape and felt-tip markers

Diamond
orange fabric
black bias seam binding
black acrylic paint and brush
black poster board or construction paper
orange yarn

Harlequin
black and orange fabric
black and orange yarn
orange poster board or construction paper

STEP-BY-STEP:

1. **Draft Paper Pattern** Figure measurements according to chart and cut out pattern. Place pattern piece on double layer of fabric and cut out. Repeat. (For Harlequin, repeat on second color fabric.) On fabric, note crotch, wrist, and ankle points as well as trim placement lines (Diamond).

2. **Stitch Center Seams** Right sides together, stitch center back seam from crotch to within 10 inches of neck edge. Press under and edge-stitch remaining seam allowance if desired. Stitch center front seam from crotch to neck edge. Combine Harlequin fabrics as desired.

3. **Finish Neck Edge** Right sides together, stitch top sleeve seams from wrist to within 10″ of center seam. Press sleeve seam open. Press neck edge under ⅝″. To form casing, sew bias seam binding inside neck opening by first stitching binding along folded neck edge, then along *remaining binding edge* (Illustration 20-8). Cut binding at sleeve seam and start

anew on other side of seam. Thread one length of ribbon through casing. When wearing, draw up ribbon, tie securely and adjust gathers. Try on to check sleeve and pants length. Adjust if necessary.

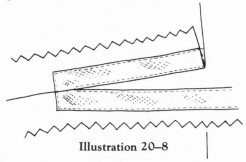

Illustration 20–8

4. **Decorate Fabric** Place cardboard or newspaper under fabric to absorb moisture. Trace, then paint, diamond shapes (See Design Sheet, page 130) on right side of fabric as shown. Let paint dry thoroughly before proceeding. Stitch seam tape on sleeve and pants edges at points 1″ and 2″ from edges.

5. **Finish Sleeve Edge** To make ruffle, stitch edges of bias seam binding to right side of sleeve 4″ from sleeve edge. Binding color should contrast to fabric color. Cut elastic the wrist measurement plus 1 inch and thread it through casing, pinning ends to prevent slipping.

6. Right sides together, stitch side seams and under arms, catching elastic ends in seams.

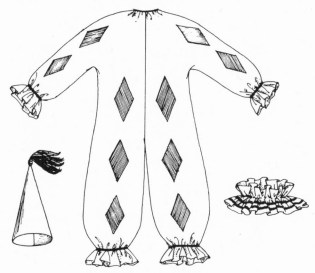

DIAMOND CLOWN

7. **Finish Pants Edge** Repeat step 5, except elastic length is ankle measurement plus 1 inch.

8. Right sides together, stitch remaining pants seam, catching elastic ends in seam.

Accessories

Neck Ruff Apply black bias seam binding 1″ and 2″ from lower edge of one piece only (Diamond Clown only). Place the two ruff pieces on top of each other, decorated piece uppermost, and stitch together 3″ from one long edge and again ½″ from first row of stitching. Thread remaining piece of ribbon through casing. Draw up ribbon, tie securely and adjust gathers when wearing.

Pointed Hat Draw triangle 12″ high with base the head measurement plus 1″. Draw curved line below base line. Roll hat one long edge to other and tape overlap in place (Illustration 20-9). Color tape with felt-tip markers if desired. Try on hat and shorten if necessary by trimming bottom. Determine a comfortable length for elastic chin strap. Staple elastic in place on sides of hat. Add pompom or tassel according to design.

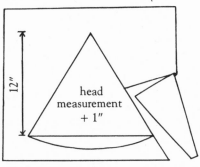

Illustration 20–9

Pompoms Wrap yarn around a 5″ wide piece of cardboard 100 times. Slide wound yarn off cardboard and tie securely in middle. Cut open all loops and trim pompom neatly. For Harlequin, make 6 black and 2 orange pompoms. Pin black ones on center seam and hat and on orange sleeve and leg. Pin orange ones on black sleeve and leg.

Tassel Wrap yarn around a 7″ wide piece of cardboard 35 times. Slide off cardboard and tie at one end; cut open the other end. About 1″ from tied edge, wind a piece of yarn tightly around tassel and secure. Attach tassel to Diamond Clown hat.

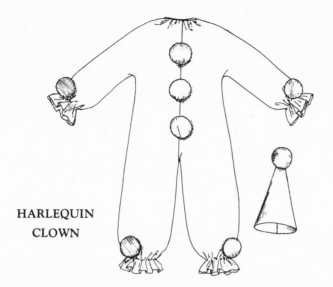

HARLEQUIN
CLOWN

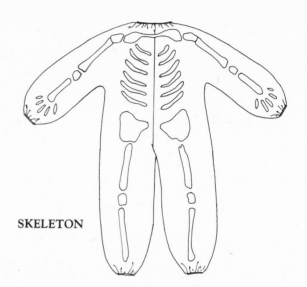

SKELETON

Makeup White powdered face and rouged cheek circles are appropriate clown makeup.

Skeleton

COLOR PLATE 11
MATERIALS:
    black fabric
    1½ yd. black ribbon, ¼" wide
    black bias seam binding
    ¼" elastic
    white acrylic paint (acrylic fluorescent paint is
        available in some art stores)
    white bathing cap (optional)

STEP-BY-STEP:
1. **Draft Paper Pattern** Figure measurements according to chart and cut out pattern. Cut pattern piece twice out of double layer of fabric. Note knee, waist, and elbow on fabric pieces.
2. **Stitch Center Seams** Follow step 2, Clown, disregarding reference to combining fabrics.
3. **Finish Neck Edge** Follow step 3, Clown.
4. **Decorate Fabric** Enlarge skeleton (see Design Sheet, page 129) and transfer to front of costume (or purchase a dangling cardboard skeleton, take apart, and trace pieces on fabric). Place costume, right side up, over several layers of newspaper to absorb moisture and carefully paint in skeleton design. Let paint dry thoroughly before proceeding with costume.

5. **Finish Sleeve Edge** Turn sleeve edge under 1" and stitch ½" from the fold forming a casing. Cut elastic the wrist measurement plus 1" and thread it through casing, pinning ends to prevent slipping.
6. Follow step 6, Clown.
7. **Finish Pants Edge** Repeat step 5 except elastic length is ankle measurement plus 1".
8. Follow step 8, Clown.
9. **Accessories** A plain white bathing cap may be worn to imitate the look of a skull.

Witch

COLOR PLATE 11
MATERIALS:
    black fabric for dress and cape
    red fabric for cape lining (optional)
    1½ yd. black ribbon, about ½" wide (dress)
    2 yd. white ribbon, about 1" wide (cape)
    black bias seam binding
    ¼" elastic
    glue
    soft rope, for waist and hat brim
    stick, twigs, twine for broom
    black poster board, 22" × 28"
    white acrylic paint

STEP-BY-STEP:
1. **Draft Paper Pattern** Figure measurements for dress according to chart and cut out paper pattern. Cut pattern twice out of double layer of

fabric. Note knee, elbow, and waist on fabric pieces.

2. **Stitch Center Seams** Right sides together, stitch center back seam from bottom to within 10″ of neck edge. Press under and edgestitch remaining seam allowance, if desired. Stitch center front seam from bottom of fabric to neck edge. Try on dress to check length. Adjust if necessary.

3. **Finish Neck Edge** Follow step 3, Clown.

4. **Decorate Fabric** Enlarge bats and arched cats (see Design Sheet, page 130). Transfer designs to skirt about 12″ from bottom on right side of fabric. Place costume, right side up, over several layers of newspaper to absorb moisture and carefully paint in designs. Let paint dry thoroughly before proceeding with costume.

WITCH

5. **Finish Sleeve Edge** Follow step 5, Skeleton.

6. Follow step 6, Clown.

7. **Finish Skirt Edge** Though no finish is necessary, skirt edge may be cut jagged or fringed if desired.

Accessories

Cape Cut cape fabric and lining pieces same length. (Cape should fall from shoulders to ankles.) Sew two long edges of cape fabric together for center seam and do same with lining fabric. Press seams open. Greatly enlarge bat or arched cat and paint on right side of cape fabric in center

of back. When paint is dry, place lining and cape right sides together and stitch around sides and top, leaving bottom edge open. Turn right side out. Press. Make casing along top of cape by stitching 1″ from edge and again 1¼″ below first row of stitching. Remove seam from casing ends and thread wide ribbon through casing. Draw up cape to fit when wearing.

Pointed Hat Follow step 9, Clown. Enlarge cat design, transfer to hat, and paint on hat front before rolling hat into cone shape. To add brim, set hat on black poster board and draw around bottom edge of hat. Enlarge this circle by adding 2″ all around outside the line and ½″ inside the line. Cut out cardboard. Slash inside circle ½″ deep about every ½″ or so. Fold up slashes and tape brim inside hat. Glue rope around crown. (Illustration 20-10)

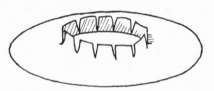

Illustration 20–10

Broom Assemble 1 sturdy, fairly straight stick and several fairly straight twigs about 18″ long. Attach twigs to broomstick by winding twine around one end, adding one twig with each winding. Wind twine several times around the whole lot of twigs to bind, then tie securely.

Note: *The Delineator* suggested such untraditional color combinations for this costume as orange and black on gray or on green, yellow on brown, and black on yellow.

Fairy Queen
COLOR PLATE 11
MATERIALS:
    pink fabric for dress
    purple fabric for cape
    sequins, metallic trims as desired
    1½ yd. pink ribbon, ¼″ wide (dress)
    2 yd. purple ribbon, 1″ wide (cape)
    ¼″ elastic
    poster board, foil giftwrap paper, glitter for
      crown
    white glue

STEP-BY-STEP:

1. **Draft Paper Pattern** Figure measurements for dress according to chart. Cut out paper pattern. Cut pattern twice out of double layer of fabric. Mark waist and trim placement lines on fabric.
2. **Stitch Center Seams** Follow step 2, Witch.
3. **Finish Neck Edge** Follow step 3, Clown.
4. **Decorate Fabric** Following design lines, sew or glue sequins or other trim to dress. Place trim on right side of fabric on front of costume (on back as well, if desired). If painting or gluing, place costume over newspaper to absorb moisture. Let dry thoroughly before proceeding with costume.
5. **Finish Sleeve Edge** Follow step 5, Skeleton.
6. Follow step 6, Clown.
7. **Finish Skirt Edge** No finish is necessary, although skirt may be hemmed if desired.

Accessories

Cape Cut cape fabric length to fall from shoulders to ankles. Sew long edges together for center seam. Press seam open. Press top edge under 2½". Make casing along top of cape by stitching 1" from folded edge and again 1¼" below first stitching. Thread wide ribbon through casing and draw up cape to fit when wearing.

FAIRY QUEEN

Crown Enlarge crown pattern (see Design Sheet, page 130) to fit head measurement plus 2" overlap. Cover crown with shiny foil paper and decorate in design shown, or as desired, using white glue and glitter and left over dress trims. Staple crown together at back to fit.

Ghost

COLOR PLATE 11

MATERIALS:

> white fabric (an old sheet is fine)
> ¼ yd. stiff white netting
> 1½ yd. white ribbon, ¼" wide
> black felt-tip marker or acrylic paint (optional)

STEP-BY-STEP:

1. **Draft Paper Pattern** Figure measurements for dress according to chart. Then cut pattern twice out of double layer of fabric.
2. **Stitch Center Seams** Follow step 2, Witch.
3. **Finish Neck Edge** Follow step 3, Clown.
4. **Decorate Fabric** No decoration is necessary.
5. **Finish Sleeve Edge** Edge may be hemmed if desired.
6. Follow step 6, Clown, disregarding reference to elastic.
7. **Finish Skirt Edge** Follow step 7, Queen.

Accessories

Hood Cut fabric shape according to the illustration and the measurements on the chart, page 123. Fold in half and stitch edge together, curving corners at top. Turn right side out. Try hood on child and, with felt-tip marker, carefully put dots where eyes, nose, and mouth should be. Remove hood, draw large ovals for eyes, nose, and mouth. Space eye circles 1" apart. Baste netting under eye area. Machine satin stitch around eyes, nose, and mouth. Cut holes out of white fabric, leaving netting intact, and trim away excess netting on wrong side. If straight stitch is used to stitch facial circles, accent outlines with acrylic paint or felt-tip marker.

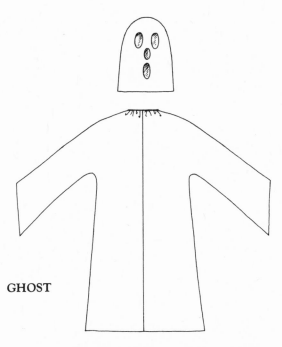

GHOST

Trick or Treating

The custom of begging on Halloween, whether for fuel for the bonfire, alms, or goodies to eat is rooted in the pagan New Year celebration. At one time, it was the aged women of the village who would go begging from house to house singing the old wail

> Soul, Soul for a soul cake;
> Pray, good mistress, for a soul-cake.

Today, the custom of begging has descended in altered form to merry bands of children. Children chant "trick or treat" in place of the hymn of the crones, and they expect to be rewarded with attractive and appetizing sweets in lieu of the soul-cake, which was a plain, slightly sweetened but generously seeded oatmeal cake. Nuts and apples and highly appropriate treats, or variations such as nut candy, taffy apples, etcetera.

Since the fairies and ghosts rampant on Halloween could be blamed for all manner of mischief, tricking has become a part of the American celebration of this festive eve. With the fairies to blame and behind the anonymity of costumes, masks, and other disguises, children feel free to indulge in innocent practical jokes such as writing with soap on windows, rolling yards with tissue paper, and ringing doorbells. Formerly, unhinging gates and moving outhouses were considered great fun.

Trick or Treat Tote Bag
MATERIALS:
    fabric 23″ × 18″
    2 fabric strips, 20″ × 3″
    heavyweight interfacing, 23″ × 3″
    acrylic paints to decorate bag (optional)

STEP-BY-STEP:
1. To form top edge of tote bag, press under one long edge of fabric 3″ and slip interfacing under fold. Topstitch ¼″ from folded edge.
2. Fold fabric, right sides and short edges together, and stitch side and bottom in ½″ seams. Clip corner. Turn and press bag.
3. Topstitch ¼″ from edges on sides and bottom.
4. For handles, fold fabric strips in thirds lengthwise and stitch ¼″ from each folded edge (Illustration 20-11). Press ends under 1″ and stitch to tote in manner shown. (Illustration 20-12)

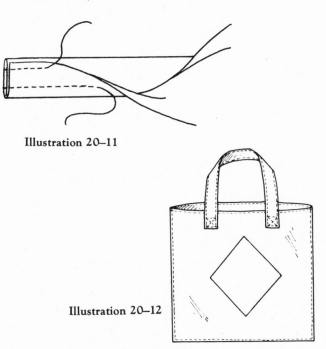

Illustration 20–11

Illustration 20–12

5. Slip cardboard or newspaper into bag to absorb moisture and paint bag with appropriate motifs as desired.

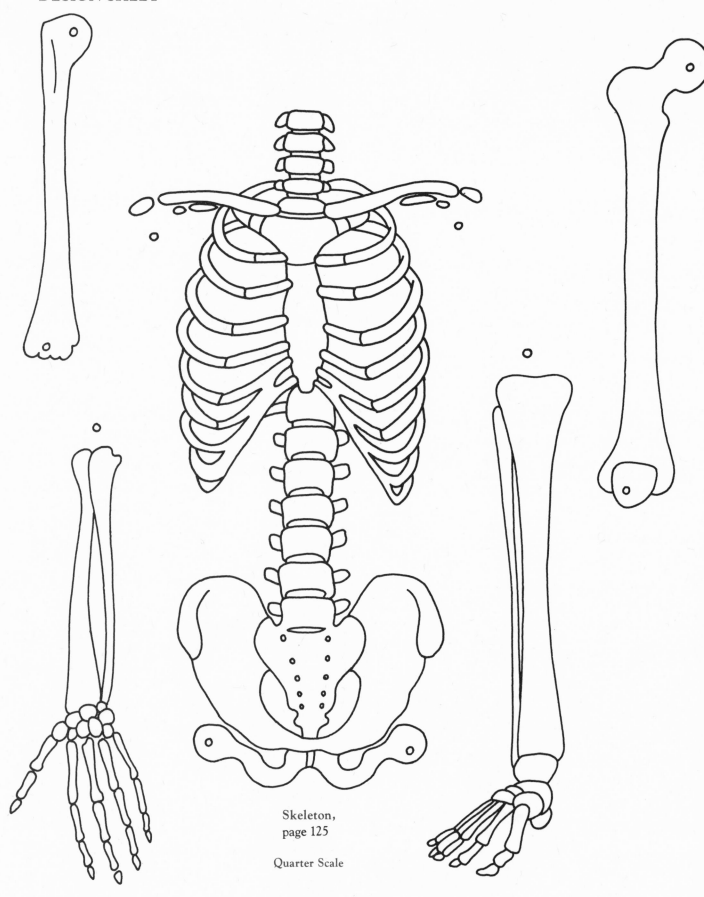

DESIGN SHEET

Skeleton,
page 125

Quarter Scale

DESIGN SHEET

Children's Party, page 116
and Occult Party, page 119

Diamond Clown,
page 124

Children's Cobweb Party,
page 116
and Occult Party,
page 119

Children's Party,
page 116
and Occult Party,
page 119

Fairy Queen,
page 126

Half Scale

Children's Cobweb Party,
page 116
and Occult Party,
page 119

The Delineator, 1927

21
Thanksgiving Day

Celebrated fourth Thursday in November

A feast to celebrate the harvest has been a part of man's history since recorded time began. The Chinese were said to have celebrated such a feast thousands of years ago. The Feast of the Tabernacles (Sukkot) a Jewish celebration, also is a harvest rite and lasts eight days. It is so named because the celebrants build booths and tents during the festival in memory of the years when the Jews had no homeland. The Old Testament is replete with commands to gather the harvest and rejoice, the most well known of which are found in Deuteronomy 16:14 and Leviticus 23:10.

The ancient Greek harvest festival was called Thesmophora and celebrated Demeter, the founder of agriculture and the goddess of the harvests. It was celebrated in Athens in November, by married women only. The symbols of Demeter were poppies and ears of corn, a basket of fruit and a little pig. The Roman goddess of the harvest, Ceres, had a festival which occurred on October 4 and was called the Cerelia. This feast was celebrated by a fast and offerings of a cow and the first cuttings of the harvest. Later there was a feast of thanksgiving.

In England, the autumnal feast was called the Harvest Home and was derived from the Druidical harvest feast. This festival began with a special service in the village church, which had been decorated for the occasion by fruit and flowers, and was followed by a large communal dinner. The English also celebrated special days of thanksgiving to commemorate, for example, the defeat of the Spanish Armada, the discovery of Guy Fawkes' Gunpowder Plot, and the recovery of George III from one of his fits of insanity. These special days of thanksgiving became so numerous, however, that by the time Cromwell ruled England, there were over one hundred such feasts to offend the severe Puritans. Later, in Holland, the Puritans were more comfortable with the respectable and religious fast days of the Dutch. The Puritans remained in Holland for ten years before venturing to the New World.

Among the major holidays celebrated in the United States, only two are really national holidays, Independence Day and Thanksgiving. Thanksgiving was proclaimed a feast day on July 30, 1623, by Governor Bradford of the Plymouth Colony, two years after the first Thanksgiving feast which celebrated the harvest of the year 1621. The spread of the feast during subsequent years was sporadic. The Bay Colony in Boston held a day of Thanksgiving on February 22, 1630. From about 1644, the Dutch settlers in New Amsterdam

132

observed a day of thanksgiving, but this was to celebrate the safe return of their soldiers from a foray with local Indians.

To the Puritan settlers who originated the holiday, Thanksgiving replaced both Christmas and New Year's. Their religious beliefs, as well as the austerity and difficulty of their lives in the rather primitive settlement, did not permit them the luxury of gay and merry holiday celebrations. Their severe living conditions required discipline and sacrifice. Another factor was that these religious dissenters objected to many of the traditional feast days of the established church, in which Christmas and New Year's were celebrated. Thanksgiving, a holiday thanking God for the harvest enabling them to survive the winter, seemed to them to be a more fitting celebration than other more joyous feasts.

The celebration of Thanksgiving sprang up haphazardly at the beginning and was celebrated, if at all, on different days in different parts of the country. Mrs. Sarah Josepha Hale is generally credited with being the motivating force behind having the last Thursday in November designated as a national Thanksgiving Day. The main vehicle of her crusade was *Godey's Lady's Book,* of which she was editor. Aside from using every pretext to promote her cause in *Godey's,* Mrs. Hale wrote numerous letters to governors, so that by 1859 she had gathered almost all the states in the Union to her cause. Her ultimate victory was given to her by President Lincoln, who in September, 1863, proclaimed the last Thursday of November as the official national celebration of Thanksgiving.

Before this, however, it had been the custom for each president to issue a separate proclamation designating a day for Thanksgiving. George Washington, during the first year of his presidency in 1789, proclaimed Thursday, November 26 as Thanksgiving Day to commemorate the adoption of the Constitution.

Keepsake

A stencil design from *Needle-Art*, 1924, develops into this bold, graphic turkey worked in reverse appliqué (see page 283) and embroidery (see page 289). The design can also be executed either entirely in appliqué, entirely in embroidery, or in needlepoint.

MATERIALS:

    good quality felt, size 15″ × 18″; burnt orange, dark green, cream, large scraps gray

    Persian yarn: red, orange, dark brown, light brown, grey, yellow, dark green

    white glue, crewel needle, sharp pointed small scissors

    2 11″ and 2 14″ canvas stretchers

    staple gun or thumb tacks

STEP-BY-STEP:

1. Enlarge design to 11″ × 14″.

2. Transfer entire design (solid lines only) to center of cream-colored felt.

3. Embroider turkey body in satin stitch using 2 strands of Persian yarn combined as follows:
   Area 1 1 red, 1 orange (eyes and mouth optional)
   Area 2 2 dark brown
   Area 3 1 dark brown, 1 orange
   Area 4 1 light brown, 1 orange
   Area 5 1 yellow, 1 gray
   Area 6 1 dark green, 1 gray
   Area 7 1 dark brown, 1 orange
   Area 8 1 dark green, 1 gray
   Area 9 1 dark brown, 1 orange
   Area 10 1 dark brown (1 strand only)

4. On embroidered cream-colored felt, cut individual tail sections out and discard.

5. Cut a piece of dark green felt 10″ × 13″, then cut a 9″ × 12″ rectangle from the center, leaving a ½″ wide frame.

6. Cut a piece of burnt orange felt 11″ × 14″, then cut a 10″ × 13″ rectangle from the center, leaving a ½″-wide frame.

7. Using dotted lines for pattern shapes, cut piece A out of gray felt, piece B out of dark green felt and pieces C and D out of burnt-orange felt.

8. Glue pieces A, B, C, and D in position under cut-out tail sections. If additional support is needed, glue a piece of lightweight fabric behind tail.

9. Assemble canvas stretchers and stretch turkey. Glue orange-felt frame in place on background then glue green-felt frame in place, butting edges together.

10. Frame.

Thanksgiving Celebration

Thanksgiving is an annual expression of gratitude for a full harvest and the main event of the day is the feast. The order of the day for an old-fashioned Thanksgiving was church in the morning and the feast in the early afternoon. During the long and hearty meal, it was the custom in some families for each member present to cite his individual cause for thankfulness. After the meal, the men retired to the barn to inspect the livestock, the children played games of athletic skill and strength, and the ladies did what ladies seem still to be doing: they cleaned up after the feast!

Family Thanksgiving

Decorations

    The decorations for the day should reflect the bounty of the harvest. Many table arrangements use seasonal flowers, colorful leaves, and the beautiful fruits, vegetables, and grains of the harvest in cornucopia or other designs. Fill a tall glass vase with celery stalks and surround with fruits, vegetables, and nuts that have been polished with a soft cloth to enhance their natural beauty. Apples or turnips may be cored to serve as candle holders.

Each grid square is equal to one square inch.

Place Cards

On the subject of place cards, an 1894 *Delineator* cautioned:

When a family gathering is to be held on Thanksgiving Day, care should be taken in seating the guests at table, to place congenial relations together and thus promote perfect harmony.

So it seems that place cards may be perfectly in order at this traditional feast.

• Make autumn leaf place cards by pressing colorful leaves and lettering a guest's name on each with markers.

• A novel potato turkey decoration could be adapted for part of a centerpiece or used as a place card. It might require a visit to a local duck pond or turkey farm to collect feathers. Tom turkeys have bronze feathers and turkey hens have white feathers. The base of the turkey is a small round potato. Use wooden match sticks (break off the heads) or halves of round toothpicks for legs. Insert three sticks into the potato, two to serve as legs and one as a support. Slit the potato on the end (Illustration 21-1). Enlarge the Turkey Head pattern (see Design Sheet, page 150) as needed to fit the potato, then trace the turkey head on stiff cardboard (shirt cardboard or poster board). Cut out the tracing, color the head brown with felt-tip markers to match the potato, if

Illustration 21–1

necessary, and draw in eyes and a mouth with a felt-tip marker. Trace wattles (see Design Sheet, page 150) on red construction paper. Cut and fold on the dotted line. Glue the band-like upper portion to the turkey's neck and allow the lower flaps to hang free (Illustration 21-2). Insert the turkey head into the slit

Illustration 21–2

as far as the dotted line or until it fits. On each side, stick in two curved feathers for wings. If no curved feathers are available, bend straight ones at intervals until they are round enough to cling to the sides of the turkey (Illustration 21-3). Insert stiff feathers for the tail. If feath-

Illustration 21–3

ers stand at varying heights, trim with scissors to an even fan. It may help to use an ice pick or awl to poke holes in the potato before inserting the feathers (Illustration 21-4). To use as a place card, write a guest's name on a paper collar and hang it around the turkey's neck. Add a ribbon leash to the centerpiece, if desired. See the finished turkeys in Color Plate 14.

Illustration 21–4

Pilgrim Centerpiece, The Delineator, *1910*
COLOR PLATE 14

This centerpiece uses corn husk dolls in an arrangement which notes the special heritage of this holiday.

CORN HUSK DOLLS

MATERIALS:
   20 corn husks (Pilgrim woman) or 10 corn husks (Pilgrim man, Indian man)
   lightweight wire (30 gauge) or needle and thread
   black yarn
   black and white felt scraps or other colors (See Clothing below.)
   tapestry needle, white glue, acrylic paints (optional), straight pins
Note: Purchase dried corn husks at a craft shop or collect and dry your own in the sunshine during corn season. Soak husks in hot water for 5 to 10 minutes until pliable and workable. May be tied using sewing thread or wired together with lightweight wire. Clothing may be sewn or glued.

STEP-BY-STEP:
Pilgrim Woman
1. **Arms** Roll tightly 3 corn husks, 2″ × 5″, to form 5″ tube and tie or wire 1″ from each end. Trim "hands" evenly so arms are 4″ long (Illus-

Illustration 21–5

tration 21-5). For sleeves, cut black felt 3½″ × 2″ and roll around arm. Glue seam.

2. **Head** Roll scraps of husks into a ¾″ diameter ball. Take 2 husks about 6″ long and at least 1½″ wide. Tie in middle and pull the 4 seg-

Illustration 21–6

ments over the ball of husk scraps. Tie tightly below ball to make neck. Tie two more husks together. Wrap these over head again and tie at neck. (Illustration 21-6)

3. **Hair** Using black yarn and tapestry needle sew hair in desired style (Illustration 21-7). Knots are not necessary; just pull yarn through husk and cut.

Illustration 21–7

4. **Body** Put arm under neck and between husks—3 in front and 3 in back—and tie husks together beneath arm to form waist (Illustration 21-8). To form shawl collar, take 2 husks 4″ × 1½″ and fold in half. Place one over each shoulder crossing over at waist. Tie tightly. (Illustration 21-9)

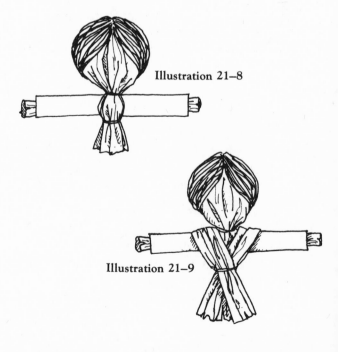

Illustration 21–8

Illustration 21–9

5. **Skirt** Use 4 pairs of husks (8 husks in all) that are long and wide. Arrange pairs of husks around waist with narrow part at waist and widest part up over head. Tie tightly around waist (Illustration 21-10) then fold husks down over tied part to form skirt. Hold skirt in place with a loose rubber band to hold shape until husks are dry. Cut felt for skirt by pattern (see Design Sheet, page 151). Fit over waist and body; lap and glue center back seam.

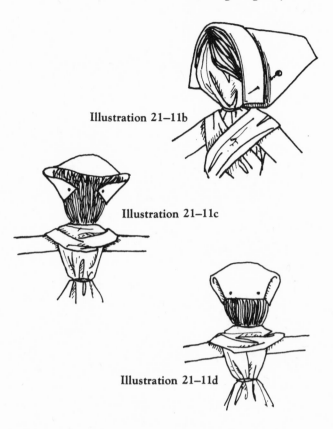

Illustration 21–11b

Illustration 21–11c

Illustration 21–11d

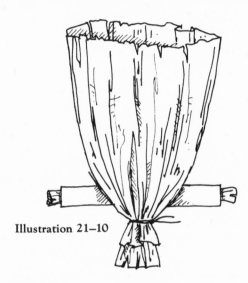

Illustration 21–10

6. **Apron** Cut 1 husk 3½″ × 2″ and tie tightly at waist. Wrap long slender strips of husk around waist and tie in back.

7. **Cap** Cut a husk 2½″ × 2″. Fold back ½″ to make a square (a). Place fold on front of hair and pin each side by pushing in a straight pin (b). Fold each side to center back and pin (c). Pull down top and pin over center back (d). When husks dry, they will hold this shape and pins can be removed. (Illustration 21-11)

8. Paint eyes and mouth if desired.

Illustration 21–11a

Pilgrim Man

1. **Arms** Follow step 1, Woman.

2. **Head and Hair** Follow step 2, Woman.

3. **Body** Follow step 3, Woman, omitting reference to shawl collar.

4. **Legs** For each leg, roll 3 husks 3″ × 5″ and tie at one end. For pants cut 2 pieces of black felt, each 3″ × 2¾″. Roll around each leg and glue seam. Tie tightly at knees. Tie legs to waist.

5. **Waistcoat** Cut black felt waistcoat by pattern (see Design Sheet, page 150). Fit on figure and glue in place on centerfront and at shoulder, lapping shoulder seam ¼″. Cut white felt collar by pattern (see Design Sheet, page 150) and fit around neck. Glue points in front and back.

6. **Hat** Glue two 2″ diameter circles of black felt together and clip through center to sit on head (see Design Sheet, page 150). Cut a strip of felt 1″ wide and long enough to roll around crown. Clip and glue in place. (Illustration 21-12)

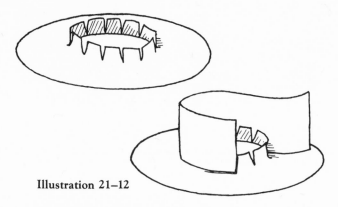

Illustration 21–12

7. **Face** Follow step 7, Woman.

Indian Man

1. **Arms** Follow step 1, Pilgrim Man. For sleeves, use rust felt.
2. **Head and Hair** Follow step 2, Pilgrim Man. Let hair fall in long, shoulder length fringe. (Illustration 21-13)

Illustration 21–13

3. **Body** Follow step 3, Pilgrim Man.
4. **Legs** Follow step 5, Pilgrim Man. For pants, cut 2 pieces of rust felt each 3″ × 3¾″, fringe one long edge. Roll around each leg and glue seam with fringed edge extending (Illustration 21-14). Do not tie at knees.

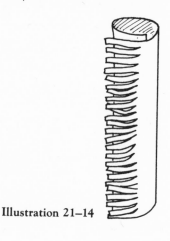

Illustration 21–14

5. **Tunic** Cut tunic (see Design Sheet, page 151) out of rust felt. Fringe lower edges. Decorate with pinked trimmings or beads. Fit over head and glue at sides and center back.

Clothing

The Pilgrims in the photo are dressed in black but other subdued conservative colors such as brown, gray, and dull red are equally suitable. The men should have ear length hair and an occasional "metal" belt or hat buckle. The women's hairdos should be severe. Women's collars, cuffs, aprons, and hats may be white felt if preferred. Men may carry muskets or staffs. The Indian garments may be made out of felt, but suede or chamois would give an added touch of authenticity. Indian men may wear beads and feathers. The garment edges can be trimmed or painted in geometric shapes to simulate embroidered details.

THANKSGIVING TABLE

MATERIALS:

 1 piece thin wood or stiff cardboard, as needed to hold food
 4 wooden skewers for legs, about 3″ long
 glue
 1 recipe cornstarch clay (see page 288)
 acrylic paints or markers to color clay pieces

STEP-BY-STEP:

1. Glue legs to table, slanting toward center.
2. Mold Thanksgiving foods and table appointments from cornstarch clay.
3. When dry, paint appropriately; plates should be pewter. Use the Old Fashioned Thanksgiving menu for food ideas. Note from the photograph that Pilgrim women baked large quantities in pans enormous by our standards.

DISPLAY

To set up the centerpiece it will be helpful to have the arrangement in an easily moveable form so you can take it off the table at feast time. The one in the photo has been arranged on a piece of foam board (available in art-supply stores) set into a flat basket with a rail-like rim and handles. The corn husk figures stand by means of straight pins inserted through the foam board and then into the legs of the figures. Trees and bushes are evergreen twigs stuck into painted spools. And for a new England winter, there must, of course, be an ample woodpile, easy to simulate with orderly stacks of twigs. Strew the "ground" with bits of hay or dried evergreen needles. You might like to add a rail fence or stone fence over in one corner protecting a crepe paper garden with cabbages, turnip tops, and pumpkins still growing among the corn stalks. A haystack in the field is another possibility. A pot made of cornstarch clay can bubble merrily over a cellophane fire.

Food for the Feast

The Thanksgiving dinner should be direct from the land. *The Delineator* in 1906 and 1910 urged a return to traditional menus, setting aside for this one day "hot house ingredients and the charms of foreign cookery." The notable feature of the Thanksgiving meal is an abundance of food, all of which is scrupulously seasonal or "put up" from the summer crops—pickles, chow-chow, and the like. Latitude in the preparation of the various foods is permitted, as long as the method remains essentially simple. Oysters or clams may be served on the half shell or in a soup. Vegetables may be mashed, creamed, or boiled and served in a butter sauce. Sweet potatoes may be candied. Cranberries may be served as sauce, jelly, or relish. All the food should be placed on the table at the start of the meal to emphasize the bountifulness of the holiday and to allow the cook to enjoy eating without having to rise frequently to bring on another course. The dinner which follows appeared in the *Delineator* as a traditional menu.

TRADITIONAL THANKSGIVING DINNER

Oysters or Clams

Celery   Chow-Chow   Pickles

Roast Turkey* with Stuffing*, Giblet Gravy*

Cranberries*

White Potatoes   Turnips

Squash   Parsnips

Onions   Sweet Potatoes

Virginia Chicken Pie*

Old-Fashioned Indian Pudding*

Mince Pie*   Apple Pie   Pumpkin Pie*

American Cheese

Assorted Nuts   Raisins

Apples, Pears, Grapes Bonbons Coffee Cider

*See below.

The *Delineator* provided some interesting information about the Thanksgiving turkey. Reading eighty or so years later, we realize just how much simpler food preparation has become. Proper selection of the bird (live, of course) was of utmost importance, according to an 1895 *Delineator* which provided the following interesting information:

What constitutes a good turkey is not difficult to decide. The best turkeys have smooth black legs, soft bills, and toes, and flesh that is white and plump. Many prefer a gobbler to a hen, but the latter will usually be found more sweet and tender. Twelve pounds is a good weight. . . . Those fortunate enough to have their own poultry yard should fatten their turkey on corn and keep it twelve hours without food before killing. The food can be so managed that the meat shall have a delicious flavor. If a gamey flavor is liked, it may be secured by feeding chopped meal, boiled rice, and chopped celery tops. This food is given but three or four days before killing. After killing, the bird should be properly bled, and after hanging six hours should be picked. Every modern housewife knows the superiority of drypicked fowls over those scalded.

A 1912 *Delineator* quoted from the early 1800's *Cook's Oracle*, by William Kitchiner, M.D.:

If you wish a turkey, especially a very large one, to be tender, never dress it till at least four or five days after it has been killed. . . . No man who understands good living will say, on such a day I will eat that turkey— but will hang it up by four of the large tail feathers, and when on paying his morning visit to the larder he finds it lying upon a cloth prepared to receive it when it falls, that day let it be cooked.

This approach was hardly suitable for a scheduled feast like Thanksgiving! There followed, in the same passage, directions for cooking the turkey before an open fireplace, a method also not applicable to today's life.

ROAST TURKEY
The Delineator, 1893

Wash a plump young turkey and rub it with salt and pepper inside and out. Stuff it. Skewer the fowl, draw the legs firmly against the body, fold the wings under the back and tie all firmly in position with clean cotton cord. Grease the turkey well with butter, olive oil, or the like, dredge with flour, and place it on a rack in a pan. Baste the fowl frequently from pan drippings, adding a little melted butter if necessary. Bake an 8–12 lb. turkey at 325° for 3½–4½ hours; a 12–16 lb. turkey for 4½–5½ hours. See How to Carve a Turkey, page 147.

BREAD STUFFING
The Delineator, 1906

1 loaf stale bread	1 tbs. summer savory
1 tbs. salt	2 tsp. thyme
1½ tsp. pepper	1 tsp. sweet marjoram
4 onions, finely chopped	½ cup melted butter
1 tbs. sage	

Break bread into pieces and cover with boiling water. Let stand about 15 minutes. Stir remaining ingredients into moist bread, adding butter last. Mix thoroughly.

OYSTER STUFFING
The Delineator, 1928

3 cups seasoned dry bread crumbs	1 pt. oysters, chopped, and liquor
½ cup melted butter	1 egg (optional)
1 tsp. salt	1 cup chopped celery (optional)
¼ tsp. pepper	
1 small onion, chopped	

Mix bread crumbs, melted butter, and seasonings, then add oysters and enough of the oyster liquor to soften the dressing. Enough for a small turkey or the crop. Double amount for large turkey.

CHESTNUT STUFFING
The Delineator, 1914

50 chestnuts, shelled and blanched	1 tbs. salt
3 tbs. butter	½ tsp. pepper

To shell chestnuts: Peel a narrow strip off one side of each chestnut. Set nuts in a pan of cold water. Bring to a boil and boil 1 minute. Remove from heat. A few at a time, take chestnuts out of water and peel off shells and inner skins. Must be done while chestnuts are warm.
The stuffing: Boil peeled chestnuts in water to cover until softened but whole and not mushy, about 15 minutes. Drain water. Add butter, salt, and pepper, Stuff turkey. Chestnuts will be whole, dry, sweet, and tender. This is a rich stuffing. Use it in the crop with a bread stuffing in the cavity.

GIBLET GRAVY
The Delineator, 1893

Boil giblets in a little salted water until they are done, then chop fine and return to the water in which they were boiled. When the turkey has been removed from the roasting pan, turn the giblets and water into the pan and let the gravy boil. The flour that has.been basted from the turkey will usually make the gravy thick enough, but if this is insufficient, dredge browned flour into the pan until the gravy is creamy as it boils up. The roasting turkey will, as a rule, impart sufficient seasoning to the gravy, but more may be added if necessary.

How to Make a Turkey Last a Week
From a 1907 *Delineator,* these hints:

- Sunday, served as a roast.
- Monday, made a stew.
- Tuesday, French Hash on toast.
- Wednesday, a rich fricandeau.
- Thursday, a delicious Pâté.
- Friday, for grilled bones.
- Saturday, soup.

If turkey was considered to be the national bird, then surely the cranberry was thought of as the national berry. Its extravagant use was urged and, as homemakers became more conscious of nutrition, cranberry concoctions ceased to be strained to remove the skins. During times when sugar was scarce or frightfully expensive, cranberry recipes using corn syrup were developed. There were even games played with cranberries (see page 148).

CRANBERRY JELLY I
The Delineator, 1893

2 cups cranberries
1 cup sugar
½ cup water

Wash cranberries and place in saucepan. Add sugar and water. As water comes to boil, cover pan and boil continuously for exactly 10 minutes. Skim the top and turn berries into a wet earthenware mold. Berries may

be strained, but flavor and wholesomeness are lessened by removing the skins.

CRANBERRY JELLY II
The Delineator, 1906

4 cups cranberries
2 cups sugar
1 cup water

Place cranberries in pan with sugar and water. Bring just to a boil, then simmer for 20 minutes. Rub through a colander and turn into molds to harden.

CRANBERRY SAUCE I
The Delineator, 1893

Follow recipe above, adding ½ cup more water and a little less sugar. *The Delineator* noted that "late in the season, cranberries are riper and require less sugar."

CRANBERRY SAUCE II
The Delineator, 1920

¾ cup water
4 cups cranberries
1¾ cups white corn syrup

Add berries to boiling water, cover, and cook until berries burst. Add syrup and boil 5 minutes longer. Pour into mold.

SPICED CRANBERRIES
The Delineator, 1907

10 cups cranberries
3½ cups brown sugar
1 cup cider vinegar
1 tbs. allspice
1 tbs. cinnamon
1½ tsp. ground cloves

Boil brown sugar with vinegar adding, after the mixture has begun to cook, allspice, cinnamon, cloves. Cook to a syrup, then add cranberries and simmer 1½ to 2 hours. Makes 4 cups. If kept in covered jar in cool place, will keep for a long time.

DATE AND CRANBERRY MARMALADE

The Delineator, 1920

4 cups cranberries	1 cup corn syrup
8 oz. pkg. dates	¼ cup brown sugar
2 cups water	

Wash berries and chop dates. Add water, cover, simmer 20 minutes. Put through a sieve, return to saucepan, add syrup and sugar, and boil 15 minutes. Pour into tumblers. Makes 4 cups.

CRANBERRY TARTS

The Delineator, 1920

1½ cups cranberries	¾ cup sugar
½ cup raisins	1 cup water

Mix the ingredients in the order given. Place in open pan and cook for 15 minutes over direct heat until quite thick. Allow to cool.

Tart shells: Line muffin tins with pie crust, and bake for 10 minutes. Fill with the cranberry mixture and return to oven just long enough to heat through. Serve hot or cold.

CRANBERRY FRAPPE

The Delineator, 1914

2 cups cranberries	1 orange, juice
2 cups water	1 cup sugar
1 lemon, juice	

Boil cranberries in water for 10 minutes until soft. Strain. Add juices and sugar. Freeze to a stiff mush. Serves 6. Excellent for sherbert during meal or as dessert.

CAPE COD COCKTAIL

The Delineator, 1924

1 tbs. sugar	¼ small banana, sliced
2 tbs. cranberry sauce	1 tbs. lemon juice
1 small piece canned apricot	

Mix ingredients thoroughly and chill. Serve as an appetizer. Serves 1.

For many years, another dish essential to the Thanksgiving feast was chicken pie, served in addition to the turkey. As homemakers began to rebel against spending so much time to prepare one so-called holiday meal, the Thanksgiving repast became streamlined and chicken pie was one of the first traditions to be abandoned. For those who want a really authentic meal, here is a delicious recipe.

VIRGINIA CHICKEN PIE

The Delineator, 1906

1 9″ double crust pie shell	½ tsp. pepper
3 medium sized potatoes	4 tbs. chicken broth
1½ cups cooked or parboiled chicken	1 large whole onion, peeled
1 tsp. salt	3 thin slices salt pork or bacon

In pie shell, layer chicken, potatoes, salt, and pepper. Pour broth over top then add salt pork on top and place onion in center. Cover with crust and slit. Bake 1 hour at 375°. Chicken broth may be used to make gravy to be served separately.

A distinctively New England dish, and therefore one served traditionally at the Thanksgiving dinner, is Indian Pudding. Old recipes for this pudding vary radically: some omit raisins, others use molasses to sweeten, others use surprisingly scant amounts of corn meal. This one has a pleasant, sweet flavor. Serve with hard sauce (traditional) or whipped cream.

INDIAN PUDDING

The Delineator Cook Book, 1928

1 qt. milk	½ tsp. salt
⅓ cup cornmeal	½ tsp. ginger
½ cup raisins	1 egg, beaten
½ tsp. cinnamon	
½ cup brown sugar	

Place milk in double boiler and when it is scalding hot, add the cornmeal, moistened with cold water, and stir constantly to avoid lumps. Cook for 10 minutes. Add sugar, cook 10 more minutes. To prevent curdling, gradually add about 1 cup of hot pudding mixture to egg, mixing constantly, then add egg mixture and spices to remaining pudding. Pour into a generously buttered 2 quart baking dish. Bake 1½ hours at 325°. Serve hot. ½ cup dates or figs may be used instead of the raisins.

In time, the pumpkin began to compete with the turkey for the spotlight on the Thanksgiving table and the harvesting of these abundant golden vegetables was a forerunner of the Thanksgiving holiday. The favored use of pumpkin was, and remains, as a pie filling, a custard laboriously made from scratch until canned pumpkin and canned pumpkin-pie filling became available. The pumpkin pie must be absolutely fresh and is therefore best baked the day of the feast.

Preparing Fresh Pumpkin for Pies

Cut pumpkin into strips, peel and remove seeds and soft pulp. Cut into 1 inch pieces. Cook with small amount of water or steam until tender. Mash pulp through colander. Refrigerate until ready to use. One medium size pumpkin should make about 6 cups of stewed pumpkin.

PUMPKIN PIE
The Delineator, 1894

1 9″ pie shell	1 tsp. cinnamon
2 cups stewed pumpkin	½ tsp. nutmeg
⅔ cup sugar	2 eggs
½ tsp. salt	2 cups milk
½ tsp. ginger	

Mix all ingredients. Pour into 9″ pie shell. Bake at 375° 1 hour or until knife inserted in center comes out clean.

PUMPKIN PIE WITH EXTRA CREAM
The Delineator, 1905

Prepare pie by recipe above or use canned pumpkin pie mix. As the pie begins to bake firm, very gently pour a cup of thick cream over it. Cover rim of crust with aluminum foil and bake until knife tests clean. This adds considerable time to baking period but results in a delicious pie with a very flaky crust.

PUMPKIN PIE WITH NUTS
The Delineator, 1905

Prepare pumpkin pie by recipe above or use canned pumpkin pie mix. Bake. Before serving, cover top with whipped cream and decorate with salted pecans.

CANDIED PUMPKIN CHIPS
The Delineator, 1921

1½ cups raw peeled pumpkin, cut in 1″ square slices	¾ cup pineapple juice
	1 tbs. ginger (optional)
1 cup sugar	Juice and grated rind of 1 lemon (optional)

Boil sugar and pineapple juice into heavy syrup. Add pumpkin and cook until pumpkin begins to soften. Let stand overnight. Drain and cook syrup until it spins a thread, 230°–234°. Add pumpkin and other ingredients to syrup and simmer until pumpkin is clear. Drain and place on lightly oiled plate. Dry until no longer sticky, about 24 hours. Roll in granulated sugar. Pack in glass jar.

Mince pie was and is another favorite at Thanksgiving. Homemade mincemeat, too, gave way to already prepared filling. Although some cooking editors found canned filling entirely acceptable, others mourned the good old days when mincemeat recipes were cherished family heirlooms. Pies may be made several days ahead of need.

MINCEMEAT (WITH MEAT)
The Delineator, 1894

½ lb. beef (round steak or piece off rump)	1 lb. green apples
	½ lb. currants
½ lb. suet	¼ lb. citron
4 tbs. candied lemon peel	1 cup sugar
1 lb. raisins	1 nutmeg grated or ½ tsp. grated nutmeg
1 cup sherry	
1 cup brandy	1 tsp. mace
1 orange (juice and rind)	2 tsp. cinnamon
2 tsp. salt	1 tsp. ground cloves

Cook beef in water gently until tender. Cool. Chop beef, suet, and orange through a meat grinder with fine blade. Put all other fruits through grinder on coarse blade. Stir in dry ingredients, then sherry and brandy. Mix well in heavy 3 qt. saucepan. Simmer 30 minutes until very hot. Pack in sterile jars to keep. Allow to age at least 2 to 4 weeks. Makes a good gift. Makes 2 quarts or 2 9″ pies.

MINCEMEAT (WITHOUT MEAT)
The Delineator, 1916

1 lb. raisins	2 oz. candied fruit peel
1 lb. golden raisins	¾ tsp. mace
12 oz. currants	¾ tsp. ground cloves
2 lb. tart peeled apples	¾ tsp. salt
1½ lb. brown sugar	1 tbs. cinnamon
⅓ lb. citron	½ cup olive oil
Juice of 1 lemon	¾ cup good quality apple
Juice of 2 oranges	cider
2 oz. candied pineapple	

Chop all fruits through meat grinder on coarse blade. Dissolve the spices and sugar in the oil and cider, add the fruit juices, and pour over fruit. When well mixed, store in a cool place 2 to 4 weeks or simmer on low heat 20–30 minutes until hot and pack in sterile jars and seal. Does not require cooking until put in pastry. Good for gifts. Makes 3 qts. or 3 pies.

MINCE PIE

1 9″ double crust pie
   shell
1 qt. mincemeat

Line pie pan with crust. Fill with mincemeat. Cover pie with an upper crust or lattice crust and bake at 450° for about 30 minutes. Pies may be made several days ahead of need and heated before serving.

MINCEMEAT PIELETS
The Delineator, 1928

6 tbs. mincemeat	1 double crust pie shell
6 tsp. applesauce	1 egg, beaten

Cut pie crust into 12 3″ circles. Spread half of the circles with 1 tsp. applesauce each, leaving a ¼″ rim clear. Over the applesauce spread 1 tbs. mincemeat. Moisten the edges with beaten egg and cover with the remaining pastry circles, making a few slits. Press and crimp the edges together and bake at 375° for 15–20 minutes or until well browned. Makes 6.

For a time, women's magazines such as *The Delineator* were doggedly determined to perpetuate the old Thanksgiving meal traditions. However, as tastes became more sophisticated, families became smaller, and economic matters intervened (rising food costs, decline in household servants), other types of menus were developed and given the stamp of social approval.

MODERNIZED THANKSGIVING DINNER, 1911

Oyster Cocktail or Bouchées[1] of Caviar
Olives and Mayonnaise
Italian Minestra[2]
Boiled Salmon, Sauce Hollandaise
Potato Balls
Roast Turkey** with Chestnut Stuffing**
or
Broiled Young Guinea Hen
with Parsley Butter
Cranberry Mold**
Mashed Potatoes   Cauliflower au Gratin
Lettuce and Tomato   Jelly Salad
Apple Tart   Nesselrode Pudding[3]
Cheese   Crackers   Assorted Fruits and Nuts
Demitasse

**See recipes elsewhere in this chapter.
[1]Bouchées: pastry shells
[2]Minestra: Soup
[3]Nesselrode: Bavarian creme with chestnut puree and optional candied ginger or kumquats added, served with sweetened whipped cream.

Thanksgiving Day   146

VEGETARIAN THANKSGIVING DINNER, 1912

Grapefruit with Maraschino Cherries or
Loganberry Jelly
Ripe Olives   Salted Nuts   Celery
Cream of Tomato Soup with Bread Sticks
Nut Turkey Roast*   Cranberry Jelly**
Baked Irish Potatoes
Sweet Potatoes (Southern Style)
Hubbard Squash   Glazed Onions
Orange and Pineapple Salad
Cheese Crisps   Pumpkin** or Cranberry Pie
Indian Pudding**
Grapes   Apples   Nuts
Cider or Grape Juice Punch

*See below.
**See recipes elsewhere in this chapter.

NUT TURKEY ROAST

The Delineator, 1913

½ cup chopped pecans   2 eggs
½ cup chopped walnuts   1 tbs. melted butter
1 cup dry bread crumbs,
plus milk to moisten

Add enough milk to moisten the crumbs and add more as it soaks in. Crumbs should be a little too thick to run. Add nuts and mix well. Turn into a small buttered bread pan and dot with butter. Bake at 325° for 30 minutes. Serves 2. Triple recipe and shape as a "turkey" roast for Thanksgiving.

And this menu from 1907 really tells a lot about the days long gone:

THANKSGIVING DINNER
FOR THREE DOLLARS FOR
SIX PERSONS

Celery
Tomato Soup with Croutons
Roast Turkey**   Sage Dressing
Potatoes   Onions   Turnips
Squashes
Cranberry Sauce**
Apple Pie   Mince Pie**
American Cheese
Coffee

**See recipes elsewhere in this chapter.

THE SONG OF THE THANKSGIVING BIRD
By John Howard Jewett
—
ALL OVER THE LAND AND FAR OVER THE SEA
OUR GLAD "GOBBLE-GOBBLE" IS HEARD,
'TIS THE NATIONAL AIR OF THE BRAVE AND THE FREE
THE SONG OF THE THANKSGIVING BIRD!

New Idea Woman's Magazine, 1906

Carving the Turkey, *The Delineator,* 1923
STEP-BY-STEP

1. Place the bird on its back on the platter or board with the drumsticks at the left. (Reverse directions for left-handed carver.) Grasp the carving fork firmly in the left hand, with the tines pointing toward the bird's neck and the tips curved away from the bird. Insert the fork into the leg in this position, being sure that one tine goes diagonally through the drumstick and the other through the second joint (thigh). With the knife cut all around the bone. (Illustration 21-15)

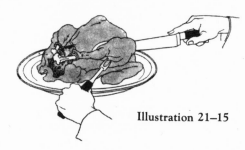

Illustration 21—15

2. Press against the side of the bird with the flat of the knife and use the fork as a lever to bend the leg back. This will separate the hip joint and the leg can be lifted off without difficulty. (Illustration 21-16)

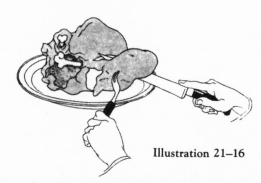

Illustration 21—16

3. Without removing the fork, lay the leg down flat, with the open end pointing to the left, and insert the knife from right to left between the tines of the fork. In this position it should rest directly over the joint and the knife should go through when pressed down. (Illustration 21-17)

Illustration 21—17

4. Next insert the fork through the side of the bird, rather low down, and hold it firmly, cutting the breast downward in thin even slices. (Illustration 21-18)

Illustration 21—18

5. Serve a slice of white meat with a slice from the second joint (thigh) to each person at the table. If more portions are needed, sever the wing in the same manner as the leg and divide it similarly (Illustration 21-19). The tip of the wing and the drumstick are not usually served, if it can be avoided, but are used for other purposes. If more than one side is needed, turn the bird on its side and remove the second leg in the manner described. Then stand it up on its back, turn the platter around and slice from the breast.

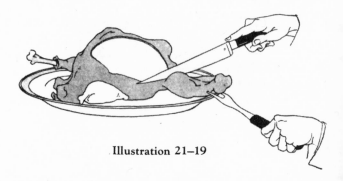

Illustration 21—19

Games

Games and activities to amuse and entertain all ages are appropriate for this family festival day. The games of athletic skill played at Thanksgiving celebrations long ago are reflected in the modern popularity of football and other sporting events on this day, to be enjoyed via television or in pick-up games played for family fun.

Thankfulness Game, The Delineator, 1907

This is a nice game for a family gathering, since the players must be well acquainted. Numbered slips of paper are distributed and each player writes an answer to the question "What are you thankful for this year?" and signs his name. The hostess collects the slips and hands out others, each bearing a list of numbers from "1" up to the number of players. The hostess shuffles the first papers, then reads aloud the various reasons for thankfulness, assigning each reason a number but not revealing the names. The listeners fill in, on the slips they have in their hands, the names which they believe to correspond with the reasons read. Prizes go to those with the most right answers. Vary the game by having each guest write both his own cause for thankfulness and what he thinks should be the source of his neighbor's gratitude.

Cranberry Crush, New Idea Woman's Magazine, 1906

Place a basket of cranberries at the head of each of two lines. At a signal, each team tries to empty its basket into a bowl at the opposite end of the line by passing one cranberry at a time from one to another, from one hand to another. The first team to do so wins.

Cranberry Guessing Contest, New Idea Woman's Magazine, 1906

Each player ventures a guess as to the exact number of cranberries contained in a dish. The berries are counted and presented as a gift to the one making the closest guess.

Cranberry Race, New Idea Woman's Magazine, 1906

A dish of cranberries, an empty dish, and a large spoon are provided for each player. The object is to transfer the cranberries from the full dish to the empty one, one spoonful at a time. Spilled berries must be picked up at once. The first player to empty his dish is the winner.

Children's Corner

Apple/Pumpkin Spin, *The Delineator, 1905*
MATERIALS:
    1 large apple
    8 small apples with stems, all same size (about 2″ diameter, flat top and bottom)
    8 10″ squares orange tissue paper
    brown button and carpet thread
    1 3½″ square green tissue paper
    1 sheet corrugated cardboard, 26″ × 19″
    fine felt-tip marker, black
    pencil

STEP-BY-STEP:
Apple/Pumpkins
1. Place each of eight small apples upright on square of orange tissue paper (Illustration 21-20). Smooth tissue paper over the apple in tiny pleats and twist the ends around the stem. Be sure covering lies flat and smooth. (Illustration 21-21)

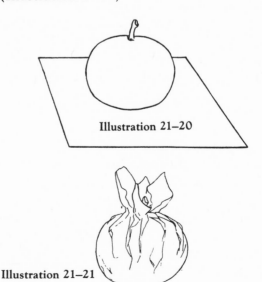

Illustration 21–20

Illustration 21–21

2. Tie one end of heavy brown thread around twisted stem. Wind thread once around the apple then once around the stem to secure it. Thread must pass over the exact center of the bottom of the apple. (Illustration 21-22)

Illustration 21-22

3. Continue to wind thread around apple and stem making even segments which resemble a pumpkin. Tie thread end and trim stem to 1″ in length.

4. Pinch green tissue square over the twisted stem. Tie a thread around the base of the stem to hold green tissue in place. (Illustration 21-23)

Illustration 21-23

Playing Court

1. Lightly pencil diagonal lines on corrugated board to locate the center of the board. (Illustration 21-24)

2. Permanently mark the center with a 2″ diameter circle then surround this circle with another one 7″ in diameter. Erase diagonal lines within the circles.

3. Permanently draw over the remaining diagonal lines and add additional lines.

4. Give number values to the sections of the court (Illustration 21-25). Place the little apple/pumpkins evenly around the larger circle.

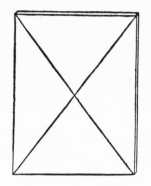

Illustration 21-24

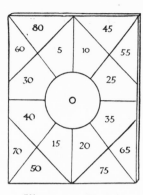

Illustration 21-25

The Game:

Stand a large, round, uncovered apple on the central small circle. The object of the game is to spin the uncovered apple so it will hit one or more of the surrounding apple/pumpkins and roll or push them onto the highest marked divisions of the court. Each player takes one spin at a time. The spinning must always be started on the small center circle.

Scoring:

• If the apple does not leave the large circle, the player loses his turn and loses 5 points.
• If the apple rolls off the board, the player gets another turn. If the apple rolls off the board again, the player loses his turn with no other penalty.
• When an apple/pumpkin lands on a line, the player loses 10 points.
• Every apple/pumpkin which lands in a division scores the number of points on that division.
• Apple/pumpkins are replaced around the circle after each turn.
• Five rounds constitute a game—the highest score wins.
• The game may be played in teams, with equal numbers of players on each side.

Bead Stringing, *The Delineator,* 1911
MATERIALS:

saucers of cleaned and dried yellow and red corn kernels; acorns; and squash, melon, and sunflower seeds

short needle
strong thread
awl, beeswax

STEP-BY-STEP:

1. Soak seeds in warm water for about an hour, then dry between soft towels.

2. String onto doubled thread. Push needle through fleshy end of corn kernel, pointed end of squash and melon seeds. (Illustration 21-26)

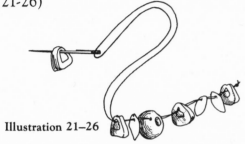

Illustration 21–26

3. Bore holes with an awl through acorns before using for beads or pendants. (Illustration 21-27) **Note:** These make lovely necklaces, belts, and other jewelry items. If preferred,

beads may be sewn to cloth like embroidery or glued to boxes, bits of wood, or cans, for accessories.

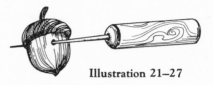

Illustration 21–27

Leaf Waxing, *The Delineator,* 1912

MATERIALS:
colored leaves
melted paraffin
newspaper

STEP-BY-STEP:

1. Dip leaves into warm paraffin to preserve color and shape.

2. Lay leaves on newspaper to cool.

3. Arrange as desired in garlands or festoons. **Note:** Make a frieze on shelf paper for the dining room. Use the leaves to decorate place cards for the Thanksgiving table.

DESIGN SHEET

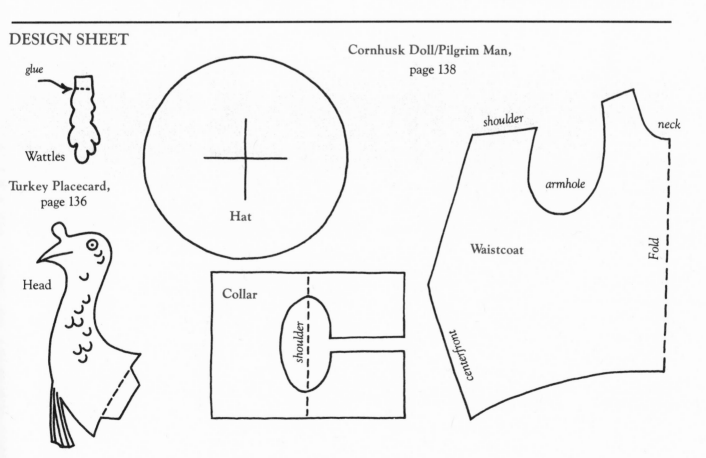

glue

Wattles

Turkey Placecard,
page 136

Head

Hat

Collar

shoulder

Cornhusk Doll/Pilgrim Man,
page 138

shoulder

neck

armhole

Waistcoat

centerfront

Fold

DESIGN SHEET

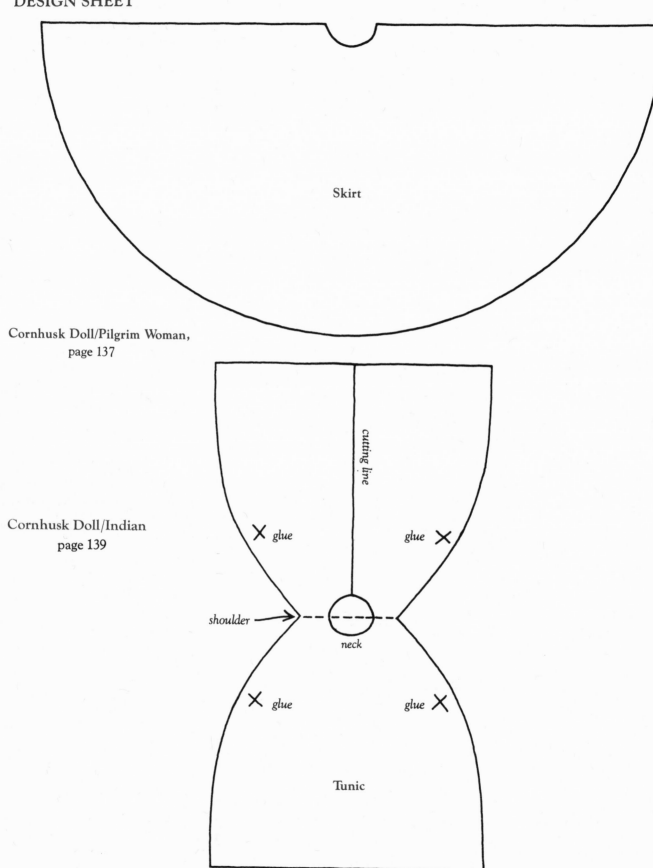

Skirt

Cornhusk Doll/Pilgrim Woman,
page 137

Cornhusk Doll/Indian
page 139

cutting line

✗ *glue*   *glue* ✗

shoulder ➜   *neck*

✗ *glue*   *glue* ✗

Tunic

Color Plate 9/Independence Day
The Delineator, July, 1927

COLOR PLATE 10/Independence Day
Paper Fireworks: Sparkling Calumet, page 97; Comet, page 98;
Skyrocket, page 99.
Girls wearing Head Wreath, page 100. Boy wearing Cocked Hat, page 100.

COLOR PLATE 11/Halloween
Halloween Costumes, pages 121-128. Costumes are Diamond and Harlequin
Clowns, Fairy Queen, Skeleton, Witch, and Ghost.

DESIGNED AND DRAWN BY MARY HAYS HUBER

No OTHER season of the whole year is so surrounded with quaint traditions as that of All Hallowe'en. The artist who originated these charming place-cards for DELINEATOR readers has caught the gay spirit of the season and portrayed all the picturesque customs associated with the day in a happy manner. Extra copies of this page, printed on heavy paper without lettering on the other side, may be obtained by sending five cents in postage to the Picture Editor, care of THE DELINEATOR, New York.

If this ghost were chasing you
Don't you think you'd hurry, too?

Patter-patter
down the stairs
A trembling
little lass
Goes to seek her
true love's face
In a looking-glass.

WITHOUT SO MUCH AS "BY YOUR LEAVE"
GATES WALK OFF ON HALLOW EVE

LETTERING BY HAROLD SICHEL

Steaming, steaming
in the kettle
Is a magic brew;
And I'm sure
when it is cooked
There'll be a fate
for you.

Young Lochinvar on a
pumpkin coach sat
Instead of a horse,
he was driving
a cat!

Splash into her flower-bed
Bobbed a roguish pumpkin head!

ON EVERY CORNER OF THE TOWN
WEIRD JACK-O-LANTERNS GLARE AND FROWN.

Over the wall a Puritan boy
Watches a gobbler strut
with joy.

Bobbing for apples,
So smooth and so bright,
Is an old-fashioned pastime—
On Hallowe'en night.

Would the yellow moon care,
Or the old witch see,
If a lover stole a kiss
Oh —— most carefully!

Humpty-Dumpty sat on a wall
Humpty-Dumpty had a great fall;
If he'd sat on a pumpkin instead
He'd never have tumbled
and
broken
his
head!

A maid
as fair as
you've ever seen
Will serve
a feast
on
Hallowe'en

Color Plate 12/Halloween
The Delineator, October, 1917

COLOR PLATE 13/Thanksgiving
The Designer, November, 1915

COLOR PLATE 14/Thanksgiving
Potato Turkey for Place Cards, page 136 and Pilgrim Centerpiece, pages 137-140.

COLOR PLATE 15/Christmas
Christmas Gift Wraps, pages 194-198. Pictured: Candy Holly, Silhouette Tin,
Crocheted Snowflake Tin, Santa Carton, Poinsettia. Christmas Food Gifts, pages
189-194.

COLOR PLATE 16/Christmas
The Delineator, Christmas, 1916

22
Hanukkah

Celebrated for 8 days beginning on the 25th day of the lunar month of Kislev (November-December)

Hanukkah is a happy midwinter festival commemorating the victory of the Maccabees over the Syrians in 165 B.C. in a battle fought to reassert the religious integrity of the Jews during a period of forced assimilation. The word *Hanukkah* means "dedication" in Hebrew and indeed the festival is also known as the Feast of Dedication as well as the Festival of Lights.

Hanukkah represents the struggle of the Jews, as a religious minority, to preserve their cultural and ritualistic identity in the face of political and military coercion. It is also a reminder that religious laxity and neglect can lead to a loss of freedom and represents a rededication to the preservation of Judaic ideals.

In the home, the kindling of lights on the Hanukkah menorah—an additional one on each of the eight nights of the festival—is an essential feature of the holiday. This practice derives from a legend regarding the war of the Maccabees. The Jews of Palestine, under the leadership of Judas Maccabeus ("The Hammer"), had successfully fought a war against King Antiochus, who wanted all of his subjects to practice the religion of Greece. At the time, Palestine was under Syrian-Greek rule. When the Maccabees returned to the temple after the war, they found only enough sacred oil to light the holy menorah for one day. By divine miracle, however, the light continued to burn for eight days.

The importance of light in this festival is also probably related to the winter folk customs, observed at the time in the Middle East and elsewhere, in which ceremonial fires were lighted at the winter solstice to urge the sun back to long days and short nights. Thus the observance of Hanukkah, like so many other festivals, is rooted in seasonal as well as historical occurrences.

The menorah is a religiously significant Jewish candelabra with a tree-like shape. The Hanukkah menorah differs from the Temple menorah in that the former has nine branches, instead of seven, one for each of the eight celebration nights and the remaining one to hold the *Shammash* or "servant candle" which is used to light the other candles.

Other traditional Hanukkah symbols are the dreydl and gelt. The dreydl is a four-sided top used for game playing. At one time, dreydl playing was employed to disguise the fact that Jews were really praying together, in places where they were forbidden to practice their religion. Hanukkah gelt is small amounts of money, commonly coins, given to children.

The Jewish community does not entirely agree on the reasons for the increasing popularity and importance of Hanukkah in the Jewish festival calendar. Some feel it has happened because of the festival's proximity to Christmas, the secular activities of which place pressure on Jewish parents to provide for their children Santa Claus and the merriment which generally accompanies the Christmas season. Others feel that its message of re-dedication is particularly appropriate in this time of general ethnic revival. Actually, Hanukkah, like many other festivals, has been alternately more or less important during its long history according to the needs of the people. And the custom of giving gifts is quite an ancient part of the Hanukkah celebration.

Hanukkah Menorah

A Hanukkah menorah may have a tree-like shape similar to the Temple menorah although any design is permissible. In a traditional Hanukkah menorah, the Shammash remains higher or lower than the other eight candles which are usually on the same level with one another. An arrangement of nine candles without any special holder complies with the spirit of the occasion as long as the flames are kept distinct one from another. Ancient Hanukkah menorahs were often made of metal or ceramic; today a wide variety of materials is used in their construction, depending on the skill of the craftsman. Many people burn olive oil instead of wax candles. Some people display electric Hanukkah menorahs in front windows as these do not require the constant supervision that candles do; however, a traditional menorah with burning flames must be used elsewhere in the home to comply with tradition. As the primary symbol of the festival, the Hanukkah menorah is found on greeting cards, decorations in the home, wrapping paper, and needlecraft projects. Colorful Hanukkah candles are available in many supermarkets as well as in Jewish bookstores. Standard household candles may also be used.

Spool Menorah, *The Young Judaean,* 1925
MATERIALS:
    8 small wooden spools
    2 large wooden spools (Wooden spools are available in craft shops.)
    white glue, hole puncher
    aluminum to cover spool tops (disposable pie plate is good)
    1 piece wood, 16″ long, ¼″ thick at least 1½″ wide (balsa is fine)
    acrylic paints to decorate (optional) or wood stain (optional)

STEP-BY-STEP:
1. Cut 4″ length off wood strip, leaving one 12″ piece and one 4″ piece.
2. Cut circles of aluminum slightly smaller than tops of 8 small spools and 1 large spool. Punch a hole in the center of each aluminum disk and glue to spool top. (Illustration 22-1)

Illustration 22–1

3. Locate exact center of 12″ wood strip and glue bottom of large aluminum-topped spool in place.
4. Glue small spools in place evenly spaced, 4 on each side of the center spool. (Illustration 22-2)

Illustration 22–2

5. When dry, glue remaining large spool directly under large spool candle holder. Center and glue 4″ strip of wood to bottom of base spool. (Illustration 22-3)
6. Stain or decorate as desired.

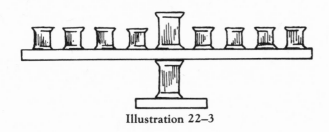

Illustration 22–3

Hanukkah Menorah Candle-Lighting Ceremony

The menorah is usually placed so it can be seen by passersby. The first candle is lit with the Shammash at sundown on the evening when the holiday begins. The Shammash is lit each night and is used to light the other candles as they are added to the menorah. The candles are placed in the menorah beginning at the right side and increasing toward the left. The candles are lit, however, from the newest addition toward the right. An increasingly popular custom with many Jewish families is for each family member to light his own menorah making a personal rededication. Before the Shammash is used for its lighting duties, special blessings are recited. After the candles are lit and the Shammash replaced, there is another traditional chant. Then the children receive a Hanukkah gift.

Hanukkah Gifts

Hanukkah gifts were formerly given only to children, but the custom is currently expanding to include exchange between husband and wife and other close relatives. In some homes, a small gift is given on each of the eight nights. If the Hanukkah gift is to be a large one, perhaps a bicycle, it is presented on the last night. One popular Hanukkah gift is gelt (money). A bank to contain the holiday gelt is, therefore, another appropriate gift. Chocolate disks covered with gold foil, imitating money, make an edible form of gelt enjoyed by most children. Embroidered items for the Sabbath table are meaningful gifts for adults. The dreydl, a traditional Hanukkah symbol, is also a popular gift item.

The Dreydl

Games of chance have a long tradition during Hanukkah and are played by adults and children alike. On each side of the dreydl is a Hebrew character, the four of which, ‎נ‎ , ‎ג‎ , ‎ה‎ , and ‎ש‎ stand for the Hebrew words *nes gadol hayah sham,* "A great miracle happened there," referring to the small amount of sacred oil which lasted for eight days. Like the Hanukkah menorah, the dreydl appears as a graphic symbol of the festival on cards, household decoration, etcetera. Because of its shape, it can be crafted into a gift box.

Clay Dreydl
MATERIALS:
    1 recipe cornstarch clay (see page 288)
    acrylic paints to decorate
    clay modeling tools or kitchen tools (knife, spatula)
    fine sandpaper (optional)

STEP-BY-STEP:

1. Form a small lump of clay into a cylinder about 2″ long and 1″ in diameter. Pinch, pull, pat, and tap dreydl into shape, taking care that handle remains sturdy and centered. (Illustration 22-4)

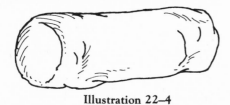

Illustration 22–4

2. Use kitchen spatula to smooth bottom of dreydl into a point, which must also be centered for balance. Make handle about 1″ long, point about ¾″ long from edge to tip. (Illustration 22-5)

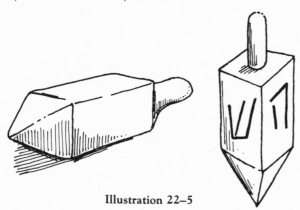

Illustration 22–5

3. The Hebrew characters ג , נ , ה and ש (Design Sheet, page 158) may be pressed into the sides of the dreydl with a sharp tool. (It is difficult to carve raised letters on the dreydl and still maintain its balance.) Or, when the dreydl is thoroughly dry, paint Hebrew characters on sides if they have not already been pressed in place. (Illustration 22-5)

4. Smooth or shape for balance with sandpaper, if necessary.

Wood Dreydl I

MATERIALS:

 1 block balsa wood, 1″ square × 1¼″ long
 1 wooden household skewer with pointed end, cut 2¼″ long

household glue, artist's knife
acrylic paint to decorate
fine sandpaper

STEP-BY-STEP:

1. Draw line around block with pencil, ¼″ from one end. Locate center point on each end and mark with pencil. (Illustration 22-6)

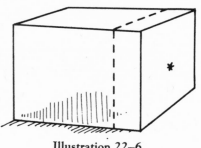

Illustration 22–6

2. With knife, carve each side diagonally from marked line toward point, shaving off a bit of wood with each stroke until sides slope evenly and point is slightly rounded. (Illustration 22-7)

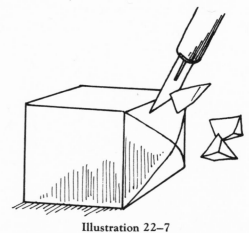

Illustration 22–7

3. On other end of block, scoop out wood in diameter of skewer, about ¼″ deep. Push pointed end of skewer into hole. Remove skewer, apply a dab of glue to point, and replace in hole. Be certain skewer is centered. (Illustration 22-8)

4. Sand edges as necessary to balance.

5. Paint appropriate Hebrew character on each side of dreydl (see Design Sheet, page 158). (Illustration 22-9) **Note:** This design is

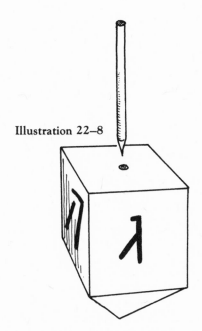

Illustration 22–8

adapted from a 1924 dreydl which was made out of melted lead poured into a hand-carved form.

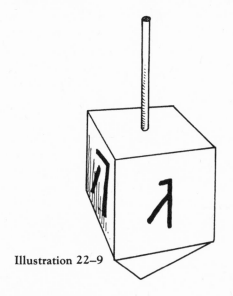

Illustration 22–9

Wood Dreydl II
MATERIALS:
1 balsa wood block, 1″ square × 2″ long
artist's knife
fine sandpaper
acrylic paint to decorate

STEP-BY-STEP:
1. Draw lines around block with pencil ¼″ from one end and ¾″ from other end. Locate center point on each end and mark with pencil.
2. With knife, carve sides from ¼″ marking to form center point, shaving off a bit of wood with each stroke until sides slope evenly. (Illustration 22-10)

Illustration 22–10

3. On other end (top of dreydl), draw a ¼″ circle around center point. Cut away wood from line around block toward top, forming a round handle.
4. Sand as necessary and paint appropriate Hebrew character on each side (see page 158).

Dreydl Song

Children are especially fond of playing dreydl and many generations of them have sung this lively song about the toy.

MY DREYDL

I have a little dreydl, I made it out of clay,
And when it's dry and ready, then dreydl I shall
  play.
Chorus
O dreydl, dreydl, dreydl, I made it out of clay,
O dreydl, dreydl, dreydl, now dreydl I shall play.
It has a lovely body, with leg so short and thin,
And when it is all tired, it drops and then I win!

Chorus

O dreydl, dreydl, dreydl, with leg so short and thin,
O dreydl, dreydl, dreydl, it drops and then I win.

My dreydl's always playful, it loves to dance and
   spin,
A happy game of dreydl, come play, now let's begin.

Chorus
O dreydl, dreydl, dreydl, it loves to dance and spin,
O dreydl, dreydl, dreydl, come play, now let's begin.

Dreydl Games

The Hebrew letters on the sides of the dreydl are an essential element of the games played with the dreydl. *Nun* ‫נ‬ stands for *nisht* ("nothing"), *gimel* ‫ג‬ for *gantz* ("all"), *heh* ‫ה‬ for *halb* ("half"), and *shin* ‫ש‬ for *shtel* ("put in").

Each player begins the game with an equal number of tokens: pennies, nuts, candies, etcetera. To start, each player places one of these tokens in a saucer which forms the pot. The dreydl is spun by each player in turn. The side which faces up when the dreydl falls determines whether he wins or loses. If it lands on *nun* the player gets nothing, *gimel* the player gets all the pot, *heh* the player takes half of the pot, *shin*, the player puts two tokens in the pot. When the pot is empty or there is only one token, each player adds two tokens to it. If a player rolls *heh* and the pot contains an odd number, the player takes half plus one. The object of the game is for one person to win all the tokens.

An alternate game involves the numerical values of the Hebrew letters: *nun* = 50, *gimel* = 3, *heh* = 5, and *shin* = 300. The object is to accumulate the highest number of points. A time limit or point goal may be set.

Hanukkah Celebration

Since potato latkes (pancakes) are the food most traditionally associated with Hanukkah, a latke party is a favorite form of Hanukkah entertainment. Other foods cooked in oil are also popular, since oil is an important element in the Hanukkah legend.

Invitations

Create invitations using a menorah or dreydl design (see Design Sheet, page 158) stamped on the front (see Card Making, page 284). A potato print would be especially appropriate!

Decorations

Use any of the Hanukkah symbols in abundance: the Hanukkah menorah, dreydl, Magen David, the hammer (sign of Judas Maccabeus), and the elephant (the animal used by Antiochus' Syrian army).

Food

LATKE PARTY

Potato Latkes* with Sour Cream   Applesauce
Doughnuts
Cider

*See below.

TRADITIONAL POTATO LATKES

4 large potatoes	½ tsp. salt
1 small onion	½ tsp. salt
1 egg	2 tbs. flour
1 tsp. baking powder	Oil for frying
1 tbs. matzoh meal	

Peel and coarsely grate the potatoes and onion. Drain well. Add egg and remaining ingredients. Drop from spoon into hot oil, about ¼" deep. Fry until brown on both sides. Serve hot.

Games
Dreydl Games

These, logically, are the evening's informal entertainment. Supply dishes of tokens for guests, and a collection of dreydls. A stuffed dreydl pillow would be a nice prize for the evening's grand winner. Supply tiny dreydl favors for each guest. Card games are also popular and may be played with a special Hanukkah deck, in which the number and face cards have been replaced with Hebrew characters.

DESIGN SHEET

Dreydl, page 154

Invitation, page 157

Godey's Lady's Book, 1866

23
Christmas

Celebrated December 25

Even before the birth of Christ, it was common to celebrate a midwinter feast. Among the Romans, this feast was the Saturnalia, a time when beggars were welcome at the doors of the nobleman's palace and slaves were permitted to share in all the pleasures of the master.

The probable source of the midwinter festivals among the pre-Christian cultures was the worship of the sun. It was believed that in midwinter the God of Life and Light drew closest to the earth before starting once again on his journey around it. It is known that during the days between the seventeenth and twenty-fifth of December, the Scandinavians, the Persians, and the Phoenicians celebrated a festival similar to the Roman Saturnalia.

With the coming of the Christian age, the Star of Bethlehem replaced the sun as the symbol for the source of light that filled the world.

Christmas was first set apart as a religious feast by Pope Telesphorus, who died in the year 138. This was a moveable feast, however, until the fourth century, when Pope Julius I fixed December 25 as the day of Christ's Mass. Since it was believed that Christ was born at midnight, Christmas Eve has always been an important part of the celebration and midnight of that day has always been specially observed, as it is today, in the custom of ringing church bells at that hour. Following more closely the Saturnalia rituals, early Christmas celebrations were boisterous and lively. The custom of singing Christmas carols, still practiced today, was in those days accompanied by dancing and the music of violins, guitars, tambourines, and organs. As time passed, the gayer aspects of the Christmas celebration shifted to New Year's and later Christian observances of Christmas became more solemn.

The practice of gift giving, on the other hand, which had earlier been a feature of New Year's Day festivities, became a part of the modern Christmas holiday. Gift giving as a part of Christmas may also be derived from the gifts brought to the infant Jesus by the three magi, who followed the star to Bethelem.

One important influence on the way Americans celebrate Christmas is the Puritans, who tempered to a considerable extent the pagan gaiety that they felt had contaminated the celebration of the holiday. The Puritans transposed a great deal of the seasonal significance of Christmas to Thanksgiving, which celebrated a good harvest.

The American celebration of Christmas is, of course, also derived from the traditions brought by the many settler who came to America's shores from other lands. From England came the singing of carols, the holly wreath, and the legend of mistletoe, which found its way into the traditional English Christmas from the Druid festivals. In early England, *waits* (bands of itinerant musicians) celebrated Christmas by singing carols and other seasonal music on Christmas Eve. They walked through the streets and stopped from time to time to sing beneath windows.

Mistletoe was hung by the Druids in their temples to provide a winter refuge for the fairies and pixies while they awaited the warmth and sunshine of springtime. This feature of Druid folklore found its way into the English Christmas festivities and was ultimately brought to America. To the Druids, mistletoe was a fertility symbol. Today, mistletoe is hung from the portal at Christmas time and whenever a young boy and girl are under it at the same time, they are obliged to kiss.

Another important feature of the traditional English Christmas to become a part of the American celebration is the use of holly, bay, and laurel in decorating the home for the season. It is thought that holly entered the holiday because the sharp leaves recall the crown of thorns worn by Jesus and the red berries drops of blood He shed. Much further back in time, it was a symbol of rejoicing at pagan festivals.

Although it is generally agreed that the Germans contributed the Christmas tree to the celebration of Christmas, there is a traditional Christmas legend which describes another origin in charming detail. Ansgarius, an early Christian, was sent among the Vikings of the North to preach Christianity. Three messengers were sent along with him—Faith, Hope, and Love—to find and light the first Christmas tree. They sought one that should be as high as Hope and as wide as Love and should have the sign of the Cross on every bough. The balsam fir seemed to meet these requirements and was chosen. To this day, it is the favorite choice for a Christmas tree.

In New York and the surrounding region, where Dutch traditions and customs predominated, social enthusiasm was concentrated on New Year's Day as the midwinter feast. Christmas was celebrated by the Dutch but only as the result of being merged with the celebration of Saint Nicholas Eve, traditionally December 5. Saint Nicholas was a bishop of the early Church who, according to legend, devoted himself to the welfare of children and had secretly enabled three dowryless maidens to marry by dropping into their open windows, on three consecutive nights, a purse of gold. As a result, little Dutch children ever since have petitioned Saint Nicholas to answer their wishes by laying out, on Saint Nicholas Eve, their wooden shoes and knitted stockings for him to fill. They, also, sing a quaint little song:

> Saint Nicholas, my dear, good friend,
> To serve you ever was my end;
> If you me now some thing will give,
> Serve you I will as long as I live.

It is no surprise, therefore, that Dr. Clement C. Moore, author of the beloved poem "T'was the Night Before Christmas" was born and reared in New York where he was surrounded by Dutch traditions.

England's Queen Victoria had a major influence on the way modern England celebrates Christmas by decorating her Christmas tree with lights, sugar ornaments, and gifts. When the idea came to America, Saint Nicholas got into the picture as the gift dispenser. Queen Victoria topped her tree with a doll to be given to a little girl named by her playmates at the school near the Royal residence as "the best girl in school." From this practice, the less frivolous custom of topping the Christmas tree with a star developed. The star represents the Star of Bethlehem.

The Scandinavian influence on the celebration of Christmas can be seen in various Yuletide customs. The English word *Yule* refers to Christmas and the festivities connected therewith. It is related to a Scandinavian word which today means "Christmas time," but originally referred to a pagan midwinter feast lasting twelve days. Scandinavian influence came to England with the Vikings and to America via both English and Scandinavian settlers. *Yule* may also be distantly related to *Nowell* (from the French *noël*, "Christmas carol"). In medieval England, people would shout or sing "Nowell" as an expression of joy to commemorate the birth of Christ. The word was also used as another name for Christmas.

The Yuletide feast is noted by the burning of the Yule Log, which was a carry-over of the earlier custom of celebrating the winter solstice with a bonfire. The fire built with the Yule Log was lit in the fireplace only after sunset on Christmas Eve and burned throughout Christmas day. The charred log that remained was placed under the bed throughout the year to prevent fires and was used to start the fire the next year. The log was soaked in water and kept in the back of the fireplace in order to burn slowly. The Yule candles were lit from the Yule Log and used in other traditional Christmas celebrations.

The traditional Christmas dishes in Old England were plum pudding, boar's head, frumenty or furmity (a dish made of hulled wheat boiled in milk), and stuffed peacock.

The practice of sending Christmas cards developed from the English custom of sending ornately decorated letters to friends offering season's greetings. Children also sent little "pieces" to demonstrate their penmanship. The first printed Christmas card is generally credited to John C. Horsley, who produced it on commission from a gentleman who was too busy to write greetings to his many friends. By 1860, the custom had spread throughout the Empire and to America, where it grew in popularity after the lithograph printing process was introduced in the 1870's.

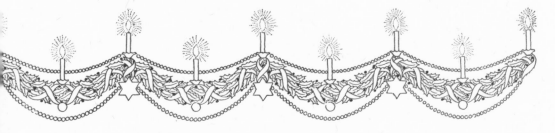

Each grid square is equal to one square inch.

Keepsake

O CHRISTMAS TREE COLOR PLATE 31

This design is from the December, 1920, cover of *The Delineator* and is worked in needlepoint, page 295, in the original colors. Miniature toys and beads are sewn on as tree ornaments. The design can also be worked in plain needlepoint, felt appliqué, or embroidery. Make it into an Anticipation Tree by sewing metal loops to the tree and metal hooks onto the ornaments and hanging one ornament each day from December 1 until December 24.

MATERIALS:

10/20 mesh Penelope canvas, size 15″ × 18″
Persian yarn: medium bright kelly green (tree), dark forest green (background), white, light yellow, medium pink, medium blue, flesh tone, black, brown, bright yellow, orange
18 or so miniature toys, beads, etcetera
green and white sewing thread, needle
11″ × 14″ very stiff cardboard, strong thread, needle

STEP-BY-STEP:

Note: Yarn yardages will be determined by stitches selected. Chain stitch and straight stitch are illustrated in Needlepoint Stitches.

1. Enlarge design to 11″ × 14″
2. Transfer design to needlepoint canvas.
3. Work needlepoint as follows:

children 1 strand basket weave, petit point
  boy's garments blue and white
  little girl's dress yellow
  big girl's dress pink and white
  all shadows blue
candles
  stick 3 strands, white, continental stitch, over 3 strand white filling
  flame 1 strand, white, petit point (irregular circle) surrounded by 1 strand, orange, petit point (equally irregular arc)

  wick 1 strand, black, straight stitch
  base 3 strands, bright golden yellow, continental stitch
star 2 strands bright golden yellow, diamond eyelet stitch
background 3 strands, dark forest green, basket weave stitch
tree 3 strands, bright kelly green, satin stitch
tree container 3 strands, bright kelly green, basket weave stitch
garland 1 strand, white, chain stitch
rays 1 strand, bright golden yellow, straight stitch around star

4. Clean and block as necessary
5. Arrange tree ornaments as desired and sew in place carefully, taking care not to disturb satin stitches.
6. Stretch and frame.

Christmas Greenery

The fragrances of Christmas are essential to full enjoyment of the season. The smell of good things cooking is a year-round pleasure, but the spicy-fresh, special smell of evergreens in the house is unique to Christmas. As *The Delineator* put it in 1920, "However little one intends to 'do for Christmas,' there is no house but the happier for the bringing into it of a little of the Christmas greenery, for with its joyous fragrance comes inevitably something of the blitheness of Christmastide itself." The Christmas tree will be the most important evergreen decoration. Let it be joined by other greenery throughout the house.

Since the generous use of greens sets a festive scene (and the more greens, the better the smell), use whatever fragrant evergreen is most abundant in your area. Plan to prune your evergreens, if you have a yard, around Christmastime and fill your house with the clippings, sending the overflow to less fortunate, apartmentbound friends. Use spruce, pine, yew, cedar, juniper, and boxwood for major indoor decorating. Since hemlock needles fall out rather quickly after having been cut, it is less satisfactory. Save those greens which are hardest to obtain, holly and mistletoe, for accents and special purposes. Other appropriate leaves are ivy, laurel, bay, and rosemary.

Decorate inside and out. Hang wreaths, crosses, stars, triangles, and sprays in windows, on doors, over, under, or around wallhung pictures; festoon garlands over doorways, from chandeliers, along the mantle, flanking the fireplace, wound among the bannisters. Fill brass and copper containers, baskets, buckets with boughs of evergreens. Keep them fresh by sticking the ends into jars of wet sand.

Among all the greens, you'll need some color. White, gold, silver, and red are traditional choices, as well as evergreen cones (natural or gilded), nuts, acorns, and sweet gum balls. A good outdoor activity for a summer or fall hike is to collect these materials in abundance so you'll be ready when wreath-making time comes around.

The pale hues of mistletoe bring out by contrast the deeper and more beautiful tints of cedar, pine, and spruce, A hanging of Southern moss with its grey, beard-like fibre provides similar contrast. A mistletoe spray over a doorway is license to kiss whoever stands beneath it. Tie a spray with bunches of red ribbon, or combine it with a few sprays of evergreen and hang from the hall chandelier or dining room entrance—any well traveled spot! Gold and silver ornaments, and tinsel and paper garlands, are also quite effective with evergreens. See page 169 for ideas.

Holly provides a gay contrast, with its red berries and shiny leaves. A holly sprig is the traditional adornment for a flaming plum pudding. Barberry, bittersweet berries, red roses, carnations, bunches of red bows, and pots of poinsettias may also be used for spots of color among all the green.

The poinsettia is a very popular gift plant. It was introduced to the United States in 1825 by Joel Poinsett, who was serving as ambassador to Mexico. The unusual plant gradually gained wide appeal as a Christmas plant. A tropical plant, it thrives best in bright light, away from drafts. The soil should be kept moist, but not soggy. With proper care, the brightly colored bracts should last for several weeks or even months. Many people discard the plant when the leaves and bracts start to drop but it can be kept growing normally and put outside during the summer months. In extreme southern parts of the United States, it is a common outdoor plant.

To persuade the poinsettia to repeat its annual Christmas show as a houseplant in northern climes, several steps are necessary. Cut the plant back hard in midsummer and repot it in one size larger pot. Bring it indoors in early September. In October, the poinsettia must begin to have absolute darkness for fourteen hours a day, with light for the remaining ten hours of the day. A good schedule is darkness from 5:00 P.M. until 7:00 A.M. This routine is necessary to encourage development of bracts and must continue until early December, when the bracts will start to fill out and develop color. One way to condition the plant is to cover it with a carton the prescribed length of time each day, or shut it away in a closet. But remember, not one ray of light during its period of darkness!

SOME sayes, that ever 'gainst that Season comes
Wherein our Saviour's Birth is celebrated,
The Bird of Dawning singeth all night long:
And then (they say) no Spirit can walke abroad,
The nights are wholesome, then no Planets strike:
No Faiery takes, nor Witch hath power to Charme,
So hallowed, and so gracious is the time.
                                        Shakespeare

Wreaths and Garlands

Wreaths, garlands, and swags can easily be made at home. Items which will hang in windows should be alike on both sides. Mist indoor decorations if they seem to be drying out. Pine, boxwood, and yew are good for inside use, fir for outside use.

Evergreen Wreath (Wire Form), *The Delineator,* 1924

MATERIALS:

    wire wreath form (available in craft shops)
    flexible wire, size 22
    evergreen boughs
    ribbons, cones, berries, or other trimmings as desired

STEP-BY-STEP:

1. Use young evergreen shoots, 4"–6" long for small wreaths, longer for large wreaths. Attach end of wire to frame and wrap around base of boughs.
2. Put 2 or 3 boughs in place at a time in front, and a larger bough in back with tips pointing in same direction. Place branches so that each overlaps the base of the next. (Illustration 23-1)

Illustration 23–1

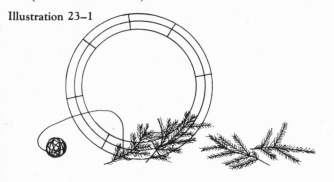

3. Continue wrapping wire around boughs in this manner until wreath is completed.
4. Check that wreath is an even thickness all around, and nice and full.
5. Add a splashy bow of red ribbon or a few cones or holly berries at the top.

Evergreen Wreath (Cardboard Form), *The Delineator,* 1919

MATERIALS:

    corrugated cardboard cut in desired shape
    button and carpet thread, needle
    evergreen boughs
    trimmings as desired

STEP-BY-STEP:

1. Sew boughs to the cardboard, covering densely. Short pieces will be easiest to handle. (Illustration 23-2)

Illustration 23–2

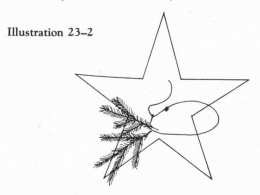

2. Add trimmings as desired. **Note:** During World War I, shield shapes were used, decorated with small American flags. Cardboard-backed wreaths are not suitable for outdoor use.

Cone Wreath (Wire Form)

MATERIALS:

wire wreath form (available in craft shops)
flexible wire, size 22
evergreen cones of various sizes and shapes,
   acorns
trimmings as desired
plastic spray varnish (optional)

STEP-BY-STEP:

1. Wrap 8″ lengths of wire around each cone
   or, using a longer piece of wire, fasten several cones together before wiring to frame.
   Two wire ends extending from each cone
   permit more secure wiring in place. (Illustration 23-3)

Illustration 23–3

2. Arrange cones symmetrically and cover frame
   densely.
3. If desired, spray with plastic varnish and
   trim with ribbon.
4. Wreath may be stored and used year after
   year.
5. Acorn caps must be wired or glued to their
   bases so they will not separate as they dry
   out. **Note:** Another cone wreath is made by
   soaking cones in water until they close up.
   Then push cones through wire frame. As
   cones dry, they open up and fit frame snugly.

Cone and Nut Wreath (Cardboard Form)

MATERIALS:

corrugated cardboard cut in desired shape
cones, nuts, acorns, sweet gum balls
white glue
trimmings as desired
plastic spray varnish (optional)
ribbon for hanger

STEP-BY-STEP:

1. Punch holes in top of shape to insert hanging ribbon when wreath is completed.
2. Glue cones, nuts, acorns, and sweet gum
   balls in place to cover densely. (Illustration
   23-4)

Illustration 23–4

3. When thoroughly dry, spray with plastic
   varnish.
4. Thread ribbon through hanging holes and
   tie in bow.

Garlands, *The Delineator,* 1919

MATERIALS:

heavy string, green if possible
flexible wire, size 22
soft evergreen boughs

STEP-BY-STEP:

1. Attach wire to string.
2. Wire individual boughs in a spiral around
   the string sliding wire between needles to
   conceal (Illustration 23-5). Lap tip of one
   bough over the base of the next to conceal
   ends. Make a full, rich-looking garland, at
   least 4″ in diameter.
3. Yards and yards of garland will be necessary
   for best decorating effect.

Illustration 23–5

4. Gay ribbon bows or rosettes at the points of a draped garland will add a bright touch.

Evergreen Mat, *The Delineator,* 1887
MATERIALS:
>   burlap or coarse cloth, about 24″ × 19″ or desired size
>   button and carpet thread, needle
>   long needled flexible evergreen boughs, such as pine

STEP-BY-STEP:
1. Sew lengths of evergreen to cloth.
2. If desired, work a message such as "Good Will" or "Welcome" into the mat with tinsel, ribbon, or contrasting color evergreens. (Illustration 23-6)

Illustration 23–6

3. Place mat inside the hall or on threshold during Christmas Day.

The Christmas Tree

A brightly ornamented tree is the single most important Christmas decoration in many households. Balsam fir has long been a popular choice for indoor decorating because of its good needle retention if kept in water. Other popular trees are the Douglas fir and Scotch pine. Whatever tree you choose, put it in a container which will keep it secure and steady and will permit the addition of water to keep it moist. Use a holder designed especially for this purpose or a small tub filled with stones.

Decoration of the base of the tree was once almost as important as decoration of the tree itself. First the container was covered with a green matting. Then a tableau was arranged beneath the tree. In 1888, *Peterson's Magazine* suggested a farm or garden arrangement on green matting with a mirror for a lake, a few dolls, woolly sheep or chickens, a fence made of tiny twigs or a wall of pieces of stone, and evergreen scraps as trees. This, the magazine wrote "will furnish to a child an amount of gratification utterly inexplicable to the adult."

Trees were decorated with a wide variety of objects. Anything that provided color, was appropriate in size, and fun was fair game. Toys and gifts were hung on the tree when possible. Paper was fashioned into chains, cornucopias, flowers, and cutout ornaments. Tarlatan (a net-like fabric) was turned into bonbon bags, stockings, and fairy gowns. Apples, oranges, nuts, popcorn, cranberries, and candy were formed into decorations. Blown eggs painted with seasonal motifs made dainty ornaments. Evergreen cones, sweet gum balls, and acorns were gilded and hung in bunches. And, of course, there were the candles.

Before electric tree lights became available, candles were used on the trees, providing sparkle and light—and quite a fire hazard. The magazines of the era cautioned that a member of the family, armed with a bucket of water and a long-handled swab, should be appointed to see that the candles did not set the tree ablaze. Today, of course, there is never any reason to use real candles on a Christmas tree and it is certainly not advisable, even for old times sake. Candles do, however, play an important role in other decorations throughout the house, especially on the Christmas table.

There were two schools of thought regarding the actual decorating of the tree. Some felt that the preparations should be surrounded with great mystery, the tree being trimmed by the older members of the household as a surprise for the young, maintaining the fiction that the gifts and ornaments were brought by unknown visitors. Other families felt, however, that the children's enjoyment of the holiday would be enhanced by participating in the making of the ornaments and decorating of the tree.

The decorations made in the home were generally of paper, fabric, or food. Many were simple to fashion and surprisingly effective on the tree. The generous use of gilt, gold and silver paper, spangles, and tinsels when making ornaments was advised in lieu of colored paper, which lacked brilliance.

Paper Ornaments

Paper ornaments provide many opportunities to recycle used gift wrapping paper, cards, shirt cardboard, ribbons, yarns, trims, tissue paper, etcetera. Saved throughout the year, quite a collection can be accumulated. Experiment with different weight papers and with different width cuts; alter or combine colors instead of sticking with the ones suggested. Plan size of decorations to compliment size and density of tree your prefer. Handled carefully, some of these items can be stored away to become a part of your family's Christmas tradition. Many of the following ornaments may be seen in Color Plates 2 and 18.

Cut Paper Chain, *The Delineator,* 1894
MATERIALS:
  strips of foil gift wrap paper, 2½" wide, any length
  scissors

STEP-BY-STEP:
1. Fold each strip in half lengthwise.
2. Cut alternately from each side of the strip, making cuts about ¼" apart, taking care not to cut through the edges. (Illustration 23-7)

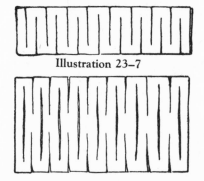

Illustration 23–7

3. Unfold the strip carefully and pull at each end to open and lengthen. (Illustration 23-8)

Illustration 23–8

4. Place this delicate chain on tree immediately or use with evergreen garlands around doorways, windows, etcetera.

Paper Link Chain, *The Delineator,* 1888

MATERIALS:

lightweight paper, brightly colored on one side, deep rich colors

glue

scissors

STEP-BY-STEP:

1. Cut paper strips 4″ long and 1″ wide. Fold colored edges toward center of strip to conceal uncolored side. (Illustration 23-9)

Illustration 23–9

2. Apply glue to one end and slip into other end to form a link.

3. Prepare second band in the same manner and slip it through the first before gluing. (Illustration 23-10)

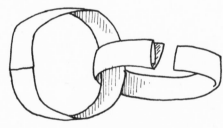

Illustration 23–10

4. Use on tree or with evergreen garlands elsewhere around the house.

Jacob's Ladder Chain, *The Delineator,* 1894

MATERIALS:

2 colors of lightweight paper, brightly colored on both sides. (If paper colored on only one side, such as foil gift wrap, must be used, choose deep colors which contrast sharply to the uncolored side.)

glue

scissors

STEP-BY-STEP:

1. Cut strips 1″ wide and of equal length from each color paper.

2. Lay strips perpendicular to each other and overlap at one end. Glue ends together. (Illustration 23-11)

3. Fold according to illustration until entire length is folded and glue end. (Illustration 23-12)

 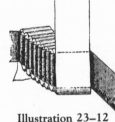

Illustration 23–11   Illustration 23–12

4. Pull ends to open out ladder. (Illustration 23-13)

Illustration 23–13

5. Use on tree, in garlands, or tuck ends of a short chain together for a unique gift wrap ornament. A 3″ wide chain made from 4′ strips can be joined at the ends for a treetop ornament.

Foil Garland, *The Delineator,* 1901

MATERIALS:

3 strips aluminum foil or foil gift wrap, any length, 3″ wide for large tree, 2″ wide for smaller tree

strong string

scissors, stapler

STEP-BY-STEP:

Note: Strips 12″–15″ long will be easiest to work with, especially if foil is used; additional strips may be added until desired length garland is reached.

1. Stack the strips and cut fringe, making cuts about ¼″ apart and 2″ deep along one side. (Illustration 23-14)

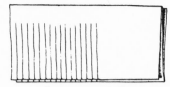

Illustration 23–14

2. If aluminum foil is being used, *very carefully* separate the layers, then restack. Twist the fringe around and around the string forming a rope of silvery fringe, stapling to string at ends. (Illustration 23-15)

Illustration 23–15

3. Aluminum foil will make a puffy rounded garland, while foil gift wrap will produce a feathery effect.

4. Use on tree or elsewhere as a garland.

Holly Garland, *The Delineator,* 1901

MATERIALS:

    4″ squares gold or silver paper
    3″ squares red paper, colored on both sides (each complete section of the garland requires 2 gold or silver and 1 red square)
    glue
    scissors
    yarn or string

STEP-BY-STEP:

1. Fold each metallic square in half then in half again, forming a small square, then diagonally into a triangle. (Illustration 23-16)

Illustration 23–16

2. Trace the holly leaf design (see Design Sheet, page 199) on folded paper as shown and cut according to the lines. Snip off corner (Illustration 23-17). Unfold.

Illustration 23–17

3. Fold red squares in same manner and trace and cut out holly berry design (see Design Sheet, page 199). Unfold berries. (Illustration 23-18)

Illustration 23–18

4. Sandwich berries between 2 leaves and glue together at center only. If two sided paper is being used, be sure shiny side is next to berries.

5. Lay each section on top of the next and glue the tips of the large leaves together at outer points. Repeat until garland is formed. (Illustration 23-19)

Illustration 23–19

6. Thread yarn through holes in center of garland. Open out by gently pulling sections. Leave yarn long enough to allow full extension of garland and tie a loop at one end for hanging. Pull up yarn and garland will lay flat for storage.

7. Use on tree, as a garland around the house or send a short section as a Christmas card.

Paper Flowers, *Peterson's Magazine,* 1888

Crepe-paper flowers look lovely on a Christmas tree and were a popular decoration in the past. To make a crepe-paper flower, refer to the directions on page 64. Instead of a blown egg center, build the flower around several additional petals, tightly rolled.

Cutout Ornaments, *Petersons Magazine,* 1888

MATERIALS:
  shirt cardboard
  foil gift wrap paper
  glue
  scissors

STEP-BY-STEP:

1. Cut hearts, diamonds, crosses, crescents, and other appropriate symbols out of cardboard.

2. Glue hanger in place on each (or punch hole and later thread hanger through hole.)

3. Fold foil paper wrong sides together and cut each shape out of doubled paper. (Illustration 23-20)

Illustration 23–20

4. Glue paper cutouts to each side of appropriate cardboard shapes. **Note:** To vary this idea, texture the ornaments as follows:

Textured Cutout Ornaments

MATERIALS:
  shirt cardboard
  glue
  scissors
  rice, mustard seed, or sand
  gold or silver paint
  yarn, ribbon or string for hangers

STEP-BY-STEP:

1. Cut out shapes as desired (see cutout ornaments).

2. Punch a hole in the top of each.

3. Brush glue on cutouts and cover thickly with rice, seed, or sand. Allow to dry, then repeat on other side. (Illustration 23-21)

Illustration 23–21

4. When thoroughly dry, gild or silver.

5. Thread hanger through hole and tie.

Cutout Snowflakes, *The Delineator,* 1895

MATERIALS:
  foil gift wrap squares of desired size
  sharp scissors
  ribbon, string, or yarn hangers

STEP-BY-STEP:

1. Fold square in half diagonally three times so that all the corners meet. (Illustration 23-22)

Illustration 23–22

2. Trace a snowflake design (see Design Sheet, page 199) onto the folded paper.

3. Cut out with sharp scissors. Unfold. (Illustrations 23-23, 24, 25)

Illustration 23–23

Illustration 23–24

Illustration 23–25

4. Hang on tree or use as a Christmas card.

Medallions, *The Delineator,* 1911
MATERIALS:
    shirt cardboard circles, about 2″ in diameter
    scraps of fringe or ruffle-type trimming to fit around circles
    16″ ribbon, about ¼″ wide, or yarn, for each medallion
    gummed stickers, bright pictures, or photos
    white glue

STEP-BY-STEP:
1. Glue ribbon across right side of cardboard circle, with one end extending about 1½″.

2. Glue trim around circle on same side as ribbon about ½″ from cardboard edge.

3. Cover center of cardboard with sticker, photo, or picture gluing over edge of trim. (Illustration 23-26)

Illustration 23–26

4. Tie medallion to tree bough or use as a Christmas card.

Snowball, *The Delineator,* 1891
MATERIALS:
    20 circles of white tissue paper, about 3½″ diameter
    needle and doubled white thread
    16″ yarn or narrow ribbon hanger

STEP-BY-STEP:
1. Lightly fold each circle twice to determine center. Open flat and pick up the center point of each section and draw it through your hand, crushing it into a roll.

2. Run the needle through the folded center point about ¼″ from the end. (Illustration 23-27)

Illustration 23–27

3. When all sections are strung, push them together as tightly as possible and tie thread to the center of the yarn or ribbon hanger. Tie ribbon into a pretty bow and hang from tree. (Illustration 23-28) **Note:** This design origi-

nated as a "shaving ball gift for papa or uncle." Any size tissue circles can be used; as the circle size increases, however, more are required for a full ball.

Illustration 23-28

Cornucopia

The cornucopia is one of the most traditional tree decorations. It may be made from a variety of papers and fabrics and lends itself to great creativity. The cone may have an open or closed top. If sturdily constructed, the cornucopia can be used as it traditionally was to conceal small lightweight gifts or candy. Cornucopia ornaments may be seen in Color Plate 18.

Cornucopia
MATERIALS:
 7" square mediumweight paper, stiff but flexible
 12" ribbon about ¼" wide
 glue
 scissors
 gummed stickers, paper scraps, adhesive trims, doilies, etcetera for trimming

STEP-BY-STEP:
1. Transfer the cornucopia shape (see Design Sheet, page 200) to paper and cut out.
2. Glue long edges together in a ½" overlap. Trim top edge if necessary to even. (Illustration 23-29)

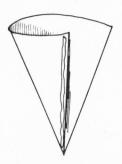

Illustration 23-29

3. Decorate top of cone as desired.
4. Glue ends of ribbon 1" below decorated edge on opposite sides of cone. If cornucopia is destined to be used as a container for a heavy object, staple ribbon hanger in place and glue trimming over staples to conceal. (Illustration 23-30)

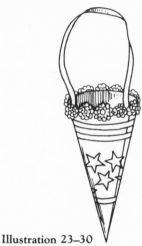

Illustration 23-30

5. Hang on tree or use as package ornamentation.

Paper Top Cornucopia, The Delineator, *1901*
MATERIALS:
 1 cornucopia (see above)
 1 strip tissue paper about 11" long and 3" wide.
 glue
 gummed sticker

STEP-BY-STEP:
1. Glue long edge of tissue paper strip around inside of cone opening, about ½" below edge. (Illustration 23-31)

Illustration 23–31

2. Fill cone using piece of crushed tissue paper down in point and to round off top (or use lightweight item such as scarf or hanky).

3. Fold tissue cover in pleats over top and hold in place with sticker. (Illustration 23-32)

Illustration 23–32

Drawstring Top Cornucopia, Godey's Lady's Book, *1874*
MATERIALS:
    1 cornucopia (see above)
    1 strip lightweight fabric 4″ wide. Length should be same as circumference of cone opening plus ¼″ overlap
    12″ cord, yarn, or ribbon drawstring
    glue
    large-eye needle

STEP-BY-STEP:
1. Fold long edge of fabric over 1″ and stitch ¼″ from fold and again ¼″ from first stitching to form casing. (Illustration 23-33)

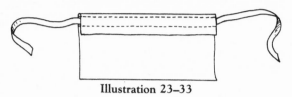

Illustration 23–33

2. Glue unstitched edge around inside of cone opening, about ½″ below edge. (Illustration 23-24)

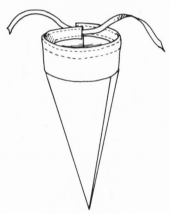

Illustration 23–34

3. Thread drawstring through casing.
4. Fill cornucopia.
5. Draw string up and tie in a bow. (Illustration 23-35)

Illustration 23–35

Fabric Ornaments

Fabric Oranges, *Pastimes for Children,* 1891

Oranges at one time were not as widely and economically available as they are today and at Christmastime they were highly prized as small gifts. They were also popular tree ornaments, the bright color standing out well against the dark green tree foliage. An 1891 article offered the following design, which turns oranges into surprise gift containers.

MATERIALS:

    orange fabric, about 15″ × 6″ (lightweight felt, flannel, etcetera)
    stuffing (fiberfill or tissue paper)
    orange thread and needle
    small gift

STEP-BY-STEP:

1. Cut 5 sections of fabric according to the pattern (see Design Sheet, page 200).

2. Join consecutive sections by placing right sides together and stitching with a ¼″ seam allowance. Leave last seam open. Trim.

3. Stuff to orange shape and insert tiny gift inside. Slipstitch remaining seam.

4. With green yarn, embroider a star on the top of the orange and leave a long loop for hanging. (Illustration 23-36)

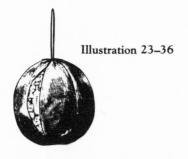

Illustration 23–36

Crochet Snowflake

Crocheted Snowflake, *Peterson's Magazine,* 1891
COLOR PLATE 18
MATERIALS:

    1 skein crochet cotton
    #8 crochet hook

STEP-BY-STEP:
Center
Chain 4. Sl st to join. Chain 5.
Rnd 1: 11 trc in circle. Sl st to join (12 stitches). Chain 8.
Rnd 2: *Trc in next stitch, chain 3.* Repeat 10 more times (12 stitches).
Point 1
Row 1: Chain 18. Turn. *Skip 5 stitches on chain and trc in sixth stitch. Chain 2.* Repeat twice. Make 11 trc over chain (treble chain). Join to Round 2 in second trc.
Note: This makes half of the point. The point is finished in the next step.
Point 2
Row 1: Chain 6. Turn. Count 6 stitches on treble chain and trc in that stitch. *Chain 2, skip a trc on treble chain and trc in next stitch.* Repeat twice. Chain 5. Turn.
Row 2: *Trc in trc stitch in Row 1.* Repeat twice. 11 trc over chain (treble chain). Join to Round 2 in third trc.
Continue until points 2 through 12 are complete. Finally, to finish Point 1, follow instructions below:
Point 1
Row 2: Chain 6. Turn. Skip 5 stitches on treble chain and trc is sixth stitch. *Chain 2, skip one stitch in treble chain and treble in next stitch.* Repeat twice. Join to Row 1 at point.
For hanging loop, chain 28 and join in same stitch.

Bonbon Bag, *The Delineator,* 1891
MATERIALS:

    15″ diameter circle fine or stiff fabric, such as taffeta, with pinked edges
    3″ diameter circle shirt cardboard
    4 ft. string, fine yarn, or gold cord
    zigzag sewing machine, thread

STEP-BY-STEP:

1. Center cardboard circle on wrong side of fabric circle. Stitch the two together with long straight machine stitches about ⅜″ from cardboard edge.

2. With widest zigzag stitch, stitch over string around edge of fabric on right side, about 1½" from edge. Do not stitch through string at any point.

3. Draw up slightly and fill bag with candy. Tie string in double bow.

4. Vary circle sizes for different size bags as desired. The tiny bags in Color Plate 2 have 2½" cardboard circles and 12" fabric circles; the large bag in Color Plate 24 has a 6" cardboard circle and a 30" fabric circle. **Note:** May be trimmed with lace or ribbon as desired.

Food Ornaments

Decorations of food are charming and, in some cases, remain edible. Wrapped candies, bunches of nuts, and wrapped cookies can be removed from the tree as a treat for small visitors. Gilded food, however, may not be eaten because of possible paint contamination. Strung food may become sticky or stale and lose its taste appeal. And besides, once the decorations are eaten, what is left to adorn the tree?

Hanging Fruit, *The Delineator,* 1915
Tie ribbons around apples and oranges or around the stems, make a pretty bow and hang.

Popcorn, *The Delineator,* 1915
String stale popcorn on strong thread, or make popcorn balls (see page 119), pressing a ribbon hanger into each as it is formed.

Cranberries, *The Delineator,* 1915
String long cranberry garlands with knots of red satin ribbon tied here and there on the strands. Or string three or four cranberries on black thread and tie closely to ends of the branches (Illustration 23-37). The berries, being light, do not cause the branches to bend and give the appearance of fruit growing on the tree.

Peanuts, *The Delineator,* 1901

• Press one end open and insert a knotted yarn or string into the opening. Release the peanut and the shell will close over the knot (Illustration 23-38). Gild or silver it with spray paint as desired.

Illustration 23–38

• Twist pieces of fringed tissue paper around individual peanuts (Illustration 23-39) and tie three or four to a piece of yarn and hang from the branches (Illustration 23-40). Give as impromptu gifts to young guests. Peanut garlands may be seen in Color Plates 2 and 18.

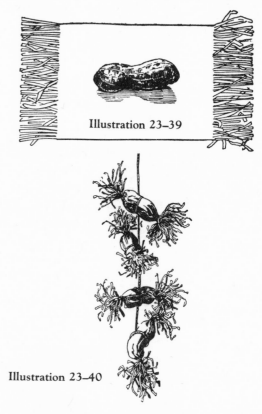

Illustration 23–39

Illustration 23–37

Illustration 23–40

Walnuts and Chestnuts

Tie string or yarn to a carpet tack and hammer into one end of a nut (Illustration 23-41). Gild or silver it and hang it on the tree. Or gild or silver it first, then apply the tack to the nut through narrow ribbon, which is used as hanger.

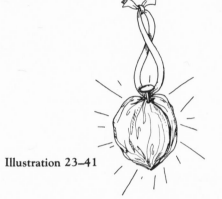

Illustration 23–41

Raisins and Nuts, *The Delineator,* 1901

String raisins and nuts into a garland, alternating varieties for an interesting design. (Illustration 23-42)

Illustration 23–42

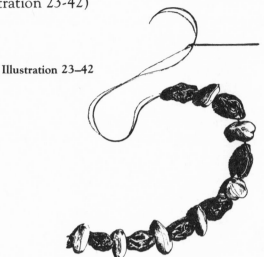

Christmas Stocking

Filling the stockings, which have long been hung with great care on Christmas Eve, is great fun. It is not necessary to have expensive or elaborate gifts, just so they look knobby and mysterious. An orange in the toe is an old tradition from those days when oranges were hard to obtain.

Of course, any old sock can serve as a Christmas stocking, but it is much nicer to create a special stocking for a young child and let it become a part of the family's yearly Christmas tradition. Many seasonal designs in this chapter can be worked into charming stockings in embroidery, needlepoint, or felt appliqué, using the basic pattern shape given for the Flannel Stocking, which dates from 1905. Several stocking designs follow. The own-

er's name can be embroidered (see cross-stitch alphabet, page 219) or appliquéd to the top of the stocking or the design can be so unique as to provide identification by association.

Flannel Stocking, *The Delineator,* 1905
MATERIALS:

    red flannel, about ½ yd.
    white flannel scraps, at least 8″ × 7″
    16″ red ribbon, about ¾″ wide
    red embroidery floss, embroidery needle
    red thread and needle or sewing machine
    8 golden jingle bells
    embroidery floss or appliqué scraps (optional)

STEP-BY-STEP:
1. Enlarge stocking pattern (see Design Sheet, page 201) to desired size; a good size is 17″

long by 6½″ at the top. Add ½″ all around for seam allowance. Make a paper pattern of stocking, heel piece, and pointed flap.

2. Fold red fabric right sides together and cut out stocking piece, observing grainline. Cut heel and flap pieces out of doubled white fabric.

3. Place right side of flap next to wrong side of stocking and stitch top edges together (Illustration 23-43). Trim seam, turn, and press. Embroider name on flap at this point if desired.

Illustration 23–43

4. On right side of stocking, feather stitch (see page 289) heel and flap edges in place about ¼″ from edges. (Illustration 23-44)

Illustration 23–44

5. Place stocking pieces right sides together and stitch all around in a ½″ seam (Illustration 23-45). Do not stitch across top. Trim and clip (trim seam allowances close at top). Turn and press.

6. Place ends of ribbon inside top edge of stocking about 1″, concealing seam allowances. Handstitch securely in place. (Illustration 23-46)

7. Tack bells in place at points of flap, heel, and toe. (Illustration 23-47)

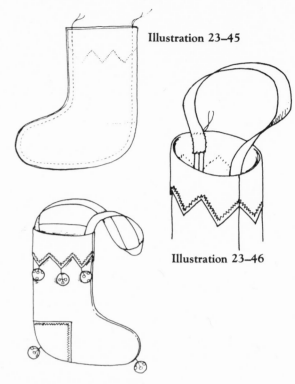

Illustration 23–45

Illustration 23–46

Illustration 23–47

Calico Stocking

MATERIALS:
  red calico fabric, about ½ yd.
  green calico fabric scraps, at least 8″ × 4″
  16″ red ribbon, about ¾″ wide
  white thread and needle or sewing machine
  zigzag sewing machine or white embroidery floss, needle

STEP-BY-STEP:
1. Prepare stocking pattern and cut out stocking, heel, and pointed flap as described for Flannel Stocking, above.

2. Place right side of flap next to wrong side of stocking and stitch top edges together. Trim seam, turn, and press.

3. Use zigzag satin stitch embroidery or hand satin stitch (see page 289) to put name on flap, if desired.

4. Satin stitch pointed edges of flap and top and sides of heel piece to stocking.

5. Place stocking pieces right sides together and stitch all around in a ½″ seam. Do not

stitch across top. Trim seams (trim seam allowance close at top) clip curves, turn and press.

6. Place ends of ribbon inside top edge of stocking about 1", concealing seam allowances. Machine satin stitch ribbon securely in place. (Illustration 23-48)

Illustration 23-48

Christmas Cards

Although the Christmas card played a vital role in spreading the tradition of greeting cards to other celebrations, Christmas remains the most important holiday for the sending of cards, and cards remain one of the very important aspects of a Christmas celebration. Although some people eschew Christmas cards as a commercial exploitation of a religious festival, there are many others who value this regular means of keeping in touch with faraway friends and of expressing their sincere good wishes to others closer to home.

Christmas cards cover a wide range of subjects in an equally wide variety of artistic interpretations. Many people feel that religious themes are most appropriate for this religious holiday—angels, madonnas, manger scenes, wise men, etcetera. Others prefer folk themes involving the secular symbols of a joyous season—Santa Claus, Christmas trees and greenery, bells, candles, and stars. Still others send cards with seemingly no relation to Christmas at all—ships, globes, snowy farm scenes.

As has been repeatedly pointed out with other projects in this book, the Christmas card is more meaningful to both the sender and the receiver if it is in some way a *personal* expression. At the very least, the card should be carefully chosen and personally signed, with, perhaps, a brief personal message from the sender. At its very best, the card is hand crafted and contains, in addition to the actual message, an implied message: "I care enough about you and our friendship to have put something extra of myself into this expression of goodwill."

The thought of hand crafting greeting cards should not intimidate the novice or the artistically less skilled. There are many methods of creating cards which compensate handsomely for lack of ability to draw or paint. Some simple printing methods require only a steady hand. Other techniques rely simply on the exercise or good taste and selective judgment, or a skill in some other area: needlepoint, perhaps, or wood cutting or calligraphy. It has never been possible for ordinarily talented people to duplicate at home the brightly colored lithographed cards which quickly became popular during the 1870's. In fact, even those who could draw and paint wouldn't possibly have had the time to create elaborate designs for each person on their list. So the craftsman quickly developed alternate means for creating cards.

Christmas Card Designs

It is the cards in the "non-art" categories which will be presented in this section. Gift tags may be adapted from this material also. Details on actual card making are treated in a separate section (see page 284) which should be read before card making begins. Many of the cards described below may be seen in Color Plate 28.

The following designs have been chosen for

their suitability to several methods of reproduction. For each design, appropriate methods will be listed, all of which are described in Card Making, page 284, or elsewhere in this book. In certain cases, when the crafting of the card is unique to that particular design, it will be discussed with the design.

Christmas Ornaments as Cards

The first group of card ideas have appeared as tree ornaments elsewhere in this chapter. There is a trend toward creating cards which "don't just sit there" and these ornament designs adapt handsomely to cards. Likewise, several ideas which are presented here as card ideas can be produced as ornaments.

Holly Garland (see page 171)

Write greetings on a stiff card and enclose in an envelope with a folded holly garland and instructions for its use.

Cutout Ornaments (see page 172)

Tie an ornament through a hole punched in a contrasting color card on which a greeting has been written.

Textured Cutout Ornaments (see page 172)

Follow the same procedure as for cutout ornaments. Test mail one to yourself to determine if the rigors of mailing will shake off the textured covering.

Snowflakes (see page 172)

Attach a snowflake through a hole punched in the card, if use as an ornament is intended. Otherwise, rubber cement the snowflake in place on a contrasting color card and add a message.

Medallions (see page 173)

Made with flat trimmings, arranged around a child's photo, these are a lovely way to record a child's growth if sent yearly, especially to grandparents.

Crocheted Snowflake (see page 176)

Attach to a contrasting color card with double-stick transparent tape; write a greeting on the card.

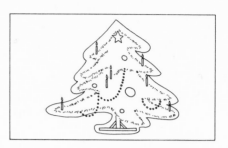

Felt Christmas Tree, *Needle-Art,* 1921
COLOR PLATE 28

This design, originally an iron-on transfer, is interpreted in torn felt appliqué. The design is also suitable for interpretation in paper collage, felt-tip marker drawing, or machine zigzag embroidery. The felt or embroidered versions can be used as tree ornaments.

MATERIALS:
    scraps of green felt (various dark shades)
    4″ × 6″ scrap felt for backing
    bugle beads and rocaille beads to decorate tree
    embroidery floss and needle
    metal ruler, double-stick transparent tape
    sewing machine and green thread
    6″ red yarn for hanger (optional)
    Note: Size fits into standard 3⅞″ × 5¹³/₁₆″ correspondence card.

STEP-BY-STEP:
1. Trace large tree outline (Design Sheet, page 201) and cut out of 4″ × 6″ felt.
2. Tear green felt scraps into small pieces by tearing sharply against metal edge. Beginning at bottom, arrange pieces with fuzzy sides toward base of tree, slightly overlapping on one side. Stitch in place across top of pieces.
3. Repeat in irregular rows to top. Very last piece should have a fuzzy torn edge all around.
4. Apply beads and embroider trunk and stand as desired.
5. Attach to correspondence card with double-stick tape.
6. Inscribe desired message on card.
    Note: To use as a tree ornament, sew optional 6″ yarn hanger in place with last tree piece at top of tree.

Felt Duck, *Needle-Art,* 1924
COLOR PLATE 28

The stuffed felt appliqué duck makes a charming seasonal card for a child and can be used as a tree ornament. The design may also be interpreted in fabric or paper collage or felt-tip marker drawing.

MATERIALS:
2 pieces yellow felt, each 4″ × 6″
scraps of white felt
scraps of fake fur, cotton, or angora yarn, white
4″ × 6″ piece polyester fleece
black and orange embroidery floss
6″ piece yellow yarn for hanger (optional)
white glue, double-stick transparent tape
fine felt-tip marker
sewing machine, yellow thread
Note: Size fits onto standard 3⅞″ × 5¹³/₁₆″ correspondence card.

STEP-BY-STEP:
1. Cut two outlines of design (see Design Sheet, page 202) from yellow felt pieces, including muff, beak, head, and boots. Cut out white hat and boots. Cut polyester fleece in shape of duck body and head, about ¼″ smaller all around.
2. Transfer hat, eye, beak, wing, and leg markings to right side of one yellow felt piece.
3. Stitch hat and boot pieces to appropriate markings.
4. Sandwich fleece between two yellow felt pieces placing piece with hat and boot appliqué on top and edgestitch together all

around with yellow thread. Position yarn hanger in sandwich.
5. Embroider beak in orange satin stitch, eye in black French knot, wing and leg indications in black stem stitch.
6. Apply furry areas: hat, muff, muffler, boot trim. Fake fur or cotton bits may be glued in position; angora yarn must be stitched.
7. Attach to correspondence card with double-stick tape.
8. Inscribe message as desired.

Snowflake, *Peterson's Magazine,* 1879
COLOR PLATE 28

This design for an antimacassar, originally worked on netting, has been adapted to embroidery on perforated paper. The design may also be worked in needlepoint or cross-stitch embroidery.

MATERIALS:
4″ square piece perforated paper
3″ square felt for backing
crewel yarns: red, dark green, medium green
needle and thread
plain card and envelope to fit
fine felt-tip marker

STEP-BY-STEP:
1. Work design using single-ply yarn throughout.
2. For ornament, use bookmark technique for backing; for card, mount using frame method (see page 286).

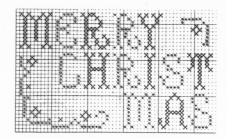

"Merry Christmas," *Needle-Art, 1924*

In the style of Victorian mottoes, embroider a Christmas message on perforated paper. See design provided (Design Sheet, page 202) or use cross-stitch alphabet, page 219, to compose alternate messages. The design may be adapted to needlepoint if desired.

MATERIALS:

    8″ × 4″ perforated paper

    red and green yarn or embroidery floss, as desired

    felt or ribbon backing, as desired

    plain card and envelope to fit

    fine felt-tip marker

STEP-BY-STEP:

1. Use single-ply embroidery if yarn, 3-ply if floss.
2. For ornament, use bookmark-backing method; for card, mount using frame method (see page 286).
3. Add your own holly or bell motifs, graphed from page decorations in this book.

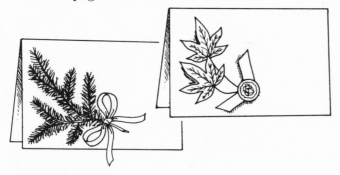

Evergreen, *The Delineator, 1923*
COLOR PLATE 28

This is a quick card anyone can make in the collage technique described below or by direct printing of the evergreen combined with collage.

MATERIALS:

    evergreen twig or ivy leaves

    hole punch and ¼″ wide red ribbon, or

    sealing wax (red), signet, and ½″ wide red ribbon, scrap

    white correspondence card or folded note and envelope to fit

    fine felt-tip marker

STEP-BY-STEP:

1. Arrange evergreen or ivy on front of card as desired.
2. Attach with sealing wax and a bit of red ribbon, or
3. Punch two holes and tie bough in place with ribbon, making a small flat bow on top.
4. Inscribe message as desired.

The Three Kings, *The Delineator, 1910*
COLOR PLATE 28

Silhouette was a popular technique for card making, either photographic or cut paper silhouette. *The Delineator* ran a short series, including this design, of simple designs printed on slightly heavier paper than the remainder of the magazine for children to cut right out of the magazine and paste together to make an actual card or tableau. The design may also be stenciled.

MATERIALS:

    dark paper

    contrasting color plain card or folded note and envelope to fit

    rubber cement

    tracing paper, sharp scissors

STEP-BY-STEP:

1. Trace design (Design Sheet, page 202) on tracing paper and transfer to dark color paper.

COLOR PLATE 17/Christmas
The Delineator, December, 1921

COLOR PLATE 18/Christmas
Christmas Tree Ornaments: Cut Paper Chain, page 169; Jacob's Ladder Chain and
Foil Garland, page 170; Cutout Snowflakes and Cutout Ornaments, page 172;
Snowballs and Medallions, page 173; Cornucopias, pages 174-175; Crocheted
Snowflake, page 176; Peanuts, page 177.

COLOR PLATE 19/Gifts
Needle-Art, Winter, 1922-1923

COLOR PLATE 20/Wedding and Anniversary
The Designer, June, 1915

COLOR PLATE 21/Birthday
Butterick Quarterly, Winter 1919-1920

Color Plate 22/Gifts
Back: Patchwork Pillow, page 237; Lace Mat, page 234; Travel Pillow, page 270.
Middle: The Apron for Everybody, page 263; Soft Photograph Case, page 236; Cord Box, page 266; Telephone Book Cover, page 241; Travel Shoe Bag, page 270.
Front: Business Card Cases, page 240; Jewelry and Make-Up Travel Cases, page 269.

COLOR PLATE 23/Gifts
Back: Embroidered Photograph Frame, page 233; Needlework Yarn Carrier, page 266; Flower Pincushion, page 229; Scissors Case, page 268.
Middle: Padded Fabric-Covered Box, page 294; Drawer Sachet, page 226, Padded Hanger Sachet, page 226; Lingerie Sachet, page 225; Sea Shell Pincushion, page 229.
Front: Round Pincushion, page 228; Napkin Ring, page 262; Folded Sachet, page 225.
Background: Embroidered Throw, page 239.

COLOR PLATE 24/Gifts
Back: Knitted Pussycat, page 255; Knitted Dog, page 256.
Middle: Elephant Toy, page 258; Ring Toss, page 260.
Front: Indoor Croquet Game, page 259; Knitted Ball, page 257.

2. Carefully cut out design.

3. Glue design to front of card.

4. Inscribe message as desired.

Note: Con-Tact® may also be used for silhouettes.

Christmas Tree, *The Delineator,* 1917

This design can be quickly interpreted in paper collage and if pieces are cut out several at one time, a quantity of cards can be easily assembled. Consider using gummed stars and seals for ornaments. Another method is to stencil the tree and the pot and decorate with paper collage.

MATERIALS:
    dark green paper for tree
    metallic paper scraps for star and ball and
        flame
    white paper for pot and candle
    red paper scraps for pot decoration
    brown paper scrap for tree trunk
    scissors, rubber cement, fine felt-tip markers
    plain card or folded note and envelope to fit

STEP-BY-STEP:

1. Trace (Design Sheet, page 203) and cut out pieces.

2. Glue tree, tree trunk, and pot in position.

3. Decorate tree and pot.

4. Inscribe message as desired.

"And Away They all Flew," *The Delineator,* 1911

Another design from *The Delineator* card se-

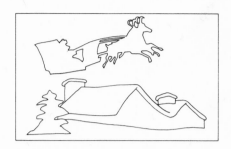

ries for children, this one can be interpreted in cut paper silhouette, as described below, or in stencil or block print, or the design may be traced and colored with felt markers.

MATERIALS:
    dark papers—green for tree, brown or red for
        house, blue or black for Santa and his rein-
        deer
    sharp scissors, rubber cement
    tracing paper
    plain card or note and envelope to fit
    fine felt-tip marker

STEP-BY-STEP:

1. Trace designs (Design Sheet, page 203) on tracing paper and transfer to appropriate colored papers.

2. Carefully cut out design.

3. Glue design to front of card.

4. Inscribe message as desired.

Deco Wreath, *The Delineator,* 1929

This wreath appeared as part of a *Delineator* Christmas greeting to its subscribers. It reflects the Art Deco style popular at the time. Interpret the design in art gum eraser stamping or paper collage.

MATERIALS:
    3 art gum erasers

artist's knife
card or folded note and envelope to fit
foam stamp pad
fine felt-tip marker

STEP-BY-STEP:
1. Cut one stamp in each of the design elements on the Design Sheet, page 203.
2. Lightly draw circle of wreath on card to serve as a stamping guide.
3. Stamp elements following illustration.
4. Add dots with felt markers.
5. Inscribe message as desired.

Abstract Tree, *The Delineator,* 1926

Part of a Christmas story illustration, interpret this abstract tree in block print or cut paper collage. To make a novel ornament, cut 2 trees out of paper colored on each side and sew or staple the two together down the center. Fold the trees apart down the center and the ornament will stand. Add a ribbon or cord hanger to use on the tree.

MATERIALS:
linoleum block printing equipment
appropriate card and envelope to fit
fine felt-tip marker

STEP-BY-STEP:
1. Transfer design (Design Sheet, page 204) to the block.
2. Cut and print design.
3. Inscribe message as desired.

Linear Tree, *Needle-Art,* 1924
COLOR PLATE 28

Use block printing to produce this design in quantity or trace over the design using fine felt-tip markers and rice paper.

MATERIALS:
linoleum block printing equipment
appropriate card and envelope to fit
fine felt-tip markers

STEP-BY-STEP:
1. Transfer design (Design Sheet, page 204) to the block.
2. Cut and print design.
3. Add details with felt-tip markers.
4. Inscribe design as desired.

Star of Beauty, *The Delineator,* 1927
COLOR PLATE 28

Choose dramatic colors for this simple design which was originally a page embellishment in *The Delineator.* The design is suitable for silk screen printing, block printing, or cut paper collage.

MATERIALS:

silk screen equipment
appropriate card and envelope to fit
fine felt-tip marker

STEP-BY-STEP:

1. Transfer design (Design Sheet, page 204) to the screen.
2. Prepare screen and print design.
3. Inscribe message as desired.

Card Messages

Card message should be personal or in some way related to the design of the card. Choose lines from poems, songs, Christmas carols, the Bible, etcetera. Two very nice messages found among the pages of *The Delineator* follow:

> With holly dress the festive hall,
> Prepare the song, the feast, the ball,
> To welcome Merry Christmas.
>
> *The Delineator,* 1903

> There is a wish we have you this Christmas tide.
> May Joy and all glad things the Season brings get to you and abide.
>
> *The Delineator,* 1927

Family Christmas Celebration

Thanksgiving is America's major feast day, its bounty paying tribute to the spirit of the day, which is thankfulness for the abundance of the harvest. Christmas, on the other hand, is a time of rejoicing and feasting for the simple joy of eating and enjoying rich foods. And these rich foods seem to be even more enjoyable, if that is possible, when they are eaten in surroundings as opulent and special as the foods themselves. Table decorations, therefore, are an important part of Christmas finery for the home, and they need not be confined to the eating or service table. Indeed, any unused nook or cranny can be dressed in the spirit of the season.

Decorations
Holly Cone, The Delineator, 1891

Make this sophisticated decoration for a special dinner table. Select a round decorative basket, or a crystal or silver bowl, as the base. Use green poster board to shape a cone which will sit securely atop the base. Sew holly leaves and berries to the cone with green thread and a strong needle, arranging the holly densely, with tips directed more or less toward the base. Heap the bowl full of candy, tiny toys, and favors and cover with the holly cone. At the end of the meal, lift the cone to reveal its lovely surprise (Illustration 23-49). Although live holly is beautiful for this decoration, the project is time consuming and you may prefer to use good quality artificial holly so that the decoration can be used for several years. With artificial holly, sew with green button and carpet thread.

Illustration 23—49

Manger Scene

Fashion a manger scene out of corn husk dolls (see page 137). Dress them in Biblical fashion, using costume history books for ideas. Make a stable of cardboard and twigs and strew about a bit of hay. (Illustration 23-50)

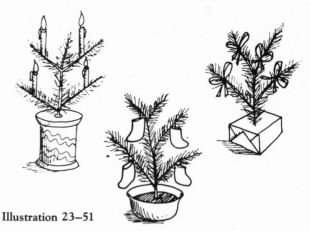

Illustration 23–51

Illustration 23–50

Mini Trees

There are many delightful ways to decorate small trees or evergreen twigs and branches for use on the table and throughout the house. Small potted evergreen trees (which may later be planted out-of-doors) are suitable for many of these ideas, especially if lights are used carefully or not at all. Or several shapely evergreen branches can be wired together and placed in a flower frog in a vase or a pot of wet sand.

• Decorate a small artificial tree with red birthday candles and gold and scarlet cornucopias (see page 174) filled with sweets. Set the tree on a lace doily. Glue or wire the candles in place (*The Delineator*, 1915).
• Arrange small white and amber lights on a tree and decorate with cellophane wrapped candies and tiny red cellophane stockings (*The Delineator*, 1933).
• Stick a bit of fir into a small box or wooden spool and decorate with tiny red-tied white boxes, red bows, or red candles (Illustration 23-51). Paint the spool red (*The Delineator*, 1916).
• Swish an artificial tree or evergreen twig in thick condensed starch. Shake off the excess starch, then shake on powdered soap, followed by gold or silver glitter. Allow to

dry, then glue on tiny red or white candles (Illustration 23-52). A decorated wooden spool makes a good stand for a well-balanced twig. Golden spools may be used for smaller twigs and are especially lovely when the tree is dusted with gold glitter. Label with a ribbon banner and use for a place card (*The Delineator*, 1924).

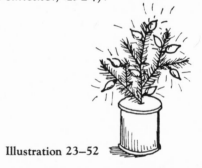

Illustration 23–52

• Spray a shapely, leafless tree branch or entire small tree with white paint. Sprinkle with gold glitter while damp and decorate as usual, emphasizing tinsel and glass (*The Delineator*, 1915).
• A gracious and beautiful tinsel tree was suggested in 1911 for the breakfast table. Drape a mini tree in gold and silver tinsel, with a small gift on it for each family member. Metallic gifts (scissors, thimble, ring, etcetera) would look especially lovely with the tinsel decorations. On one side of the tree, place a fancy green basket filled with highly polished red apples and decorated with a sprig of mistletoe. On the other side, fill a red basket with white grapes and decorate with holly (*The Delineator*, 1911).

Food

Families, as well as religious and ethnic groups, have their own food traditions for Christmas Eve and Christmas Day breakfast and dinner. And without those certain dishes to trigger sweet memories, Christmas, for many, just wouldn't be Christmas.

In households with children, Christmas Day usually begins rather early and a hearty breakfast will be appreciated by all (except perhaps children in those families where tradition insists that breakfast must precede gift opening!)

CHRISTMAS BREAKFAST

Grapefruit
Hot Cereal with Cream
Omelet   Sausage
Fruited Christmas Crescent*
Coffee

*See below.

FRUITED CHRISTMAS CRESCENT

The Delineator, 1935

2 pkg. dry yeast	or
1 cup lukewarm milk, scalded	1 tsp. dry lemon rind
	1 cup raisins
½ cup sugar	½ cup currants
4 cups flour	½ cup walnuts, chopped
½ cup melted shortening (lukewarm)	½ cup mixed citron, orange, and lemon peel
2 eggs (room temperature)	or
½ tsp. salt	1 tsp. dry orange rind and
⅛ tsp. nutmeg	1 tsp. dry lemon rind
Grated rind from 1 lemon	1 egg, beaten

In large mixing bowl stir yeast with 1 cup flour, sugar, and lukewarm milk. Let the sponge sit until light, 10–15 minutes. Stir in shortening, eggs, 2½ cups flour, lemon rind, salt, and nutmeg. (Use more flour if needed so mixture is easy to handle.) Beat well and knead until light, 8 to 10 minutes. Add ½ cup flour to fruits and walnuts and stir until well

coated with flour. Divide dough, placing ⅓ in lightly greased medium-size bowl to rise. To other ⅔, add flour-coated fruit mixture and mix well. Place this dough in a large, lightly greased bowl. Cover doughs and let rise 1½ to 2 hours. Punch down doughs. Roll out plain dough into a thin sheet. Shape fruit dough into a crescent and place on plain dough as shown. Fold plain dough around the crescent (Illustration 23-53). Pinch seam together. Place on a lightly oiled cookie sheet and cover with lightly greased plastic wrap. Let rise in refrigerator overnight or set out at room temperature 1½ to 2 hours. Bake at 325° for 1 hour. Brush with beaten egg for last 10 minutes of baking. Dust with confectioner's sugar before serving. Can be baked ahead and reheated for serving.

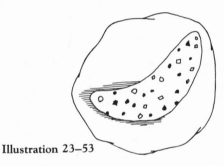

Illustration 23–53

Although for many people, a Christmas turkey is as essential as a Thanksgiving turkey, other main courses are equally appropriate on this day. Since many of America's other Christmas customs are of English origin, why not try a traditional English Christmas dinner from 1912 as a delicious alternative?

ROAST BEEF CHRISTMAS DINNER

Grapefruit and Oyster Cocktail
Celery   Olives   Pickles
Cream of Celery Soup
Roast Beef with Yorkshire Pudding
Creamed Onions   Sweet Potatoes
Browned Irish Potatoes
Pineapple Salad
Plum Pudding* with Brandy Sauce Cranberry Tart**
Raisins   Nuts   Sweetmeats
Coffee

*See below.
**See recipe, page 143.

PLUM PUDDING
The Delineator, 1886

¾ cup dry bread crumbs	1 tbs. cinnamon
¾ cup raisins	1 tsp. cloves
6 eggs, separated	⅓ cup chopped apple
¼ cup chopped suet	2 tbs. flour
⅓ cup sugar	½ cup milk

Butter a 1 quart tin or mold. Beat the egg yolks and whites separately. Add sugar to yolks and beat well. Add suet and spices, then apple and bread crumbs. Fold flour into raisins and add to mixture above, alternately with milk. Fold in egg whites. Steam 3 hours in mold, covered tightly with greased foil. Tie foil on so steam does not condense onto pudding. Place on a metal rack in a large saucepan with 2″ of water or so water comes only half way up the mold. Serves 6. (To prepare pudding up to 1 month ahead, steam as directed above, cover and refrigerate. To serve, resteam covered as above for 1½ hours.) Turn out on a plate to serve. Pour 151 proof rum (about ¼ cup) around the pudding and ignite. Allow to burn about one minute before serving. Garnish pudding top with holly sprig. Serve with hard sauce. *The Delineator* called this a nice light pudding and indeed it is. If pudding is given as a gift, be sure to enclose directions for covering and steaming for serving.

Another English Christmas food tradition which has been adopted by many Americans is a roast goose dinner.

CHRISTMAS GOOSE DINNER

Cape Cod Cocktail[1]
Celery   Olives
Roast Goose, Apple and Celery Stuffing*,
Giblet Gravy[2]
Creamy Mashed Potatoes   Baked Squash
Buttered Brussels Sprouts
Pimiento and Green Pepper Salad
French Dressing
Crisp Wafers
Plum Pudding*, Hard Sauce
Mixed Nuts   Raisins   Candies
Fruits
Coffee

*See below.   [2]See recipe, page 142.
[1]See recipe, page 143.

APPLE AND CELERY STUFFING
The Delineator, 1928

1 tbs. minced onion	1 cup minced apple
2 tbs. butter	1 cup soft bread crumbs
1 cup minced celery	salt, pepper

Saute onion in butter. Add celery and apple and cook 5 minutes. Add bread crumbs, salt and pepper.

Christmas Food Gifts

An important part of Christmas feasting has always been the sharing of the bounty with friends, family, and the poor. In early Christmas tradition, even the most humble visitors were made welcome at high houses and generously fed.

Although any food prepared in the cook's own kitchen, and perhaps with its ultimate source in the cook's own garden, is a thoughtful gift, the foods traditional to the holiday are especially appropriate. Since the decorative and festive features of the Christmas menu are largely borne by the desserts and confections prepared for the occasion, any hostess is sure to appreciate food gifts which she can add to her own Christmas table.

Summer is the time to start thinking about Christmas gift foods. Jams, jellies, conserves, pickles, relishes, and sauces can be canned beyond the family's need with an eye toward gift packages, Homemade herb vinegars and jars or bunches of dried herbs will delight the gourmet cooks on your list, as will small pots of growing herbs, started well enough in advance to be lush and healthy. A dried pressed-flower arrangement or potpourri is a delightful (and very old-fashioned) garden gift which is always well received.

Many gifts of holiday foods can be prepared along with the family's own supply. Some of these items—mincemeat, plum pudding, fruit cake—should be made well in advance of the holiday so that the last minute rush is avoided. Other favorites to prepare in quantity for gift giving are cranberry sauces and marmalades, pumpkin chips, candies, cookies, small cakes, candied fruits, and roasted nuts. In the case of cookies, cakes, and candies, the cook has great opportunity for creative expression in the decoration of the item, making the goodies as much fun to make and give as to receive.

When planning a gift of food, remember that an assortment of different foods is more fun to receive than a big box of one item. Pack three different jams or three different vinegars in a bread basket. Tuck a small plum pudding and two small fruitcakes, one light and one dark, into a stenciled tin. Fill the spaces with plastic-bagged candies or cookies. Arrange layers of dried fruit and shelled nuts in a clear glass container. There are gift wrap suggestions following each food below and more in the Gift Wrap section on page 292.

Many of the recipes in this book may be prepared for gift giving. Although every cook has special favorite recipes, it may be interesting to try others for their historical value. Candy and fruitcake recipes follow. Elsewhere in the book are found recipes for mincemeat pudding (page 144), cranberry sauce (page 142), date and cranberry marmalade (page 143), and pumpkin chips (page 144). Many of these gift foods are pictured in Color Plate 15.

Christmas Candies

Fudge and fondant of infinite variety (including violet flavored) were the popular favorites for homemade gift candy in the early decades of this century. Since recipes for these can be found in any good general cookbook, they are not given here. Instead, here are some interesting tidbits to fill the corners of a candy box for a nice candy gift. Remember that candy gifts can be tailored to the precise tastes of the receiver: lollipops for children, old-fashioned candies for older folks, rich assortments for others.

FRUIT CARAMELS
The Delineator, 1923

½ cup raisins	½ cup citron
½ cup dates	2 tsp. lemon juice
½ cup figs	2 tsp. orange juice
½ cup grated coconut	Granulated or powdered
½ cup nut meats	sugar

Put all fruits and nuts through a food chopper and mix thoroughly with fruit juices. Form into ¾″ balls and roll in granulated or powdered sugar. A very easy candy. Yields 50 balls.

FRICASEED PECANS
The Delineator, 1901

1 cup pecan halves	Salt
3 tbs. butter	

Melt butter in heavy frying pan and stir in pecans. Let pecans roast slowly (on medium-low heat) and stir often. Nuts are done when slightly brittle to break. Drain off surplus butter and drain nuts on paper towel. Just before dry, sprinkle with salt to taste and place in glass jars. Increase recipe for gifts.

CANDIED ORANGE PEEL

The Delineator, 1913

Fresh orange peel from
    one or more oranges
Granulated sugar in
    quantity equal to
    amount of peel

Hot water in quantity
    equal to amount of peel

Cut orange peel into long strips ¼″ wide. Place in heavy saucepan and cover with cold water. Bring to boil. Drain off water and bring to boil again. Drain and repeat. After boiling and draining three times, measure peel and add equal quantity sugar and water. Cook until white of pulp is translucent. Remove from syrup and roll in granulated sugar. Let dry overnight and place in glass jar.

GLACÉ NUTS AND FRUITS

The Delineator, 1913

1 cup sugar
½ cup boiling water
½ tsp. cream of tartar
3 tbs. sugar, caramelized
    (melted over high heat
    until brown)
Blanched nuts of any
    kind

Assorted candied fruits
Dates or figs
Strawberries, seedless
    grapes, seedless orange
    sections (if juicy fruits
    are used do not prick
    while dipping as juice
    will spoil glacé)

To the caramelized sugar, add additional 1 cup sugar and boiling water. When dissolved, add cream of tartar. Boil until candy thermometer registers 300°–305°. Remove from heat and pour into top of double boiler over boiling water. Dip nuts and fruits. Place on greased marble slab or stoneware plate until cool. Store loosely covered.

LOLLIPOPS

The Delineator, 1920

2 cups granulated sugar
½ cup water
Flavoring as desired
⅛ tsp. cream of tartar

12 lollipop sticks (craft
    or popsicle sticks)
Red food coloring

Combine ingredients in heavy, tall, narrow saucepan over high heat. Cook until temperature on candy thermometer registers 305°. Caution: mixture is very hot and can cause a bad burn. Carefully add a few drops of food coloring. Allow mixture to thicken slightly, about 2 minutes. Heavily grease a flexible cookie sheet. Pour thickened mixture into circles about 2″ diameter on cookie sheet. Press a stick into each circle after it is poured and drop a tiny additional dab of hot mixture over top of stick to enclose it. When hard, carefully remove from sheet and wrap in plastic wrap. Makes 12.

PARISIAN FIGS

The Delineator, 1900

1 lb. large whole dried figs
⅔ cup walnuts
⅔ cup almonds

⅔ cup raisins
1 tbs. brandy, maraschino,
    or lemon juice to flavor

Halve figs and remove seedy center and set aside. Put walnuts, almonds, and raisins through a food chopper and add fig seeds. Stir in flavoring. Fill fig shells with this mixture and roll in granulated sugar.

SALTED PEANUTS

The Delineator, 1911

Shell freshly roasted peanuts and soak in hot water to remove the skins. Wipe on a clean towel, mix with a little melted butter, sprinkle liberally with salt, place in a hot oven to crisp.

Packing Candies

Sweets should be carefully packed. Foil, doilies, waxed paper, and bonbon cups may be used. All candies should be perfectly dry when placed in the box. Moist candies like caramels should be wrapped in waxed paper. Bonbon cups may be used for larger candies. Place the candies in layers or sections, separating them with cardboard or strips of candied orange peel (Illustration 23-54). In the 1890's, home-

Illustration 23–54

fashioned bonbon bags (see page 176) were considered to be a charming way to present a small candy gift. Candies placed in a bag or cloth-covered box should be individually wrapped. Other suitable Christmas wraps are Santa Carton (page 195) and Silhouette Tin (page 197). On a plain box, Candy Holly (page 198) makes an appropriate ornament.

Christmas Cakes

Cakes are much in demand as a holiday food and therefore make ideal holiday gifts. Fruitcakes baked weeks ahead ripen and improve with keeping, but they should be wrapped in waxed paper and kept in an airtight container. Icing or decorations, if any, should be added only a day or two before use.

LIGHT FRUITCAKE

The Delineator, 1926

½ cup shortening	¼ lb. citron
¾ cup sugar	1 cup grated coconut
2 cups flour	¼ lb. candied orange peel
1 tsp. baking powder	¼ lb. candied pineapple
¼ tsp. salt	¼ lb. candied lemon peel
½ cup light fruit syrup, any kind	¼ lb. candied red cherries
	½ lb. blanched almonds
½ lb. white raisins	4 egg whites

Cream shortening and sugar. Add 1 cup flour, baking powder, and salt alternately with fruit syrup. Mix other cup of flour with fruits and add to cake mixture. Fold in beaten egg whites. Bake at 250° in paper-lined pans for 2½ hours. Then increase to 300° for ½ hour or until cake tests for doneness. Makes 2 4″ × 8″ loaves.

DARK FRUITCAKE

The Delineator, 1924

½ lb. butter	Juice and grated rind of 1 lemon
1⅓ cups brown sugar	
2¾ cups flour	Juice and grated rind of 1 orange
5 eggs	
½ cup molasses	½ cup tart jelly, such as currant
½ cup strong coffee	

1½ lb. raisins	1 tsp. cinnamon
1 lb. currants	½ tsp. baking soda
½ lb. citron	1½ tsp. baking powder
½ lb. dates	⅓ cup blanched, slivered almonds to sprinkle on top
1 tsp. nutmeg	
½ tsp. mace	
½ tsp. ground cloves	

Cream butter and sugar, then add molasses, coffee, lemon, orange, and jelly. Add well-beaten eggs. Reserve 1 cup of flour and mix with fruits. Mix and sift remaining dry ingredients and add to creamed mixture. Stir in floured fruits. Bake in greased paper-lined pans. Sprinkle almonds on top. Bake at 300° for 2 hours with a shallow pan of water on a lower rack of the oven for steaming. Remove water and bake 1 more hour or until cake tests for doneness. Makes 5 lbs. of cake or 3 4″ × 8″ loaves.

Decorating Cakes and Cookies

Since many holiday meals are unusually rich in themselves, fairly simple cakes, beautifully decorated, are a nice counterpoint for desserts and tea time. Plain cake and sponge cakes (recipes for each can be found in any general cookbook) are used. Sponge cake cuts particularly well without crumbling. The gift cakes make up rather quickly, as the shapes are simply cut or stamped with cutters out of a 1″ thick sheet cake, placed on a rack, and then frosted in one operation. Decorations are then applied. These may include red and green icing, sugars, angelica, candied fruit, nuts, sprinkles, small candies, citron, and coconut. In addition to the designs shown here, other simple seasonal motifs can be interpreted in edibles. The designs are from *The Delineator*, 1923, in an article entitled "Cakes that Saved the Day." (Illustrations 23-55).

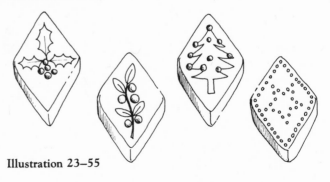

Illustration 23–55

Larger versions of the cakes simply provide a larger canvas for creativity (Illustration 23-56). Adapt the concept of the Fortune Cake (see page 118) and bake small gifts into a cake. Include coins, a thimble, a small whistle, porcelain figures, tools, toys—the only criterion is that the items not melt. A perennial favorite with children is a house made of cake. The simple one which follows can be further embellished as desired.

Illustration 23–56

House of Cake, *The Delineator,* 1923

Bake two sponge cakes in the same size square pans. Cut each in half to make four rectangles. On a square platter or a piece of foil-covered cardboard, stack the four halves with frosting between the layers. Trim the top two layers to form a roof. Cut a chimney out of the

Illustration 23–57

remaining pieces of cake and fasten it on the roof temporarily with a hat pin. Frost the entire house and yard with cooked white frosting to represent snow. Remove the hat pin when the frosting is dry. Make windows out of chocolate bars (four squares) and door out of the same (six squares). Let frosting drip over the window corners as if snow had hardened there. Make a walkway with pebble candies, add evergreen twig trees frosted with snow. Place a tiny Santa or fabric wisp of smoke atop the chimney. (Illustration 23-57)

Packing Cakes

Cake houses are best presented without a wrapping, so as to avoid damage to the decorations.

Small frosted cakes and loaf cakes and plum pudding may be wrapped in Silhouette Tin and Poinsettia (page 197). All cakes should be wrapped in plastic wrap, aluminum foil, or waxed paper before the decorative wrap is applied. Handle small frosted cakes as you would candies. Loaf shapes fit nicely into long baskets or into shoe boxes which can be covered with fabric (see page 293. As with cookies and candies, an assortment of cakes makes a more interesting gift. Bake fruitcakes and fruit breads in cans, package with a small plum pudding, and tuck the three into a pretty basket.

Christmas Cookies

During the early years of the twentieth century, cookies seemed to lag behind cakes and candies in popularity for gift giving. Today, however, that is hardly the case, and each year, countless dozens of cookies are turned out to be given as gifts, used as tree ornaments, or simply enjoyed by appreciative family and friends. Although any cookie qualifies as a Christmas cookie, holiday preferences seem to lean toward mysterious, spicy cookies; rich, fruity cookies; and simple sugar cookies to be decorated as elaborately as desired. Because every cook has her favorite recipes, none are included here.

Packing Cookies

Cookie gifts should include an assortment of flavors and textures designed to appeal to the eye as well as the taste buds. For mailing, wrap cookies individually or in pairs. Although soft cookies should be stored in an airtight container and crisp ones in a container with a loose-fitting lid, a gift cookie assortment probably will not spend enough time in the box for this to be a concern. So, put cookies in anything you like. Use doilies, foil, and plastic wrap in the containers. The Santa Carton (page 195) and Silhouette Tin (page 197), among others, are nice cookie containers.

Christmas Gift Wraps

The most traditional Christmas gift wrap, considered to be in perfect taste, was plain white tissue paper tied with narrow satin ribbon, either holly printed or plain red. Frequently, a sprig of evergreen with a small candle adorned the package (Illustration 23-58). Cornucopias, of course, were also used to contain lightweight

Illustration 23—58

gifts which could be hung from the tree. They were a favorite hiding place for money gifts. Another favorite Christmas tradition was to hang shiny coins from a small artificial tree, a sure hit with the young recipients.

Food gifts were presented in a variety of ways. Many cooks choose to ornament glass containers simply by adding ribbon and an evergreen or holly sprig. Others decorated boxes or tins with seasonal motifs. Jars or cans of cookies were tucked into baskets or cache pots. Candies, for some reason, were usually presented in more elaborate containers—bonbon bags or boxes.

Often, decorated boxes were created just to delight the recipient or to make a simple gift seem more special. Sometimes, the box itself might be part of the gift: a dainty hanky would be contained in a padded, scented box intended for later use as a hosiery, lingerie, or jewelry container. See page 294) for information about covering boxes.

Basic gift wrap techniques and other general wrapping ideas appear on page 292. The ideas which follow below are especially oriented toward Christmas gifts and some are particularly well suited for oddly shaped items and food gifts. Some are illustrated in Color Plate 15 The Easter Berry Basket (page 68) makes a lovely gift food container if worked in seasonal colors.

House of Cards, *The Delineator*, 1925

MATERIALS:
- 5 Christmas cards with horizontal designs, about 6″ wide × 4″ high
- 2 Christmas cards with vertical designs, about 4″ wide × 7″ high
- red or green yarn
- sharp pointed yarn needle
- scissors

STEP-BY-STEP:
1. Cut the 5 horizontal design cards to be exactly the same size. Use only the decorative front of the cards for the box and center designs in the 4″ × 6″ space whenever feasible. (Illustration 23-59)

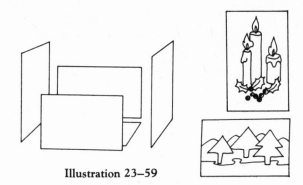

Illustration 23–59

2. Cut the 2 vertical design cards to be the same width as the height of the horizontal cards.

3. Join cards in the shape shown, using the blanket stitch (see page 289), alternating stitches back and forth between the cards.

4. Cut the tops of the end cards into equal points to form gables. (Illustration 23-60)

5. Trim 2 remaining horizontal cards as necessary to fit smoothly over the points and join along one long edge.

6. Stitch roof to house on 3 sides leaving a flap opening through which to fill the house. Blanket stitch around any free edges. (Illustration 23-61)

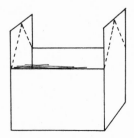

Illustration 23–60

Illustration 23–61

7. Add a yarn loop, center front, to tie the box together. Or, for real security, overcast edges together through blanket stitch loops!

Santa Carton, *The Delineator,* 1906
COLOR PLATE 15
MATERIALS:

    1 round cereal box, about 6″ × 3½″

    red crepe paper (or fabric, if permanence is desired)

    white polyester quilt batting or fleece

    black ribbon, about ⅝″ wide

    1 sheet stiff white paper, about 9″ × 12″

    rubber cement

    scissors

    small silver buckle or buckle cut out of silver paper

    five felt-tip markers or watercolors to paint face

STEP-BY-STEP:

1. **Head** Cut and shape a tapered cylinder to fit top of cereal box and extend about 4″ above it. Diameter at top point should be about 3″. Slash wide lower edge about ½″ deep and glue to outside edges of carton lid. Overlap and glue cylinder seam. (Illustration 23-62)

Illustration 23–62

2. **Body** Cut batting 6″ wide, long enough to fit around box with about a 3″ overlap in front. Glue batting to box bottom edges even. Cover with red crepe paper, cut to fit around box, overlapping in front (Illustration 23-63). Cut 1¼″-wide batting strips.

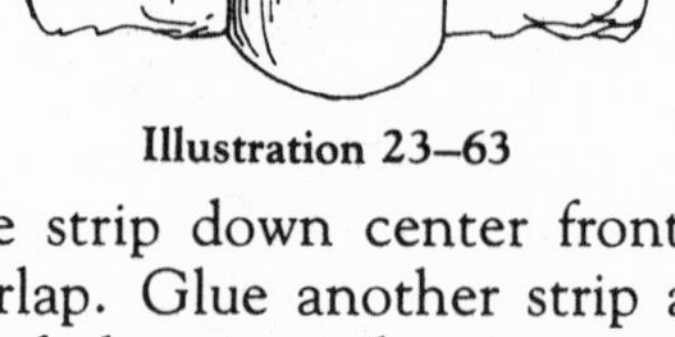

Illustration 23–63

Glue one strip down center front, covering coat overlap. Glue another strip around the bottom of the coat, butting against front piece. Position black ribbon belt around body and glue to coat in front. Glue buckle in place (Illustration 23-64). At top, glue

Illustration 23—64

excess crepe paper coat to carton, pleating and tucking as necessary. Take care not to interfere with opening and closing of cover. (Illustration 23-65)

Illustration 23—65

3. **Arms** Cut paper pieces 4″ × 4″. Fill with a bit of batting, roll into a cylinder and glue. Glue ½″ strip of batting around the lower edge of each sleeve. Flatten upper edge of each sleeve and glue to carton at shoulder position. (Illustration 23-66)

Illustration 23—66

4. **Face** Paint facial features on head (see Color Plate 15). Cut a half circle of batting about 5″ wide and 3″ deep. Glue to face. Trim and pull batting into beard and mustache shape. Work

batting away from eyes and mouth (Illustration 23-67). Add bushy eyebrows if desired. Glue batting piece to cover back of head from beard edge to beard edge.

Illustration 23—67

5. **Hat** Cut a piece of crepe paper as shown, measuring about 13″ wide by 6″ high. Glue into triangular cone-shape hat. Glue hat to head. Glue 1″-wide batting strip around edge of hat and a batting puff at end of cap peak (Illustration 23-68). Arrange peak as desired. **Note:** This makes a really special gift box. Or as a table centerpiece, it could contain surprise favors for each guest. Make various size Santas according to round cartons available.

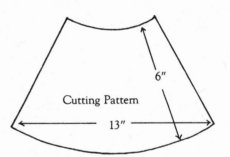

Cutting Pattern
6″
13″

Illustration 23—68

Silhouette Tin, *The Delineator,* 1920
COLOR PLATE 15
MATERIALS:

    metal can with cover
    spray paint
    paper to cut silhouettes
    fine scissors
    plastic varnish, paintbrush

STEP-BY-STEP:

1. Spray-paint can and cover.
2. When thoroughly dry, paint with clear plastic varnish and while tacky, apply previously cut out silhouettes.*
3. Apply several more coats of varnish as desired, following instructions on can. (Illustration 23-69)

Illustration 23–69

*Use Christmas motif shapes and card designs (see Design Sheet, pages 201-204), or cut silhouettes of family members for a particularly meaningful container.

Note: Con-Tact® paper makes an excellent silhouette material and eliminates the need for varnish.

Poinsettia, *The Delineator,* 1922
COLOR PLATE 15
MATERIALS:

    1 piece stiff cardboard diameter of gift
    2 pieces red crepe paper to fit around gift plus 1″ overlap (Paper should be height of gift plus about 6″.)
    white glue
    scraps of green and yellow crepe paper, about 6″ × 10″
    2 ft. ribbon, about ½″ wide

STEP-BY-STEP:

1. Cut deep pointed scallops at top of double strip of red crepe paper. Glue the unscalloped edge to the bottom of the cardboard disk. Glue a neat seam up the back.
2. Cover bottom of disk with red crepe paper scrap if desired.

Illustration 23–70

3. Deeply fringe green and yellow paper. Roll together and twist end. (Illustration 23-70)
4. Insert gift into bag and tie top with ribbon. Fold scallops over in pretty arrangement.
5. Tuck fringed tuft into the center of the closed bag. **Note:** Adjust dimensions of cardboard and crepe paper to wrap a variety of odd-sized bundles such as bottles, toys, and plum puddings.

Bonbon Box, *The Delineator,* 1900
MATERIALS:

    1 shallow box about 1″ deep
    white satin fabric to cover box
    rubber cement
    acrylic paints or embroidered appliqué
    ribbon, about ¼″ wide, as needed depending on box dimensions

STEP-BY-STEP:

1. Cover box with white satin.
2. Paint a floral design in the center of the cover or attach embroidered appliqué.
3. Make slits in the satin along opposite sides of top and weave ribbon through slits, tucking ends under satin at each end.
4. Attach tiny bows at opposite corners.

Candy Holly, *The Delineator,* 1920
COLOR PLATE 15
MATERIALS:
  several round wrapped candies
  artificial holly leaves
  red tissue or crepe paper
  white glue
  green floral tape

STEP-BY-STEP:
1. To customize a plain box, wrap candy balls in red paper and cover paper stems with floral tape.

2. Arrange with artificial holly leaves and glue in place on box top. (Illustration 23-71)

Illustration 23–71

"Merry Christmas"

The Delineator, 1911

DESIGN SHEET

Holly Garland/Berries, page 171

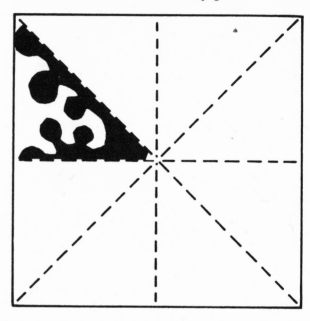

1. Fold square along dotted lines. Use 3″ squares for Holly Garland/Berries and 4″ squares for Holly Garland/Leaves and Cutout Snowflakes.
2. Trace pattern onto folded paper.
3. Cut on lines.
4. Unfold and press.

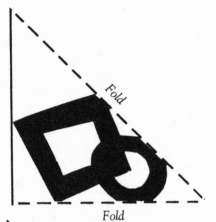

Cutout Snowflakes, page 172

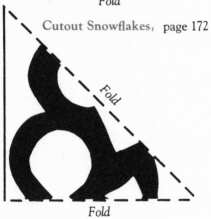

Holly Garland/Leaves, page 171

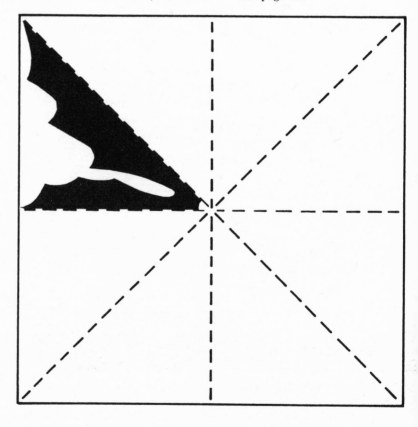

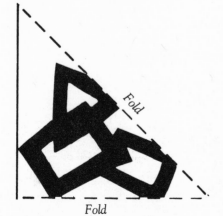

DESIGN SHEET

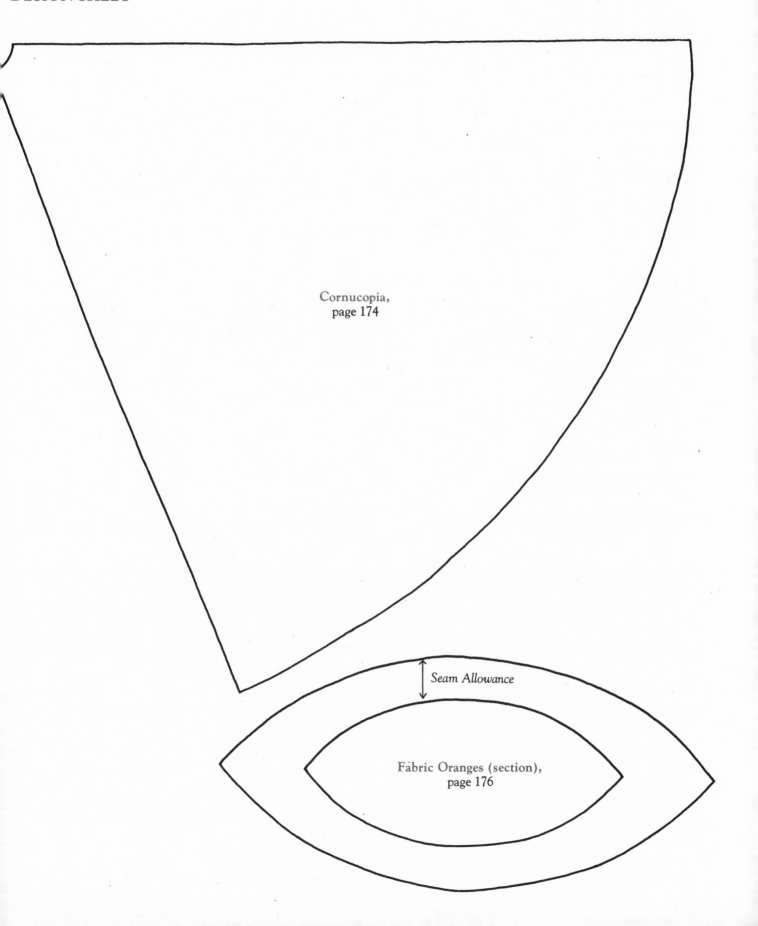

Cornucopia,
page 174

Seam Allowance

Fabric Oranges (section),
page 176

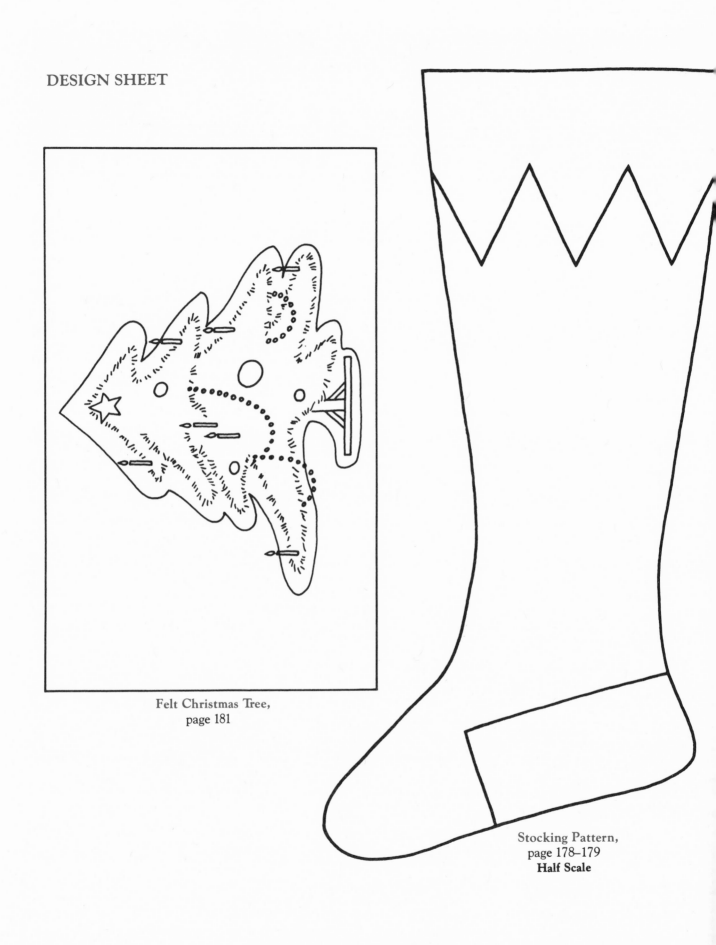

DESIGN SHEET

Felt Christmas Tree,
page 181

Stocking Pattern,
page 178–179
Half Scale

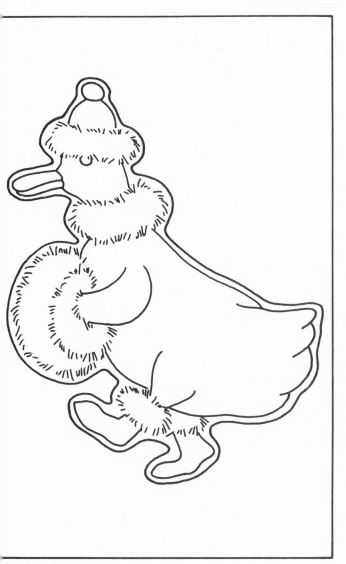

Felt Duck, page 182

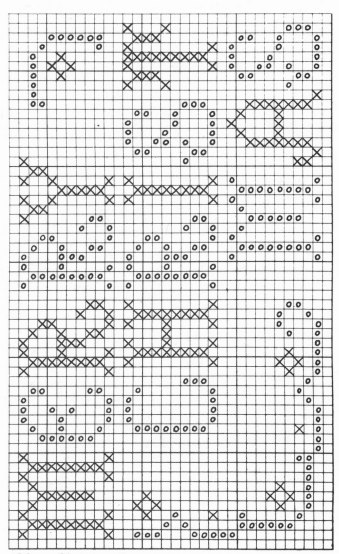

"Merry Christmas," page 183

RED ☒
GREEN ☉

The Three Kings, page 183

Christmas Tree, page 184

Deco Wreath, page 184

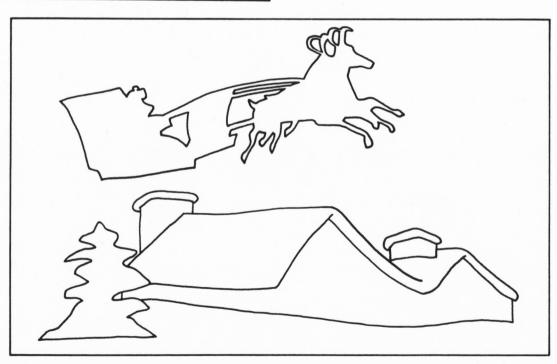

"And Away They All Flew," page 184

Linear Tree, page 185

Abstract Tree, page 185

Star of Beauty, page 185

The Delineator, 1902

24 Personal Celebrations:

Birthdays & Wedding Anniversaries

Personal holidays do not depend on seasonal, religious, or patriotic events. Everyone has a birthday and every married person has a wedding anniversary. These events are important and most people want to celebrate or observe them. An editorial in *Godey's Lady's Book* delightfully expressed some thoughts on such celebrations:

What untold delights would be lost to the juvenile world if the celebration of Christmas, New Year's Day, and the Fourth of July was henceforth and forever annihilated! And what minor pleasures and joyful anticipations would fade in dim distance were the family holidays or birthday and wedding-day to be forgotten.

We know that in some households, they are scarcely recognized; but in others, even "baby" may have his birthday, and become at once an individual of importance. There is no prettier picture in all that Mary Howitt has written than her description of the simple feast in those wonderful anniversaries given in "Our Cousins in Ohio." The little hero or heroine of the day not only a receiver of the great plum-cake—manufactured after the most harmless of receipts, but entirely satisfactory to all parties concerned—the brothers and sisters in neat array, even father and mother invited guests at the tea-table.

We like to see, first of all, wedding-day remembered between the heads of a household by some trifling gift, calling forth tender and grateful recollections of a time when it seemed so easy to love and to cherish, so unnatural to give utterance to a quick word or harsh reproof. It is true, regret, and loss, and self-upbraiding must, with more genial feelings; but they are as dew and showers to freshen the heart, hardened by the cares of the world and the attrition of daily petty offences.

Perhaps the milestones will come too quickly hereafter. If we wreathe them now with garlands, we may then be thankful to sit awhile beside them in the shade, for shadows lengthen as the eventide creeps on and number, with thankful recollection, the blessings of the way. A happy childhood carries its own brightness to another generation, springing up with the same glad anticipations, and birthdays are among its brightest recollections.

Godey's Lady's Book, 1856

BROWN △ PINK ▱
MEDIUM GREEN Ⓞ MEDIUM RED ⊠

Note: The corner motif for the MARRIAGE SAMPLER is graphed in the upper righthand corner. Arrows indicate the vertical and horizontal centerlines. The other motifs can be used to decorate and enhance the sampler. The alphabet on page 219 can be used to create your special message.

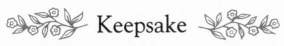

Keepsake

MARRIAGE SAMPLER COLOR PLATE 30

The marriage sampler is composed of cross-stitch elements from many sources, principally *Needle-Art*, 1900–1925, when cross-stitch and filet crochet were extremely popular needlework forms, providing many charming graphed patterns. The Marriage Sampler in the photo features the rose, the flower for June. Personalize the sampler you design by choosing colors and motifs indicative of the month of the celebration. The design may also be needlepointed.

MATERIALS:

1 piece fine white linen or even-weave fabric, 15″ × 18″

Persian yarn: red, pink, light brown, dark brown, kelly green, metallic gold (Although design in photo is worked in Persian yarn, cotton embroidery floss would be equally beautiful.)

graph paper (8 squares to the inch) or 8 mesh needlepoint canvas

embroidery needle

2 11″ and 2 14″ canvas stretchers

thumb tacks or staple gun

STEP-BY-STEP:

Note: Sampler may be worked in counted-thread embroidery (cross-stitch). Methods are discussed in Embroidery, page 290. Use 1-ply Persian yarn throughout, except for dark brown color. If using cotton embroidery floss, experiment with various plies for best effect.

1. Plan design from elements provided. It is advisable to plot design on graph paper of the appropriate size before beginning work. Eight squares to the inch is a good workable size. Indicate colors on paper with felt-tip markers or colored pencils.

2. Transfer design to canvas, if using cross-stitch over canvas method. If using counted-thread method, you will work from graph paper.

3. Work embroidery. Do frame first, then letters, then corners. Embroider over heart, bell, and ribbon with metallic yarn.

4. Clean if necessary and block or press lightly.

5. Stretch and frame.

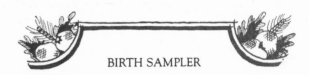

BIRTH SAMPLER

Plan a sampler to honor a birth or birthday using the cross-stitch motifs on Design Sheet, page 220. Use the basic central shape from the Marriage Sampler but substitute the children's corner motif and other cross-stitch elements as desired. For inscription, use cross-stitch alphabet, Design Sheet, page 219. Use colors associated with the flower or gem for the birth month. The design may be worked in needlepoint instead of cross-stitch embroidery.

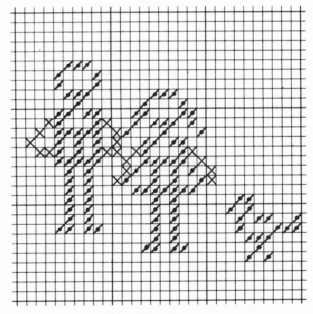

CHILDREN'S BIRTH SAMPLER

Corner Motif

Birthdays

Most adults do not particularly wish to *celebrate* a birthday, although many do like to observe the day in some special manner, and everyone likes to be remembered with a card or gift. Children, on the other hand, relish birthdays. They are eager to grow up, unconcerned with growing old, and a birthday is very special indeed. A child's birthday should be a little festival, at least while the child is still young. And since a child cannot fully enjoy anything alone, a children's party is a delightful way to celebrate a birthday.

Birthday parties began with the belief that spirits gather around a birthday celebrant. Since it was further believed that these spirits could cause harm, friends and relatives gathered so that their good wishes and presence could protect the birthday person from the spirits. Gifts brought even greater protection. So the birthday party evolved, intended to protect the person from evil and ensure a good coming year.

Birthday candles hark back to the early Greeks and Romans, who thought them to have the magical ability to carry messages to the gods. The celebrant makes a secret wish on the candles and if all are blown out with one puff, the wish will be granted. It is customary to have on the cake one candle for each year, and one to grow on. Playful birthday spanks are also rendered for good luck.

Game playing at a birthday party, in addition to providing merriment, originally provided a chance for the celebrant to demonstrate his development, both mental and physical, during the past year since his last birthday.

Of great interest to many people are the birthstone, flower, and character traits associated with each month. Gems were supposed to be endowed with magical qualities and it was the possession of these attributes which made them of such special value to older civilizations. Many people feel that wearing their birthstone will bring good luck. The stone colors and flowers serve as appropriate themes for party decorating and for gifts. The twelve signs of the zodiac correspond roughly to the twelve months of the year and are important to astrologers to predict good or bad luck and plot a horoscope. The signs are given below:

AQUARIUS The Water Bearer, January 20–February 18

PISCES The Fish, February 19–March 20

ARIES The Ram, March 21–April 19

TAURUS The Bull, April 20–May 20

GEMINI The Twins, May 21–June 20

CANCER The Crab, June 21–July 22

LEO The Lion, July 23–August 22

VIRGO The Virgin, August 23–September 23

LIBRA The Balance, September 24–October 23

SCORPIO The Scorpion, October 24–November 21

SAGITTARIUS The Archer, November 22–December 21

CAPRICORN The Goat, December 22–January 19

These astrological signs also provide card and gift ideas and themes.

Month	Flower	Stone
JANUARY	Snowdrop	Garnet
FEBRUARY	Primrose	Amethyst
MARCH	Violet	Bloodstone
APRIL	Daisy	Sapphire
MAY	Hawthorn	Emerald
JUNE	Honeysuckle	Agate
JULY	Waterlily	Ruby
AUGUST	Poppy	Sardonyx
SEPTEMBER	Morning Glory	Chrysolite
OCTOBER	Hop Blooms	Opal
NOVEMBER	Chrysanthemum	Topaz
DECEMBER	Holly	Turquoise

Birthday Parties

Since birthday parties are more important to children than to adults, the party plans which follow are for children. Adult parties can be clever, original, and different, but most children will be happiest if given exactly what they expect: games, food, and favors. Children enter with zest and heartiness into any plans for their enjoyment and games well planned beforehand and competently led are usually successful. When guests are all one sex, they are usually easier to entertain. Should the group be mixed, however, the clever hostess will see to it that the guests do not separate into two groups, since to get them back together is almost impossible. Both games with prizes and games played just for fun should be planned.

Food must be plentiful and decorative. Ice cream and cake have for many years been the expected birthday party fare. The cake occupies the place of honor and is usually the primary table decoration. It must carry the proper number of candles—one for each year (or, as at a party in 1898, one for each guest). The candles are allowed to burn for a bit before they are blown out and the cake is cut. A Fortune Cake (see page 118) is a popular birthday cake idea for older children. Decorate cakes with animal crackers or alphabet noodles colored with food coloring and formed into words and names.

Favors and prizes are treasured by young party guests and can be customized to any party theme or group. A Jack Horner pie (see page 28) or bonbon bags (see page 176) can be used as party decorations before becoming, ultimately, favors.

Mother Goose Party, The Delineator, 1930

The invitations to this party for young children should ask each child to dress like his or her favorite Mother Goose character.

Decorations

Cut a Ring around the Rosy place decoration for each child. Fold a square of colorful paper diagonally in half, then in half again and

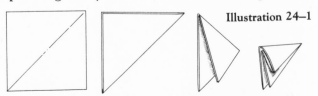

Illustration 24-1

again (Illustration 24-1). Enlarge the double figure design (see Design Sheet, page 218) and trace it on the folded triangle. Cut it out carefully with sharp scissors. Then unfold it and smooth it out, ironing with a dry iron to remove the creases (Illustration 24-2). This design may be used on invitations also.

Illustration 24-2

Games

Mother Goose Search, The Delineator, *1930*

Have one child go from the room leaving behind some part of his costume (Little Boy Blue's horn, for example) which is then hidden from sight. Appoint another child to say "warm" or "cold" and bring the first child back to search for the hidden object. "Warm" means that the searcher is close to the object, "cold" that he's going away from it. Let each child have a turn.

Peanut Race, The Delineator, *1930*

Divide guests into pairs by height. Place a large pan of peanuts at one end of the room, two empty baskets at the other end. One pair at a time competes, each carrying one peanut at a time on a spoon from the pan to his basket. The player getting a predetermined number of peanuts into his basket wins. Each pair competes, then winners may compete and so forth until a grand winner is determined.

Making Pictures, The Delineator, *1930*

Before the party, glue pictures (toys, Mother Goose characters, animals, etcetera) on cardboard squares and cut each square in half. Set aside one half of each picture. At the party, spread the remaining halves among three large pans. Give each child half of one picture and have him find the matching half in one of the pans. When he matches one set, he is given another half and continues to play. The one matching the most pictures in a specified time is the winner.

Food

The centerpiece is a cake decorated with pink frosting and Mother Goose shapes representing each guest (these may be paper cutouts, tiny dressed dolls, or decorated cookies which may then serve as favors). The menu suggested was:

Sweet Sandwiches
Milk
Ice Cream
Cake

Indian Party, The Delineator, 1916

Invitations

Print folded notes with a feather motif (see Design Sheet, page 218).

Decorations

Use Indian pictures cut from magazines and children's books. Construct a small teepee in one room with a "bear skin" rug cut out of acrylic fake fur. Provide a headband made of construction paper feathers (see Design Sheet, page 218) attached to a stiff paper band for each guest (Illustration 24-3). Table favors will be candy-

Illustration 24—3

filled canoes cut from wood-grain wallpaper, which resembles bark. Place the bottom of the canoe pattern (see Design Sheet, page 218) along the folded edge of the paper; cut out, leaving the fold intact; glue the canoe ends together (Illustration 24-4). Table decorations may be miniature Indian village scenes created from paper, vines, twigs, a mirror lake, tiny dolls, or corn husk dolls (see page 137).

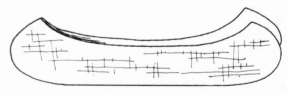

Illustration 24—4

Games

Heap Big Indian Chief, The Delineator, *1916*

One player is blindfolded, placed in the center of a circle of the other players, and given a stick. The other players dance around Indian style until the player in the center taps the floor with the stick. When all are still, he points toward one player who must say "Heap Big Indian Chief." If the blindfolded player guesses the voice, he rejoins the circle of dancers and the discovered player takes his place in the center of the circle.

Drop the Moccasin, The Delineator, *1916*

Players stand in a circle. One player, "It," walks around the outside of the circle and drops a moccasin behind another player, who must pick it up, then chase "It" around the circle. "It" attempts to reach the vacated spot without being caught. If he does so, the chaser becomes "It."

Feather Hunt, The Delineator, *1916*

Guests hunt for chicken or turkey feathers which have been hidden about the house or lawn. Prizes may be awarded for the most feathers found or specially marked feathers.

Food

Two different menus were suggested for this party:

Teepee-Shaped Cookies with Citron Poles and a
Flattened Raisin Entrance
Chocolate and Strawberry Ice Cream
Cake
Lemonade
or
Baked Apple with Cream
Cocoa
Cookies Tied with Ribbon
Ice Cream Garnished with Popcorn
and Cake

More Birthday Ideas

Birthday Surprise Cake, *Modern Priscilla, 1927*

Select two square boxes, fairly deep, one about 1″ smaller than the other. Prepare cake frosting, candles, and decorations as desired. Ice and decorate the lid of the larger box as if it were a cake. Then wrap tiny gifts to go inside the bottom of the smaller box—small toys, tiny dolls, marbles, etcetera. Cover and wrap the box containing the toys, then set the decorated lid over all. Light the candles (watch carefully) and watch surprised eyes when the "cake" is lifted (Illustration 24-5). This is a nice idea for a child who happens to be sick on his birthday and needs some extra cheering up or as a means of distributing party favors.

Illustration 24–5

Half-Birthday, *The Delineator,* 1898

This charming idea from 1898 was developed by a young lady whose birthday fell during the summer, when all her friends were scattered. The date celebrated is half a year after the birthday and the "half" idea is a theme throughout—cakes are cut in halves, ice cream molds are halved, half cups of beverages are served, etcetera. Gifts should also be in halves—half a box of candy, half a dozen handkerchiefs, or half a gift from one person, the other half from another.

Birthday Cards

Cards For Children

Chicks Having a Ball, *Needle-Art,* 1921
COLOR PLATE 26

Make this simple card using art gum eraser stamping in combination with collage or trace the design, transfer it to card and color with felt tip markers.

MATERIALS:
   1 art gum eraser
   fine felt-tip marker
   chenille chicks, one for each year
   plain card or folded note and envelope to fit
   white glue

STEP-BY-STEP:
1. See art gum eraser printing, page 286. Cut and print ball section in size necessary to hold chicks. Complete circle with felt markers.
2. Glue chenille chicks in place balanced on ball or draw chicks with markers.
3. Inscribe message such as "Sitting on top of the world on your birthday!" and "Have a ball on your birthday."

Jolly Clown, *Needle-Art,* 1921
   Paper collage with felt-tip marker details fashion this cheerful clown. Fabric collage is another suitable technique.

MATERIALS:
   bright papers for clown's costume and hat
   fine felt-tip markers
   plain card or folded note and envelope to fit
   rubber cement

STEP-BY-STEP:
1. Trace design to colored papers as desired.
2. Glue pieces in place.
3. Draw or trace face with felt-tip marker.
4. Inscribe message such as "This jolly clown has birthday wishes for you."

"I'm Late, I'm Late," *Needle-Art,* 1924
   Combine various scraps of fabric to fashion this card which a young child will enjoy, especially if the fabrics are of various textures.

MATERIALS:
   striped fabric for fence
   fuzzy fabric (velour) for rabbit
   cotton ball for tail
   green yarn for grass
   glue
   needle
   fine felt-tip marker
   plain folded note and envelope to fit

STEP-BY-STEP:
1. Trace various pattern pieces and transfer to appropriate fabrics. Cut out pieces.
2. Glue fabrics in place on card. Glue on grass details. Glue on cotton tail.
3. Inscribe message, such as "Hope this bunny isn't too late to wish you a Happy Birthday."

Cards for Adults

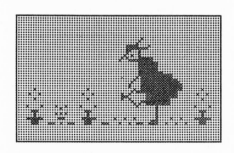

A Garden of Wishes, *Needle-Art, 1921*

This design has been adapted from a cross-stitch border for hot-iron stamping. Work it in **embroidery on perforated paper** or adapt to needlepoint, mosaic paper collage, or cork stamping.

MATERIALS:

needlepoint canvas or perforated paper, about 3″ × 4″
embroidery floss as desired
plain double-folded note and envelope to fit
fine felt-tip marker
artist's knife, metal ruler

STEP-BY-STEP:

1. Work design.
2. Cut a frame out of top layer of folded note.
3. Mount embroidery behind cutout.
4. Inscribe message, such as "A garden of wishes for your birthday."

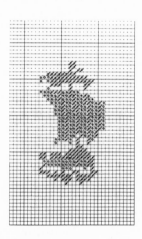

Ship Ahoy, *Needle-Art, 1924*

Work this stately ship on perforated paper and turn it into a bookmark for a card for a gentleman friend. The design may also be worked in needlepoint.

MATERIALS:

perforated paper, about 3″ × 4″
ribbon or leather, width of finished work, desired length
embroidery floss
plain folded note and envelope to fit
fine felt-tip marker

STEP-BY-STEP:

1. Work design and finish edges as for bookmark, using ribbon or leather strip.
2. Insert bookmark into folded note.
3. Inscribe message in note as desired.

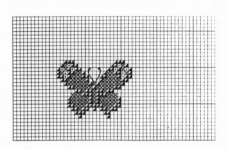

Fluttering Butterfly, *Needle-Art, 1924*

This butterfly can be interpreted in needlepoint with embroidered details or in perforated paper embroidery.

MATERIALS:

10 mesh needlepoint canvas, about 5″ square
Persian yarn
embroidery needle
double folded plain note and envelope to fit
artist's knife, metal ruler, transparent tape
fine felt-tip marker

STEP-BY-STEP:

1. Work design.
2. Cut frame out of top layer of folded note. Mount needlepoint behind frame and tape in place.
3. Inscribe message in card.

Sweet Bouquet, *Needle-Art,* 1920
COLOR PLATE 26

Use an assortment of trimming scraps to create this lovely design. The design can also be traced to rice paper with felt-tip markers for a different interpretation.

MATERIALS:

scraps of ribbons, eyelet, pretty strings, trims, laces, fabrics, and embroidered appliqués
glue
fine felt-tip marker
plain card or folded note and envelope to fit

STEP-BY-STEP:

1. Lightly trace design to card for positioning elements.
2. Make cone shape out of eyelet or lace scrap and glue to card.
3. Tie bow and glue to card.
4. Fashion flowers by rolling trims and ribbons to desired sizes and gluing in place. Make other flowers by gluing one shape on top of another.
5. Cut leaves out of green fabric.
6. For fun, drop perfume on several of the more prominent blossoms.
7. Inscribe desired message inside card.

Wedding Anniversaries

Celebrating wedding anniversaries with some sort of simple entertainment is a charming way to observe a notable and happy occasion with one's friends. The origin of the themes for the anniversaries is unknown (maybe they were devised by some enterprising shopkeeper) but, according to an 1894 *Delineator* booklet entitled "Weddings and Wedding Anniversaries," the "anniversaries have been recognized by the following titles for many years and are variously celebrated." The booklet gave the following list. (Modern additions and changes to this list are in parentheses.)

One year, cotton (paper) wedding
Two years, paper (cotton) wedding
Three years, leather wedding
(Four years, silk or flowers wedding)
Five years, wooden wedding
(Six years, iron wedding)
Seven years, woolen wedding

(Eight years, bronze wedding)
(Nine years, pottery wedding)
Ten years, tin wedding
(Eleven years, steel wedding)
(Twelve years, silk or linen wedding)
(Thirteen years, lace wedding)
(Fourteen years, ivory wedding)
Fifteen years, crystal wedding
Twenty years, china wedding
Twenty-five years, silver wedding
Thirty years, pearl wedding
Thirty-five years, lace (coral and jade) wedding
Forty years, ruby wedding
(Forty-five years, sapphire wedding)
Fifty years, golden wedding
Fifty-five years, emerald wedding
(Sixty years, diamond wedding)
Seventy-five years, diamond wedding

The early anniversary designations are rather fanciful. Indeed, it clearly seems to be a case of "any excuse for a party" and the themes provide many opportunities for clever decorations, favors, and gifts. Games and activities are not strictly necessary but can be planned to co-ordinate with the theme. Observance of later anniversaries are genuine occasions for celebration, however, and are generally marked by more formal entertainment.

Parties for early anniversaries are always given by the couple themselves. The later parties may be given by the children of the couple, although it is entirely correct for the couple to do it themselves, if the young people cannot or do not. A fiftieth anniversary celebration is almost always planned by the family of the celebrating couple and in many communities is considered to be a newsworthy event, one which is celebrated by a wide circle of friends and relatives.

At a typical traditional formal anniversary celebration described by *The Delineator*, the host and hostess received their guests beneath a floral wedding bell, an umbrella, or a canopy, after which they mingled with their guests. The celebration was usually an evening party with dancing, which was found to be more practical and in better form than to attempt to duplicate the original wedding festivities, which may have taken place in the morning. Often the silver or gold engraved invitations bore the words "No gifts received" in an effort to avoid "making such occasions the opportunity for display or a draft upon the generosity of acquaintances." (And at this point in their lives, most couples had more possessions than they needed anyway.) As many as possible of the friends who assisted at the first ceremony were present at the anniversary. The refreshment table usually featured a beautifully frosted cake with the dates of the marriage and the wedding anniversary conspicuously displayed.

Anniversary Parties

Cotton Wedding Anniversary

Invitations

Wrap invitations in white cotton and tie with cotton cords in various colors. Ask guests to dress in cotton fabrics. Select cord colors to match whatever flowers are in season. A September 1894 *Delineator* chose blue and yellow and used asters and goldenrod throughout. Substitute yellow zinnias for goldenrod in deference to your allergic friends!

Decorations

Arrange flowers in containers appropriate to the color scheme. Wind the stair bannister with blue cloth and yellow leaves. Have a basket heaped with real cotton bolls. The hostess wears muslin. Favors are cotton items: handkerchiefs, scarfs, sachets, etcetera. On the tables, arrange blue and white checkered cloths and blue and white china. Yellow zinnias, purple asters, and bursting cotton bolls form the centerpiece. Have zinnia boutonnieres for the men, asters for the women.

Food

BREAKFAST BUFFET

Canteloupe on ice
Deviled Oysters on the Half Shell
Thin Celery Sandwiches
Ham Omelet
Broiled Blue Fish with Lemon Sauce
Potato Chips   Salmon Croquettes
Corn Muffins   Butter
Coffee   Lemonade
Yellow and Purple Plums and Grapes on Cracked Ice
Chocolate Sponge Cake

Wooden Wedding Anniversary

Invitations

Write invitations on thin wood and deliver in envelopes made of wood-grain wallpaper. Use this verse from 1926:

"Wood" you be inclined to grace
Our board with your convivial face,
To celebrate, in antic mood,
Our Wedding-feast of seasoned wood?

Decorations

Construct a rustic arch of boughs with bark, lichen, Spanish moss. Hang Spanish moss on chandeliers, picture frames, mantles, doorways, etcetera. Add some draped greenery and pots of blooming plants for color. Have baskets of wood about and provide soft mellow (yellow) light. Favors are wooden items: boxes, bowls, utensils, etcetera. Decorate the table in gray and green. Use no cloth on a wooden table; instead, arrange a mirror down the center with vines along the sides and bunches of violets here and there. Use imitation wood-grain paper for place mats.

Food

Use wood or imitation wood plates, bowls, cups, serving pieces and eating utensils. This menu is from 1894:

Raw Oysters on Half Shell
Celery Salad   Beef Croquettes   Chicken Salad
Cheese Wafers   Sardine Sandwiches
Lettuce Salad with Egg
Maraschino Sherbet
Grapes   Bananas   Oranges

Crystal Wedding Anniversary, *The Delineator, 1926*

Invitations

Write invitations on the whitest cards available and sprinkle with silver glitter. Use with verse:

At fifteen years, we still can truly say
"A thousand blessings on our wedding-day"
Come now and see, as in a crystal bubble,
How doubled joy has meant divided trouble.

Decorations

Use white and green exclusively. Cover the floor with white fabric, have potted palms and ferns on stands and in white containers in front of mirrors. Use candles in glass candelabra. Sconces should have frosted lamp shades. Arrange for a fountain banked with greenery. The hostess may wear her wedding gown embellished with crystal beads. Favors will be glass paperweights, crystallized fruits, rock crystal candy, etcetera. Arrange, in a crystal vase, several glittering evergreen boughs (see page 187). Hang crystal pendants like icicles from the branches. Set the table entirely with glass. Let the centerpiece be a block of ice, with bouquets of flowers and fruits frozen within, surrounded by a border of mirrors and vines.

Food

Iced Bouillon: Russian Salad Galantine
Cheese Wafers   Sandwiches
Olives
Moulded Lemon Jelly with Wine Ices
Salad in Halved Cucumber Containers
Vanilla Ice in Snowball Form Frosted with Sugar
Assorted Iced and Sugared Cakes
Coffee in Glass Cups

Plan Your Own Party

Paper Wedding Anniversary, *The Delineator, 1926*

With many a lightsome jest and merry caper,
We mean to give a party frilled in paper.
The first year we are through, and that's a sign
  (They say!)
The worst is over, and the rest is fine
  (They say!).

Tin Wedding Anniversary, *The Delineator, 1926*

Our 'leventh year we usher in
With bright festivities of tin,
Pray join us in the cheerful clatter
Of clinking cup and tinkling platter.

Ring Around the Rosy, page 210

Headband/Feather, page 211

Fold

Canoe, page 211

Invitation, page 211

Chicks Having A Ball, page 212

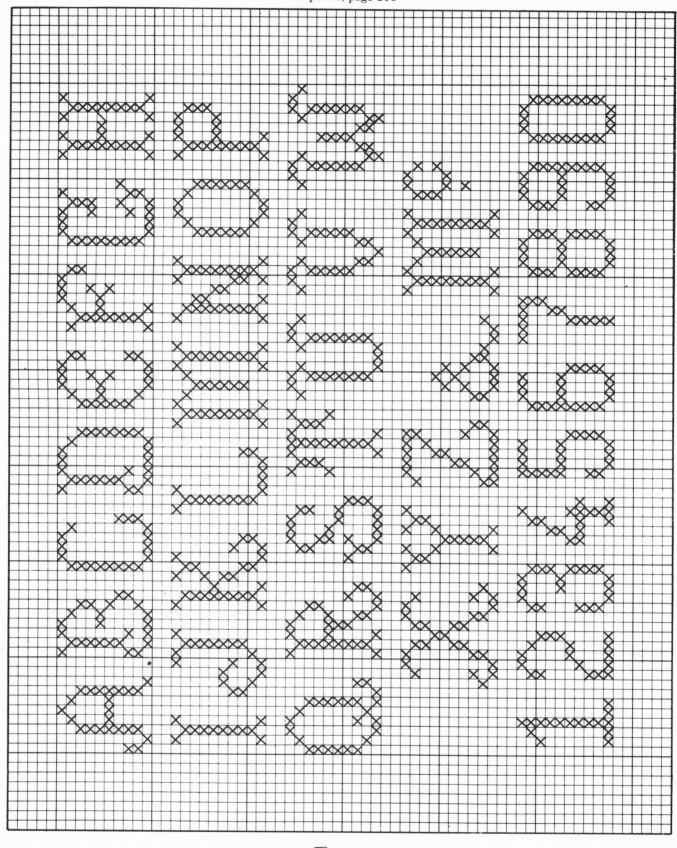

MEDIUM GREEN ⊙   ORANGE ◪

MEDIUM RED ⊠   MEDIUM BLUE ◪

BLACK ■   PINK ◹

MEDIUM YELLOW ⊡   BROWN ◬

Jolly Clown, page 213

"I'm Late, I'm Late," page 213

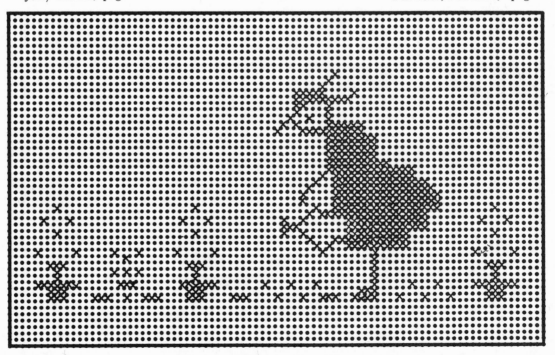

A Garden of Wishes, page 214

Ship Ahoy, page 214

Sweet Bouquet, page 215

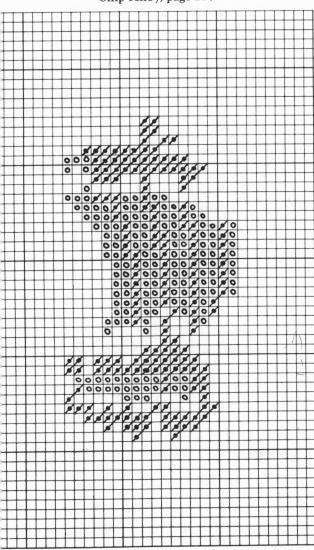

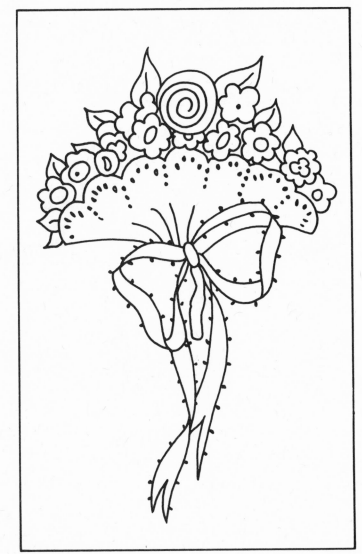

MEDIUM GREEN ⊙
MEDIUM BLUE ◪

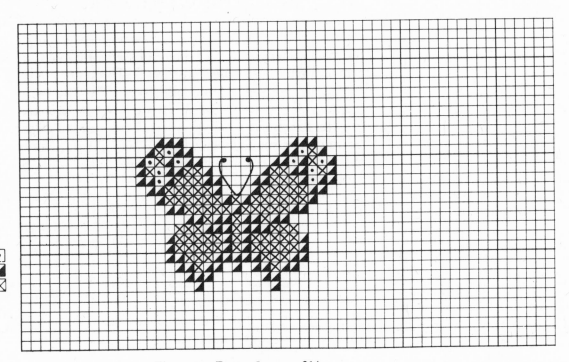

MEDIUM YELLOW ⊡
ORANGE ◰
MEDIUM RED ⊠

Fluttering Butterfly, page 214

25
Gifts

Gifts are a part of many holiday and personal celebrations. A gift can be elaborate or simple, but it is usually more meaningful if it has been made by hand or personalized by the giver in some way. It becomes, then, a gift of time and thought and effort, valuable far beyond its actual material worth. The giver reaps from giving, and the holiday celebrant from celebrating, in direct proportion to the personal effort expended, a fact which was realized long ago.

The gift projects presented below have been selected from the hundreds on the pages of *The Delineator, Peterson's Magazine,* and *Godey's Lady's Book* for their nostalgic interest as well as their relevance to today's way of life. They have been grouped by type and include a particularly generous sampling of three extremely popular gift items from the late 1800's—pincushions, sachets, and photo frames.

Clothing, of course, was popular for gifts, but it has not been included in this collection of gift projects because of the obvious complications of sizes and the fact that styles have changed so many times during the time span covered by this book.

There is a gift here for everyone. Everything is in the interpretation and styling of the item. Let need and taste be your guide to combining fabrics, colors, and designs which are suitable and absolutely perfect for a given occasion and recipient. Many of the projects also make ideal bazaar items.

The projects in this section range widely, in terms of skills required. Although some projects do require special needlecraft techniques, the majority can be successfully completed by anyone even modestly handy with scissors and glue or needle and thread. There are many projects which involve merely decorating a purchased item. This was a popular approach to gift making, one whose possibilities are often overlooked today.

In the pages which follow, instructions for specific projects are given. Some can be made by children. When a specific craft or technique is part of the project, there will be a reference to the appropriate pages in the Craft Basics section.

Sentiments to Send with Gifts

by Ethel Colson

With a box of Candy
"Sweets to the sweet," the wise old saw
    I quote because 'tis fitting,
And tribute pay unto the law
    With gladness unremitting,
"Like unto like" is also true,
Wherefore these candies haste to you.

With Embroidery or Needlework of Any Kind
May all your years be glad and bright,
    Deep-filled with pleasant days,
And all your hours know sweet delight
    Of love that lives and stays!
With each such wishes, true and kind,
    Each Christmas (New Year) (birthday)
        should begin,
While some of these must surely bind,
    Because **they've been sewed in!**

For Any Sort of Holiday Remembrance
Here's a thought of joyous cheer
For Christmas and for all the year!

With a Laundry Bag, Soap, etc.
This gift is clean, as you may see,
So every time you'd cleaner be
Just send a pleasant thought to me!

With an Affectionate Gift of Any Kind
Good luck to you, and varied cheer,
    All sorts of wishes tender,
And may they hold for all the year,
    So prays (hopes) the loving
        (friendly) sender.
May life be good and glad and gay,
    No matter where you find it,
And may you meet no briefest day
    But leaves a smile behind it!

With Cutlery, Scissors, Pins, or Other
"Sharp-Edged" Present
The heart (thought, love) that sends this
    gift to you
Is "true as steel," yet tender, too.
While never superstitious fear
Need rise to chill our Christmas (joyous)
    (birthday) (loving) cheer.
The friendship that has stood time's test
May safely smile at all the rest.

The Delineator, 1910

Sachets

Sachets were considered "delicate conceits" and were much favored for those gifts one wanted to give but didn't want to put too much time into. They serve much the same purpose today, the difference being that they are a bit unusual and not commonly received. The fragrance in the sachet is imparted by sachet powder, for which heavily scented dusting powder may be substituted if necessary. Sachet fragrances vary widely and should be selected with the recipient in mind (musk for men, violets for romantics). And coordinated with the mood of the covering of the sachet. (See mail order list for sachet powder source.)

The sachet powder may be sprinkled or spooned into a sachet bag alternately with the batting. When filling a sachet with a long shape, gently pull apart the batting into two layers, sprinkle powder on one layer, top with the second layer and slide gently into the bag. When styling sachets, do not overlook the possibilities of using ribbons in lieu of fabric and purchased appliqués for embroidered accents.

Folded Sachet, Peterson's Magazine, 1891

COLOR PLATE 23

This is a lovely sachet, to embroider or not as desired. The sachet in Color Plate 23 uses the original color scheme.

KEY TO CRAFT TECHNIQUES: Read through the project and then check for general information in the Craft Basics chapter beginning on page 282. Techniques and skills are listed alphabetically with complete how-to information.

MATERIALS:
- 16″ pink ribbon, 3″ wide
- 16″ green ribbon, 3″ wide
- 1 yd. green ribbon, 1″ wide
- 15″ polyester batting, 2½″ wide
- silk embroidery floss: medium pink, light pink, dark green, medium green, light green, and black
- sachet powder
- beads, buttons, or ornaments (optional)
- marking equipment, embroidery needle, pink or green sewing thread

STEP-BY-STEP:
1. Transfer designs from Design Sheet, page 247 to each end of green and pink ribbons on right side.

2. Embroider design as follows:

    stems 4 strands, dark green, stem stitch
    leaves 6 strands, medium green and light green, satin stitch
    flowers 6 strands, medium pink and light pink, satin stitch
    buds 6 strands, medium pink, satin stitch
    details 2 strands, black, straight stitch, French knot

3. Stitch ribbon ends, right sides together with embroidery at opposite ends, in a ½″ seam. Turn right sides out. Edgestitch one long edge together. Sprinkle sachet powder on batting and insert between ribbons. Edgestitch remaining long edge.

4. Fold sachet over, with pink embroidered end shorter and on top. Gather loosely and tie with a double bow about 2½″ below fold.

5. Sew beads, buttons, or ornaments to sachet ends as desired.

Lingerie Sachet, The Delineator, 1886

COLOR PLATE 23

The original was made in lavender brocade and tied in a "bewilderment of loops and ends that are gracefully careless looking." Choose delicate colors, fabrics, laces, and ribbons.

KEY TO CRAFT TECHNIQUES: Read through the project and then check for general information in the Craft Basics chapter beginning on page 282. Techniques and skills are listed alphabetically with complete how-to information.

MATERIALS:
- 1 piece fabric, 10″ × 4″ (If fabric is very sheer, use a double layer.)
- 2 yds. ribbon, about ¼″ wide
- 6″ gathered lace, about 1¼″ wide
- polyester fiberfill or cotton batting
- sachet powder
- needle and thread, sewing machine (optional)

STEP-BY-STEP:
1. Fold fabric right sides together to form 4″ × 5″ rectangle and stitch along sides. Press seams open and turn.
2. Turn under fabric edges at top ¼″ and ¼″ again and hem.
3. Stitch edge of lace to top of bag, folding under raw end of lace where lace overlaps.
4. Stuff bag, to within 1″ of top with fiberfill or batting sprinkled with sachet powder.
5. Tie top of bag in multiple bows.

Drawer Sachet, The Delineator, 1900

COLOR PLATE 23

The long narrow shape of this sachet distributes fragrance evenly throughout the drawer.

KEY TO CRAFT TECHNIQUES: Read through the project and then check for general information in the Craft Basics chapter beginning on page 282. Techniques and skills are listed alphabetically with complete how-to information.

MATERIALS:
- 1 yd. embroidered ribbon, about 1½″ wide
- 1½ yd. narrow ribbon, about ⅛″ wide, contrasting color
- polyester fiberfill
- sachet powder
- needle, thread

STEP-BY-STEP:
1. Cut embroidered ribbon into two 18″ pieces.
2. Edgestitch embroidered ribbon pieces, wrong sides together, along each long edge. Stuff puffs of fiberfill, alternately sprinkling with sachet powder, into tube, leaving about 2″ unstuffed at each end.
3. Cut narrow ribbon in half and tie in a double bow about 2″ from each end.
4. Notch ends of ribbon.

Padded Hanger Sachet, The Delineator, Holiday Souvenir, 1899-1900

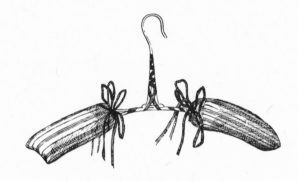

COLOR PLATE 23

This practical and really lovely gift imparts a faint delicate fragrance to the clothing it supports. Wide ribbon may be substituted for fabric.

KEY TO CRAFT TECHNIQUES: Read through the project and then check for general information in the Craft Basics chapter beginning on page 282. Techniques and skills are listed alphabetically with complete how-to information.

MATERIALS:
- 2 7″ × 8″ pieces of smooth fabric
- 1 wooden dress hanger, about 16″ long
- 4 ft. ribbon, about ¼″ wide
- 2 3″ × 12″ pieces polyester batting
- 2 6″ × 18″ pieces polyester batting
- sachet powder
- needle, thread, sewing machine (optional), bodkin or safety pin

STEP-BY-STEP:
1. Wrap narrow batting piece around end of

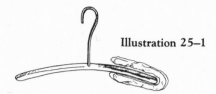

Illustration 25-1

hanger (Illustration 25-1). Wrap wide batting piece around arm, sprinkling layers with sachet powder. Tighten batting to a diameter of about 6″. Catchstitch batting in place along side and across end (Illustration 25-2). Repeat for other end of hanger.

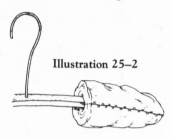

Illustration 25-2

2. To make sachet bags, fold fabric right sides together lengthwise and stitch side and one end in ½″ seam. Press seam open. Turn right side out. Repeat for other bag.

3. Turn open edge of bag inside ½″ and stitch ⅜″ from edge forming a casing. Repeat for other bag.

4. Open stitching in seam of casing. Cut narrow ribbon in half and thread one piece through casing of each bag.

5. Slip bag over padded hanger end, draw ribbon up tight and run one end of ribbon around hanger hook then tie in a double bow at sachet bag. Repeat for other end.

Hanging Star Sachet, The Delineator, 1893

Adapted from a pincushion, this sachet can be tied over a closet rod. The original was made in pink china silk with silk embroidery around the star. Use the same color today with darker pink star.

KEY TO CRAFT TECHNIQUES: Read through the project and then check for general information in the Craft Basics chapter beginning on page 282. Techniques and skills are listed alphabetically with complete how-to information.

MATERIALS:
- 2 8″ circles of lightweight fabric
- 1 scrap stiff fabric, contrasting darker color
- 1 piece lightweight cardboard
- 5 puffs polyester fiberfill
- embroidery floss to match lighter fabric
- ½ yd. ribbon, about ½″ wide
- sachet powder
- needle, thread, sewing machine (optional), white glue

STEP-BY-STEP:
1. Mark center of circle with tailor tack. Stitch circles, right sides together, around edges in a ½″ seam, leaving an opening for turning. Clip curves and turn. Press edges of opening under ½″.

2. Insert 5 puffs of fiberfill sprinkled with sachet powder into circle to fill loosely. Slipstitch opening.

3. Divide circle into 5 equal parts with pins, with a puff of fiberfill in each section. Gather each section with running stitch from edge to center and secure in center. (Illustration 25-3).

4. Fold ribbon in half and stitch fold to edge of sachet between two sections.

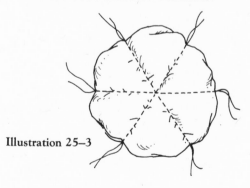

Illustration 25-3

5. To make star for front, cut paper pattern (see page 101) which measures 2¾" point to point. Trace and cut star out of cardboard. Cut star pattern out of contrasting fabric adding ½" turn under allowance all around.

6. Wrap star fabric around cardboard star and glue in place on back mitering points and clipping corners.

7. Slipstitch star to sachet so that star points fall between puffed sections. Embroider edges of cardboard-covered star through fabric only, using long and short stitch.

8. Tie ribbon ends into loop with bow at top. Untie to hang around closet rod.

Pincushions

Pincushions were another popular gift item. The Victorian age abounded with them, generally ornate monstrosities with rows of lace, beads, or ribbon, often in designs hollowed out to hold a scent bottle in the middle. The pincushions were often quite large, for use with dressing, hat, and stick pins, no doubt, and were filled with every conceivable stuffing—bran, hair, and sawdust, to name a few. Later, cotton batting became a practical filler, although sawdust remains the best filler for the "serious" pincushion. (When using a sawdust filling, make a muslin inner bag to prevent leakage.) Cotton batting runs a close second because it is easy to work with. Avoid polyester fiberfill, which may dull the pins. Emery cushions were also common. Smaller than pincushions, and not quite as ornate, they set about their serious task of keeping those pins and needles sharp and rust free.

Round Pincushion, The Delineator, 1877

COLOR PLATES 2 and 23

The original was a pillbox covered with embroidered kid. The pincushion pictured uses ribbon, crepe, and a spray-can top. To use a spray-can top with a rim, coordinate ribbon color with cap color and let rim show or glue ¼" ribbon over rim. Glue felt circle on bottom of cap to hide any advertising messages.

KEY TO CRAFT TECHNIQUES: Read through the project and then check for general information in the Craft Basics chapter beginning on page 282. Techniques and skills are listed alphabetically with complete how-to information.

MATERIALS:
- 1 spray-can top
- 1 piece ribbon or trim, same width as cap and long enough to reach around cap with 1" overlap
- 1 piece ¼" ribbon to fit around cap twice
- large scrap muslin
- large scrap lightweight fabric to cover cushion
- sawdust or cotton batting
- white glue, rubber bands

STEP-BY-STEP:
1. Cut muslin diameter of cap plus 3" all around. Baste around edges and draw up to form a bag. Pack tightly with sawdust, testing fit into cap periodically. When bag is tightly packed and proper size, twist rubber band tightly around end of bag (Illustration 25-4). Avoid pleating around edges of bag. Pound and mold to refine shape, which should be a cylinder slightly rounded on top. (Illustration 25-5)

Illustration 25–4

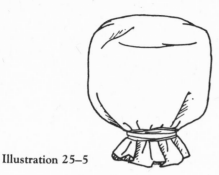

Illustration 25–5

2. Stretch scrap of cover fabric smoothly and tightly over stuffed muslin and secure in place with rubber band. Avoid pleats along sides.

3. Cover cap by gluing wide ribbon along edges. Turn ribbon end under ½″ and overlap ½″ for neat finish. Glue narrow ribbon around top and bottom edges of cap.

4. Put glue around rim of cap on inside and tightly fit stuffed unit into cap.

Sea Shell Pincushion, The Delineator, 1893

COLOR PLATE 23

A novel way to use shells gathered on a vacation at the shore, the original design featured two shells glued together, one stuffed as a pincushion, the other left open for rings, keys, etcetera.

KEY TO CRAFT TECHNIQUES: Read through the project and then check for general information in the Craft Basics chapter beginning on page 282. Techniques and skills are listed alphabetically with complete how-to information.

MATERIALS:
- 1 or 2 large sea shells, fairly deep (If 2, choose similar shape and size.)
- several smaller shells for trimming (optional)

- scrap of muslin twice the size of the shell
- scrap of silk or velvet fabric to cover cushion
- sawdust or cotton batting
- needle, thread, sewing machine, white glue, emery paper

STEP-BY-STEP:
1. Polish edges of shell with emery paper.
2. Trace shape of shell on double layer of muslin and cut out, allowing ¼″ for seam allowance all around. Cut shell shape out of velvet, allowing 1″ extra all around.
3. Stitch muslin shapes together around edges in ¼″ seam, leaving an opening. Clip curves, turn, and pack tightly with sawdust. Overcast opening. Pound and mold into a shape which fits into shell.
4. Wrap velvet around muslin bag, easing around edges, and stitch in place on back.
5. Check fit of bag in shell, then glue in place.
6. Ornament with smaller shells (optional).

Flower Pincushion, The Delineator, 1881

COLOR PLATES 23

This design can be made into many different flowers depending on the colors chosen. Let a garden be your inspiration and make a daisy with a yellow center and white petals, a sunflower with a brown center and yellow petals, a poppy with a black center and red petals.

KEY TO CRAFT TECHNIQUES: Read through the project and then check for general information in the Craft Basics chapter beginning on page 282. Techniques and skills are listed alphabetically with complete how-to information.

MATERIALS:
- ¼ yd. 45″ imitation suede, felt, or equivalent scraps

- 12″ × 14″ remnant of cotton print, coordinating color
- sawdust or cotton batting for stuffing
- small piece lightweight cardboard
- scissors, needle, thread

STEP-BY-STEP:

1. Transfer petal pattern (see Design Sheet, page 247) to cardboard and cut 45 petals out of suede.

2. Cut one 10⅝″ circle and one 3½″ circle from cotton fabric. Easestitch 1⅜″ and 3¼″ from edge of large circle and ½″ from edge of small circle.

3. Make 3 circles of petals. Pleat one petal by folding on the long line and bringing short lines together on right side of petal. Secure pleat with one or two whipstitches, using matching thread. Lap next petal over pleated petal, whipstitch in place, pleat, whipstitch, lap next petal and continue around circle in same fashion until 15 petals are joined. Lap last petal over first and stitch together securely. Repeat with remaining petals.

4. Draw up easestitching row closest to center of large circle so that the petal circles will fit. Pin petals in place, then stitch to fabric close to edge of petals. Place next circle over first so that petals are staggered and do not cover the points of the first row of petals. Stitch in place. Repeat with last circle of petals.

5. Draw up easestitching row closest to edge on large circle to form a pouch for stuffing. Stuff so that center of flower is plump and remainder of cushion is filled tightly. Pull up remaining easestitching to enclose stuffing. Lap raw edges of circle and tack together securely.

6. Cut one 2″ circle from lightweight cardboard. Draw up ease-stitching on small fabric circle and place cardboard circle inside. Draw up ease to fit snugly and smoothly and tack raw edges of fabric circle together with whipstitching.

7. Place fabric-covered cardboard circle over raw edges of fabric on cushion bottom and, using doubled thread, whipstitch circle to cushion.

Pansy Pincushion, The Delineator, 1883

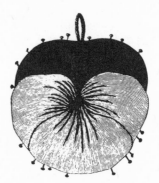

COLOR PLATE 2

A pretty flower pincushion, this would also be a lovely sachet. Make small ones of felt for New Year's favors and stuff with cotton batting, eliminating seam allowances and muslin inner bag. Muslin step is necessary only when pincushion is being stuffed with sawdust.

KEY TO CRAFT TECHNIQUES: Read through the project and then check for general information in the Craft Basics chapter beginning on page 282. Techniques and skills are listed alphabetically with complete how-to information.

MATERIALS:

- scraps of velvet or flannel in 2 pansy colors as desired: 2 yellows, purple and yellow, purple and lavender, black and yellow, brown and yellow, purple and white
- large scrap muslin
- embroidery floss, black
- sawdust or cotton batting
- 6″ cord, yarn, or ribbon (optional)
- needle, thread, sewing machine

STEP-BY-STEP:

1. Cut pattern C out of doubled layer of muslin. Cut pattern A out of color 1 and pattern B and C out of color 2. See Design Sheet, page 248.

2. Stitch top edge of piece B on stitching line. Clip curves and corners. Press edge under.

3. Lap pressed edge of piece B over piece A and slipstitch or edgestitch in place.

4. Embroider details according to pattern pieces in stem stitch.

5. Stitch muslin pieces together with ¼″ seam

allowance, leaving opening. Clip curves and turn.

6. Stitch cover pieces right sides together with ¼" seam allowance, leaving an opening. Clip curves and turn.

7. Insert muslin bag into cover bag. Pack muslin bag tightly with sawdust and overcast opening. Turn in edges of cover bag ¼" and slipstitch.

8. Stitch ends of optional ribbon, yarn, or cord in place on back of pincushion.

Star Pincushion, The Delineator, 1882

COLOR PLATE 2

Use different patterned fabrics, as for New Year's pincushion favors, or enlarge the pattern to 3"-long diamonds and decorate plain fabric with embroidery, as in the original. Use white embroidery on various solids.

KEY TO CRAFT TECHNIQUES: Read through the project and then check for general information in the Craft Basics chapter beginning on page 282. Techniques and skills are listed alphabetically with complete how-to information.

MATERIALS:
- scraps of 5 different fabrics
- sawdust or cotton batting
- embroidery floss
- needle, thread, sewing machine
- 6" ribbon or cord (optional)

STEP-BY-STEP:
1. Trace diamond (Design Sheet, page 248) and embroidery designs on 5 different fabrics, enlarging if desired. Work embroidery as desired.
2. Cut out embroidered pieces and one

additional piece of each different color, adding ¼" all around to all pieces.

3. Piece embroidered fabrics together and plain fabrics together into two stars.

4. Right sides together, stitch edges of stars in ¼" seam, matching like colors, leaving an opening.

5. Pack star tightly with batting. Slipstitch opening and handstitch ends of optional ribbon or cord in place.

Photograph Frames

Fabric-covered frames for photographs were favorite gifts during the era when "to kodak it" was a common phrase. People were fascinated by cameras, and portraits were considered especially suitable gifts for Valentine's Day, anniversaries, and birthdays. The portraits were often presented in a lovely frame or soft folding photo case.

The frames in this section have been chosen from among the many elaborately decorated ones presented in the magazines. They make lovely gifts with or without photographs. A pretty print fabric or gift wrapping paper inserted behind the opening makes a nice presentation in the absence of a photograph. The frames have a common basic construction, as do the mats which surround the frame opening. Embroidery was the needlework from popularly used to ornament the mats, which were often padded. The frame may have an easel back, stand as part of a group, or hang.

The instructions for the Basic Photograph Frame below will serve as a guide for the construction of the designs which follow.

Basic Photograph Frame

KEY TO CRAFT TECHNIQUES: Read through the project and then check for general information in the Craft Basics chapter beginning on page 282. Techniques and skills are listed alphabetically with complete how-to information.

MATERIALS:
- mat or illustration board, enough to cut out desired shape at least twice and one optional

easel stand. Shirt cardboard is suitable for some frames and children can work with it more easily.

• fabric to cover one frame shape (and back, optional). Firmly woven fabrics such as muslin, broadcloth, and taffeta are easiest to work with, but the lovely effects possible with velvets, brocades, and silks can be worth the extra effort.

• lightweight batting or polyester fleece

• ornamental materials: ribbon, lace, embroidery floss and yarn, cord, appliqués, etcetera.

• strong glue or stapler with short staples

• white glue

• sharp scissors, utility knife, metal ruler and metal shapes (see below)

• ½" wide ribbon for hinge (used with easel back) 5"–7" long

• self-sticking hanger (for hanging frame)

STEP-BY-STEP:
Cut Mat

1. Cut 2 or 3 pieces of mat board into desired size. Cut easel 2½" wide × ¾ of height of frame.

2. Cut desired shape hole out of center of mat board(s), leaving one piece whole to serve as back of frame.

   • Use utility knife and cut slowly, going a little deeper with each cut. Do not attempt to cut all the way through with the first cut.

   • Use a metal ruler to guide straight edges (Illustration 25-6) for proper relationship between metal ruler and mat board. Ruler should

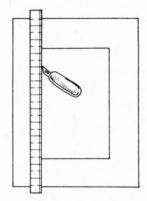

Illustration 25–6

shield the mat, not the hole. Used carefully, a tin can of proper size may be used to guide round edges. Be on the lookout for other interesting metal shapes which might be suitable templates.

• Some products, such as tissues and fancy soaps and powders, are packaged in containers made of stiff cardboard with interestingly-shaped, die-cut openings. These can often be utilized in frames.

• Precut mats are available in art supply stores. If used, step 2 can be omitted.

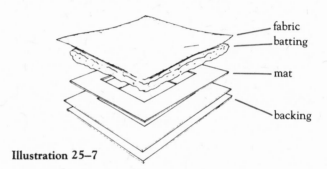

fabric
batting
mat
backing

Illustration 25–7

Cover Mat (See Illustration 25-7 for components and order.)

3. Mark mat opening shape and outside corners of frame on cover fabric, using tailor tacks. If mat covering fabric is going to be embroidered, do it now.

4. Cut out fabric in frame shape, adding 1½" all around. Do not cut out mat opening.

5. To pad frame, cut two layers of batting in frame shape, with cut-out mat opening. Glue batting to frame.

6. Stretch cover fabric over padded mat around edges. Securely fasten to back of board using glue or staples. Staples must not show on right side. Miter corners. Do not stretch too tightly. If you want a covered frame back, cover a frame piece without mat opening in the manner just described.

7. Cut fabric out of mat opening, leaving 1" turn-under allowance all around.

   • For rectangular or square opening, clip into corners, stopping ¼" from corner. Put a tiny dab of white glue at ends of cuts, if fabric has tendency to ravel. Stretch edges to back and glue.

• For rounded opening, clip curves similarly but handle very carefully. Many clips may be necessary to turn a smooth edge.

• Place frame under heavy weights (i.e., books) after each gluing to assure a tight, flat bond, or hold edges in place with paper clips while drying.

Assemble Frame

8. Staple or glue optional second board with mat opening behind fabric-covered board. Use of this piece helps stabilize frame.

9. Position photo as desired behind cutout in mat. Glue in place with a dab of glue in each corner or, for removable photo, trace outline of photo on back of frame.

10. Staying outside the traced line (see step 9), fasten back of frame to front with glue or staples, on top, one side, and bottom. If photo is to be permanently enclosed, fasten all sides.

11. Choose display method:

• **Easel back** Score and bend easel 1½″ from one end. Glue or staple this end to back of frame. Glue one end of ribbon hinge to lower end of easel. Adjust ribbon length as desired and glue other end of ribbon to back of frame. (Illustration 25-8)

• **Standing group** Slipstitch sides of several identical frames loosely together. Position at desired angle to stand.

• **Hanging** Attach a self-adhesive hanging hook to back.

Illustration 25–8

Embroidered Photograph Frame, Peterson's Magazine, 1882

COLOR PLATE 23

The original colors for this "new and exceedingly pretty affair" were 3 shades of blue silk embroidery on black satin fabric, with moss green shades for the leaves, wood color for the stems. The original frame was part of a group. The frame shown in Color Plate 23 is embroidered in warm pinks on muslin. It has an easel back and a 2½″ × 4½″ opening, which will hold a 3½″ × 5″ photo, a common size.

KEY TO CRAFT TECHNIQUES: Read through the project and then check for general information in the Craft Basics chapter beginning on page 282. Techniques and skills are listed alphabetically with complete how-to information.

MATERIALS:

• basic frame materials and equipment (see Basic Photograph Frame, page 231.)
• 10″ × 13″ natural color muslin
• cotton embroidery floss: dark kelly green, red, light pink, violet
• ½ yd. lightweight polyester batting
• marking equipment, embroidery needle

STEP-BY-STEP:

1. Transfer embroidery design (see Design Sheet, page 249) to center of fabric. With tailor tacks, indicate corners of center opening and frame edges.

2. Embroider design as follows:

stems 3 strands, dark kelly green, stem stitch
leaves 6 strands, dark kelly green, satin stitch

flowers 6 strands, red, light pink, and violet, satin stitch

3. Clean and block as necessary.

4. Construct mat following steps 1–7 in Basic Photograph Frame section, using the embroidered fabric in step 6.

5. Assemble frame following steps 8–11, applying easel back as in step 11.

Lace Mat, Godey's Lady's Book, 1898

COLOR PLATE 22

The original frame was made in red silk with crocheted lace tacked flatly around the opening and ribbon binding on the edges. The mat shown in Color Plate 22 is covered in natural color muslin, with natural color ruffled lace placed away from the actual opening for a different interpretation.

KEY TO CRAFT TECHNIQUES: Read through the project and then check for general information in the Craft Basics chapter beginning on page 282. Techniques and skills are listed alphabetically with complete how-to information.

MATERIALS:
- basic frame materials and equipment (see Basic Photograph Frame, page 231.)
- ½ yd. muslin (or other fabric)
- ½ yd. lightweight batting
- 1 yd. lace
- 2 precut oval mats
- fabric glue

STEP-BY-STEP:
1. Mark oval lightly on fabric using mat as a guide.

2. Pad mat with two layers of batting. Glue batting to mat.

3. Measure and mark lace placement by marking 1″ all around oval on fabric. Do not cut out oval. Pin lace to marking. Stitch by machine (Illustration 25-9). Press.

Illustration 25–9

4. Stretch muslin in place on padded mat surface. Glue to back of mat. Use paper clips to hold fabric in place while glue dries. Miter corners with glue. Let dry.

5. Cut oval opening 1″ from marking. Clip oval to within ¼″ of marking. Saturate clips with glue and press to back of mat board.

6. Glue on another oval mat (slightly smaller oval) to finish back.

7. Use as a mat or construct a frame according to Basic Photograph Frame section.

Folding Photograph Case, Peterson's Magazine, 1871

A traveler would welcome this novel item. The original was covered with brown silk and featured black beaded embroidery around the frames. The instructions below are for a case styled in leather or imitation leather for a gentleman. Use fabrics such as calico, chintz, or brocade for a lady. For fabrics other than leather, purchased bias seam binding can be used on the edges. A ribbon tie will be appropriate for a lady's case. The case measures 6½″ × 5″ folded.

KEY TO CRAFT TECHNIQUES: Read through the project and then check for general information in the Craft Basics chapter beginning on page 282. Techniques and skills are listed alphabetically with complete how-to information.

MATERIALS:

- basic frame materials and equipment (see Basic Photograph Frame, page 231.)
- ¼ yd. leather or imitation leather, at least 36″ wide
- 1 scrap contrasting color leather or imitation leather, 5½″ × 8½″ (optional—see step 2 below)
- white glue
- needle, thread, sewing machine (optional)
- artist's knife

STEP-BY-STEP:

1. Cut two pieces mat board each 6½″ × 5″ (pieces A) and 1 piece 5½″ × 4″ (piece B). Cut desired frame ovals (see Design Sheet, page 248) in piece B.

2. Cut two pieces of leather each 6½″ × 10″ (pieces A) and one piece 5½″ × 8½″ (piece B—may be contrasting color if desired). Cut binding strips: two each 10½″ × 1⅛″; two each 6½″ × 1⅛″; one tab 7″ × 1⅛″; one tab holder 2¾″ × ½″; one picture holder 5″ × 1½″.

3. Position tab on right side of one leather piece A, centered and 2½″ from the edge, and stitch in place across end (Illustration 25-10). Position tab holder on right side of other piece A, with edge of holder 2½″ from edge of fabric. Stitch ends in place (Illustration 25-11).

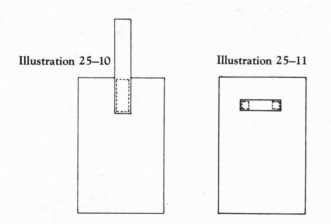

Illustration 25—10   Illustration 25—11

4. Lightly glue wrong side of leather piece A to both sides of cardboard piece A, wrapping leather around board along one long edge. Matching edges, glue wrong side of leather piece B to one side of cardboard piece B with cutouts (Illustration 25-12). Cut leather away

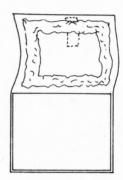

Illustration 25—12

from openings. Wrap leather around cardboard piece B and glue other side. Cut out openings carefully as this will become right side of frame. Leather will extend ½″ beyond long edge on right side. Glue leather picture holder strip on wrong side of frame cutouts. (Illustration 25-13)

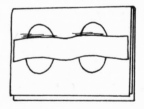

Illustration 25—13

5. Glue extension of piece B to wrong side of piece A, which has tab attached. Piece B should be ½″ from each end of piece A, but must match along cut edges. (Illustration 25-14)

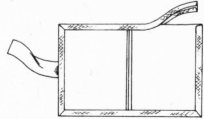

Illustration 25—14

6. Finger press 6½″ binding strips in half lengthwise and glue around long raw edges of pieces A, overlapping ½″ on each side. (Illustration 25-15)

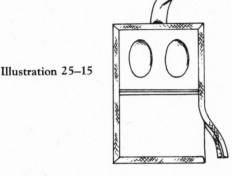

Illustration 25–15

7. Place unbound edges of pieces A toward each other, right sides down, ½″ apart. Finger press remaining binding strips (10½″) and glue around remaining edges of pieces A. Trim binding at corners to miter. Glue binding to itself in space between frame covers. Use paper clips to hold glued edges while drying.

Soft Photograph Case, The Delineator, 1887

COLOR PLATE 22

The original of this "beautiful ornament for a table" was light olive green velvet with a pale gold, quilted silk lining. Thick silk cord bordered all the edges and silk embroidery ornamented the case. Use this type of case as a recipe file, for memo pad/date book, small sewing kit, or lingerie holder. Adjust the size to the purpose. The two cases below for photos hold 8″ × 10″ (case A) or 5″ × 7″ or snapshots (case B). Construction is the same for each case.

KEY TO CRAFT TECHNIQUES: Read through the project and then check for general information in the Craft Basics chapter beginning on page 282. Techniques and skills are listed alphabetically with complete how-to information.

MATERIALS:
- double-faced quilted fabric:
  ½ yd., at least 36″ wide, for large case (A)
  ¼ yd. for small case (B)
- purchased bias seam binding, about ⅞″ wide
  2¼ yd. for large case (A)
  1¾ yd. for small case (B)
- ½ yd. grosgrain ribbon, about 1½″ wide, to match binding

STEP-BY-STEP:
1. Cut out case according to measurements on Illustration 25-16 or Illustration 25-17.

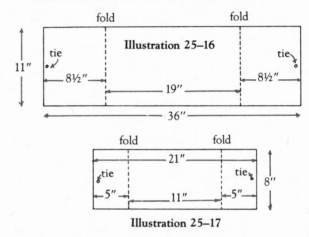

2. Bind 2 short edges, following binding package instructions. (Illustration 25-18)
3. On fold lines, fold bound edges toward center of case on inside; press. Cut ribbon in half and notch one end of each piece. Position unnotched ends on outside of case in center of folded edge, matching edges. Machine baste around all edges. (Illustration 25-19)
4. Bind all edges, rounding off corners. To bind, open out binding and sew to inside of case stitching in fold. Ease in curves around corners and trim away excess fabric. Turn binding over edges and slipstitch on outside. Note: Sew on binding in ½″ seam for case A and ¼″ seam for case B. Self-fabric binding may be used if preferred.

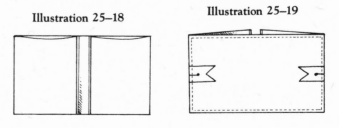

Illustration 25–18   Illustration 25–19

Pillows and Throws

Pillows as gifts provide ample opportunity for creative expression. Needlework techniques suitable for pillows vary widely and there is practically no limit to what can be done in the way of color, design, and ornamentation of pillows. A bit of sachet powder sprinkled in with the pillow stuffing adds an extra dimension.

Pillow covers may be made to fit foam rubber forms or they may more easily be stuffed to the desired plumpness with polyester fiberfill. If care has been taken with the selection of the covering materials, these pillows may then be washed. Although some pillows do have zipper closures installed in one seam, a simple overcast or slipstitched seam is quick and easy to do and less bulky than a zipper.

Many variations on the blanket theme are possible, too, and it is a quick way to make a fancy gift out of a plain piece of fabric (a special large remnant perhaps?). Many fabric weights are suitable. Monograms add to the personal nature of a throw and various fringe styles are interesting to experiment with.

Patchwork Pillow, The Delineator, 1895

COLOR PLATE 22

The version shown is interpreted in tiny calico prints and solids. *The Delineator* suggested "crazy" patchwork as well, with ornamental embroidery on the seams of the fancy silk, satin, and velvet fabrics, and cautioned that some sections of a very dark color were essential to the design. To recreate the pillow photographed, use these colors: color A, black print; B, blue print; C, red print; D, black solid; E, white solid; F, yellow print; G, blue solid.

KEY TO CRAFT TECHNIQUES: Read through the project and then check for general information in the Craft Basics chapter beginning on page 282. Techniques and skills are listed alphabetically with complete how-to information.

MATERIALS:
- generous scraps of fabrics above, 4 prints, 3 solids
- ½ yd. fabric for pillow backing (may be one of patch fabrics)
- polyester fiberfill
- scissors, needle, thread, sewing machine (optional)

STEP-BY-STEP:

1. Using templates P1–P7 (see Design Sheet, page 250), cut the following:

   P1 (16 times) 4 color A, 4 color B, 8 color C
   P2 (16 times) 8 color D, 8 color E
   P3 (8 times) 4 color B, 4 color A
   P4 (4 times) 4 color C
   P5 (20 times) 12 color F, 4 color A, 4 color B
   P6 (4 times) 4 color C
   P7 (8 times) 8 color G

   When cutting add ¼″ all around each piece for seam allowance and observe straight of grain.

2. Stitch pieces together by hand, ending stitches ¼″ from each seam end to enable exact matching at corners. Block is composed of squares (Illustration 25-20). Piece each square separately, then join squares to form block.

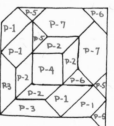

Illustration 25–20

3. Using pieced pillow front as a pattern, cut a back out of fabric. Place front and back right sides together and stitch all around, leaving an opening. Clip corners. Turn and stuff. Slipstitch opening.

Lace and Ribbon Pillow, The Delineator, 1882

Originally a "tidy," this design adapts to a lovely pillow. Use embroidered satin or brocade ribbons or treasured antique ribbons and lace. For a delicate boudoir pillow, use white, ecru, or pale colors.

KEY TO CRAFT TECHNIQUES: Read through the project and then check for general information in the Craft Basics chapter beginning on page 282. Techniques and skills are listed alphabetically with complete how-to information.

MATERIALS:
- 16" ribbon, 1" wide, color A
- 8" ribbon, 1½" wide, color B
- 16" ribbon, 2" wide, color C
- 43" ribbon, 1½" wide, color D
- 59" lace, 2" wide
- polyester fiberfill
- 11½" × 12" fabric for backing pillow
- needle, thread, pins, sewing machine (optional)

STEP-BY-STEP:
1. Cut 1" and 2" ribbons into two 8" pieces each.
2. Lap long edges of ribbons slightly and stitch together along edge. (Illustration 25-21)

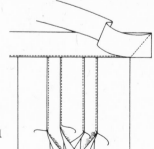

Illustration 25–21

3. Overlap and stitch remaining 1½" ribbon around lapped ribbon section, mitering corners.
4. Overlap and stitch lace around ribbon section, mitering corners.
5. Press edges of pillow back fabric under ½" all around. Wrong sides together, pin pillow back to pillow front matching pressed edge of back and ribbon edge (Illustration 25-22). Pin care-

Illustration 25–22

fully to avoid damaging ribbon. Stitch, leaving an opening on one side.
6. Stuff pillow and slipstitch opening.

Star Patchwork Pillow, The Delineator, 1883

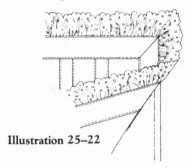

Originally presented as a lamp mat, this design makes an interesting shape pillow with its unusual seven-segment star. Among the color combinations suggested were crimson and pale blue, myrtle and pink, sage and ceil, and terra-cotta and orange, in velvet and satin fabrics. Tassels were added to the corners.

KEY TO CRAFT TECHNIQUES: Read through the project and then check for general information in the Craft Basics chapter beginning on page 282. Techniques and skills are listed alphabetically with complete how-to information.

MATERIALS:
- generous scraps of fabrics in 2 colors
- embroidery floss, crewel yarn, or pearl cotton
- ½ yd. fabric for pillow back
- polyester fiberfill
- needle and thread, sewing machine (optional)

STEP-BY-STEP:
1. Trace one diamond and one square pattern (see Design Sheet, page 250) on templates. Trace on fabric and add ¼″ seam allowance all around. Cut seven diamonds out of one color and seven squares of the other.
2. Piece star together out of the diamond shapes, sewing sides A together.
3. Piece squares to star in design shown.
4. Work stem stitch over seams.
5. Using pieced pillow front as a pattern, cut a back for the pillow from fabric. Place right sides together and stitch front to back leaving an opening. Clip corners, turn, and stuff. Slipstitch opening.

Satin Shapes—Heart, Star, and Leaf, The Delineator, 1926

Make shaped pillows in satin, the glamour fabric of the late Twenties and early Thirties. The leaf design is adapted from a *Delineator* pen wiper design from 1885. For heart, star, and leaf designs see Design Sheet, pages 251 and 252. Choose bright red for the heart, blue or gray for the star, and autumnal hues for the leaf.

KEY TO CRAFT TECHNIQUES: Read through the project and then check for general information in the Craft Basics chapter beginning on page 282. Techniques and skills are listed alphabetically with complete how-to information.

MATERIALS:
- satin fabric as desired, according to pattern and size chosen
- polyester fiberfill
- needle and thread, sewing machine (optional)

- cable cord, ¼″ diameter (optional) or purchased covered cording

STEP-BY-STEP:
1. Enlarge chosen pattern to desired size.
2. Cut shape out of doubled fabric. If edge is to be corded, cut a 1¾″ wide bias strip to cover cording or use purchased covered cording. Strip must be large enough to reach around edges of pillow, plus 1″ for turn-under allowance.
3. Cover cording, turning under ends of covering ½″ at either end. Baste cording to pillow front, matching cording edge and pillow edge.
4. Place pillow back over pillow front, right sides together, enclosing cording. Stitch, leaving an opening. Clip curves and corners. Turn cover. Stuff. Slipstitch opening.

Embroidered Throw, The Delineator, 1895

COLOR PLATE 23

Carriage robes were a necessity in the days before cozily heated automobiles and this design was proposed for that purpose. Our interpretation in pink could grace the foot of a bed to be used for a quick nap. Work in acrylic yarns, washable fabric for a crib blanket. Worked in a darker fabric (navy on brick, ecru on forest green), the throw would make a nice stadium blanket or it could be kept in the car—its original intent fulfilled!

KEY TO CRAFT TECHNIQUES: Read through the project and then check for general information in the Craft Basics chapter beginning on page 282. Techniques and skills are listed alphabetically with complete how-to information.

MATERIALS:
- 2 yd. soft warm fabric, at least 54″ wide (select weight according to preference)
- tapestry wool. Design is worked in 3 strands of yarn, fringe is full strand (4-ply). 8½″ fringe requires 1 skein to cover 12″ of fabric.
- embroidery needle, scissors, fine crochet hook
- ¾ yd. lightweight lining fabric (optional), needle, thread

STEP-BY-STEP:

1. Straighten ends of fabric by cutting on a thread all the way across. Hem selvage edges if unsightly.

2. Transfer design to fabric with edge of design 4″ from edge of fabric, parallel to cut edges. Note: If fabric is extremely spongy, hot iron transfer pencil may be the most suitable transfer method.

3. Embroider design, using stem stitch throughout (see Design Sheet, page 252).

4. Press fabric ends under ½″ and make yarn fringe over pressed edge, thereby hemming blanket as fringe is applied (Illustration 25-23). Loosely wind yarn around 8½″ wide cardboard; cut one edge of yarn resulting in 17″ pieces of yarn to make fringe.

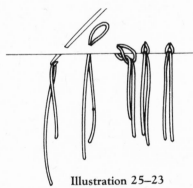

Illustration 25–23

5. To cover back of stitching (optional): Cut 6″ wide strips of lining fabric and stitch ends together. Cut into two strips long enough to extend across blanket plus 1″. Press edges under ½″ and slipstitch in place over back of embroidery.

Desk Accessories

Tasteful gifts for the gentleman have often been a problem for the home gift maker who wants to make something other than clothing. And during the Victorian era, propriety had also to be considered: the gift could be neither too personal nor too formal. A handsome desk accessory often seemed to be just the right thing and in addition gave one the pleasant opportunity to work with supple, sweet-smelling leathers.

The gifts in this section are styled for both men and women and often are made of paper and fabric instead of leather. By making fabric choices carefully, coordinated sets of desk accessories for a businessman or woman can be easily assembled.

Business Card Case, The Delineator, 1881

COLOR PLATE 22

A nice gift for a businessman or woman, the size and color can be customized to suit any taste, any size business card. The original was silk-embroidered kidskin; our versions of ribbon, topstitching, and imitation suede make up much more quickly.

KEY TO CRAFT TECHNIQUES: Read through the project and then check for general information in the Craft Basics chapter beginning on page 282. Techniques and skills are listed alphabetically with complete how-to information.

MATERIALS:
- scraps of leather or imitation suede
- scraps of lining fabric
- scraps of fusible interfacing
- 1 yd. ribbon, color A, ⅜″ wide
- 1 yd. ribbon, color B, ⅜″ wide
- scissors, thread, needle, sewing machine, white glue (optional)

STEP-BY-STEP:

1. Check business card for which case is intended, to be certain dimensions are suitable. Adjust if necessary. Trace cover pattern, piece A, and flap pattern, piece B (see Design Sheet, page 253). Cut one piece A from suede and one from fusible interfacing. Cut one piece A from lining, adding ½″ all around. Cut four pieces B from suede.

2. Apply fusible interfacing to wrong side of the lining. Press lining edges under ⅝″ all around, mitering corners.

3. Apply ribbon to right side of cover (piece A), following placement lines (Illustration 25-24),

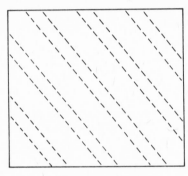

Illustration 25–24

extending ribbon ⅜″ to ½″ beyond all edges. Turn ribbon extension to underside of cover and tack or glue in place.

4. Wrong sides together, position lining over cover and pin in place, being sure that lining does not extend beyond the edge of cover. From the suede side, stitch lining in place ¼″ from raw edge.

5. With wrong sides together, stitch two flaps together ⅛″ from grooved edge, as shown. Repeat with remaining flaps.

6. Position flaps over lining and pin in place. Stitch in place from the right side on top of or next to the first row of stitching. Secure threads.

7. Fold complete card case in half and press crease.

Variation: *Card Case with Topstitching*
COLOR PLATE 22

Follow steps 1 and 2 above. For step 3, topstitch a design, stitching on the right side of cover, using the wide side of the sewing machine pressure foot as a guide for spacing. Pull all threads to wrong side and tie ends. Follow steps 4–7 to complete case.

Telephone Book Cover, Godey's Lady's Book, 1857

COLOR PLATES 22 and 32

Originally designed as a notebook cover, this gift has been adapted to serve as a telephone book cover. A smaller size would cover a paperback book. This cover will fit a standard size telephone book with a binding that is 1″ thick. Dimensions may be changed to fit a book with a different binding thickness.

KEY TO CRAFT TECHNIQUES: Read through the project and then check for general information in the Craft Basics chapter beginning on page 282. Techniques and skills are listed alphabetically with complete how-to information.

MATERIALS:
- ½ yd. imitation suede
- ½ yd. 45″ lining fabric, print or solid
- 1 yd. fusible interfacing, lightweight
- 2 yd. ribbon, color A, ⅜″ wide
- 1 yd. ribbon, color B, ⅜″ wide
- scissors, thread, needle, sewing machine

STEP-BY-STEP:

1. Make a pattern, following Illustration 25-25. Pattern may be made from tissue paper or Stacy's Trace-A-Pattern®. Mark fold lines on pattern. Enlarge and trace ribbon placement design (see Design Sheet, page 253) onto pattern, being careful to center it in the correct panel.

Illustration 25-25

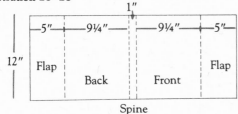

2. Place pattern on suede and cut one thickness. Remove pattern. Place pattern on fusible interfacing and cut one. Using pattern again, cut one from lining, adding ½" all around.

3. Apply fusible interfacing to wrong side of lining. Turn and press raw edges of lining to inside ⅝" from edge all around. Miter corners.

4. Carefully pin and baste ribbons to pattern tissue, following design lines. Baste pattern with applied ribbon to the right side of the suede cover. Stitch ribbon to suede through pattern. Pull all threads to the wrong side and secure by tying in square knits. Be sure to stitch both edges of ribbon. Remove pattern piece (tear paper or trim Trace-A-Pattern®) very carefully close to ribbon.

5. Position lining and suede wrong sides together. Pin lining in place, being sure that it does not extend beyond the edge of the suede.

6. On the suede side, stitch lining to suede ¼" from edge.

7. Turn flaps to inside on fold lines and pin in place. Stitch in place on top of first row of stitching.

Covered Bookends, The Delineator, 1901

These bookends are covered with a piece of needlepoint, but the technique for covering can be adapted to other needleworked pieces or to decorative fabric. Use dark, rich shades. Dimensions, yardages, measurements are determined by the specific bookends purchased.

KEY TO CRAFT TECHNIQUES: Read through the project and then check for general information in the Craft Basics chapter beginning on page 282. Techniques and skills are listed alphabetically with complete how-to information.

MATERIALS:
- 1 set purchased metal bookends, right-angle design
- needlepoint canvas sufficient to cover one side of each rack
- yarn to work needlepoint design
- firmly woven backing fabric
- rayon cord, about ⅛" diameter (optional)
- needle, thread, sewing machine

STEP-BY-STEP:

1. Work needlepoint for each bookend. Use the tulip design from *Peterson's Magazine*, 1891, on Design Sheet, page 254. To determine size, trace outline of the upright portion of bookend onto canvas, allowing at least 1" extra canvas all around. Center and transfer design to shape on canvas. Work background one extra stitch in each direction. Block needlepoint as needed. Machine stitch close to needlepoint stitches all around. Cut out canvas about 1" from work.

2. Using canvas as a pattern, cut backing piece for each bookend.

3. Pin needlepoint and backing right sides together. Working with needlepoint on top, stitch the two together around top and sides, stitching exactly next to the needlepoint stitches. Trim seam to ⅜". Turn bottom up 1" all around and hem. Turn and press.

4. Slide finished cover over metal bookend.

5. Overcast rayon cord in place around top and sides (optional).

Paper-Clip Caddy, *The Delineator, 1886*

A familiar folded paper shape makes a charming desk accessory styled in a handsome wallpaper. Paper colored on each side may be used. If so, omit steps 5–7 below. Corners of original were ornamented with hand-painted designs.

MATERIALS:
- wallpaper cut as follows (do not use vinyl paper):

  1 9″ square
  1 4½″ square
  4 2¼″ squares

- rubber cement, scissors

STEP-BY-STEP:
1. Fold 9″ square in half diagonally in each direction to determine center point (fold 1 and fold 2). Fold so that wrong sides of paper are together. Unfold.
2. Fold each corner toward center (WX, XY, YZ, ZW). Crease well. (Illustration 25-26)
3. Turn folded unit over and fold corners toward center again. Crease well. (Illustration 25-27)

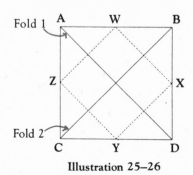

Illustration 25–26

Illustration 25–27

4. Turn unit back over. Open outside folds out to form a compartment at each corner. (Illustration 25-28)

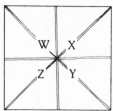

Illustration 25–28

5. Fold 4½″ square in half diagonally, right sides together, and on the square wrong sides together. Spread rubber cement on wrong side of square and glue in place over center part of caddy.
6. Fold each 2¼″ square in half diagonally, right sides together. Spread rubber cement on wrong side of each piece and glue to inside of corner folds. (Illustration 25-29)

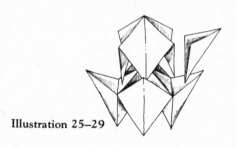

Illustration 25–29

7. Trim excess paper from corner folds if necessary.

Memo-Paper Holder, *The Delineator, 1888*

Make this as a companion to the paper-clip caddy. Substitute white glue and children can handle this and its companion piece. Paper colored on each side may be used. If so, omit step 5. Original featured embroidered corners.

MATERIALS:
- wallpaper cut as follows (do not use vinyl paper):

  1 9″ square
  4 2¼″ squares

- rubber cement, scissors
- loose sheets memo paper, about 2½″ square

STEP-BY-STEP:
1. Fold 9″ square in half diagonally in each direction to determine center point (fold 1 and fold 2). Crease well. Fold so that wrong sides of paper are together. Unfold. (Illustration 25-30)
2. Fold each side to meet at center line (folds AB and CD).
3. Fold a square in each corner (fold on DE and DF, for example).
4. Spread rubber cement over square ABCD and press folded area into glue.
5. Fold each 2¼″ square in half diagonally, right sides together. Spread rubber cement on wrong side of each square and glue inside corner flaps, over fold, covering wrong side of paper which is exposed in these areas. (Illustration 25-31)
6. Fit memo paper in place under corner flaps.

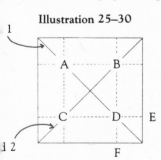

Illustration 25–30

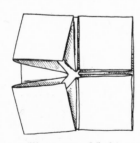

Illustration 25–31

Decorated Stationery, The Delineator, 1916
Stenciling or stamping are techniques for creating lovely stationery. Especially nice are seasonal designs (which can be found in each major holiday chapter).

KEY TO CRAFT TECHNIQUES: Read through the project and then check for general information in the Craft Basics chapter beginning on page 282. Techniques and skills are listed alphabetically with complete how-to information.

MATERIALS:
- 1 package good quality folded notes or correspondence cards
- appropriate printing equipment
- ½ yd. satin ribbon to tie around cards
- fabric or paper to cover box (optional)

STEP-BY-STEP:
1. Print design as desired. Some designs suitable for stenciling and stamping are on the Design Sheet, page 254. Consider the design positions in Illustration 25-32.

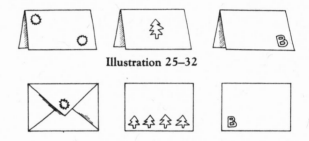

Illustration 25–32

2. When thoroughly dry, stack envelopes first, then cards on top. Tie ribbon around stack, finishing with flat bow or knot before placing in box. (Illustration 25-33)
3. Cover box if desired.

Illustration 25–33

Plant Gifts

"It must be acknowledged," it was written in *Godey's Lady's Book* in 1857, "that the common earthen red flower pot is scarcely in keeping with drawing-room or boudoir furniture." There followed in succeeding issues of the magazine numerous designs to fill the need for "an elegant fancy flower-pot within which the common article may be placed . . . uniting utility with decoration of the home apartments."

Cache pots remain an item well liked by many plant lovers, although the possibilities of hand crafting them in various forms other than ceramic and basketry have not been widely explored.

The cache pots which follow are interesting variations and should make any plant more loved. At the very least, the pot will be more attractive! And for a touch of color among all those foliage plants, place whimsical wooden butterflies here and there in the pots.

Cone-work Flower Pot, Godey's Lady's Book, 1876

COLOR PLATE 32

Cone-work is an unusual craft technique which was employed by the Victorians to create picture frames, Christmas tree decorations, boxes, and other decorative items such as this flower pot. The work is easy to do but time-consuming, as it must be done in stages so that each row can dry before the next is applied.

MATERIALS:

• 1 plastic flowerpot and saucer, about 6″ diameter (Choose a dark color to blend with cones.)
• 6 or 7 large pine cones separated into individual petals (Prepare individual petals by trimming ends evenly.)

• 4 or more small cones
• silicone adhesive
• clear spray varnish (optional)

STEP-BY-STEP:

1. **Rims of Pot and Saucer** Glue 2 or 3 overlapping rows of petals on rims, starting at top. First row should extend slightly above edge of rim. On pot, glue top 2 rows with petals vertical and 3rd row with petals horizontal. On saucer glue 2 vertical rows. (Illustration 25-34)

2. **Body of Pot** Squeeze glue in a circle 2½″ in diameter on one side of the pot and position a radiating row of petals. (Illustration 25-35)

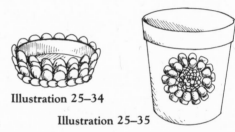

Illustration 25–34

Illustration 25–35

4. Squeeze glue in a circle just inside large circle and place another row of smaller petals.

5. Squeeze glue in center and imbed base of small cone. If any blank spots show, put glue directly on end of cone petal and press into open space.

6. Repeat on each of the three remaining sides of pot. Fill in any blank spaces by putting glue directly on cone petal and pressing into the open space.

7. Spray thoroughly dry work with clear varnish, if desired.

Covered Cache Pot, The Delineator, 1878

The basket-like construction of this article makes it a container suitable for other purposes. It can serve as a wastepaper basket or pencil caddy, if a bottom is added. The design can also be adapted to embroidery on perforated paper, a technique suggested in the directions accompanying the original.

KEY TO CRAFT TECHNIQUES: Read through the project and then check for general information in the Craft Basics chapter beginning on page 282. Techniques and skills are listed alphabetically with complete how-to information.

MATERIALS:

- mat board or illustration board
- fabric or wallpaper to cover (print) and line (solid)
- 10 ft. ribbon about ½″ wide
- flat bias trim (amount determined by size of panels) to go around edge of each panel (optional)
- hole punch, utility knife
- glue

STEP-BY-STEP:

1. Plan cache pot to fit a specific pot. Trace diameter of top of pot on paper. Draw a square around tracing ⅛″ from line (a). One side of this square represents width of one panel of cache pot. Measure height of pot with ruler for other dimension of panel (b). Curve top of pattern above height measurement (c). (Illustration 25-36)

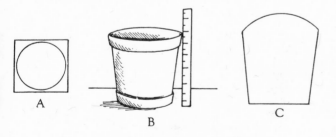

Illustration 25–36

2. Cut four pieces of mat board by pattern determined in step 1.

3. Cut fabric or paper for cover by pattern plus 1″ all around. Cut fabric or paper for lining by pattern.

4. Wrap covering around panels and glue in place on back. Miter corners, clip curves as necessary. Glue lining in place over back of panels. If desired, glue bias trim around edges of panels as in original pot, mitering corners, easing curves.

5. Punch holes in all four corners of each panel and tie panels together with ribbon. Each tie will take about 14″ of ribbon.

6. Slip cover over pot.

Woven Ribbon Basket, The Delineator, 1887

Directions for a variation of this basket appear on page 68). The original is pictured here. The idea easily adapts to a cache pot, especially if plastic ribbons are used.

MATERIALS:

- 1 wire basket, or several plastic berry baskets
- ribbons to fit between mesh and around baskets
- ribbon for bows (optional)
- spray paint (optional)

STEP-BY-STEP:

1. Spray-paint basket as desired.

2. Weave ribbons through mesh, paying particular attention to corners.

3. Arrange presentation as desired:

- several plants in a long wire basket
- several plastic berry baskets woven together with a small plant in each
- one special pot of herbs tucked into a berry basket woven in kitchen colors

Fern Vase, Godey's Lady's Book, 1876

COLOR PLATE 15

Godey's succinct directions read: "The vase is of glass, ornamented with fern leaves stuck on and varnished." The ornamentation is lovely for glass canister gift containers and plastic cache pots or flowerpots as well.

MATERIALS:
- glass vase or jar
- fresh fern leaves, pressed several days in a telephone book
- polyurethane varnish, paintbrush, spray adhesive

STEP-BY-STEP:
1. Spray adhesive on front of fern leaves and arrange on outside of the container as desired. Press into place while adhesive is tacky.
2. Varnish over fern leaves several times to seal area. Follow label directions for polyurethane drying time between coats.

DESIGN SHEET

Folded Sachet, page 225

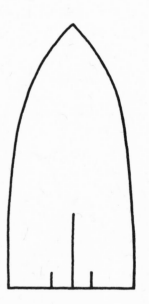

Flower Pincushion (petal),
page 229

Fold on long line by bringing short lines together.

WITH EASTER WISHES

JUST A LITTLE BIT O' RHYME TO WISH YOU JOY AT EASTER-TIME!

A Box of Easter Joy!

HERE'S TO EASTER, HERE'S TO YOU, HERE'S TO ME— AND BUNNY TOO!

EXTRA copies of this page, printed on heavy paper without lettering on the other side, may be obtained by sending five cents in postage to the Picture Editor, care of THE DELINEATOR, New York City.

If I seem to be in trouble, Please don't believe it true; With all my Easter greetings I'm headed straight for you

Mr. Bunny humbly begs Acceptance of his Easter-eggs.

Little maid and rabbits gay Sing and dance on Easter-day.

We may be very very small And young and shy and pink, But our Easter wish is just as big As two wee things can think.

My Easter wishes are head-high

We are busy, scratching up an Easter wish.

Here four blithe young maidens go, wearing each a new chapeau

COLOR PLATE 25/Cards   *The Delineator,* April, 1917

COLOR PLATE 26/Cards
Top: White Lace, page 21; Easter Chicks, page 59.
Middle: Magen David, page 109; Sweet Boquet, page 214; Ruffles and Violets,
page 20.
Bottom: Chicks Having A Ball, page 212; Golden Lace, page 19.

COLOR PLATE 27/Ca

The Delineator, February, 1

A little lass sat on a cushion
And busily did she knit:
Into one sock she stuffed her heart
And called it doing her bit.

Although I'm far away in France
Sweetheart you will find me
Sending all my love back home
To the Girl I left behind me

I wish I were
the Valentine
I'm sending
you to-day
I'd nestle close
against your heart
And love you dear
alway.

North South
East West
You're the one
I love best
On ship or sea
or Battle line
Still you are
my Valentine

A hundred Hearts
would be too few
To carry all
my love for you
The one I send
is true as gold
And worth itself
a hundred fold

A jolly jolly Jack
was he
Ne'er sighing
Though start
Until he met
a Red Cross Nurse
And straightway
lost his heart

Flowers I'm sending you today
Because my lips won't tell
What these blossoms boldly say
I love you all too well.

Gordon Ross

COLOR PLATE 28/Cards
Top: Linear Tree, page 185; Star of Beauty, page 185.
Middle: Felt Christmas Tree, page 181; Felt Duck, page 182.
Bottom: Snowflake, page 182; Evergreen, page 183; The Three Kings, page 183.

COLOR PLATE 30/Keepsakes
Marriage Sampler, page 208; Spring Frolic, page 53; Freedom's Song, page 92; To My Valentine, page 16.

COLOR PLATE 31/Keepsakes
O Christmas Tree, page 164; Happy New Year, page 6; Turkey Time, page 134; The Nice Old Witch, page 116.

COLOR PLATE 32/Keepsakes
Keepsake displayed. Pictured: Happy New Year, page 6; Cone-Work Flower Pot,
page 245; Butterfly Marker, page 255; Telephone Book Cover, page 241.

DESIGN SHEET

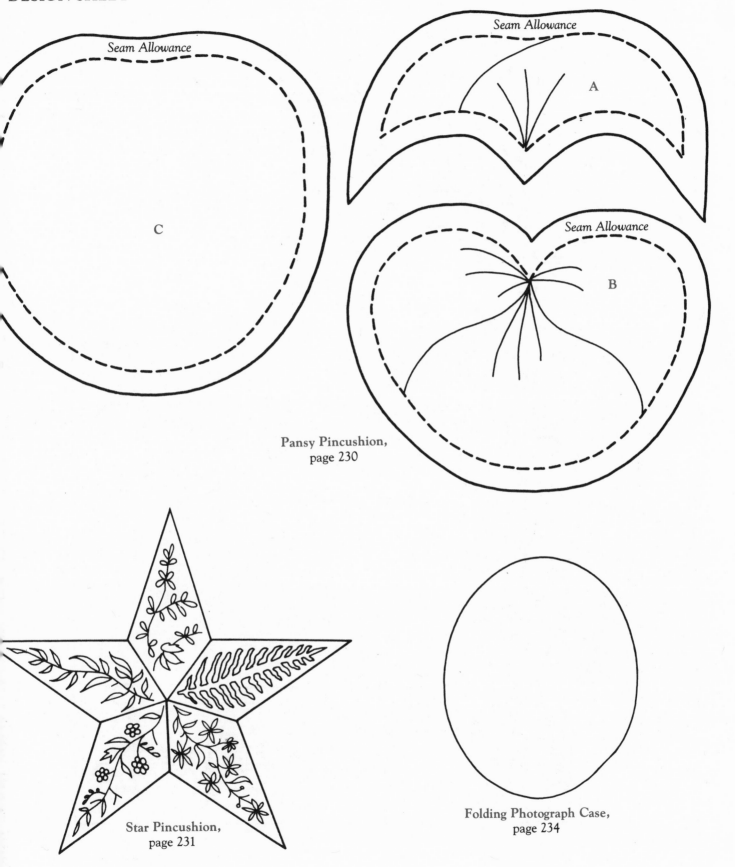

Seam Allowance

Seam Allowance

A

C

Seam Allowance

B

Pansy Pincushion,
page 230

Star Pincushion,
page 231

Folding Photograph Case,
page 234

Embroidered Photo Frame,
page 233

DESIGN SHEET

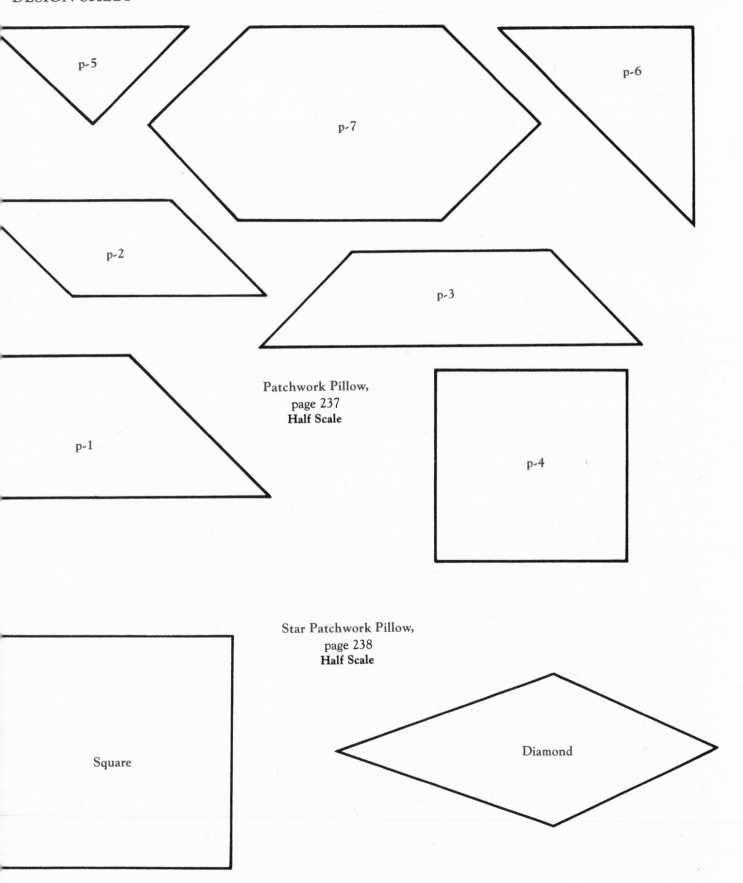

p-5

p-6

p-7

p-2

p-3

p-1

Patchwork Pillow,
page 237
Half Scale

p-4

Star Patchwork Pillow,
page 238
Half Scale

Square

Diamond

DESIGN SHEET

Satin Shapes/Leaf,
page 239
Half Scale

Satin Shapes/Star,
page 239
Half Scale

DESIGN SHEET

Satin Shapes/Heart,
page 239
Half Scale

Embroidered Throw,
page 239

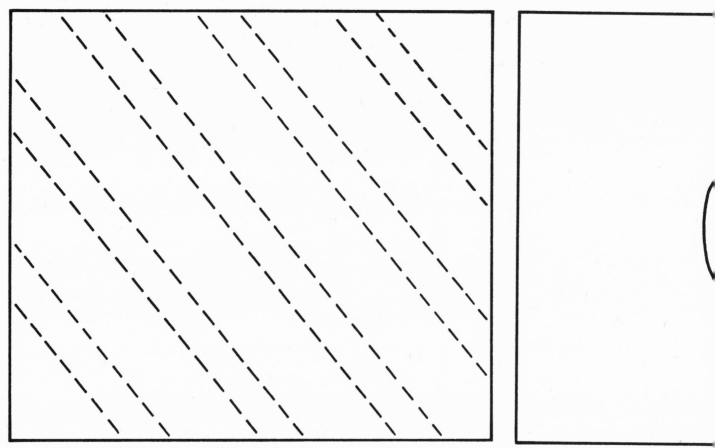

Business Card Case, page 240

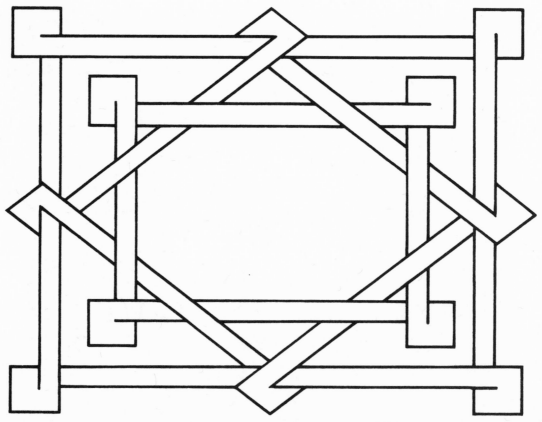

Telephone Book Cover (front), page 241
Half Scale

**DESIGN
SHEET**

Covered Bookends,
page 242

Decorated Stationery/Designs,
page 244

Garden Markers, Needle-Art, 1923

COLOR PLATE 32

Garden markers are used in gardens to indicate rows after seeds are planted and before they sprout. The same butterflies on short sticks make charming house plant ornaments and could be color keyed to care requirements—yellow/orange for a plant which likes to be kept on the dry side, blue/green for a plant which likes a lot of water.

KEY TO CRAFT TECHNIQUES: Read through the project and then check for general information in the Craft Basics chapter beginning on page 282. Techniques and skills are listed alphabetically with complete how-to information.

MATERIALS:
- ⅛" thick balsa wood, 3" × 4"
- ⅜" dowel, 18" long (for outdoor markers) or wooden skewers or plastic cocktail stirrers (for houseplant markers)
- assorted color enamel paints, acrylic paints, or permanent felt-tip markers, fine brush
- polyurethane varnish, 1" wide brush
- utility knife or small saw
- epoxy glue

STEP-BY-STEP:
1. Transfer design (see Design Sheet, page 270) to wood and cut out along outer outline.
2. Paint design in desired colors on both sides of balsa shape. Allow to dry thoroughly.
3. Varnish butterfly back, fronts, and sides. Allow to dry.
4. Notch top of dowel and glue butterfly to sides of notch.

Toys

Toys are especially rewarding to make. Children are so uncritical; they generally will not notice slight imperfections because they are so delighted to receive a gift.

Toys, like the other gift projects, involve a wide range of skills and can be as simple or as fancy as the spirit moves. Knitted toys have long been favorites. Thanks to polyester fiberfill and synthetic yarns, today's knitted toys can be made completely washable.

Several of the projects which follow were submitted by readers to *The Little Delineator*, a magazine within a magazine. Each month, *The Little Delineator* sermonized on safety and manners, offered colorfully illustrated fantasy stories and poems starring "Deli Bear," and encouraged its young readers to share their ideas. The best gift ideas received cash awards. $10.00 must have seemed quite a fortune to a young girl or boy in 1923.

Knitted Pussycat, Needle-Art, 1924

COLOR PLATE 24

Young children will love this cuddly kitten. Our cream-colored one is soft and pretty; knit one in black for a Halloween spook, or try variegated yarn for a calico effect. If work appears uneven, block pieces before assembling.

KEY TO CRAFT TECHNIQUES: Read through the project and then check for general information in the Craft Basics chapter beginning on page 282. Techniques and skills are listed alphabetically with complete how-to information.

MATERIALS:
- 2 oz. brushed acrylic yarn, cream, worsted weight
- odds and ends of black and blue acrylic yarn, fine, for details
- ½ yard blue ribbon, about ¾" wide
- #5 knitting needles
- polyester fiberfill
- yarn needle, 2 large safety-pins or yarn holders

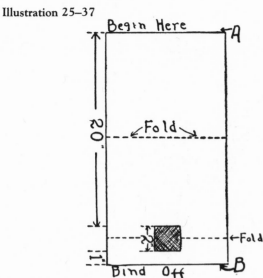

Illustration 25–37

STEP-BY-STEP:

1. **Body:** With cream yarn, cast on 30 stitches and work in stockinette stitch (knit one row, purl one row, repeat) until work measures 20″. (Illustration 25-37)

2. **Paws:** In next row, knit 12 stitches, slip them off on a safety-pin; bind off 6 stitches, knit on remaining stitches for 2″; slip them on a safety pin. Knit the stitches on first safety-pin for 2″. Join feet together with 6 cast-on stitches. Knit across all stitches for ½″, bind off. (see diagram) Fold at dotted lines in diagram so that A and B meet. Handstitch the sides of cat together and across A and B, leaving the opening between the feet. Stuff cat with fiberfill, making it full but soft. Overcast between the feet and across.

3. **Ears:** Measure 1½″ in from corner along top fold and draw it down to a similar point at side

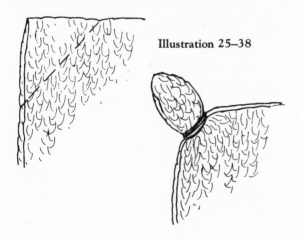

Illustration 25–38

seam. Tack it securely with cream yarn. The finished ear should look like illustration. Make other ear in same manner. (Illustration 25-38)

4. **Face** Embroider the face (see Design Sheet, page 270). Measure down 2¼″ from top fold and with blue yarn embroider the eyes, using the satin stitch, with black pupils and outlines in outline stitch. Make the nose and mouth black, using stem and satin stitches.

5. **Legs** With black blanket stitches taken ½″ long, divide each foot into 5 toes. Work stem stitch, starting at inside of foot, up the front of body for 3 inches. Do the same to the other foot. Join lines across top with a downward curved line of black outline stitching. (Illustration 25-39)

Illustration 25–39

6. **Tail** With cream yarn and needles, cast on 8 stitches. Knit stockinette for 7½ inches. Bind off. Fold in half lengthwise. Overcast the long edge and one short edge together. Stuff firmly with fiberfill; sew opening. Sew one end of tail to back of cat between feet. Bring the other end around back of one foot and to the side of cat. Tack to side.

Knitted Dog, Needle-Art, 1923

COLOR PLATE 24

A soft, squishy, washable dog will delight any young child. If the child has a pet dog in his family, color this one to match: a black spotted dalmatian, a black mini-schnauzer, or a brown beagle with black and white blotches. If work appears uneven, block pieces before assembling.

KEY TO CRAFT TECHNIQUES: Read through the project and then check for general information in the Craft Basics chapter beginning on page 282. Techniques and skills are listed alphabetically with complete how-to information.

MATERIALS:

- 2 oz. brushed acrylic yarn, white, worsted weight
- odds and ends of brown acrylic yarn, same weight, for details
- 5 inches brown braid or ribbon about ½" wide
- no. 5 knitting needles
- polyester fiberfill
- yarn needle, needle and thread, large safety pin or yarn holder

STEP-BY-STEP:

1. **Body** With white yarn, cast on 10 stitches and work in stockinette stitch (knit one row, purl one row, repeat) until work measures 3½". Slip stitches off on a safety pin. This completes back of one leg. Cast on 10 stitches, knit for 3½", cast on 4 stitches, and slip stitches off safety pin onto needle. Knit across all stitches until work measures 17" from cast-on stitches. Knit 10 stitches and slip stitches off on a safety pin. Bind off 4 stitches, knit remaining 10 stitches for 3½". Pick up stitches from safety pin. Continue to knit for 3½" more. Bind off. Fold the knitted strip in half. Overcast side. Stuff with fiberfill, overcast between legs.

2. **Arms** With white yarn, cast on 7 stitches and knit for 4". Bind off. Fold in half lengthwise and overcast sides and one end. Stuff with fiberfill and gather remaining opening. Overcast to sides of dog, measuring down 3" from top of head. Sew braid around neck, drawing neck in a little.

3. **Ears** With white yarn, cast on 6 stitches, knit 4 rows. Decrease 1 stitch at each end of every other row until 2 stitches remain (5 rows) Bind off. Repeat with brown yarn. Sew ears to each other (one brown, one white) and to dog's head, with brown in front as shown.

4. **Details** With brown, embroider the face (see Design Sheet, page 270) using satin stitch and stem stitch. Work blanket stitch across paws as shown. Embroider two patches of color on body, using duplicate stitch (see Design Sheet, page 270).

Knitted Ball, The Delineator, 1894

COLOR PLATE 24

This ball is a classic knitted toy and works up quickly using odds and ends of yarns. Choose bright colors. Knit a ball with different yarn textures to give baby a subtle learning experience.

KEY TO CRAFT TECHNIQUES: Read through the project and then check for general information in the Craft Basics chapter beginning on page 282. Techniques and skills are listed alphabetically with complete how-to information.

MATERIALS:

- small quantities sport weight acrylic yarn, 3 colors
- no. 5 knitting needles
- polyester fiberfill
- yarn needle

STEP-BY-STEP:

1. Cast on 30 stitches and knit across plain. Turn and *knit all but last 7 stitches; leave them on the needle, pass the yarn between the needles, turn and knit back, leaving the last 7 stitches at that end; turn back and knit all but 6; turn again and knit as before, leave 5 at each end, then 4, then 3, then 2, then 1; then knit all*.

2. Add new color and repeat from*. Repeat for each new color and knit nine gores in all.

3. Loosely slip and bind the last gore and sew the two edges together after filling the ball firmly with fiberfill.

MUSIC

Elephant Toy, The Delineator, 1888

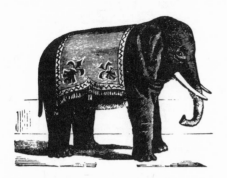

COLOR PLATE 24

The original instructions for this toy insisted on the use of gray flannel or camel's hair for a "real looking elephant." There were even tusks of bone crochet hooks. A bright print or acrylic fleece would make a pretty contemporary version. The blanket on the elephant in the photo is decorated with fringe and rickrack. Embroidery stitches, ribbons, even lace for a "lady" elephant would be pretty.

KEY TO CRAFT TECHNIQUES: Read through the project and then check for general information in the Craft Basics chapter beginning on page 282. Techniques and skills are listed alphabetically with complete how-to information.

MATERIALS:
- ½ yd. gray corduroy or other fabric, 45" wide
- large scrap red flannel, felt, or velvet for blanket
- 28" rickrack, 13" fringe, or other trims to decorate blanket
- 2 tiny black buttons or beads or black embroidery floss for eyes
- needle, thread, sewing machine
- polyester fiberfill

STEP-BY-STEP:
1. Transfer elephant pattern (pieces A–E, see Design Sheet, pages 271–274). Body (piece A) should measure 8" high along front legs. Seam allowances of ¼" have been included in the pattern pieces.

2. Cut two each of body (piece A) and underbody (piece B); cut one tail (piece C) and four ears (piece D). Transfer all position marks to body piece.

3. Right sides together, stitch notched seam of underbody, leaving seam open between notches.

4. **Ears** Right sides together, stitch two ear pieces together, leaving notched edge open. Clip curve and trim corner. Turn. Turn notched edges in ½". Press. Repeat with other ear pieces for second ear. Stitch open edge of ears to body pieces at marks (Illustration 25-40). Stitch eyes in place.

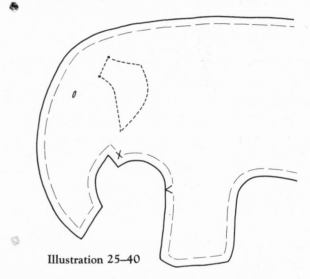

Illustration 25–40

5. Right sides together, pin underbody to one body piece, matching notches. Ease and stretch pieces to fit. Stitch. Repeat with other body piece.

6. **Tail** Press straight end of tail ½" under. Press tail in half lengthwise wrong sides together. Open and press raw edges in to meet at fold. Refold. Edgestitch along open side. Baste tail to one body piece at mark, matching edges.

7. Pin elephant bodies right sides together and stitch, ending stitching at underbody seam. Take care to keep tail enclosed during this stitching. Clip curves, trim corners. Press seams flat. Turn and firmly stuff with fiberfill. Stuff trunk and legs first, then body. Overcast opening, turning raw edges under ¼".

8. **Blanket** Cut two blanket pieces (E) of red fabric. Right sides together, join notched seam. Press seam open. If hem is necessary, turn edges under ¼″ all around and machine hem. Stitch fringe along curved edge. Stitch rickrack ¼″ from fringe and edges or use other trims as desired. Tack blanket to elephant's back with notched end toward elephant's head.

Indoor Croquet Game, *The Delineator, 1926*

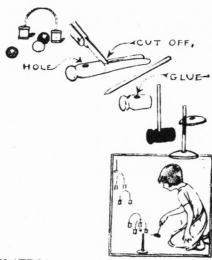

COLOR PLATE 24

Game may be played on table top or floor. Children will enjoy setting up difficult playing fields.

MATERIALS:
- 8 ft. vinyl tubing, ⅜″ diameter
- 8 ft. stiff wire (stem wire)
- 2 4″ dowels, about ⅜″ diameter to fit inside spool
- 16 small wooden spools
- 4 one-piece wooden clothespins (no springs)
- 4 wooden utility skewers, about 3/16″ diameter, 4½″ long
- 4 marbles or small firm balls, each a different color
- white glue, small saw, drill, 4 colors paint to match balls, sandpaper

STEP-BY-STEP:
Wickets (make 7)
1. Paint spools as desired.

2. Cut wire and tubing into 7 10″ lengths.
3. Curve wire into smooth horseshoe shape and insert through tubing. Fit each end of tubing into a spool. Generously glue each end into spool. (Illustration 25-41)

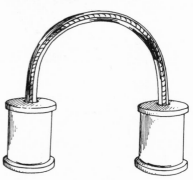

Illustration 25–41

Mallets (make 4)
4. Cut heads off clothespins, just above the prongs, to form mallet heads. Cut pointed ends off skewers. Sand as necessary.
5. Drill a hole in middle of each clothespin head, about ¼″ deep, diameter of skewer. (Illustration 25-42)
6. Glue skewer into hole.
7. Paint one mallet to match each ball.

Stakes (make 2)
8. Glue ¼″ dowel into each of 2 remaining spools. (Illustration 25-43)

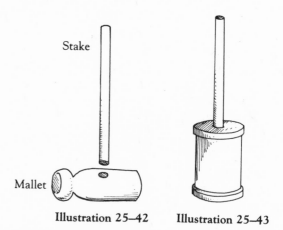

Illustration 25–42   Illustration 25–43

9. Paint as desired.

Game
1. Set up croquet field as shown. (Illustration 25-44)

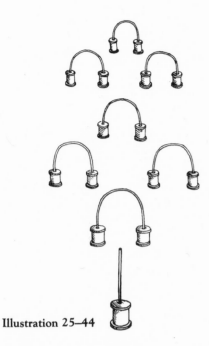

Illustration 25-44

2. Each player uses mallet and coordinating ball.

3. Player must hit his ball through each wicket to stake and back. Player may continue his turn until a wicket is missed, at which point another player takes his turn. Follow rules for lawn croquet.

• **Variation** Make and use more wickets to make the game more complicated.

Ringtoss Game, The Delineator, 1923

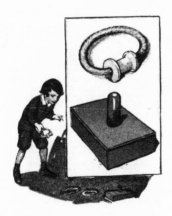

COLOR PLATE 24

This game won a first prize of $10.00 for the young man who submitted the idea. It can be easily made by a child.

MATERIALS:
- 1 fairly sturdy box, about 1½″ deep × 12″ × 8″
- 1 broom handle or 1″ dowel, 6″ long
- 3 small spools (wooden preferred, but plastic will work)
- 3 pieces stiff rope, each 15″ long, about ⅜″ diameter
- glue, knife, acrylic paints (optional)

STEP-BY-STEP:
Stake
1. Paint stake if desired.
2. Cut hole in center of box lid just large enough for broom handle or dowel to fit into snugly.
3. Force stake into hole and glue to bottom of box. (Illustration 25-45)

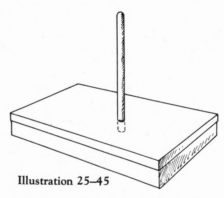

Illustration 25-45

Rings (make 3)
4. Paint spools if desired.
5. Glue rope ends into spool, inserting each end half way into spool. (Illustration 25-46)

Illustration 25-46

Game
1. Toss rings at stake. Score a point for each ringer. Player with most points wins.

• **Variation** Make more than one stake and place stakes at various distances from tosser.

Assign point values based on difficulty of stake position.
• **Variation** Paint each spool a different color and assign different point values to each color.

Crazy Cutouts Notebook, *The Delineator*, 1908

This is a gift a child can make for another child. This is a good rainy day or sickbed activity.

MATERIALS:
• spiral notebook, 9″ × 6″ (a partially filled notebook is fine)
• magazines, old greeting cards, other sources of pictures
• white glue, scissors

STEP-BY-STEP:
1. Cut pages of notebook in half from outer edge to spiral, about ⅓ of the way down from the top of the notebook.
2. Cut figures of men, women, children, and animals from magazines and cards. Cut in half.
3. Glue top halves to upper parts of the pages, absolutely centered and flush with lower edge. Glue bottom halves on lower part of pages, centered and flush with upper edge, so that they will join the heads. (Illustration 25-47)

Illustration 25–47

4. Decorate cover.
5. When the book is finished, the fun is in matching the pages. The various

combinations—a woman's body and a lion's head, a child's head and a man's body—will cause great amusement.

Jacob's Ladder, *The Delineator*, 1893

This toy has fascinated children and adults for many years. It is a rainy day activity for older children and uses materials one usually has around the house. Overlap the ribbon a scant 1″ in each instance.

MATERIALS:
• 8 pieces shirt cardboard (or ¼″ balsa wood), each 3″ × 4″, decorated as desired with paints, markers, pasted pictures, etcetera
• 10½ ft. narrow ribbon or seam tape, cut into 21 6″ pieces
• white glue or transparent tape (if wood, use glue)

STEP-BY-STEP:
1. Fasten two pieces of ribbon to the upper edge of block #1 on the front, pass ribbon over the top and down the back, and over the top and to the front of block #2 and fasten the ends. (Illustration 25-48)
2. Fasten a ribbon to the bottom of block #1 on the front. Carry it under the bottom of block #1, down the back of #2 and around the bottom. Fasten to the front of #2. (Illustration 25-49)
3. Fasten a ribbon at the center back top edge of block #2, carry ribbon down the front of #2 and fasten to the center back top edge of block #3.

4. Fasten two ribbons on back of block #2 at lower edge and pass them over the front of #3, around the bottom, and fasten to the back lower edge of #3. (Illustration 25-50)

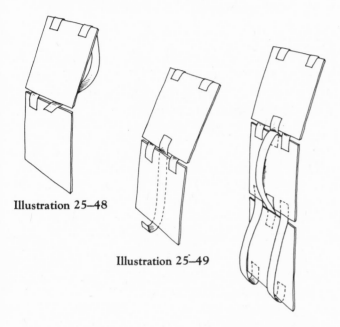

Illustration 25–48

Illustration 25–49

Illustration 25–50

5. Fasten 2 ribbons on the top front edge of #3, pass over the top down the back of #3, and fasten over the top front edge of block #4.

6. Fasten a ribbon to the center front lower edge of #3. Carry it down the back of #4 and fasten over the center front lower edge of #4.

7. Continue in this manner. Blocks 2, 4, and 6 are done alike and 3, 5, and 7 are alike.

8. To use: Hold block #1 as shown. Blocks will fall one over the other, folding as they fall.

Kitchen Gifts

Kitchen gifts aren't really for the kitchen—they're for the person who is using the kitchen, and that can be just about anyone. The gifts which follow are suitable for that "anyone." Some are to make things easier, and some are just to make things fun or pretty. Today, things for the kitchen don't necessarily stay in the kitchen, so choose snappy colors in keeping with the ambiance of the rest of the house. Use easily cleaned materials whenever possible for kitchen items.

Napkin Ring, Godey's Lady's Book, 1856

COLOR PLATE 23

The design on this ring can be adapted to other forms of needlework, notably cross-stitch embroidery or embroidery on perforated paper. The original was worked in beads of red, white, and green. The napkin rings in the photo are styled in lovely pastel shades and worked in petit point. The button closure is clever and easy to make. Instructions below are for one ring.

KEY TO CRAFT TECHNIQUES: Read through the project and then check for general information in the Craft Basics chapter beginning on page 282. Techniques and skills are listed alphabetically with complete how-to information.

MATERIALS:
- ½ yd. 24 mesh needlepoint canvas
- cotton 6-strand embroidery floss: yellow, light blue, dark olive, light pink, dark pink
- 6¾″ ribbon or felt, width of finished needlepoint (about 3″)
- 2¼″ ball buttons
- 2⅜″ plastic rings
- needle, thread, embroidery needle, white glue (optional)

STEP-BY-STEP:
1. Work needlepoint, following color key on design (see Design Sheet, page 275). Use six strands of embroidery floss for brick stitch and three strands of floss for cross stitch.

2. Clean and block needlepoint as necessary.

3. To back napkin rings, machine stitch edges of needlepoint and trim edges of canvas to ½″ all around. Turn edges of needlepoint canvas under all around, mitering corners, and glue or catchstitch edges in place. Turn ribbon under ½″ at each end.

4. Stitch wrong side of ribbon or felt to wrong side of needlepoint all around, using machine edgestitch or hand slipstitch.

5. Sew plastic rings at corners of one end of backed needlepoint. Embroider blanket stitch over rings to cover.

6. Sew buttons at corners of the other end of blocked needlepoint. Place buttons so that they will fit smoothly into the loops when napkin ring is buttoned.

7. To use, button napkin ring around napkin.

The Apron for Everyone, The Delineator, 1914

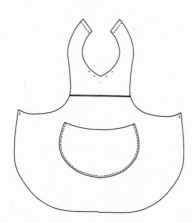

COLOR PLATE 22

The magazine presented this as a "cleaning apron." One pocket was to be used as a repository for small objects belonging in other rooms and the other for trash and other things to be disposed of. So as the cleaner made her rounds, steps were saved and hands kept free for cleaning. Our apron is reversible and has pockets on both sides. The pattern may be enlarged to any size and is suitable for a man, woman, or child. Yardages below are for one adult apron. There will be plenty of fabric left over to make matching potholders, if desired.

KEY TO CRAFT TECHNIQUES: Read through the project and then check for general information in the Craft Basics chapter beginning on page 282. Techniques and skills are listed alphabetically with complete how-to information.

MATERIALS:
- 1½ yd. 45″ cotton fabric #1 (print)
- 2 yd. 45″ cotton fabric #2 (print or solid)
- 1 button (woman's and child's apron)
- thread, sewing machine

STEP-BY-STEP:
1. Enlarge apron and pocket pattern (see Design Sheet, page 275) proportionately to desired size. For a size 10 woman, apron should be about 36″ long from shoulder to hem, which is several inches above the knees.

2. Cut one apron (piece A) and two pockets (piece B) from each of the two fabrics. Cut bias strips 2″ wide from fabric #2. Cut enough pieces to make one continuous strip 7–8 yd. long. Cut bias strips 2″ wide from fabric #1. Cut enough for a bias piece 2 yd. long. Transfer pocket placement lines to apron pieces.

3. Construct pockets. With wrong sides together, pin one pocket of fabric #1 to one pocket of fabric #2. Repeat for second pocket. Bind each pocket with contrasting bias binding. With right sides together, stitch bias strip to pocket ⅜″ from edge. Turn bias strip to inside of pocket, press, and pin in place. Do not turn under raw edge. On right side of pocket, stitch bias strip in place by "stitching in the ditch" just alongside the seam where bias was sewn to fabric.

4. Stitch each pocket to an apron front in position indicated on pattern. Stitch through center front of pocket and around edges. Leave top of pocket unstitched.

5. Stitch center back neck seam ¾″ from edge. Press seam open.

6. With wrong sides together, pin aprons together. For woman's apron, easestitch ¼″ from neckline edge between dots. Draw up easestitching slightly. Try on apron and ease to fit smoothly over bust. Remove apron and

apply binding to neckline and other edges of apron. With right sides together, pin bias strip to apron and stitch ⅜″ from edge. Miter corners. Turn bias strip to inside over seam and press. Turn raw edge of bias strip under enough so that it extends ⅛″ beyond and covers stitching line. Pin in place. From the right side, stitch binding in place by "stitching in the ditch" alongside the bias binding same as for pocket.

7. Closure. For woman's or child's apron, make buttonhole on one back corner and sew button to the other. For man's apron, make a buttonhole ½″ long on each back corner. To make tie, cut a strip of fabric 2″ wide and 2 yards long on the straight of grain (do not use bias). With wrong sides together, fold and press strip in half lengthwise. Turn in raw edges to meet at fold and press. Turn ends in. Edgestitch strip along all edges. Thread tie through buttonholes. Draw up to fit and tie in knot or bow.

Goose Pot Holder, The Delineator, 1891

Useful and ornamental, originally this was an "iron holder." Small sizes make nice pincushions and tree ornaments.

KEY TO CRAFT TECHNIQUES: Read through the project and then check for general information in the Craft Basics chapter beginning on page 282. Techniques and skills are listed alphabetically with complete how-to information.

MATERIALS:
- large cotton fabric scraps, plain and quilted
- polyester fiberfill
- 2 tiny black buttons or beads or black embroidery floss for eyes
- cotton embroidery floss, yellow and other color as desired
- scissors, needle, thread, sewing machine (optional)

STEP-BY-STEP:
1. Cut two goose body shapes (piece A) from unquilted fabric and one goose underbody (piece B) from quilted fabric (see Design Sheet, page 276.)

2. Right sides together, stitch two body shapes from dot to dot, leaving notched edge unstitched (Illustration 25-51). Stitch using a ¼″ seam allowance. Trim corners, clip curves, and turn. Sew eyes in place.

3. Stuff beak and head tightly. Wind yellow floss tightly around beak. Embroider wing shape on each side of body in stem stitch, using second color floss.

4. Press seam allowance under ¼″ around edges of goose body and underbody (Illustration 25-52). Matching notches, stitch underbody to goose with blanket stitch, stopping when nearly done to stuff goose (Illustration 25-53). Arrange stuffing so goose divides in half lengthwise on bottom. Do not overstuff. After stuffing, complete stitching and fasten thread securely.

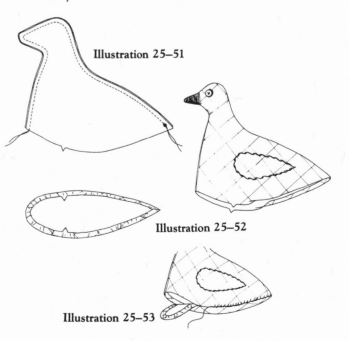

Illustration 25–51

Illustration 25–52

Illustration 25–53

Ornamental Cork, Godey's Lady's Book, 1866

The late Victorians felt the urge to decorate simply everything, thus this whimsical cork for a wine bottle. The original was green with sequins. Make yours in a neutral shade (white with silver, gold, or crystal) or in colors to match your china.

KEY TO CRAFT TECHNIQUES: Read through the project and then check for general information in the Craft Basics chapter beginning on page 282. Techniques and skills are listed alphabetically with complete how-to information.

MATERIALS:
- 80″ fine wire
- scraps of lightweight fabric such as crepe
- long cork of diameter suitable for wine bottle
- sequins to complement fabric (optional)
- needle, thread, zigzag sewing machine, white glue

STEP-BY-STEP:
1. Cut wire into 20 4″ lengths. Bend each length into petal shape with point at one end and lose wires at other end. (Illustration 26-54)
2. Set sewing machine for close zigzag stitch and stitch wire shapes to fabric, leaving each wire end exposed for about ⅜″ to ½″ (Illustration 25-55). Carefully cut petals apart close to stitching. Do not cut through stitching.

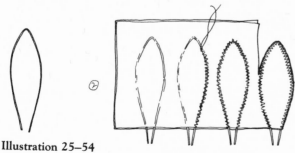

Illustration 25—54

Illustration 25—55

3. Cover top ½″ of cork with fabric, overcasting by hand to hold fabric in place.
4. Force wire ends of petals into top of cork in a circular pattern. After poking a hole with the wires, remove each petal and put glue on the wire and reinsert into proper hole.
5. When glue is thoroughly dry, bend petals as desired into a pleasing arrangement.
6. Sew a single sequin to the end of each petal, if desired.

Permanent Shopping List, The Delineator, 1916

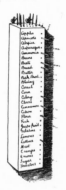

This clever grocery reminder is a good project for a boy or girl using the instructions given below. A more substantial version can be made by using a piece of painted wood (2″ × 4″ × 12″) carefully lettered and featuring drilled holes with golf tee markers.

MATERIALS:
- 1 box, 2″ × 2″ × 12″ (empty waxed paper or plastic wrap box with cutting edge removed)
- white Con-Tact® paper 12″ × 15″
- fine felt-tip marker, permanent black
- round toothpicks, about 30
- awl, nail, needle, or ice pick

STEP-BY-STEP:
1. Cut Con-Tact® paper into one piece 12″ × 10″ and 2 pieces each 4″ × 4″ squares.
2. Cover box ends with 4″ × 4″ squares. (Illustration 25-56)
3. Wrap large piece of Con-Tact® paper around box, with 1″ overlap in rear.

4. Print common grocery items on front of box with marker.

Illustration 25–56

5. Poke small hole beside each item in list and an equal number of holes in top of box.
6. To use: Store toothpicks in holes on top of box and use to mark grocery items as needed.
7. Poke hole in back of box and hang in kitchen.

Cord Box, The Delineator, 1898

COLOR PLATE 22

This clever concealment can be made for the desk or the kitchen. For the desk, cover the box with leather or fabric with embroidered designs (like the original) or paper coordinated with other desk accessories (see pages 240–244). For the kitchen, use vinyl wallpaper or Con-Tact® paper.

KEY TO CRAFT TECHNIQUES: Read through the project and then check for general information in the Craft Basics chapter beginning on page 282. Techniques and skills are listed alphabetically with complete how-to information.

MATERIALS:
- 1 ball cord or twine
- 1 sturdy box large enough to contain ball or cord. Box lid must extend full depth of box.
- decorative fabric or Con-Tact ® paper
- glue, scissors, eyelet, and eyelet punch

STEP-BY-STEP:
1. Cover box lid with decorative fabric or Con-Tact® paper.
2. Punch a hole in the center of the box lid and hammer eyelet in place following instructions with eyelets.
3. Place cord in box and draw cord end out through hole in box lid.

Containers

There is always something to carry or store and for this reason containers have long been popular gift items. There are as many containers as there are things to contain. Each project below is custom designed for its special purpose and custom styled for a special recipient.

Needlework Yarn Carrier, The Delineator, 1882

COLOR PLATE 23

The needlework nut will appreciate this carrier to keep the yarns for that current project neat and orderly. Adapt the idea in felt to a larger yarn storage unit by making the carrier several feet long, with assorted-size sections to hold the numerous odds and ends and quantities of yarn that most needleworkers end up with and just can't seem to file away neatly. Width of carrier below can be adjusted so that the length yarn most often used will fit in the carrier comfortably.

KEY TO CRAFT TECHNIQUES: Read through the project and then check for general information in the Craft Basics chapter beginning on page 282. Techniques and skills are listed alphabetically with complete how-to information.

MATERIALS:
- ½ yd. imitation suede
- 1 yd. cotton print lining fabric
- 1 yd. fusible interfacing
- scissors, needle, thread, marking equipment, sewing machine

STEP-BY-STEP:
1. Enlarge cover pattern (piece A) and yarn holder pattern (piece B) proportionally, to measure 18″ long by 10″ wide (Design Sheet, page 277). For additional carrying room, lengthen and add sections.
2. Cut cover (piece A) one each from suede, lining, and fusible interfacing. Transfer stitching lines to right side of lining only. Cut one yarn holder (piece B) from suede and transfer stitching lines to wrong side of piece. For ties, cut a 2″ wide strip of lining fabric on the straight of grain, 1 yd. long. For binding, cut bias strips 2″ wide from lining fabric. Make enough for a continuous 2 yd. strip.
3. Apply fusible interfacing to wrong side of lining fabric.
4. With wrong sides together, pin lining to suede. Bind raw edges with bias strip. Place right side of bias strip against right side of suede, matching raw edges, and stitch ⅜″ from edges. Turn bias strip to lining side, over seam allowance. Turn in the raw edge so that the bias strip just covers the stitching line. Slipstitch in place through lining only.
5. Position wrong side of yarn holder (piece B) against lining so that stitching lines match. Stitch in place. Backstitch to secure stitching. (Illustration 25-57)

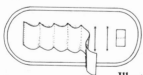

Illustration 25–57

6. Cut two pieces of lining, 2½″ square, and tack in place above yarn holder for needles.
7. Fold and press long strip of lining in half lengthwise, wrong sides together. Turn in raw edges to meet at fold line and pin in place. Turn ends in ¼″. Edgestitch all edges of strip.

Fold in half crosswide and press. Position tie at dot on suede side and stitch to binding strip securely.

Work Pocket, Peterson's Magazine, 1871

Here is a simple folded bag which can be interpreted in many sizes, many fabrics, for many purposes. The original was presented as a "receptacle for (needle) work or to contain a nightdress." It was made out of ticking, "a work now very popular," ornamented with silk embroidery. Make a canvas clutch handbag, or brocade evening clutch using this basic pattern. Add extra interfacing for stability if you wish to attach a cord handle.

KEY TO CRAFT TECHNIQUES: Read through the project and then check for general information in the Craft Basics chapter beginning on page 282. Techniques and skills are listed alphabetically with complete how-to information.

MATERIALS:
- ¾ yd. ticking fabric, gray and white stripe
- ½ yd. lining fabric
- ½ yd. heavyweight non-woven interfacing fabric, 10″ × 22″
- embroidery floss: red, blue, black
- 1 yd. double-folded bias seam binding about ⅝″ wide
- closure as desired: snap, button, Velcro®
- needle, thread, sewing machine

STEP-BY-STEP:
1. Cut 10″ × 22″ rectangles of each of the fabrics: tucking, lining, and interfacing. Cut one end of each by flap pattern (see Design Sheet, page 278).
2. Work embroidery on ticking as follows (Illustration 25-58):
   white stripes 6 strands, alternating blue and red, herringbone stitch

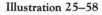

Illustration 25–58

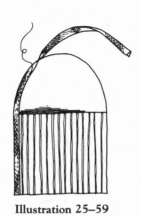

Illustration 25–59

gray stripes 6 strands, red, couched with 2 strands, black; 2 strands black, cross-stitch

3. Place ticking and lining wrong sides together with interfacing between. Baste edges together.

4. Fold bottom end of bag up 8½". Bind one fold, curve, and other fold. Tuck ends of binding under and overcast. (Illustration 25-59)

5. Apply closure.

Scissors Case, The Delineator, 1878

COLOR PLATE 23

Scissors will last longer if they are kept in their own special pouch. This one holds a variety of scissors styles and sizes. Extra pockets can be added for special needs. Coordinated with the yarn carrier (page 266), it makes a lovely gift for a needlecrafter.

KEY TO CRAFT TECHNIQUES: Read through the project and then check for general information in the Craft Basics chapter beginning on page 282. Techniques and skills are listed alphabetically with complete how-to information.

MATERIALS:
- 12" × 18" rectangle of suede or imitation suede
- ½ yd. coordinating cotton print for lining and binding
- ½ yd. lightweight fusible interfacing
- needle, thread, sewing machine

STEP-BY-STEP:

1. Cut one of each pattern piece—A, B, C and pockets A, B, C (Design Sheet, pages 279 and 280) from suede and lining. Cut two of each pattern piece from the interfacing. Cut bias strips 1⅛" wide from lining fabric, for a total length of 3 yd.

2. Apply fusible interfacing to the wrong side of each piece of suede and lining, following manufacturer's directions.

3. With wrong sides together, pin each lining section to its appropriate suede section. Baste.

4. Bind top edge of each pocket. With right side of binding against right side of suede, stitch in ¼" seam, pivoting at point. Turn and press binding to inside and pin in place. From suede side, stitch binding in place by "stitching in the ditch" alongside the binding edge. On wrong side of each pocket, trim away excess binding leaving ¼" beyond stitching. (Illustration 25-60)

Illustration 25–60

5. With lining sides together, pin and baste each pocket to its corresponding piece.

6. To make strap for holder B, cut a strip of lining fabric 1" wide and 4" long on the straight of grain. With right sides together, fold strip lengthwise and stitch in a ⅛" seam. Turn, press, and edgestitch both long edges. Position strap on suede side of holder B as indicated on pattern and baste in place. Trim away any excess strap.

7. Bind each completed holder. With right side of binding against suede side of holder, raw edges together, stitch with a ¼" seam allowance. Turn and press binding over edge to pocket side of holder. Turn under raw edge of binding so that the folded edge extends ⅛"

beyond the stitching line. Baste in place. From suede side of holder "stitch in the ditch" through the folded edge of the binding catching all layers of suede and binding. (Illustration 25-61)

8. Assemble holders. Match positioning dots and whipstitch completed holders together through the edge of the binding. Use a double thread for strength and take several stitches to secure end of stitching. (Illustration 25-62)

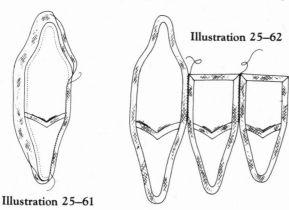

Illustration 25–62

Illustration 25–61

9. Turn flap down on fold line and press. Fold case and tuck point under strap.

Traveling Cases, The Delineator, 1922

COLOR PLATE 22

Proposed as a gift for a June bride, this set would be appreciated by any traveler and can be styled in many different manners to suit many personalities. Some pieces are suitable for gentlemen. The original set was in satin with an appliqué design. Ours is styled in three coordinating cotton prints.

MATERIALS:
    1 yard red print
    1 yard white print
    ½ yard vinyl
    ½ yard light batting
    10 yards bias binding
    pillow form
    1 snap (optional)

Make-Up Case

STEP-BY-STEP:

1. Cut a rectangle 12½" × 18½" from each of the following: red print, vinyl, batting, white print. Round corners with a teacup as a template.

2. Cut three vinyl pockets 12½" × 5½". Bind both long edges on two of the pockets and one edge on the third (bottom) pocket.

3. Place white print, right side down, and layer, in order: batting, red print, vinyl, and pockets. Machine baste all around. (Illustration 26-63a) Stitch across the bottom bound edge of the two top pockets. Make smaller pocket compartments by stitching vertically through all layers.

4. Make a ribbon tie by stitching through folded bias binding. Bind the edges of the case with bias binding (Illustration 26-63b) catching the center of the tie in the binding (see page 300).

Jewelry Case

Make as Make-Up Case except cut 10½" × 5½" rectangles. Or, omit top pocket and substitute a fabric strip with a snap closing to hang necklaces. Leave the center section of the second pocket unstitched at the bottom so the necklaces can hang through this area and be secured. (Illustration 26-64)

Illustration 26–63a

Illustration 26–63b

Illustration 26–64

Shoe Bag

STEP-BY-STEP:

1. Cut a rectangle 28" × 12".

2. Fold in half, right sides together, and sew up side seams.

3. Make a casing at the top (see page 302) and insert a ribbon tie.

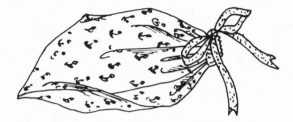

Pillow

STEP-BY-STEP:

1. Cut two rectangles of print fabric equal to the pillow form dimensions. Cut two rectangles 3 inches shorter lengthwise.

2. Place the two smaller rectangles together with wrong sides together and bind one of the short edges. This forms the pocket for the back of the pillow.

3. Pin the pillow cover to the pillow form with seam allowances extending. Pin the pocket to the back of the pillow.

4. Machine baste around the pillow using a zipper foot to stitch close to the pillow form. Bind the edges with bias binding (see page 300) to enclose the seam allowances and finish the pillow.

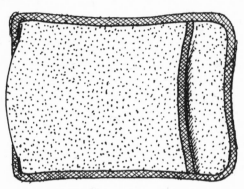

DESIGN SHEET

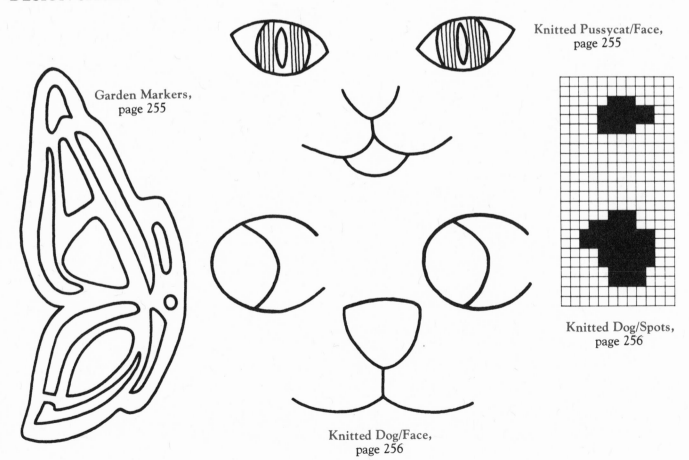

Garden Markers, page 255

Knitted Pussycat/Face, page 255

Knitted Dog/Spots, page 256

Knitted Dog/Face, page 256

DESIGN SHEET

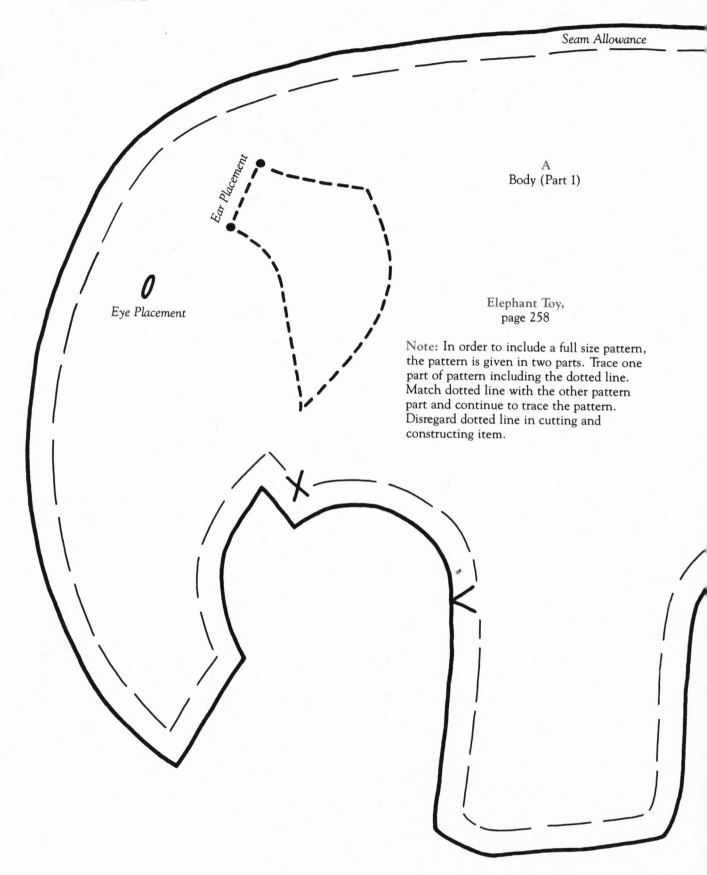

Seam Allowance

A
Body (Part 1)

Ear Placement

Eye Placement

Elephant Toy,
page 258

Note: In order to include a full size pattern,
the pattern is given in two parts. Trace one
part of pattern including the dotted line.
Match dotted line with the other pattern
part and continue to trace the pattern.
Disregard dotted line in cutting and
constructing item.

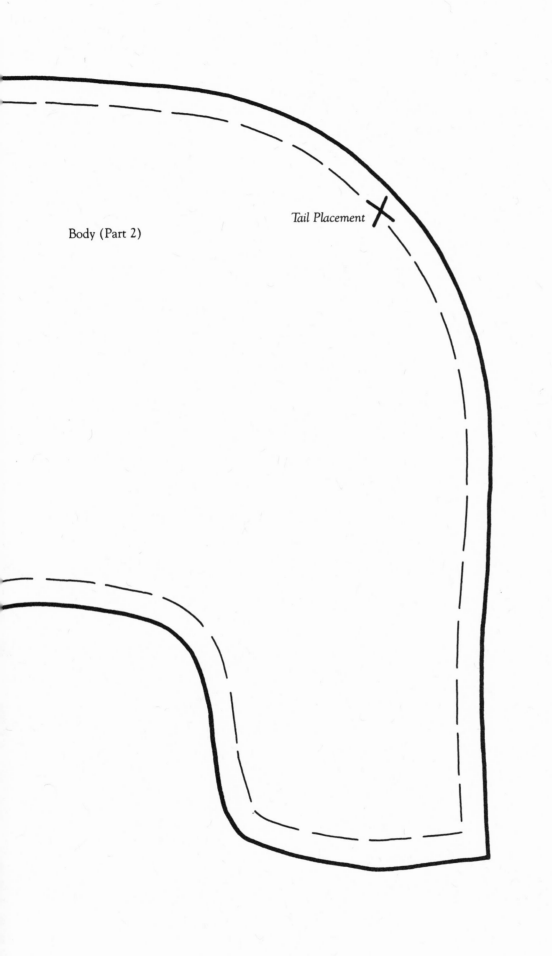

Body (Part 2)

Tail Placement

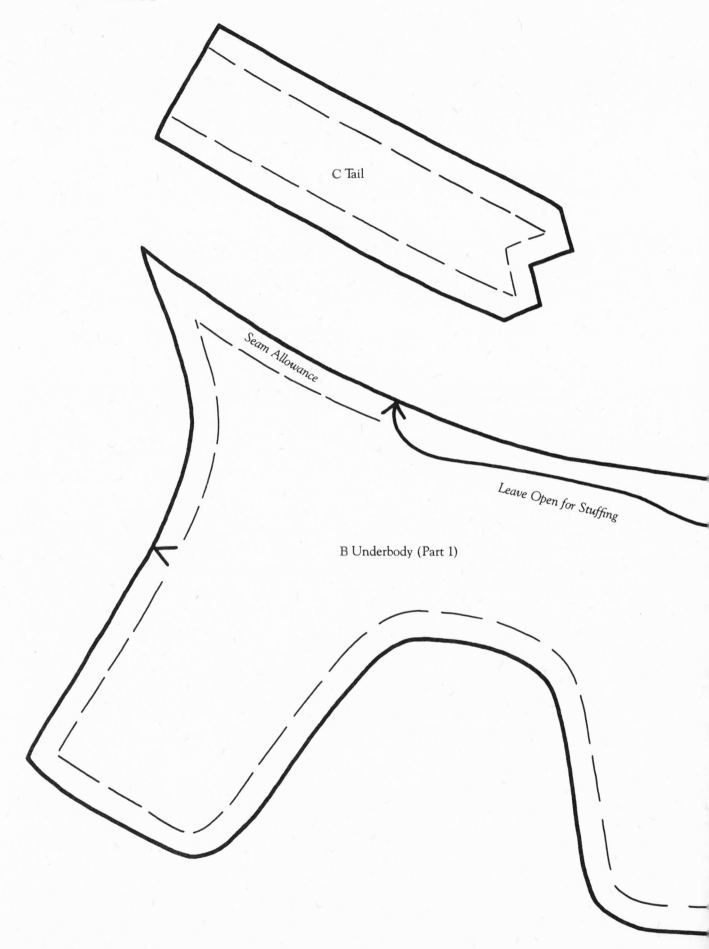

C Tail

Seam Allowance

Leave Open for Stuffing

B Underbody (Part 1)

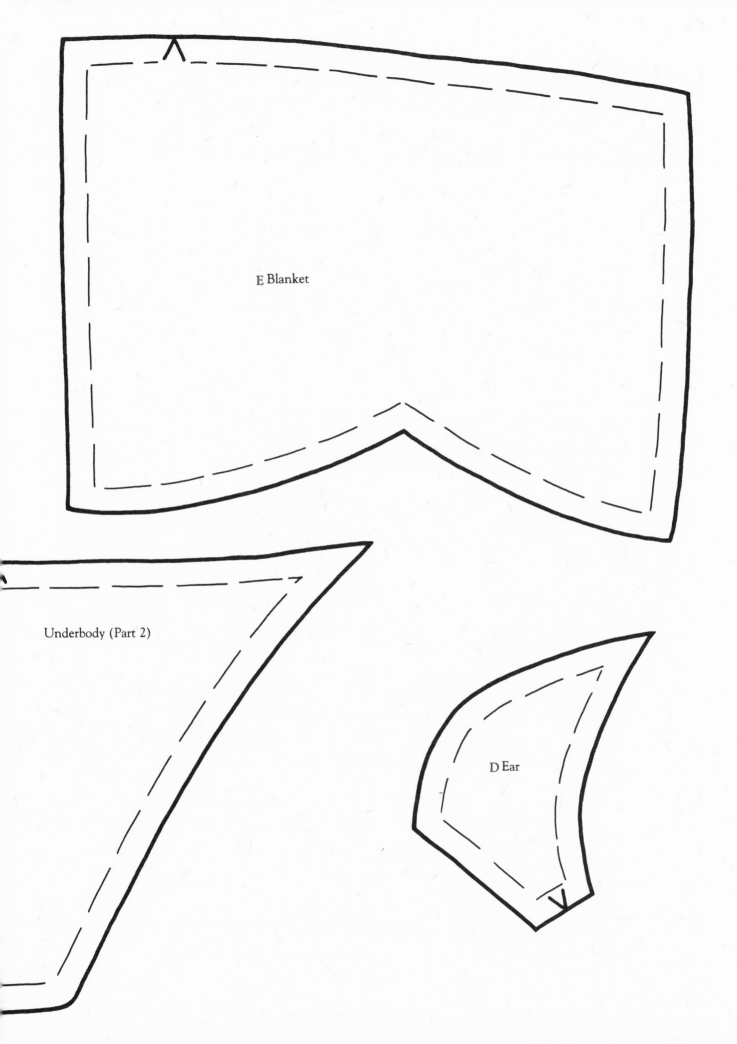

E Blanket

Underbody (Part 2)

D Ear

DESIGN SHEET

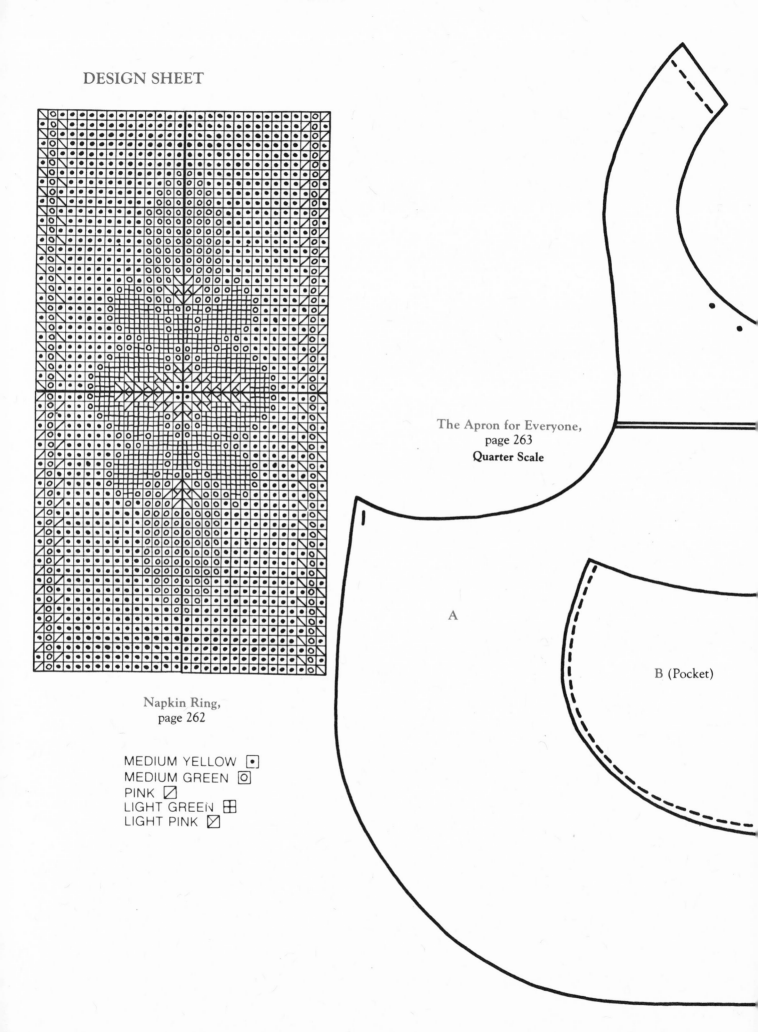

Napkin Ring,
page 262

MEDIUM YELLOW ▪
MEDIUM GREEN ⊡
PINK ◨
LIGHT GREEN ⊞
LIGHT PINK ⊠

The Apron for Everyone,
page 263
Quarter Scale

A

B (Pocket)

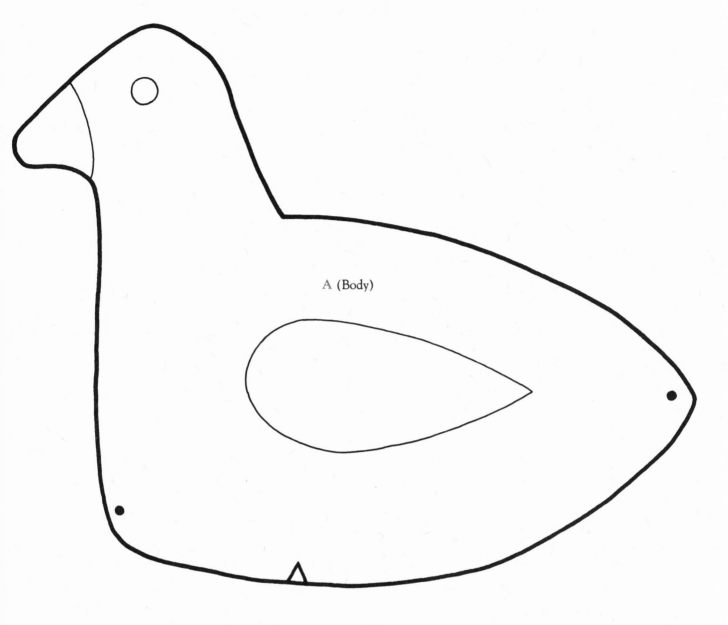

A (Body)

Goose Pot Holder, page 264

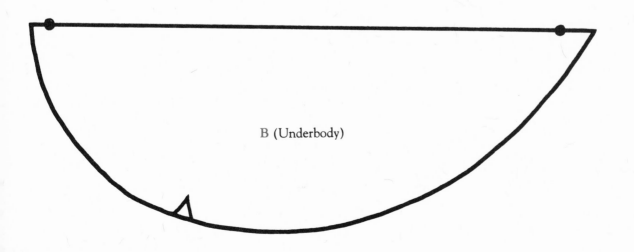

B (Underbody)

DESIGN SHEET

B (Yarn Holder)

Yarn Holder Placement

A (Cover)

Needlework Yarn Carrier,
page 266

DESIGN SHEET

Note: Only the pattern for the curved flap is given. Trace flap onto fabric and continue the outline for the work pocket from the widest part of the flap. The work pocket pattern should measure 22″ in total length.

Work Pocket/Flap, page 267

DESIGN SHEET

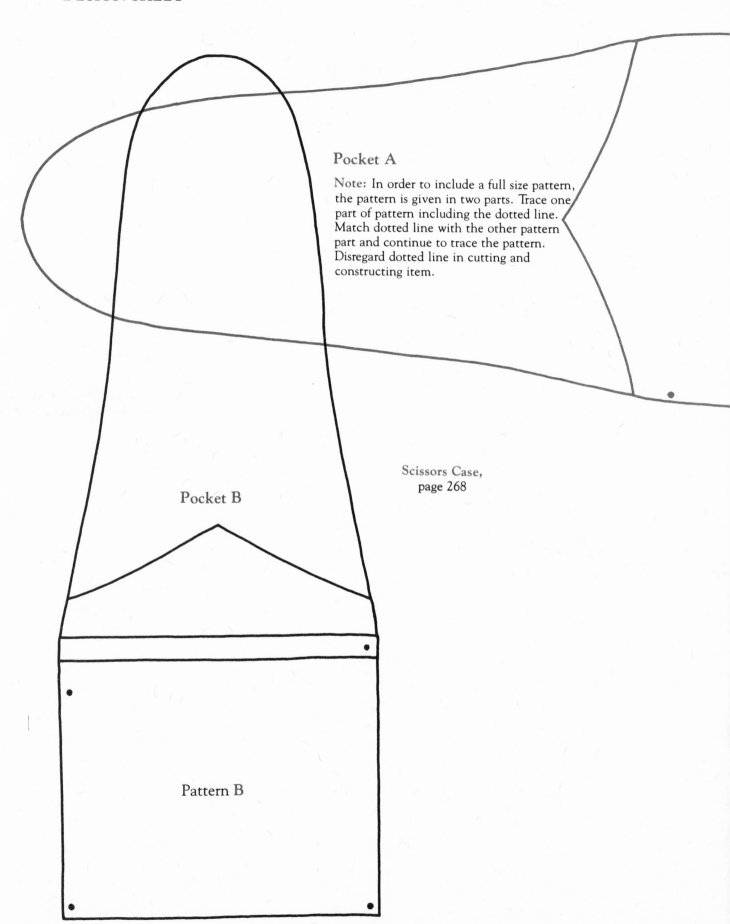

Pocket A

Note: In order to include a full size pattern, the pattern is given in two parts. Trace one part of pattern including the dotted line. Match dotted line with the other pattern part and continue to trace the pattern. Disregard dotted line in cutting and constructing item.

Scissors Case,
page 268

Pocket B

Pattern B

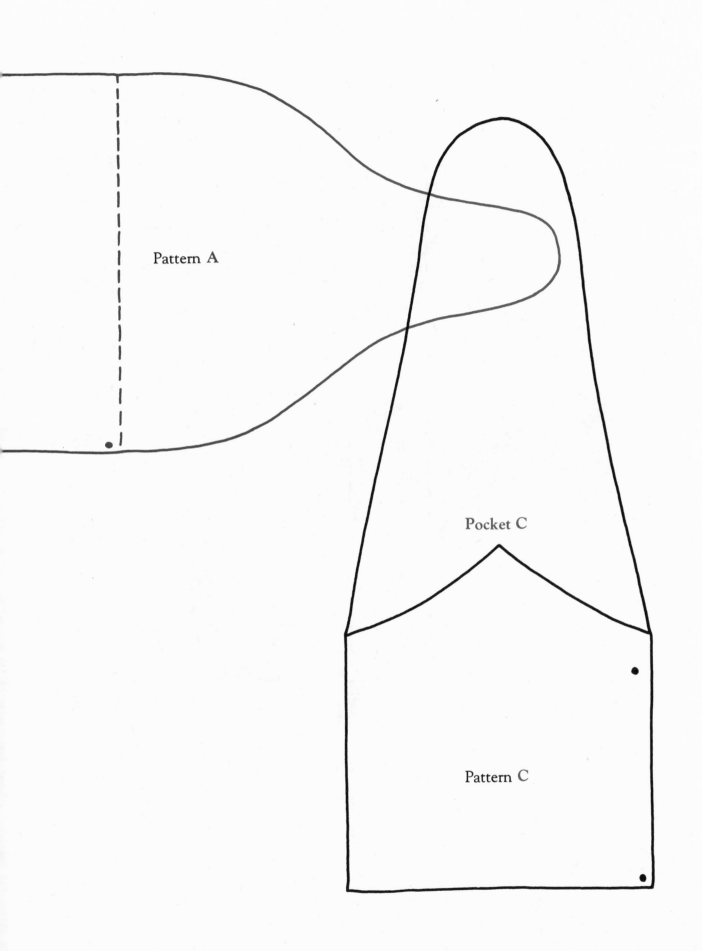

Pattern A

Pocket C

Pattern C

Needle-Art, 1923

26
Craft Basics

Appliqué

Appliqué is a form of textile embroidery in which designs are created by attaching one fabric to another. Appliqué is done by machine or by hand with invisible or visible stitches. Detail and linear qualities can be added to bold shapes with embroidery, beading, or quilting. Appliqué shapes can be lightly stuffed with fiberfill before stitching is completed to add surface interest.

Appliqué with Turned Edge

MATERIALS:
- lightweight fabrics
- polyester or mercerized cotton sewing thread, embroidery floss, or yarn
- hand sewing needles, sharps; machine sewing needles, size 14; embroidery needles

STEP-BY-STEP:
1. Transfer design to background fabric for placement of each shape to be appliquéd. Transfer individual shapes to selected fabrics and add ¼″ turn-under allowance to each appliqué.
2. Stitch around each appliqué by hand or machine, ¼″ from the edge.
3. Turn edges of appliqué to wrong side on stitched line and press lightly. Clip curves and miter corners and points (Illustration 26-1) to create a smooth edge. If desired, cut a template out of shirt cardboard in the exact shape of the appliqué and press appliqué edges back over template. (Illustration 26-2)
4. Pin appliqués in position on background fabric

and stitch in place by hand or machine. Use a straight (Illustration 26-3) or zigzag stitch (Illustration 26-4) close to the edge for machine appliqué. For hand stitching, use the slipstitch (Illustration 26-5), or running stitch (Illustration 26-6), or a decorative stitch like the blanket (Illustration 26-7) or chain stitch. If desired, add embroidered details.

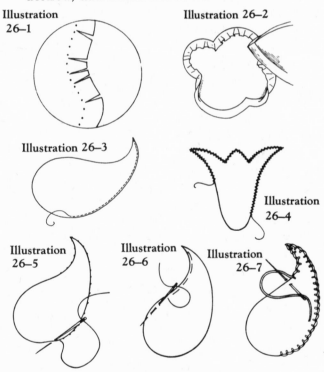

Illustration 26–1

Illustration 26–2

Illustration 26–3

Illustration 26–4

Illustration 26–5

Illustration 26–6

Illustration 26–7

Appliqué with Raw Edge

MATERIALS:
- light-, medium-, or heavyweight fabrics, felt, leather, or imitation suede
- thread, needles same as for Appliqué with Turned Edge

STEP-BY-STEP:

1. Transfer design to background fabric for placement guide. Transfer individual shapes to selected fabrics and cut out appliqués. Do not add seam allowances.
2. Position individual appliqués on background fabric and baste in place by hand or machine with straight or zigzag stitch.
3. Sew design in place using a machine satin stitch (tightly spaced zigzag stitch), enclosing all raw edges with stitches. For hand work, substitute tightly spaced blanket stitches. Add embroidered details if desired.

Appliqué with Fusibles

A fusible is a lightweight, thermoplastic web that joins two fabrics by fusing when heat, moisture, and pressure are applied with an iron. They are marketed in several widths and lengths and are usually available where fabrics are sold. Current brand names of this material include Pellon® Fusible Web, Stacy Stitch Witchery®, Poly Bond® by Coats and Clark, and Armo Stylus® Fusible Web.

MATERIALS:
- same as for Appliqué with Turned Edge
- fusible web

STEP-BY-STEP:

1. Transfer design to background fabric, appliqué fabric, and fusible web. Do not add turn-under allowances. Carefully cut shapes from appliqué fabric and fusible web.
2. Place fusible web between the appliqué and background fabric and follow product directions for fusing (Illustration 26-8). (A paper

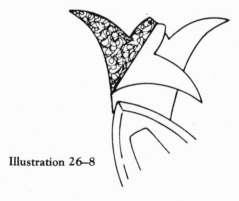

Illustration 26–8

towel placed between the iron and the appliqué will help prevent the bonding agent from sticking to the iron soleplate.) Allow work to cool on the ironing board to prevent unbonding, wrinkling, or shifting that could occur until the agent is completely cool.

3. Add embroidery stitches by hand or machine. Fusibles tend to stiffen fabric, making hand embroidery more difficult to execute.

Reverse Appliqué

The traditional method for this form of appliqué is to cut away and narrowly hem shapes within shapes. A design for reverse appliqué must be segmented or contain shapes within shapes. Usually, the shapes should be at least ¼″ apart. When lightweight fabrics like percale or broadcloth are being used, three to five layers of fabric can be worked. With heavier fabrics like felt or imitation suede, use fewer layers because it might be difficult to stitch through too many layers.

MATERIALS:
- same as for Appliqué with Raw Edge
- fabric glue

STEP-BY-STEP:

1. Arrange fabric in layers as desired. The bottom layer will remain uncut and serve as the backing fabric. The top layer will probably be the predominant color.
2. Transfer design shapes to be cut out of top layer onto fabric. Transfer shapes within shapes as you work.
3. Baste the layers together around the edges and diagonally across the center in both directions.
4. With sharp-pointed embroidery scissors, pierce top layer of fabric and cut away shapes, one at a time. For a turned edge, allow ¼″ all around design line for turn under. Clip corners and curves. Slit areas too small to be cut out. For a raw edge, cut on exact design lines.
5. Stitch edges in place through all layers. For turned edges, turn edge under with tip of needle as you sew. Use slipstitch or an embroidery

stitch (Illustration 26-9). For raw edges, stitch close to edge by hand or machine or use fabric glue. Machine satin stitch may also be used.

Illustration 26–9

6. Cut out shapes to expose progressive layers and proceed as above. Fold hems of top layers over edges of underlying ones when cutting away several layers at one time.

Stuffed Appliqué Shapes

MATERIALS:
- same as for appliqué with turned edge
- polyester fiberfill

STEP-BY-STEP:
1. Transfer appliqué design to fabric. Cut two each of the entire shape of the appliqué, adding ¼″ seam allowance all around. Felt and leather fabrics do not require the additional ¼″.
2. Set aside one piece to serve as a back. Complete appliqué on remaining major piece, adding other appliqué pieces and embroidered details, if any, last.
3. Turn under edges of appliqué front and back if necessary.
4. Place appliquéd front and plain back shapes wrong sides together and edgestitch around edge, adding 8″ ribbon or yarn loop for hanger at top and pausing with needle in work to stuff with fiberfill before completing stitching. Stitching may be done by hand or by machine. Stuffing may also be a piece of polyester fleece inserted sandwich-like before stitching begins.

- For pincushion, stuff tightly.
- For card or ornament, stuff lightly.
- For sachet, add sachet powder (or dusting powder) with stuffing and stuff lightly or as otherwise desired.

Blocking

Press appliqué lightly over a padded surface from the wrong side. Appliqué should retain its slightly puffy look and pleats and folds in the appliqué pieces should be avoided.

Card Making

Select a card-making method that is right for your card design and needs. The methods in this section concentrate on simple techniques and readily available equipment and materials. Photographic cards are not covered, as they are best done by professionals.

MATERIALS:
- **Paper and Envelopes**
  - Use standard paper sizes and get special effects by means of various folds. (Illustration 26-10)

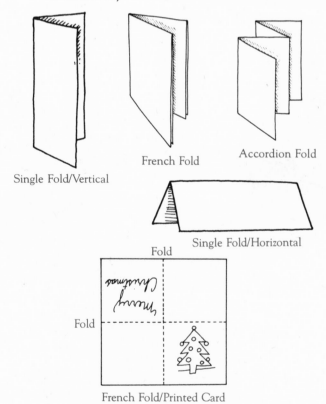

Single Fold/Vertical

French Fold

Accordion Fold

Single Fold/Horizontal

Fold

Fold

Merry Christmas

French Fold/Printed Card

- Use paper stiff enough to stand by itself when folded (double or French fold may be slightly lighter). Try construction paper, watercolor paper, coated paper, bristol (postcard weight and heavier), and rice paper.

• Use the folded card stock with coordinated envelopes carried in art stores or other common stationery items such as folded notes and correspondence cards.

• Use newsprint, tissue paper, shelf paper, or solid-color gift-wrap paper.

• Use a standard size envelope. Plan your card around the envelope to eliminate frustration and extra work. Envelope sizes vary widely. The envelope should be about ¼″ larger than the card in length and width. Padded or assembled cards may need larger envelopes to accommodate the extra dimension. Envelope may be decorated with a printed motif from card design if appropriate. To make your own envelopes, follow folds in Illustration 26-11.

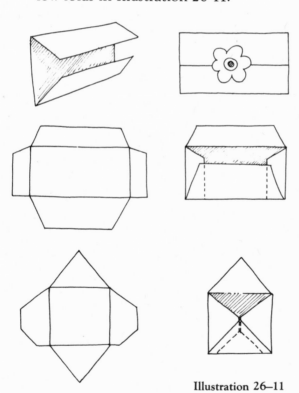

Illustration 26–11

• **Basic Equipment**
  • printing equipment as needed
  • rubber cement
  • metal ruler and artist's knife for all paper cuts

• paper cutter (optional, but nice for serious card making)

• **Lettering**
  • Fine felt-tip pen, fountain pen, and ink. Use your best flowing handwriting to inscribe your message, or slant the letters upright for a bit of a change.
  • Transfer letters. These are sold in art supply stores under brand names such as Letraset®, Artype®, and Prestype®. You transfer the words or letters to your card by gently rubbing the transparent sheets which carry the letters. There are many alphabets, colors, and letter sizes to choose from as well as borders, symbols, and textures. Unfortunately, the letters once applied are rather fragile and may crack.
  • Calligraphy is an art form in itself, out of which entire cards can be created. With some practice and the proper equipment (fountain pen with interchangeable wide nibs, ink, bond paper, and several alphabets to copy) you can become proficient in this art.

Hand Assembled Cards

Cards can be put together from bits of paper, yarn, fabric, appliqués, nature and other such materials. See Valentines (page 8), Easter cards (page 59), and Christmas card designs (pages 180–186). Keep in mind potential mailing problems if using fragile components. Complicated collage cards will be time-consuming to construct.

MATERIALS:
  • collage components as desired
  • rubber cement (preferable) or white glue (for children)
  • background card or folded note, and envelope to fit
  • pencil, tracing paper

STEP-BY-STEP:
1. Trace and cut out all paper and fabric components. Foreground pieces may overlap background pieces for interest.
2. Lightly trace design position onto card.

3. Glue parts in place, starting with largest or background pieces.
4. Clean off excess glue (if rubber cement).
5. Allow to dry well before inscribing message.

Cards with Mounted Designs

Cards which are designed to be something other than just a card may be mounted for presentation in several ways:

- Tie a paper ornament through holes punched in the card; arrange to hang on the front of the card. A card in a color contrasting to the ornament makes a dramatic presentation.
- Attach a felt, patchwork, or other fabric ornament or pincushion to a card by the use of double-stick transparent tape. Stitched and stuffed ornaments are discussed in Appliqué (page 284) and Patchwork (page 299).
- Use cutout frames to dramatically present bookmarks, photos, and flat ornaments (such as those embroidered on perforated paper and needlepoint). Cut the frame out of the front of a French fold card, center the item, and mount it with tape to the card behind the opening as in Illustration 26-12. (See Mat Cutting, page 232).

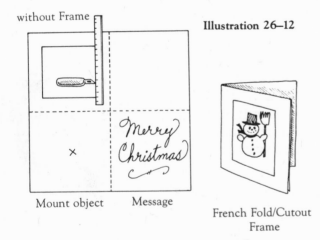

Illustration 26–12

without Frame

Mount object   Message

French Fold/Cutout Frame

Stamping

Use for quantity printing of small, moderately detailed designs. Additional details may be added with felt markers. This technique is suitable for decorating wrapping paper.

MATERIALS:
- poster, tempera, or acrylic paints, or foam stamp pad
- absorbent paper such as construction, rice, or wrapping paper
- art gum eraser, cork, potato, or styrofoam cubes to carve stamp
- artist's knife or utility knife
- pencil
- glass sheet or enamel tray
- brayer (optional) or ½" paintbrush

STEP-BY-STEP:
1. Trace design onto stamp medium with pencil.
2. Trace design placement lightly on card.
3. Carefully cut away excess material from around design on stamp. Do not cut under design as this weakens printing area. Cuts should slant away from design. (Illustration 26-13)

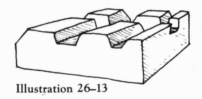

Illustration 26–13

4. Distribute paint or ink on stamp with brayer, brush, or stamp pad.
5. Make impressions on paper with stamp, pressing evenly.
6. Allow to dry.
   Note: Corks have grain lines which should be taken into consideration when design is positioned prior to carving, as these grain lines may appear in the finished print.

Linoleum Block Printing

Use for quantity production of cards. Choose a design with simple lines and shapes for a first attempt, although with practice quite nice detail can be achieved. Negative or positive prints are possible, depending on how the block is cut. A negative print is made by cutting out lines and leaving large areas to carry ink; a positive print is just the opposite with large areas cut out and lines carrying the ink.

MATERIALS:
- linoleum block from art store
- carbon paper, tracing paper, pencil
- lineoleum cutting tools
- inks (watercolor or oil)
- brayer and glass sheet or enamel tray
- newspapers, rags
- absorbent printing paper ¼″ larger than design all around

STEP-BY-STEP:
1. Wash linoleum block to remove any oil residue.
2. Transfer design to tracing paper. Tape tracing to linoleum **design side down.** Insert a piece of carbon paper between tracing and linoleum, carbon side down, before tracing design to ensure a sharp image on linoleum. Transfer design to linoleum. Image will be in reverse. (Illustration 26-14)

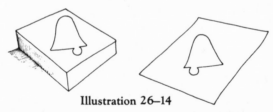

Illustration 26–14

3. Carve design, cutting away from yourself. Use "V" gouge to cut outlines and larger "U" gouges to remove large quantities of linoleum. Cutting depth should be uniform throughout.
4. Roll brayer in printing ink on glass or tray, then on cut linoleum block.
5. Place paper on inked block and roll over with rolling pin or clean brayer, or rub with the bowl of a tablespoon.

Stencil Printing

The number of good quality prints possible depends on the durability of the stencil material used. Letters are somewhat difficult to satisfactorily stencil. Suitable for decorating wrapping paper.

MATERIALS:
- stencil paper (heavy oiled paper) or mediumweight acetate
- artist's knife
- tracing paper
- absorbent printing paper
- paint (oil, acrylic, or spray)
- plate for palette (if more than one color being used)
- square-end stencil brush or bit of damp sponge
- paper clips

STEP-BY-STEP:
1. Transfer design to tracing paper and then to stencil paper.
2. Place heavy cardboard under stencil paper to protect working surface and with artist's knife, cut away design areas to be stenciled. Leave "bridges" to reinforce the design and keep large areas from shifting during printing.
3. Position stencil over printing paper and secure (paper clips are fine). If spray paint is being used, cover all exposed paper edges.
4. Print by quickly dabbing color over edges of stencil toward center of design to prevent color from bleeding under the stencil and causing a ragged edge.
5. Allow color to set before slowly lifting stencil to remove.
6. Allow to dry thoroughly.

Silk-screen Printing

Although this is a more advanced method of printing, it does not have to be complicated. Large quantities of simple prints can be produced. Use either moderately expensive silk-screen sets or the method with simpler equipment described below.

MATERIALS:
- embroidery hoop (a large one is easiest to work with)
- fine silk, nylon, or organdy fabric
- acrylic paint and brush
- rubber bowl scraper
- absorbent printing paper
- tempera paint for printing

STEP-BY-STEP:
1. Trace design onto fabric and stretch as tight as possible in hoop, forming silk screen. Design must be positioned in hoop so that hoop can rest squarely on the table with design on bottom. (Illustration 26-15)

Illustration 26–15

2. With acrylic paint, paint away areas you do *not* wish to print. Areas must be smoothly and completely blocked out. Allow to dry.
3. Place printing paper under silk-screen with design correctly aligned.
4. Dab paint on blocked area of screen. Press rubber scraper across screen, forcing paint to print through unblocked fabric.
5. Clean paint from screen before next use.

Cornstarch Clay

This clay is ideal for small objects that are planned, precisely shaped, and finely detailed, as the surface of the clay does not change during the drying period.

MATERIALS:
- 2 cups baking soda (1 lb. box)
- 1 cup cornstarch
- 1½ cups cold water

Note: Add food coloring to water to color entire batch of clay or add food coloring to portions of cooled clay. Color lightens as clay dries, so while clay is damp, color should be intense.

STEP-BY-STEP:
1. Stir baking soda and cornstarch together in a pan.
2. Quickly add cold water. Stir slowly until mixture thins and becomes smooth.
3. Cook over medium heat, stirring constantly, until thickened to consistency of mashed potatoes.

4. When mixture is too thick to stir and has dull surface, turn onto a plate and cover with a damp cloth until cool.
5. Knead like dough and form desired shapes. Clay may be held in refrigerator in plastic bags for a week or more.
6. Model clay shapes or roll out to even thickness and cut into shapes with a knife, cookie cutter, etcetera, or cut into slabs pasted together with white glue after drying.
7. Allow to dry at room temperature up to two days or place in oven which has been preheated to 350° then turned off. Turn object occasionally so that all surfaces may dry.
8. If color was not added when clay was made, paint objects with acrylic paints or felt-tip markers, then coat with acrylic medium if desired.

Crochet

Basic crochet stitches are illustrated in many books, pamphlets, and magazines. Only basic stitches are used in projects. Even beginners will be able to complete the projects with a little practice.

Embroidery

Embroidery is the surface decoration of fabric with stitches. Embroidery can be combined with other forms of needlework, including patchwork and appliqué.

MATERIALS:
- **fabrics** smooth, loosely woven fabrics or perforated paper (a cream-colored card-weight paper with 16 holes to the inch in either direction).
- **yarn** thread, cotton embroidery floss, matte cotton, pearl cotton, crewel yarn, tapestry yarn. Embroidery floss and crewel and tapestry yarns can be separated into *plies* or individual strands for various thicknesses as desired.
- **needles** slender needles with a sharp point and a long eye, called embroidery/crewel needles.
- **hoop** available with an adjustable screw in 6″ and 8″ diameters.

Embroidery Stitches

These are some basic embroidery stitches to use to execute the projects in this book.

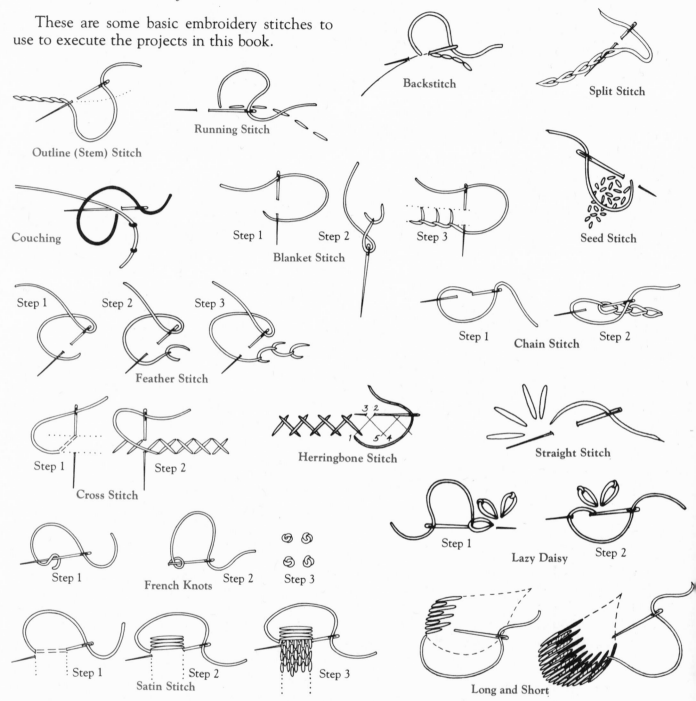

Basic Embroidery

STEP-BY-STEP:
1. Prepare and press fabric. Transfer design to fabric.
2. Assemble hoops and fabric (Illustration 26-16). Move hoops from one area to another as work progresses. To protect the completed stitching, tissue paper may be placed between the hoops and stitches. Always remove hoops at the end of a work session to prevent hard creases from forming in the fabric.

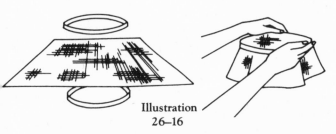

Illustration 26–16

3. Begin embroidery by tying a knot in the end of the yarn and passing the yarn from the right side to the underside of the fabric about ½″ from the starting point on a design line. Take a few embroidery stitches along the design line, catching the yarn with each stitch. When you reach the knot, clip it off. When you finish each yarn, weave the yarn end into a few stitches on the back of the work. (Knots to begin and end a yarn are usually not recommended, because they may untie, allowing pulled stitches which ultimately destroy the piece. They may also create lumps in your work.)

4. When embroidery is completed, clean if necessary. Press or block.

Blocking

Place work face down on a thickly padded surface, such as a thick towel folded several times, and steam press with light pressure.

Embroidery on Perforated Paper

Any cross-stitch or needlepoint design can be easily interpreted on perforated paper. Use the half cross-stitch, cross-stitch, backstitch, or satin stitch. Test yarn or thread on a scrap of paper to be certain yarn is not too thick. Generally, the background in a perforated paper project is not embroidered.

STEP-BY-STEP:

1. Transfer design to paper. Cutting down center of a row of holes, cut out paper, allowing an extra 1½″ all around. Tape edges of paper with masking tape to prevent tearing. Design or background may be tinted with wide point, waterproof felt-tip markers before work begins.

2. Work design, observing the following points:

   • Use a sharp point, very slender embroidery needle.
   • Begin and end stitching as suggested for regular embroidery, that is, no knots.
   • Glue yarn ends to back of design or they will be visible from the right side.
   • Always work through one hole at a time, going up and down in two separate movements to prevent tearing paper.
   • Avoid tugging on yarn.

3. Frame or mount as desired:

   • **bookmark** Overcast through holes to ribbon, felt, or leather strip.
   • **card** Tape in place beneath mat cutout (see Card Making, page 284).
   • **framed** Mount on paper same color as background of design. Unlike most needlework, framed perforated paper projects are usually covered with glass.

Cross-stitch Embroidery (Counted-Thread Embroidery)

Use an even-weave fabric and work each stitch over an exact number of threads in each direction. Cross-stitch is usually worked from a graph. Each graph square represents a counted square of fabric (or, in the case of gingham, a check). The symbols in the squares are often keyed to color schemes. Cross-stitch should be worked in horizontal rows. Work all the threads of the first half of the crosses in the same direction and make all the cross threads run in the opposite direction.

Stretching Embroidery for Framing

1. Assemble canvas stretchers (available in art-supply stores).

2. Center embroidered piece on frame. Fabric will extend beyond all sides. (Illustration 26-17)

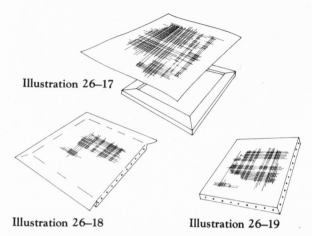

Illustration 26–17

Illustration 26–18   Illustration 26–19

3. Tack or staple each side beginning at the center and working to each corner (Illustration 26-18). Do one side at a time. Miter corners. Check repeatedly that design is remaining centered.

4. Fabric should be smooth and taut. (Illustration 26-19)

5. Frame as desired.

Enlarging and Reducing Designs

Grid Method

With a grid, a design can be translated to any size, larger or smaller, and will stay in proportion.

STEP-BY-STEP:

1. Decide how much to enlarge or reduce the design. Place a grid of exact squares over the design if it is not already marked off in squares (Illustration 26-20). This grid may be drawn on tracing paper. A shortcut is to overlay the original design with transparent graph paper or fine wire screen. The design may also be traced onto graph paper eliminating the need to construct grids.

2. Prepare another grid with the same *number* of squares as the first grid. Number the squares along the side and letter the squares along the top of both grids for easy reference while drawing. Construct grids carefully since precision is important to an accurate size adjustment.

To enlarge design: The prepared grid should have larger squares than the original design

(Illustration 26-21). For example, if the design to be enlarged is superimposed with a grid of ⅛″ squares, translate it onto a grid of ¼″, ½″ or 1″ squares.

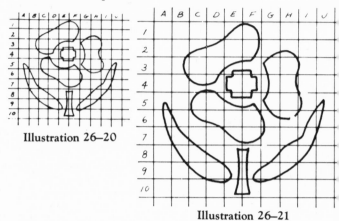

Illustration 26–20

Illustration 26–21

To reduce design: The prepared grid should have smaller squares than the original design. When a pattern has more than one piece the pieces must be adjusted proportionately. For example, if a ½″ grid has been superimposed over the pattern and the enlargement is to be drawn on a 1″ grid, all pieces must be drawn in the same scale so that the pieces will fit together properly.

3. Translate outline to grid one square at a time. Follow design carefully, checking square by square as you go.

Photostating and Photocopying

Designs may also be enlarged or reduced directly from the book by photostating, a photographic process that produces either a negative image or a positive image in either matte or glossy finish. Ask for a positive image because it is easier to use and a matte finish because it is usually less expensive. If you would like to reverse the direction of the design, ask for a "reverse image." You will receive both your original design and the finished "stat." Find a source for photostating by checking the Yellow Pages of your phone directory under "photocopying."

Some office copying machines have the ability to reduce images. This is a quick, inexpensive method to use when size reduction can be approximate.

Gift Wrapping

Gifts are wrapped to contain, protect, and conceal them for presentation. The wrapping may be a disposable covering, it may be a box specially covered with reuse intended, or it may be a custom container uniquely suited to the particular gift it contains. A gift wrap is part of the gift and, if it can be reused, it is an extra gift. Bows, ribbons, and other ornaments are often used to decorate gift packages.

Wrapped Boxes

Disposable purchased gift wrapping paper is the quickest way to prepare a gift for presentation.

- **Covering:** For outer wraps, use light- to mediumweight gift wrapping paper, fabric, or tissue paper. For inner box stuffing use tissue paper. Home-printed papers are especially nice (see Card Making, page 284). Printed paper designs should be appropriate to the size of the gift box.
- Narrow transparent tape, double-stick tape, ruler, scissors, gummed stickers (optional).
- Flat, uncluttered working surface.
- Ribbons, ornaments (see below).

Ribbons and Ornaments

- **Ribbons** For elegance use woven cloth ribbons of satin, velvet, moiré, or grosgrain. When using paper ribbons, use generous quantities for best appearance. Thick acrylic gift-yarns, string, and cords are also suitable. Size of bow should be in proportion to package.
- **Ornaments** Symbols of the occasion for the gift are good package decorations, for example, cornucopias, paper snowflakes, evergreen twigs at Christmas; candles, noisemakers, balloons on birthdays; hearts, cupids, artificial flowers on Saint Valentine's Day, etcetera.

Covered Boxes

Cover the box lid; covering the box bottom is optional. Very special boxes which are gifts in themselves are covered inside and out, top and bottom. Remember that the bottom of the box is always slightly smaller than the top, so the covering for each must be measured separately.

MATERIALS:
- **coverings** self-adhesive plastic paper such as Con-Tact®, wallpaper, light- to mediumweight fabric
- **adhesive** rubber cement for paper coverings, fabric glue for fabric coverings
- polyester fleece and fiberfill for padding fabric covered boxes (optional)
- trims for fabric-covered boxes such as lace, ribbon (optional)
- ruler, pencil, scissors, needle, thread, tape measure, double-stick tape

Paper-Covered Box
STEP-BY-STEP
1. Covering box lid: Make a paper pattern before cutting decorative paper and fold to check for fit. To make pattern, trace box lid adding depth of box top plus ½″ to each of the 4 sides.
2. Center pattern on decorative paper design, if any; trace shape onto paper and cut out.
3. Transfer crease and clip lines to wrong side of paper (Illustration 26-22). Cut and crease on appropriate lines *very accurately*. Make all creases toward wrong side of paper folding over a ruler for an absolutely straight crease.

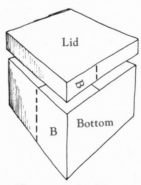

Illustration 26–22

4. Apply rubber cement along turn under A and flap B. Wrap A and B around box, with box edges and corners lined up on crease lines. Do both corners of same end of box then repeat

procedure at opposite end of box. Always plan arrangement so that on box lid, flaps B are glued to box end, instead of box side. (Illustration 26-23)

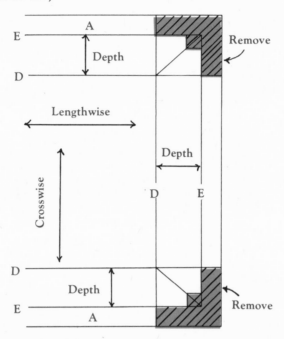

Illustration 26–23

5. Apply rubber cement along turn under C and wrap around box.

6. Covering box bottom: Follow procedure for box lid except, when cutting out pattern, adjust crease and clip lines in corners so that flap B will be glued to side of box rather than end of box. (Illustration 26-24)

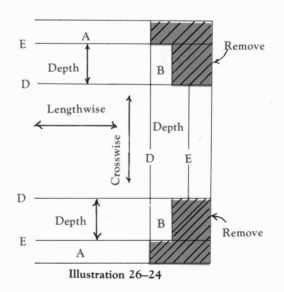

Illustration 26–24

Self-Adhesive Plastic Paper
STEP-BY-STEP:

1. Follow instructions for Paper-Covered Box above, steps 1 and 2. Measure pattern for box on back of self-adhesive paper and cut out carefully.

2. Fold all crease lines toward wrong side, sharply creasing with thumbnail.

3. Remove paper backing from plastic very carefully to avoid tearing at corner cuts. Cut away excess paper as you work to make working easier.

4. Align folded box edge exactly on crease D (see illustration). Smooth paper on top of box lid.

5. Smooth up side A and flap B. Trim away any excess of flap B that extends over top of box lid then smooth turn under A into place.

6. Smooth up side and turn under C.

7. Rub turn-under edges inside box with thumbnail for tight, neat seal.

8. Repeat steps 1–7 above for bottom of box, making adjustment as noted in step 5 of Paper-Covered Box.

Fabric-Covered Box
STEP-BY-STEP:

1. Covering box lid: Make a paper pattern before cutting fabric and fold to check for fit. To make pattern, trace box lid adding depth of box lid plus ½″ to each of the four sides.

2. Center pattern on fabric design, if necessary. Place pattern on straight of fabric grain. Trace pattern shape to fabric and cut out.

3. With pencil, lightly transfer crease and clip lines to wrong side of fabric, as shown in illustration. Cut and crease on appropriate lines *very accurately*. Make all creases toward wrong side of fabric, folding over a ruler for an absolutely straight crease.

4. Fold and glue triangle C to section C.

5. Apply glue along turn under A and triangle A. Wrap glued pieces around box with box edges and corners lined up on crease lines. Gently stretch fabric to fit smoothly, keeping grain straight. Do both corners of same end of box, then repeat procedure at opposite end of box.

Always plan arrangement so that on box lid, triangles B are glued to box end, instead of box side.

6. Apply glue along turn under C and wrap around box. Rub fabric edges inside box with thumbnail for tight seal.

7. Covering box bottom: Follow procedure for box lid, except fold and glue triangle A to section A, which is the side of the box rather than the end.

8. Glue rickrack or other flat trim along edge of fabric inside box bottom.

Padded, Lined, Fabric-Covered Box
STEP-BY-STEP

1. Shape a handful of fiberfill to dimensions of top of box lid, making fiberfill slightly puffy in the middle. Loosely glue to box lid.

2. Cover fiberfill on top of box lid with a piece of polyester fleece. Glue fleece along box lid edges, cutting out corners of fleece so edges butt together. Use piece of fleece large enough to mold attractive curve to lid of box. (Illustration 26-25)

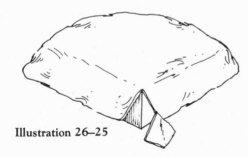

Illustration 26–25

3. With tape measure, measure short edge of box lid, up the side, around the top and down the other side to the opposite edge. Do not pull tape tightly. Add twice the lid depth plus 1½″ to this measurement. Measure lengthwise around box in same manner and add twice the lid depth plus 1½″ to this measurement. Cut a piece of fabric to these dimensions.

4. Center fabric, wrong side up, over box lid. Smooth fabric and pin corners together snugly. Stitch seam as pinned. Trim seam, turn, and fit cover over box top. (Illustration 26-26)

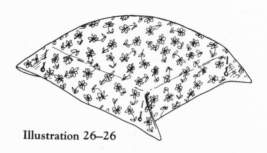

Illustration 26–26

5. Place a row of double-stick tape or glue inside box lid at fold. Press fabric to tape snugly all around.

6. Cut a piece of shirt cardboard slightly smaller than exact measurement of inside of box lid. Check fit of cardboard in top, then cover with fabric glued or taped to back. Miter fabric corners when covering cardboard. Glue covered piece into box.

7. Whipstitch lace around outside edges of box lid.

8. Cover box bottom according to directions in step 7 of Fabric-Covered Box (page 294). To make pattern, trace box bottom shape and add twice the box bottom depth plus ½″ to each of the four sides. Cut out corners following illustration for Fabric-Covered Box.

9. Line bottom of box same as lid, step 6 above.

Cutout-Decorated Box
MATERIALS:
- 1 solid-color gift box
- designs cut from old greeting cards
- spray adhesive
- small sharp scissors, pencil
- acrylic varnish, 1″ brush

STEP-BY-STEP:

1. Arrange cutout designs on box as desired.

2. To match designs on bottom with overlapping box lid, turn design to wrong side, position as desired extending under box lid. Draw light pencil line at edge of lid. Cut design in half on this line and match halves when gluing.

3. Spray adhesive on back of designs following instructions on can. Press onto box. Work on one side at a time.

4. When designs are firmly in place, coat box

with acrylic varnish, following drying-time instructions on jar between coats. Use several coats to seal cutouts smoothly. **Note:** Test acrylic varnish on box to be certain there will be no unsightly blotching of the basic box covering caused by the varnish. If this occurs, cover decorated box with transparent self-adhesive plastic paper instead of varnish. If this method is used, avoid using embossed designs for decorating the box, as they will not press smoothly under the plastic paper.

Custom Containers

Custom containers are used to wrap oddly shaped or outsize items. Several of these containers appear as projects elsewhere in this book. Instructions for the containers shown in Color Plates 15 and 24 may be found as follows: Poinsettia, page 197; Santa Carton, page 195; Silhouette Tins, page 197; Fern Vase, page 247; Bonbon Bags, page 176.

Purchased items such as baskets, cache pots, and jars make unique gift containers, especially for home-crafted items.

Knitting

Basic knitting stitches are illustrated in many books, pamphlets, and magazines. Only basic stitches are used in projects. Even beginners will be able to complete the projects with a little practice.

Needlepoint

Needlepoint is counted-thread embroidery done on even-weave fabric or stiff canvas.

MATERIALS:
- **Canvas** Needlepoint canvas is a cotton fabric woven in open, regular squares and stiffened for body and easy stitching. The size of canvas describes the number of mesh (threads) per inch. For example, #10 canvas has 10 mesh to the inch. Canvas ranges in size from very coarse (#3) to very fine (#40) and is sold by the yard.

Duo (Penelope) canvas has two threads for each mesh, so that it can be split for finer detail or be used for petit point. (Illustration 26-27)

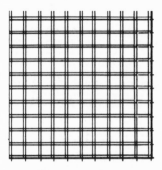
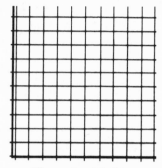

Illustration 26–27   Illustration 26–28

Note: Petit point refers to needlepoint worked on fine canvas, 16 or more mesh per inch (8 to the inch Penelope or 16 to the inch mono).

Mono canvas has one thread for each mesh and is suitable for many designs. Bargello should always be worked on mono canvas. (Illustration 26-28)
- **Yarn** Many yarns in a wide array of colors are available for needlepoint. The yarns most commonly used for needlepoint are Persian wool, tapestry wool, and crewel yarn. Persian wool is a three-stranded yarn which can be divided for use on several canvas sizes. Tapestry wool is a tightly twisted, four-ply yarn which is not easily separated and is not used on canvas smaller than 14 mesh per inch. Crewel yarn, a fine, two-ply yarn, can be used with several threads together to cover many different canvas sizes. Other yarn possibilities include rug wool, embroidery floss, metallic yarns, pearl cotton, chenille, and silk floss. Estimate the amount of yarn needed. Simply calculate the number of square inches to be covered by each color. Make generous estimates for oddly shaped areas. Multiply the number of square inches for each color by the amount of yarn needed to cover one square inch of canvas. Since this amount will vary with the stitch used and the canvas size (mesh per inch), it will be necessary to work a square inch of canvas to determine how much yarn it takes. Buy enough yarn to finish a project since it may be difficult to match color later on.

- **Needles** Use tapestry needles with a blunt point and large eye.
- **Stitches** The three stitches most often used for needlepoint are:

Continental which requires more yarn than half cross-stitch because it creates a padded effect on the back of the work which increases the durability and wearing qualities of the work. It is best used for outlining, fine details, and filling in small areas. Should not be used for entire large work. (Illustration 26-29)

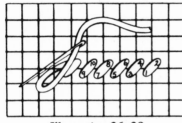

Illustration 26—29

Basket Weave which is recommended for filling in backgrounds as well as any other areas of the design. Has the padded effect and durability of continental stitch and uses more yarn than half cross-stitch. (Illustration 26-30)

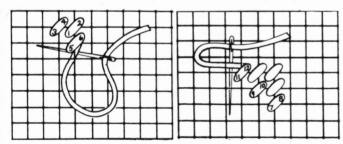

Illustration 26—30

Half Cross-stitch which requires the least amount of yarn and results in the thinnest completed fabric. Worked only on duo (Penelope) canvas. (Illustration 26-31)

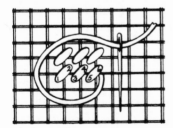

Illustration 26—31

Needlepoint Stitches

The needlepoint stitches illustrated here are some of the basic and most often used.

Odd numbers indicate that the needle is coming to the front of the work at the beginning of a stitch.

Even numbers indicate that the needle is going to the back of the canvas at the completion of a stitch.

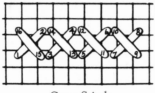

Cross Stitch

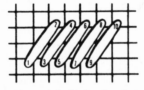

Slanted Goblelin Stitch

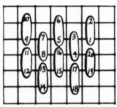

Brick Stitch

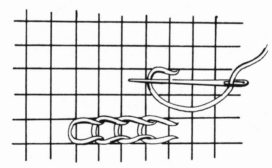

Chain Stitch

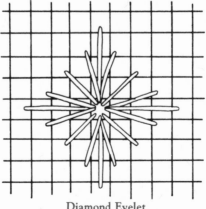

Diamond Eyelet

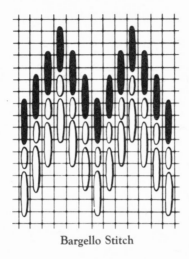

Bargello Stitch

Basic Needlepoint

STEP-BY-STEP

1. Cut canvas to the desired size, allowing at least a two-inch border all around design for blocking, mounting, and stitch shrinkage (canvas is drawn up when stitches are taken). Bind the edges with masking tape to prevent raveling and to make the canvas easier to hold. (Illustration 26-32)

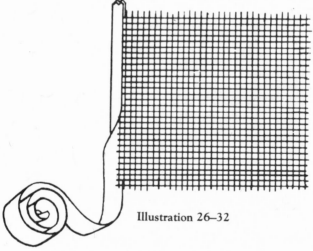

Illustration 26–32

2. Transfer design to canvas or work from a graph. To read a graph, remember that each *square* represents an *intersection* of threads in the canvas (Illustration 26-33). Always count intersections of the canvas threads (mesh), *not* holes in the canvas. When working from a graph, locate the center of the graph and the center of the canvas and begin there.

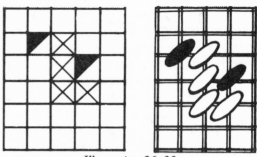

Illustration 26–33

3. To begin stitching, tie a knot in the end of a piece of yarn and pass the yarn from the right side to the underside of the canvas about ½" from the beginning point within the design area. Take a few stitches along the row, catching the yarn with each stitch. When you reach the knot, clip it off (Illustration 26-34). The

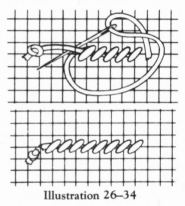

Illustration 26–34

yarn will be secured on the underside by the stitches. As you finish each yarn, pass the yarn end under a few stitches on the back of the work (Illustration 26-35). Begin working in

Illustration 26–35

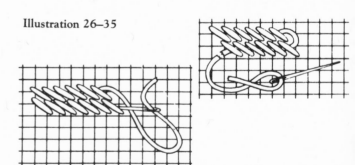

the center of the canvas and work the design areas first and the background last. Add beads or embroidery after canvas is blocked. If the design includes curves and diagonals, remember that needlepoint canvas is basically geometric and that curves and diagonals are made up of small geometric steps that give the appearance of a curve. (Illustration 26-36)

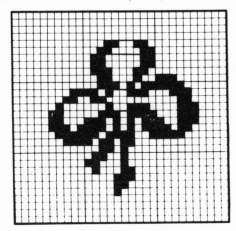

Illustration 26–36

4. When needlepoint is completed, clean if necessary and block or press into shape.

Blocking

Cover a wooden board with brown paper or a blocking cloth. Mark dimensions of canvas on blocking surface with pencil, taking care to square corners. Working from center to corners, dampen work with sponge and warm water while stretching it face down to match the board markings and tacking to board. Use rust-proof tacks or pushpins placed at ½″ to 1″ intervals. Allow to dry at least 24 hours, as long as 48.

Needlepoint in Projects

Stitched to Fabric Pieces (Pillows, Book Covers, Bookends)
STEP-BY-STEP:
1. Machine stitch twice around the edges of the piece, using a short stitch. Trim excess canvas to ½″ all around.
2. Complete project construction, incorporating completed needlepoint. Stitch on the needlepoint side when completing seams and keep stitching just on the edge of the needlepoint stitches to prevent unworked canvas from showing at seams.

Backed with Fabric or Ribbon (Belts, Bands, Napkin Rings)
STEP-BY-STEP
1. Trim canvas to 1″ all around. Clip curves.
2. Turn under unworked canvas to wrong side of work, mitering corners when necessary, and catchstitch in place.
3. To add a backing, trace around the completed shape on a piece of firmly woven lining fabric and add ⅝″ seam allowance all around.
4. Cut lining, then press seam allowance to wrong side; miter corners and clip curves if necessary.
5. Slipstitch lining in place on back side of needlepoint. Grosgrain ribbon or a strip of felt or leather may be used for a lining on a long, narrow item like a belt.

Overcast Edges (Belts, Pockets, Appliqués, Napkin Rings)
STEP-BY-STEP
1. On duo (Penelope) canvas, trim canvas leaving three rows of double threads on all sides. Crease canvas back on center pair of threads.
2. Use a double yarn to overcast edges, taking a stitch in each hole. Use matching or contrasting yarn. (Illustration 26-37)

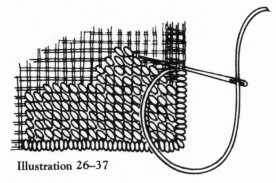

Illustration 26–37

Stretched and Framed
STEP-BY-STEP
1. Cut mat board, illustration board, or chip board to exact size of needlepoint piece.
2. Center board on back of needlepoint and turn unworked edges of canvas back over board.
3. With carpet thread and heavy needle, lace opposite canvas edges together, mitering corners.

4. Frame.
   Note: Needlepoint may be stretched on can-vas stretchers if desired. See technique in em-broidery, page 291.

Patchwork

Patchwork is a very old method for forming a large piece of fabric from many smaller ones.

MATERIALS:
- **Fabrics** Cotton or cotton blends in dress or shirt weights. Other possibilities include silks, corduroy, velveteen, and lightweight wools.
- **Thread** For both machine and hand piec-ing, use cotton or polyester thread in a neutral or matching shade.
- **Needles** Use size 8 to 10 sharps for hand piecing. Use size 14 machine needle for machine piecing.

Basic Pieced Patchwork

STEP-BY-STEP:
1. Preshrink and press all fabrics, whether newly purchased goods or recycled scraps. Transfer design parts to appropriate fabrics, using the template method (page 309). Be sure to add seam allowances of ¼″ all around each piece. Observe grainlines.
2. Cut pieces carefully. Piecework requires pre-cise measuring and cutting of design elements.
3. Begin by joining one small unit to another. Then join that unit to another and continue until large sections of completed patchwork can be joined. Press each seam open or to one side before crossing it with another.
   Piecing by hand Use a small running stitch. Begin with a knot or small backstitch and con-tinue taking three or four stitches. End with a backstitch.
   Piecing by machine Join units and stitch, using 10 to 12 stitches per inch. Guide pieces carefully with cut edge against the appropriate seam allowance line on the throat plate.

Masking tape can be applied to the throat plate for a stitching guide (Illustration 26-38). Since each seam will be crossed by another seam, backstitching is not necessary.

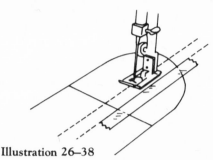

Illustration 26–38

Piecing hexagons and parallelograms For pieces that have bias edges, paper patterns are helpful in piecing and maintaining the shape. Cut a number of paper patterns exactly the size and shape of the finished patchwork piece. Use construction paper or paper of a similar weight. Center paper pattern on cut fabric and fold seam allowances over paper. Baste through seam allowances, paper, and fabric (Illustration 26-39). Join by holding two pieces with right sides together. Whipstitch along the edge to be joined (Illustration 26-40). Take special care matching and stitching corners (Illustration 26-41). To remove paper patterns, clip basting. The paper patterns can be used several times.

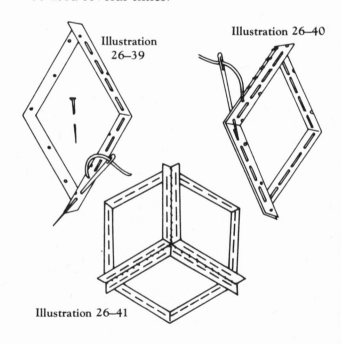

Illustration 26–39

Illustration 26–40

Illustration 26–41

4. Press completed work and use in project construction as planned.

Stuffed Patchwork Shapes

See Stuffed Appliqué Shapes (page 284) for procedure.

Blocking

Patchwork should be pressed lightly from the wrong side, stretching the seams lightly to reduce puckers and even out tension. Care should be taken never to press creases or pleats into the work, as a slight puffiness is a part of the charm of patchwork.

Sewing

Many projects in this book require knowledge of simple, basic sewing. The terms and techniques you will encounter are included in the alphabetical list which follows. Although many of the projects are more quickly and easily completed with the use of a sewing machine, hand sewing will, in most cases, be a satisfactory procedure and the techniques described here are generally applicable to either hand or machine work.

MATERIALS:
- assorted hand and machine sewing needles
- cotton or polyester thread as desired
- beeswax to smooth thread (optional)
- thimble
- scissors
- pins
- iron and ironing board
- 6″ sewing gauge
- sewing machine

Basting

Basting holds fabric pieces together to facilitate final stitching in some tricky procedures. It is usually done with a single thread using even running stitches about ¼″ long and ¼″ apart (Illus-

tration 26-42). Basting may also be done with pins (Illustration 26-43). To machine baste, set machine on longest stitch and loosen upper tension.

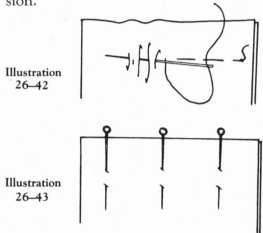

Illustration 26–42

Illustration 26–43

Bias Seam Binding, Self-Fabric

STEP-BY-STEP:
1. Cut strips on true bias (see Grain, page 304) in desired width. Cut ends on straight grain and join, pressing seams open. (Illustration 26-44)

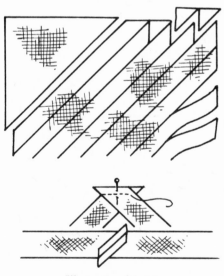

Illustration 26–44

2. Make bias binding by folding strip in half lengthwise and pressing lightly. Open and turn cut edges of binding in so one side is a scant ⅛″ wider than the other. Press. Refold center crease and press. (Illustration 26-45)

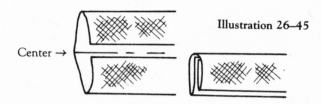

Illustration 26–45

3. To shape strip to match an inward curve, stretch the two folded edges, for an outward curve stretch the center edge. (Illustration 26-46)

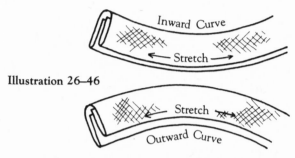

Illustration 26–46

4. To apply binding, open and pin narrower edge of binding to right side of fabric. Keep raw edges even. Stitch along crease (Illustration 26-47). Turn binding to inside and pin over seam, keeping folded edge along stitching. Slipstitch folded edge to seam. (Illustration 26-48)

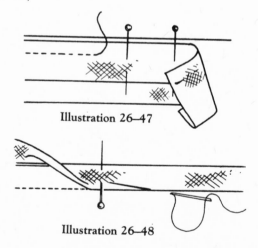

Illustration 26–47

Illustration 26–48

Alternatively, as binding is turned to inside, pin it so that the long folded edge covers the line of stitches and, from the right side, stitch in the seam ("stitch in the ditch") to catch the folded edge. (Illustration 26-49)

5. To bind corners, apply binding, backstitching at corner pivot point. Fold strip diagonally to

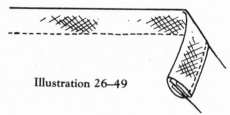

Illustration 26–49

go around corner and pin. Stitch adjoining edge along crease from edges of fabric through corner to end. Turn binding to inside over seam, forming a miter on outside. On inside, form second miter in opposite direction. Pin binding over seam, then sew binding and folds of miter in place. (Illustration 26-50)

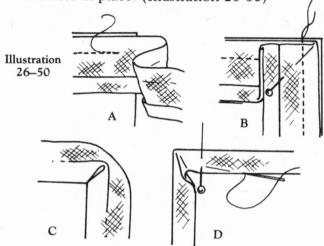

Illustration 26–50

A

B

C

D

Bias Seam Binding, Purchased

STEP-BY-STEP:
Double-Fold Binding

Follow procedure in steps 3–5 (6, if necessary) for Self-Fabric Bias Seam Binding, above.

Alternatively, place binding around edge with narrower folded edge of the tape on top. Edge-stitch through all layers. (Illustration 26-51)

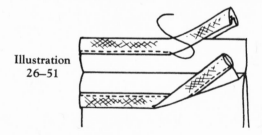

Illustration 26–51

Single-Fold Binding

Follow procedure in steps 3–5 (6, if necessary) for Self-Fabric Bias Seam Binding, above.

Bias Cording

Cut true bias strips from fabric (see Bias Seam Binding, Self-Fabric, step 1). Strips should be wide enough to go around filler plus an extra 1″–1½″. For filler use cable cord which is available in various diameters in most notions departments. Wrap bias strip around filler with wrong sides of fabric next to filler. Match raw edges of fabric. With zipper foot, machine baste close to but not on the filler.

Buttonholes, Machine-Worked

This type of buttonhole is best suited to washable items and is fast to make with a machine buttonhole attachment or a zigzag sewing machine, following the machine manual instructions. Make machine buttonholes after item has been interfaced and faced.

Casing

Applied Casing

An applied casing may be bias or straight grain self-fabric, or bias tape.

STEP-BY-STEP:
1. Cut casing to desired width plus ¼″ seam allowances on long edges (except when using bias tape). Length is as needed plus ½″ for finishing ends.
2. Press seam allowances under ¼″ on long edges.
3. Open one folded edge of casing and pin to right side of fabric with raw edges even. Turn casing ends in ¼″. Stitch ¼″ from raw edges.
4. Turn casing to inside and edgestitch remaining fold. (Illustration 26-52)

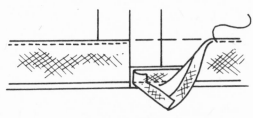

Illustration 26–52

Cut-in-One Casing

The cut-in-one casing is an extension of fabric, folded in like a hem.

STEP-BY-STEP:
1. Allow for casing width when cutting.
2. Turn under edge along foldline and pin.
3. Turn in raw edge ¼″, press, and edgestitch, leaving an opening for inserting drawstring. (Illustration 26-53)

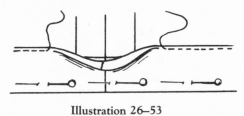

Illustration 26–53

Catchstitch

This stitch holds two layers of fabric in place flexibly and flatly. Work from left to right. Take a small horizontal stitch right to left in upper layer of fabric then just beyond edge of upper layer take same stitch diagonally from the first stitch in the under layer. Don't pull too tightly. (Illustration 26-54)

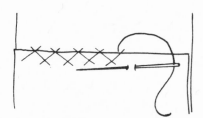

Illustration 26–54

Clipping

This is a process in which small cuts or clips are made in the seam allowance at even intervals (Illustration 26-55), the distance between clips depending on the sharpness of the curve, to enable the curve to turn smoothly. (See also Notching, page 304.) Clipping is also done directly into an inward corner so that it may be turned. Often the area is reinforced by short machine stitches on the seam line for a distance of 1″ on either side of the point. (Illustration 26-56)

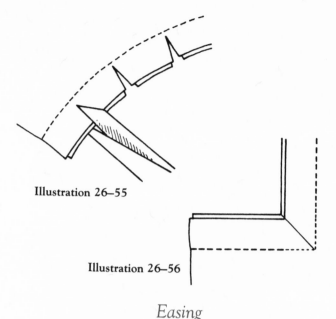

Illustration 26–55

Illustration 26–56

Easing

The easestitch is a long machine stitch (6 stitches per inch) done on a long edge (sometimes curved) to prepare it to join a shorter edge by controlling the fullness in the longer one. One of the stitching threads is pulled to draw edge up to desired length (Illustration 26-57). When the difference between the two lengths is not great, easing may be done by pinning the long edge in place then stretching out its fullness during stitching.

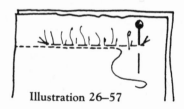

Illustration 26–57

Edgestitching

This is a row of stitching done parallel to and about $1/16''$ from a seam or turned edge. Edge can be further finished with hand overcast, machine zigzag, or pinking. (Illustration 26-58)

Illustration 26–58

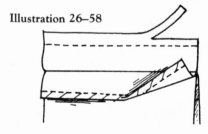

Gathering

To gather by hand, make two even rows, $1/4''$ apart, of small running stitches and pull rows up to gather. To gather by machine, make two rows of the longest machine stitch, $1/4''$ apart, with a loosened top tension. Pull bobbin thread to gather.

Grain

Woven fabric has two sets of yarns or thread interwoven at right angles to one another. The long finished edges of the fabric are *selvages*. Lengthwise grain parallels the selvages and is called *straight of grain*; crosswise grain runs from one selvage to the other. *Turn bias* is a diagonal at a 45° angle to any straight edge or grain of a fabric whose lengthwise and crosswise grains are perpendicular (Illustration 26-59). To straighten grain, cut along a crosswise thread, if one can be seen clearly. Or snip through the selvage and pull a crosswise thread until the fabric puckers then cut across this thread sliding the puckers ahead of the scissors.

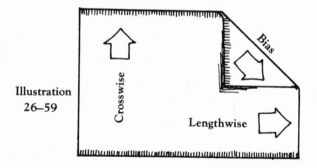

Illustration 26–59

Hemming Stitch

Take a tiny stitch in the fabric then bring needle diagonally through hem edge $1/4''$ away. Take next tiny stitch even with stitch in hem edge. Space stitches about $1/4''$ apart. (Illustration 26-60)

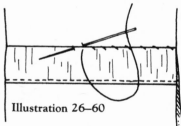

Illustration 26–60

Machine Stitching

Place fabric right sides together with seam allowance edge at right. Stitch evenly, keeping stitches an even distance from the edge. Use seam allowance line or masking tape on throat plate to guide raw edge of fabric (Illustration 26-61). For general straight stitching, use 10–12 stitches per inch. *Zigzag stitching* is done on a zigzag sewing machine. The machine is set to stitch wide or narrow stitches, far apart or close together according to need. Refer to sewing machine manual. Zigzag stitch is often used in appliqué.

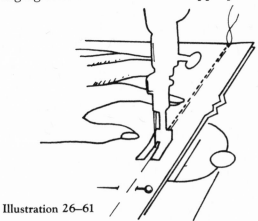

Illustration 26–61

Mitering

To miter trims, follow the procedure below.

STEP-BY-STEP:
1. Stitch both edges of trim to garment, ending stitching at opposite sides of corner. (Illustration 26-62)
2. Fold trim back and crease.
3. Fold trim at a right angle to stitched section; press.
4. Open trim and stitch along diagonal crease. (Illustration 26-63)

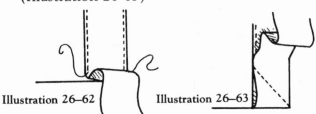

Illustration 26–62   **Illustration 26–63**

5. Fold trim to finished position and stitch both edges in new directions. (Illustration 26-64)

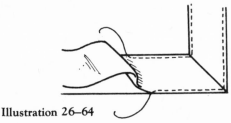

Illustration 26–64

This is a neat way to finish points and turn corners with a minimum of bulk.

STEP-BY-STEP:
1. Fold the point down. (Illustration 26-65)
2. Fold one side toward the center. (Illustration 26-66)
3. Fold the other side toward the center. Crease. (Illustration 26-67)

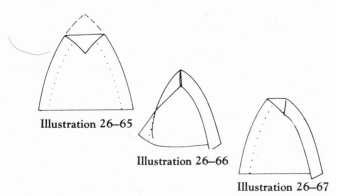

Illustration 26–65

Illustration 26–66

Illustration 26–67

Notching

This is a process in which small wedges or notches are cut out from the seam allowance at evenly spaced intervals to enable an outward curve to turn and press smoothly (Illustration 26-68). See also Clipping, above.

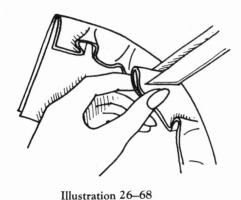

Illustration 26–68

Overcast Stitch

This stitch prevents raw edges from raveling. Take slanted stitches over the edge evenly spaced and uniformly deep (Illustration 26-69). Stitches may be close together to bind a raw edge.

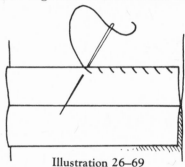

Illustration 26–69

Preshrinking

Fabrics which will be washed for cleaning should be washed before cutting to remove finishes and permit preshrinking. Simply wash and dry as anticipated for the finished project.

Pressing

Seams should be first pressed open, even if they will eventually be pressed together in a turned edge. Press lightly with the tip of the iron, using heat and steam appropriate to the fabric being pressed. Pressing tools, such as a seam roll for straight seams, a tailor's hem for curves, and a point presser for corners, are useful but not essential.

Seam Allowance

The distance from the seam to the fabric edge is the seam allowance. It is specified in each instance in the projects in this book. On some sewing machines, guidelines on the throat plate help in stitching an even seam.

Securing Stitching

For machine stitching, backstitch at beginning and end of the seam to secure (Illustration 26-70). For hand stitching, knot one thread end when beginning to sew, and take a few tiny back stitches in the seam to secure when ending the

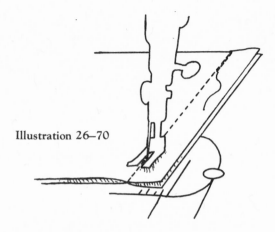

Illustration 26–70

seam. In cases where machine backstitching would show, pull threads through to wrong side or between fabric layers and secure.

Slipstitching

This stitch provides an almost invisible finish. Slide the needle in one folded edge and out picking up a thread of the second layer at this spot. Stitches should be even, ¼″ apart. (Illustration 26-71)

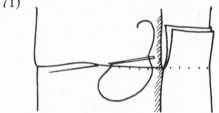

Illustration 26–71

Topstitching

A row of stitching done according to a design or parallel to and ¼″ from a seam or turned edge. (Illustration 26-72)

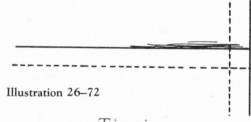

Illustration 26–72

Trimming

- **Corners** To reduce bulk when corner is turned, cut seam allowances diagonally across tip. (Illustration 26-73 and 26-74)
- **Seams** To reduce bulk on seams which are

turned and enclosed, cut one side of the seam allowances narrower than the other for a smoother edge. The longer seam allowance should be against the outside fabric. (Illustration 26-75)

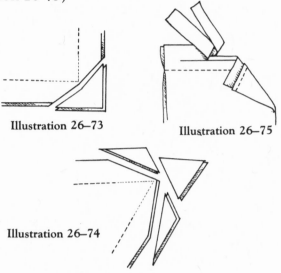

Illustration 26–73

Illustration 26–75

Illustration 26–74

Tubing

Tubing filled with its own seam allowances is used for drawstrings and hanging loops.

Self-filled Cut bias strip four times the desired finished width in the desired length. Fold bias strip in half lengthwise, right sides together, and stitch a seam halfway between fold and raw edges, stretching slightly. Leave both ends open. Turn by passing a needle and thread attached to one end of strip through tube. (Illustration 26-76)

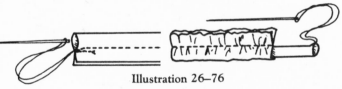

Illustration 26–76

Quick tubing Cut bias strip desired length and four times finished width. Fold edges to center of strip then together; edgestitch. (Illustration 26-77)

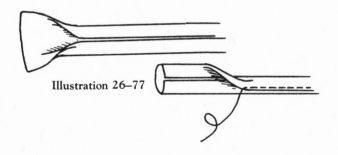

Illustration 26–77

Whipstitch

This stitch holds two finished edges together or tacks a raw edge in place. Insert needle at a right angle to the edge, forming slanted stitches. (Illustration 26-78)

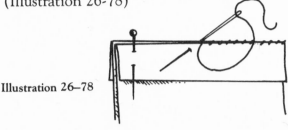

Illustration 26–78

Transferring Designs

To Fabric

MATERIALS:
- Dressmaker's carbon, dressmaker's chalk pencil. Do not use ordinary carbon paper. Dressmaker's carbon paper is designed for use on fabric and is available in a range of colors. Choose a color close to your fabric color.
- Pencil, stylus, or tracing wheel.
- Tissue paper.
- Tracing paper.

Dressmaker's Carbon Tracing
STEP-BY-STEP
1. Trace design onto tracing paper.
2. Tape fabric to hard, flat surface or pin to cutting board with right side up.
3. Position design on fabric and secure on two adjacent sides. (Illustration 26-79)
4. Slip dressmaker's carbon between fabric and design. Be sure to place waxed side of carbon paper next to fabric. On some fabrics like satins and suedes, the pressure of the tracing wheel will leave a mark without the use of carbon.
5. Go over all design lines with pencil, stylus, or tracing wheel. Check to see if enough pressure is being applied to transfer the design to the fabric. Start at the top and work down to prevent smudging the lines with the pressure and movement of your hands. Use the pencil or stylus for complex designs and the tracing wheel for simple designs.

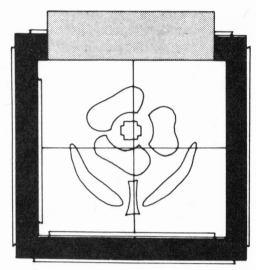

Illustration 26–79

6. Remove carbon, pins, and tape, On dark or lightly napped fabrics, go over the carbon marks with a dressmaker's chalk pencil or thread trace all lines to insure permanency of marking

Direct Tracing on Tissue Paper, Sheer Fabric, or Canvas

Use on clothing. Suitable for linear designs worked in beading, braiding, quilting, and embroidery.

STEP-BY-STEP:

1. Trace design directly onto tissue paper, sheer fabric, or canvas.
2. Baste tissue or canvas to right side of fabric; baste sheer fabric to wrong side of fabric.
3. Work design through fabric *and* tracing, which serves as a guide and prevents puckering.
4. To remove paper when work is completed, gently pull both sides of paper at same time for a clean tear. If sheer fabric tracing was used, trim away excess fabric around worked design and pink or overcast edges. Pull away canvas thread by thread.

Hot Iron Transfer Pencil

These pencils make the ease of hot iron transfer available to the needleworker who wants to use designs other than those available for hot iron stamping. The pencils are available in needlework and craft shops.

STEP-BY-STEP:

1. Trace design onto tracing paper.
2. Draw over back of design with hot iron transfer pencil. Use a fine point.
3. Transfer design to fabric following instructions with pencil. Press slowly with heat suitable for fabric. Lift a corner of the design to check for adequate transfer.

Tailor Tacks

This is a good method for marking fabrics which might be marred or damaged by other marking methods and for marking positioning points of appliqués or frame cutouts.

STEP-BY-STEP:

1. Use a long double strand of white cotton thread with no knot in the end.
2. Take a single short running stitch through the fabric and pattern at the point to be marked. Leave a 1"–2" thread end.
3. Take a second stitch across the first and draw the thread up to form a large loop. (If other symbols are to be marked nearby, carry the thread loosely to the next symbol and repeat.)
4. Snip end of thread 1"–2" from last marking. Clip connecting loops and threads, if any. (Illustration 26-80)

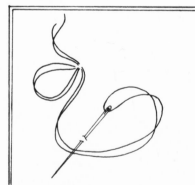

Illustration 26–80

5. Raise pattern carefully and force thread tack through paper.
6. Gently roll back upper layer of fabric and cut threads between layers so that tufts of thread

remain in each layer of fabric. Tufts indicate points that have been marked. This step is not necessary when only one layer is being marked.

Templates

Transfer with templates in needlework such as appliqué and in patchwork where motifs are repeated. A template can be made of brown paper, oak tag, plastic, or sandpaper. It should be durable enough to use several times without fraying.

To make a template, draw or trace each design shape on graph paper. Use a ruler to ensure accuracy. Cut out graph paper shapes and glue them onto template material. Cut out templates (Illustration 26-81). Accuracy in measuring, transferring, and marking is essential. For most hand appliqué, machine appliqué, and patchwork, use templates in the following manner.

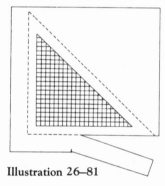

Illustration 26—81

STEP-BY-STEP:
1. Make two templates. One template should be a duplicate of the design piece and the other template the design piece plus seam allowances. (Seam allowances for patchwork and appliqué are usually ¼″ or ⅜″ wide.)

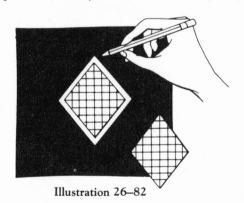

Illustration 26—82

2. On fabric, trace around largest template first. (Illustration 26-82)
3. To mark seam allowances, center the other template within the marked area and trace around it. For some machine appliqué and appliqué with fusibles, no seam allowance or turn-under allowance is required.

Transferring Designs to Paper

MATERIALS:
- soft lead pencil
- hard lead pencil
- tracing paper
- kneaded eraser or art gum eraser (optional)
- masking tape or paper clips (optional)

STEP-BY-STEP:
1. Place tracing paper over design to be transferred. Trace design onto tracing paper with hard lead pencil.
2. Rub wrong side of tracing all over with soft lead pencil.
3. Position tracing as desired right side up over transfer area. Hold tracing in place with paper clips or tape.
4. Trace over design with hard lead pencil. Design will transfer to surface under tracing paper. Handle carefully to prevent smudging.
5. After work is completed, carefully erase any pencil marks or smudges which remain visible.

Craft Materials Source List

A special effort has been made throughout this book to use materials which can be easily found in most communities. Explore dime stores, art supply stores, fabric shops, office supply stores, stationery stores, card shops, grocery stores, needlework shops, craft stores and hardware stores. Some materials may be ordered through national mail order organizations such as Lee Wards, Elgin, Illinois 60120.

The following items may not be available locally and may be ordered from:

Aphrodesia Products, Inc.
28 Carmine Street
New York, New York 10014
Sachet powder and pot pourri

Sewmakers, Inc.
1619 Grand Avenue
Baldwin, New York 11510
Perforated paper

Index

All Saints' Day. *See* Halloween
Appleseed, Johnny, 75
Applique, 282–284
  spring frolic keepsake, 52, 53
  turkey keepsake, 134, 135
  valentine keepsake, 16–18
  witch keepsake, 115–116
April Fool's Day, 46
April's Gowk Day, 46
Arbor Day, 75
Ash Wednesday, 48–49

Baskets
  Easter, 66, 68
  May 78–79
Beverage recipes
  cider flip, 118
  Christmas punch, 10
  "half-dozen" punch, 10
  lemonade, 95
  Prince of Wales punch, 11
Birthday
  cards for adults, 213–214
  cards for children, 212–213
  decorations, 210, 211
  games, 210–211, 211–212
  invitations, 210
  parties, 210–212
  surprise cake, 212
  zodiac signs, 209
Bookends, covered, 242
Boxes, covered, 293–295
Bread recipes
  challah, 108
  fruited Christmas cresent, 188
  hot cross buns, 54

Cache pots, 245–247
Cake and cookie recipes
  decorations for cakes and cookies, 192–193
  fruit cake, 192
  Hamentashen, 39
Candlemas Day, 13
Candy and nut recipes
  candied orange peel, 191
  candied pumpkin chips, 144
  fricaseed pecans, 190
  fruit caramels, 190
  glacé nuts and fruits, 191
  lollipops, 191
  Parisian figs, 191

popcorn balls, 119
salted peanuts, 191
taffy apples, 118–119
Card case, business, 240
Card making. *See also* Greeting cards
  equipment, 285
  hand assembled cards, 286
  lettering, 285
  linoleum block printing, 287
  materials, 284–285
  mounted designs, 286
  silk-screen printing, 288
  stamping, 286
  stencil printing, 287–288
Chapman, John, 75
Children's projects
  apple pumpkin spin, 148–149
  bead stringing, 149–150
  calendar, picture, 11–12
  clothespin soldiers, 102
  cocked hat, 100
  diary, 11
  double heart valentine, 23–24
  Easter top, 58
  head wreath, 100–101
  Jacob's ladder, 261–262
  leaf waxing, 150
  paper fireworks, 96–100
  star badge, 101
  stars, 101–102
  valentine card sachet, 25
Chinese New Year, 2
Christmas, 160–162
  cards, 180–186
  carol singing, 160, 161
  decorations, 186–187
  Dutch traditions of, 161–162
  English traditions of, 161, 162
  food, 188–189
  food gifts, 189–193
  gift wraps, 194–198
  greenery, 164–169
  keepsake, needlework, 164
  Puritan influence on, 160–161
  Scandinavian influences on, 163
  stockings, 178–179
Christmas tree, 161, 162
  decoration, 168–177
  ornaments, 173–179
Clay modeling, 154–155, 288–289
Columbus Day, 111

Containers
  berry basket, 68
  bonbon box, 197
  bunny box, 66–67
  custom, 295–296
  egg satchel, 67
  lily basket, 66
  May baskets, 78–79
  needlework yarn carrier, 266–267
  poinsettia, 197
  scissors case, 268–269
  traveling cases, 269
  work pocket, 267–268
Cookies. *See* Cake and Cookie recipes
Corn husk dolls, 137–139
Costumes
  Halloween, 121–130
  Purim, 39–40
Craft techniques
  appliqué, 282–284
  card making, 284–288
  clay modeling, 288–289
  coloring eggs, 61
  embroidery, 289–291
  enlarging designs, 291–292
  linoleum block printing, 287
  needlepoint, 296–300
  ornamenting eggs, 61–62
  patchwork, 300–301
  reducing designs, 291–292
  sewing, 301–308
  silk-screen printing, 288
  stencil printing, 287–288
  transferring designs, 308–310
Crochet
  valentine keepsake, 16–18

Dart board, 30–31
Dart board, 30–31 Decoration Day. *See* Memorial Day
Decorations
  children's birthday party, 210, 211
  Christmas, 186–187
  Easter, 54–55
  Halloween, 116–117, 119, 121
  Hanukkah, 158
  Independence Day, 94
  Lincon's Birthday, 36
  May Day, 79–80
  New Year's Day, 10
  New Year's Eve, 9
  Saint Patrick's Day, 43
  Saint Valentine's Day, 27, 28, 32

Thanksgiving, 134, 137–140
  wedding aniversary, 216–217
Designs
  enlarging and reducing, 291–292
  transferring, 308–310
Desk accessories, 240–244
Dessert recipes
  baked apple variations, 118
  Cape Cod cocktail, 143
  cranberry frappe, 143
  cranberry tarts, 143
  gelatin eggs, 57
  Indian pudding, 143–144
  mincemeat, 144–145
  mincemeat pielets, 145
  mince pie, 145
  plum pudding, 189
  pumpkin pie, 144
Dodd, Mrs. John Bruce, 87
Dolls, corn husk, 137–139
Druids, 2, 42, 76, 112–114, 132

Easter, 48–51
  and Ash Wednesday, 48–49
  and Blossom Sunday in Germany, 50
  cards, 59–60
  and Collop Monday, 53
  decorations, 54–55
  food, 56–57
  games, 57
  gift giving, 50, 51, 58–59
  and Good Friday, 50
  greetings, 51
  and Holy Thursday, 50
  and Holy Saturday, 50–51
  hot cross buns, 50, 54
  keepsake, needlework, 53
  and Lent, 48–49
  and Mardi Gras, 49
  and Maundy Thursday, 48, 50
  and Olive Sunday in England, 50
  and Palm Sunday, 49–50
  rabbit as symbol, 51
  and Shrove Tuesday, 49, 54
Easter eggs, 51
  containers, 66–68
  decorated, 60–66
Egg recipes
  egg nests on toast, 56
  Eggs Susette, 56
  stirred egg omelet, 56
Embroidery, 289–291

birth sampler, 208
challah cover, 108
Independence Day
    keepsake, 92–93
marriage sampler, 208
matzah cover, 73
New Year keepsake, 5–6
throw, 239–240
valentine keepsake, 16–18

Father's Day, 87–88
Flag Day, 85–86
Flag display, 86
"Fool's errand," origin of
    phrase, 46
Fortune cake, 118
Fortune eggs, 55
Fortunes, walnut, 6–7
Frames, photograph, 231–236

Games
    children's birthday party,
        210–212
    Easter, 57
    Halloween, 117–120
    Hanukkah, 157
    Independence Day, 95–96
    Passover, 73–74
    Saint Patrick's Day, 43–44
    Saint Valentine's Day,
        29–31, 32–33
    Thanksgiving, 148, 149
    Washington's Birthday, 37
Garnish and relish recipes
    cranberry jelly I, 142
    cranberry jelly II, 142
    cranberry sauce I, 142
    cranberry sauce II, 142
    date and cranberry
        marmalade, 143
    spiced cranberries, 142
Gift ideas
    Christmas food, 189–190
    Easter, 58
    Hanukkah, 154
    Valentine, 26
Gift wrapping
    boxes, 292
    boxes, covered, 293–295
    Christmas, 191, 193–194,
        194–198
    custom containers,
        295–296
    ornaments, 293
    ribbons, 293
Gifts
    containers, 266–269
    desk accessories, 240–244
    kitchen, 262–266
    photograph frames, 231–236

pillows, 237–239
pincushions, 228–231
plant, 244–247, 255
sachets, 224–227
throw, 239–240
toys, 255–262
Good Friday, 50, 54
Greenery
    Christmas decorating with,
        164–165
    garlands, 167–168
    gumdrop tree centerpiece,
        36
    evergreen mat, 168
    wreaths, 166, 167
Greeting cards
    adult birthday, 213–215
    children's birthday,
        212–213
    Christmas, 180–186
    Easter, 59–60
    Rosh ha-Shanah, 108–110
    Saint Valentine's Day,
        19–25
Groundhog Day, 13

Hale, Mrs. Sarah Josepha,
    133
Half-birthday, 212
Halloween, 112–114
    costumes, 114, 121–129
    decorations, 116, 119, 121
    and English Harvest
        Home, 132
    food, 117–119
    games, 117, 119–120
    invitations, 116, 119, 121
    Irish influence on, 114
    keepsake, needlework, 116
    masks, 121–122
    trick or treating, 114, 126
Hanukkah, 152–153
    decorations, 158
    dreydl, 152, 154–156
    games, 157
    song, 156–157
    food, 157
    games, 157
    gelt, 152, 154
    gifts, 154
    invitations, 157
    menorah, 151, 152,
        153–154
Holly, 161, 165

Independence Day, 90–91
    Centennial of 1876, 91
    decorations, 94
    fireworks, 90, 91
    food, 94–95

games, 95–96
invitations, 94
keepsake, needlework, 92
living flag, 102
paper fireworks, 96–100
parade, 90, 91
Invitations
    children's birthday party
        210, 211
    Halloween, 116, 119, 121
    Hanukkah, 157
    Independence Day, 94
    May Day, 79
    Saint Patrick's Day, 43
    Saint Valentine's Day, 27,
        32, 33
    wedding anniversary,
        216–217

Jack Horner pie, 28
Jack-O'lantern, 114
Jewish holidays
    Hanukkah, 152–153
    High Holy Days, 106–107
    Pesah, 71
    Purim, 38–39
    Rosh ha-Shanah, 106–107
    Sukkot, 106, 132
    Yom Kippur, 196, 107

Keepsakes
    birth sampler, 208
    Christmas, 163–164
    Easter, 53
    Halloween, 115–116
    Independence Day, 92–93
    marriage sampler, 208
    New Year, 5–6
    Saint Valentine's Day,
        16–17
    Thanksgiving, 134–135
Kitchen gifts
    apron, 263–264
    cord box, 266
    goose pot holder, 264
    napkin ring, 262–263
    ornamental cork, 265
    permanent shopping list,
        265
Knitting, 255–257

Labor Day, 104–105
Lent, 48–49
Lincoln's Birthday, 35–36
    decorations, 36
    food, 36
    place cards, 36
Lollipop dolls, 28–29

Main dish recipes

giblet gravy, 142
nut turkey roast, 146
roast turkey, 141
Virginia chicken pie, 143
Mardi Gras, 49
Maundy Thursday, 48, 50
May baskets, 78–79
May Day, 76
    activities, 80
    baskets, 78–79
    decorations, 79–80
    food, 80
    in Moscow, 76
    invitations, 79
Maypole dance, 76, 80
McGuire, Peter J., 104
Memorial Day, 83
Menorah, Hanukkah, 152,
    153–154
Menus
    children's birthday party,
        211, 212
    Christmas breakfast, 188
    Christmas dinner,
        traditional
        English, 188, 189
    Easter dinner, 56
    Easter family breakfast, 56
    Easter formal buffet
        brunch, 56
    Fourth of July picnic, 95
    Halloween Feast, 118
    Hanukkah latke party, 157
    Independence Day
        American Flag dinner,
        95
    Labor Day picnic, 105
    Lincoln's Birthday family
        dinner, 36
    May Day informal
        breakfast, 80
    New Year's Day buffet,
        9–10
    New Year's Day dessert
        buffet, 10
    New Year's Day tea, 10
    New Year's Eve formal
        dinner, 9
    Saint Patrick's Day family
        meal, 43
    Saint Patrick's Day party,
        43
    Saint Valentine's Day
        party, 32, 33
    Thanksgiving dinner,
        traditional, 140
    Thanksgiving dinners,
        modern, 145–146
    Washington's Birthday
        sweets, 37

wedding anniversary
breakfast buffet, 216
wedding anniversary party,
217
Mistletoe, 161, 165
Mooney, William, 111
Moore, Dr. Clement C., 162
Morton, J. Sterling, 75
Mother's Day, 81

Needle crafts. See Appliqué;
Embroidery;
Keepsakes; Needlepoint;
Patchwork
Needlepoint, 296–300
Christmas keepsake,
163–164
Easter keepsake, 52, 53
Halloween keepsake,
115–116
Independence Day
keepsake, 92–93
New Year, 2–3
customs, 3–4
gift of pins for, 8
keepsake, needlework, 6
resolutions, 4
wishing cards, 7
wishing tree, 6–8, 9, 11
New Year's Day, 2–3, 4, 9
food, 3, 9–10
open house, 10–11
New Year's Eve
celebration 8–9
customs, 3–4
dinner party, 9
Noisemakers, 40–41
Nuts. See Candy and nut
recipies

Open house on New Year's
Day, 10–11
presidential, 4
Ornaments, Christmas tree
fabric, 176
food, 176–177
paper, 169–175

Palm Sunday, 49–50
Paper baskets, 78–79
Paper fireworks, 96–100
Paper ornaments for
Christmas tree, 169
cornucopia, 174–175
cutout ornaments, 172
cutout snowflakes, 172–173
cut paper chain, 169–170
foil garland, 170–171
holly garland, 171–172
Jacob's Ladder chain, 170
medallions, 173

paper flowers, 172
paper link chain, 170
textured cutout ornaments,
172
Passion Play, 50
Passover. See Pesah
Patchwork, 300–301
Pesah, 71
games, 73–74
matzah, 72
matzah cover,
embroidered, 73
Seder, 71–72
Photograph frames
basic, 231–233
embroidered, 233–234
folding case, 234–236
lace mat, 234
soft, 236
Pillows, 237
lace and ribbon, 238
patchwork, 237–238
shaped, 239
star patchwork, 238
Pincushions, 228
flower, 229–230
for Wishing Tree, 8
pansy, 230–231
round, 228–229
sea shell, 229
star, 231
Place cards
Easter, 54
Halloween, 117
Lincoln's Birthday, 36
Lollipop dolls, 28–29
Thanksgiving, 136
Poinsettia, 165
Pomanders, 8
Potato pancakes, 157
Purim, 38–39
costumes, 39–40
grager, 38, 40–41
Hamentashen, 39, 41

Robin Hood legend and May
Day, 76
Rosh ha-Shanah, 106–107
Ross, Betsy, 85–86

Sachets, 25, 224
drawer, 226
folded, 225
hanging star, 227–228
lingerie, 225–226
padded hanger, 226–227
Saint Nicholas, 161–162
Saint Patrick's Day, 42–43
food, 43
games, 43–44
party, 43–44

Saint Valentine's Day, 14–15
cards, 18–23
cards, children's, 23–25
dart board, heart for,
30–31, 34
decorations, 27–28, 32, 33
food, 32, 33
games, 29–31, 32–33
gifts, 26
invitations, 27, 32, 33
keepsake, needlework,
16–18
party prizes, 33
place cards, 28–29
sentiments, 25–26
Sandwiches, 105
Sewing
basting, 301
bias seam binding,
302–303
bias cording, 303
buttonholes,
machine-worked, 303
casing, 303
catchstitch, 304
clipping, 304
easing, 304
edgestitching, 304
gathering, 304
grain, 304
hemming stitch, 305
machine stitching, 305
materials, 301
mitering, 305
notching, 306
overcoat stitch, 306
preshrinking, 306
pressing, 306
seam allowance, 306
securing stitching, 306
slipstitching, 306–307
topstitching, 307
trimming, 307
tubing, 307
whipstitching, 308
Shrove Tuesday, 49, 54
Society of St. Tammany, 111
Stationery, decorated, 244
Stuffing recipes
apple and celery stuffing,
189
bread stuffing, 141
chestnut stuffing, 141
oyster stuffing, 141
Sukkot, 106, 132

Table decorations. See
Decorations
Telephone book cover,
241–242
Thanksgiving, 132–133

corn husk dolls, 137–139
decorations, 134–140
food, 140–146
games, 148, 149
keepsake, needlework, 13
place cards, 136
turkey carving, 147
Throw, embroidered,
239–240
Tote bag, trick or treat, 126
Toys. See also Children's
projects
corn husk dolls, 137–139
dart board, 30–31
dreydl, 154–156
elephant, 258
grager, 40–41
indoor croquet game, 259
knitted ball, 257
knitted dog, 256–257
knitted pussycat, 255–256
ringtoss game, 260–261
Tree decorations
Christmas, 169–177
New Year's, 6–8, 9
Turkey
carving, 147
selection, 140–141
uses for leftover, 142

Valentine's Day. See Saint
Valentine's Day
Verse
to accompany gifts, 224
for Saint Valentine's Day,
25–26

Washington's Birthday, 35
decorations, 36
food, 37
games, 37
Watch Night services, 3–4, 8
Wearing of the green, 43
Wedding anniversary
decorations, 216, 217
food, 216, 217
invitations, 216–217
themes, 215
Woodworking
dreydl, 155–156
garden markers, 255
grager, 40–41
indoor croquet game,
259–260
Jacob's Ladder, 261–262
menorah, 153–154
ringtoss game, 260–261

Yom Kippur, 106–107